Edited by Paul A. Djupe

Religion and Political Tolerance in America

Advances in the State of the Art

TEMPLE UNIVERSITY PRESS
Philadelphia • Rome • Tokyo

TEMPLE UNIVERSITY PRESS
Philadelphia, Pennsylvania 19122
www.temple.edu/tempress

Published 2015

Library of Congress Cataloging-in-Publication Data

Religion and political tolerance in America : advances in the state of the art / edited by Paul Djupe.
pages cm. — (Social logic of politics)
Includes bibliographical references and index.
ISBN 978-1-4399-1232-4 (hardback) — ISBN 978-1-4399-1233-1 (paper) — ISBN 978-1-4399-1234-8 (e-book) 1. Religion and politics—United States. 2. Democracy—Religious aspects. 3. Toleration—Religious aspects. I. Djupe, Paul A.
BL2525.R4612 2015
322′.10973—dc23

2014047590

♾ The paper used in this publication meets the requirements of the American National Standard for Information Sciences—Permanence of Paper for Printed Library Materials, ANSI Z39.48-1992

Printed in the United States of America

9 8 7 6 5 4 3 2 1

Contents

Acknowledgments

This book came together quickly after years of development. That is, once I decided to pursue the book, an outstanding group of contributors quickly agreed and then worked diligently to produce the chapters contained herein. I thank them for contributing such excellent work and for being such cooperative and, especially, creative collaborators.

The impetus for pursuing this project was the realization that over the years I and coauthors had produced a coherent body of work on religion and tolerance that simply called for a book treatment. I am grateful they were willing to follow my inkling that the impact of that body of work would be greater if assembled here rather than dispersed across the social sciences in journals. The earliest work that spurred this line of inquiry was with the peripatetic, indefatigable, unstoppable Brian Calfano. Brian is all over this volume, from front to back, and the volume is frankly only possible with his partnership across these seven highly productive years. And I could go on similarly about working with each of my coauthors—it has simply been a lot of fun working with them.

Several of these chapters would not be possible without support from a Jack Shand Research Grant (administered by the Society for the Scientific Study of Religion): Small grants funded the clergy component of Chapter 2, enabling the first look at how clergy's tolerance affects that of members, and the survey data used initially for Chapter 11 (how tolerance arguments affect persuasion), which also enabled the exploration of religious value effects in Chapter 7.

I thank Temple University Press for its support. More specifically, I thank Alex Holzman, who encouraged this volume as he transitioned into retirement, and Aaron Javsicas for picking up the ball and carrying it forward with enthusiasm and great attention to detail and process. There are substantial (publishing) house effects here that work in favor of the research. Simply put, Temple does great work.

Last, but not least, I thank the Worthington public schools for keeping Bear and Gustie so well stimulated during daylight hours. But more apropos, every day the boys point out every instance of perceived unfair treatment and offer poignant reminders that they have rights not yet counterbalanced by concern for their extension to others. While I appreciate the practical lessons in democratic politics happening right under my nose, I am a bit more appreciative of playing with Legos and taking bike rides. In the maelstrom of opening the Commissary, Kate was ever mindful to create space for me to work on this book. I am lucky to be a part of this tiny, evolving society and to have such a supportive, loving partner to codirect it.

Religion and Political Tolerance in America

Introduction

PAUL A. DJUPE

Take a moment and write down the most unpopular groups to you in America today. The likely set of answers varies depending on your politics, but it is more than likely that religion is well represented in the set you record. People who challenge religious faith, like Michael Newdow, who sought to remove "In God We Trust" from American currency; people who take religious dictates to extreme positions, like the Westboro Baptist Church, which advocates against tolerance of gays and lesbians by protesting at military funerals; and all the people in between suggest that religion is an important element in the politics of American life and remains a flash point for American politics.

Should these people be allowed to say and do such things? Should atheists be allowed to run for public office? Should Christian fundamentalists who believe in creation be allowed to teach biology? Should any religious believer be allowed to advocate for the imposition of religious law in America? You may not disagree with any of these groups, but the key question confronting us in this volume is what you think when you do disagree with at least one. Do you "put up" with the group you disagree with or not? Putting up with such a group is called *political tolerance*, which entails the extension of equal rights and liberties regardless of viewpoint. Political tolerance is the bedrock of democracy because, without it, politics would quickly devolve into an endless cycle of violence rather than the peaceful (if not agreeable) resolution of conflict through debate, compromise, and fair and open procedures.

Because religion is implicated in the set of groups that challenge basic notions of what it means to be an American does not mean that religion is necessarily tied to intolerance and therefore poses a challenge to democracy. While some religious (and irreligious) groups do offer challenging positions, religion is also bound up in how people think about democracy and the extension of equal rights. Further, religion shapes how people respond to intolerance when they experience it themselves. The important point for now is that there is no single variable that we can use to describe the nature of that religion.

There is a reason why this book appears in the series *The Social Logic of Politics*. "Religion" is an incredibly complicated set of ideas and social institutions that structure how people live and interact with others. Religious beliefs concern the divine, but they also offer explicit guidance about whether and how to engage with others. Religious institutions, such as houses of worship, are engaged in shaping the particular beliefs and values individuals hold. But they are also organizations in which more or less diverse sets of people interact to learn and solve collective problems. Thus houses of worship constitute tiny publics whose institutions and interactions may generalize to the broader public. Moreover, these tiny publics exist within larger publics and, of course, have preferences over how those larger publics are governed, preferences that more than likely involve the extension of rights and liberties to all or some.

Political tolerance is, by its nature, a product of social considerations. We build support for this essential democratic norm when our social experiences mimic the conditions democracy was meant to address: Disagreement is experienced over the pursuit of collective ends. Our support for an equal playing field for all to participate is maintained when our attitudes leave space for the rightness of other accounts and the legitimacy of claims for competing interests. Of course, that support is bolstered when we believe that there is some mutual respect for our own position. These are all social considerations, through which people carefully consider other groups in society and make difficult choices about whether they and society can afford to include them in debates and governing processes.

This is an edited volume, and therefore no single argument is advanced. The contributors all have different conceptions of what religion is, how it should be measured, and how it relates to the social considerations of political tolerance. What we all agree on is that political tolerance is a vibrant area in which to understand how religion and politics relate and elaborate the social logic at play. Published after a period of relative dormancy in this literature, this volume represents new and innovative research that should reinvigorate this line of work for a generation. The additional value is that this work allows us to continue to wrestle with perhaps the fundamental question of the place of religion in democratic society.

From the beginning of the United States, there was considerable debate about the necessity of religious faith for the maintenance of limited government. Though there was a diversity of beliefs on this question, we might summarize them using the poles of James Madison and John Adams. Madison, most famously in his *Memorial and Remonstrance* ([1785] 2000), argued that freedom never flowed from a tight connection of religion with the state. Freedom, in his view, was sustained only by a riot of diversity in intensely held belief so that there could never be a majority view that could be used to oppress a minority. Put simply, for Madison disagreement was the solution to guarantee freedom (see also Jelen and Wilcox 1990; Sullivan, Piereson, and Marcus 1982). Adams, on the other hand, viewed too much disagreement as the problem: "It is Religion and Morality alone which can establish the principles upon which Freedom can surely stand" (quoted in Reichley 1985: 104). Democracy breaks down if claims on it are fundamentally at odds such that compromise is not possible.

It is notable that both Madison and Adams presume that religious groups hold tenaciously to convictions that stand at odds with other groups' values. That is, both Madison and Adams agree, at base, about the nature of religious groups. Instead, they vary in how institutions aggregate and process disagreement—for Madison disagreement maintains stability, while for Adams disagreement courts anarchy. But what if their assumption about religious groups in society does not hold? We can relax parts of their assumption systematically—that (1) groups (or portions of them) may not hold their values tenaciously, (2) their values may not be at odds with other groups (or their minority status is variable), and (3) their deeply held convictions are concerned not (or not only) with the distribution of goods in narrow, particularistic ways but with universal values of how people are treated.

This, in essence, is what the academic literature investigating religious influences on political tolerance has done. Each chapter that follows in this volume builds on this foundation, so you will not find a comprehensive review of the religion and political tolerance literature there. I provide that in this chapter. The nice feature about this literature is that, until recently, it is conceptually quite orderly. It draws on the same definitions of religion and uses many of the same measures (though almost never all at the same time). The challenging feature of this literature is that the specific findings are quite variable, for a variety of reasons that I discuss.

Religion and Political Tolerance in Review: A Proxy War

All modern empirical tolerance work builds from Samuel Stouffer's monument *Communism, Conformity, and Civil Liberties* (1955). Working amid the virulently anti-Communist politics of the late 1940s and 1950s, Stouffer finds very limited support for the extension of civil liberties to avowed Communists in the mass public, but more support for their rights among elites. It is from this observation that we have an elitist theory of democracy, in which elites maintain the rules of the game in the face of mass defection from constitutionalism for their political enemies (see also McClosky 1964). Interestingly, he elided the inclusion of clergy from his otherwise comprehensive collection of elites. But Stouffer also briefly investigated the connection of church attendance and civil liberties extensions, finding that higher church attendance was correlated with weaker support for civil liberties. This is not surprising, given the common construct of the time of "godless Communism."

This conclusion is rather unsatisfying from the perspective of modern social science. Just what does this relationship of intolerance with church attendance mean? Does it simply mean that more religion means more intolerance (as Madison might argue)? Since some groups demand or encourage more church attendance from their adherents (evangelical Protestants for instance), the people who attend church often are not the same kinds of religious people who attend less, and the religion experienced among high attenders is generally different from the religion experienced by those who attend less often.

If that is true, then does a church attendance effect mean that the adoption of certain kinds of beliefs and values is linked to intolerance? If so, then we should measure those independently. But church attendance may also signal that people hold particular sets of beliefs and values more fervently, perhaps even dogmatically (holding that they are true and without error). Higher church attendance may also mean that people are interacting with a less diverse set of people than they might if they were pursuing other activities. It may mean that they are attending in an area that is particularly threatening. Or church attendance effects may indicate that people happen to receive information in church that, while not overtly religious, still bears on their tolerance judgments. And the kinds of people who frequently attend church may be different from those who attend less regularly in other ways that bear on tolerance, such as educational attainment and gender.

This discussion is not meant to imply that sorting out church attendance effects is our central goal. Instead, this brief exercise indicates the kinds of questions that could be asked of any simple correlation of a religious attribute (a belief, behavior, value, or experience) and tolerance. You might now understand why I subtitled this section "A Proxy War"—researchers have used general purpose measures intending them to mean something else, and we continue to argue over just what that meaning is (even when our statistical models grow more "complete").

This discussion is important for a number of reasons, some of them normative. Understanding the particular mechanisms of influence may implicate religion as essentially antidemocratic, as believers see greater threats from those who do not share the faith. It may implicate a particular cognitive style as intolerant, or it may highlight the social organization of the church as problematic for the extension of civil liberties. If intolerance should be corrected, which is debatable, then which mechanism connecting religion to intolerance are we constitutionally able to alter?

But this set of concerns begs a more basic question. In Stouffer's analysis, we are seeing only that church attenders are more opposed to the equal rights of *Communists*. This does not mean that others in society are willing to apply equal protection to groups that they might dislike more. Thus, later work, starting with the General Social Survey[1] in 1972, began to list a selection of unpopular groups—generally including Communists, atheists, homosexuals, racists, and militarists.

Even that may not be enough diversity to capture the full extent of intolerance in America. That is, by the late 1970s, researchers were noting the steady increase in tolerance in comparison to Stouffer's results (e.g., Davis 1975; Nunn, Crockett, and Williams 1978). One reason for that may have been that the groups once considered unpopular were simply not salient threats anymore (Sullivan, Piereson, and Marcus 1979). As a fix, John Sullivan, James Piereson, and George Marcus (1979, 1982) proposed a "content-controlled" (1979: 785–786) method, in which individuals were allowed to select or propose a group they liked the least. Once a group was selected, people were asked whether they would extend civil liberties when the group engaged in hypothetical actions such as running for public office, marching, and teaching. When Sullivan, Piereson, and Marcus implemented this method, they found a "pluralistic intolerance" (1979: 793)—intolerance was higher and more widespread in the population than in earlier accounts using the "Stouffer method" of asking tolerance questions about predetermined groups.[2] This technology may be particularly important for the perceived tolerance levels of religious groups (see Chapter 5), since the General Social Survey list was slightly tilted to groups on the left.

With a baseline selection of groups that is widely seen as unbiased, we can build a firmer foundation of understanding how religion might bear on political tolerance. To begin, I review the literature addressing four essential questions that I alluded to previously.

Are Religious Effects Actually a Function of Demographic Differences?

The first pieces of research beginning in the 1970s to pick up where Stouffer left off investigated whether religious groups differed in their tolerance levels. Religious minorities, including Jews, were found to be more tolerant than Catholics and Protestants, implicating the minority experience in America (Beatty and Walter 1984; Filsinger 1976; Nunn, Crockett, and Williams 1978; Roof and McKinney 1987). This complicates the picture, since Jews also tend to have higher levels of educational attainment than even mainline Protestants (Roof and McKinney 1987), so it has not been clear whether Jewish tolerance is a function of values, experience, or education, though Wald (2015) argues it is a function of interests. Certainly, one of the justifications for the low tolerance scores of evangelicals was their lower level of socioeconomic status (Reimer and Park 2001; Roof and McKinney 1987; Wilcox and Jelen 1990).

In systematic analyses, when demographic differences, such as education, age, and gender, across groups were accounted for, religious group identifications played a somewhat lesser role, though they generally did not disappear (Beatty and Walter 1984; Bobo and Licari 1989; Burdette, Ellison, and Hill 2005;

Ellison and Musick 1993; Gibson 2010; Reimer and Park 2001; Wilcox and Jelen 1990; but see Burge 2013; Eisenstein 2008). All post-1990 analyses incorporate controls for demographic differences and at least some religious effects persist, especially since differences in socioeconomic status between evangelicals and others have declined (C. Smith 2000). Instead, researchers have concentrated on identifying different religious beliefs and behaviors that may be linked to tolerance judgments.

Are Religious Effects a Result of Holding Particular Religious Beliefs?

The simple answer is yes (e.g., Burdette, Ellison, and Hill 2005; Ellison and Musick 1993; Gibson 2010; Green et al. 1994; Tamney and Johnson 1997; Wilcox and Jelen 1990), but there are (at least) two ways to think about religious belief effects. First, people may differ in their political tolerance levels because of the specific content of their beliefs. Second, it may matter more the way in which those beliefs are held—this claim is addressed in the next section. Back to the first claim, some may believe that the specific values or activities of a group are sinful and thus may oppose their operation in society as a result. For instance, evangelicals are more likely than others to believe that homosexuality is a sin (e.g., Burdette, Ellison, and Hill 2005; Reimer and Park 2001; C. Smith 2000). Similarly, there is no mystery why religious believers of almost all varieties view atheists with some disdain, especially when they are described (as in the General Social Survey) as "against all religion and churches" (Djupe, Calfano, and Back 2013; Edgell, Gerteis, and Hartmann 2006; Filsinger 1976). It is clearly difficult to explicitly grant rights to those seen working against divine dictates and the practices and beliefs of your group.

In a generally overlooked chapter, Clyde Nunn, Harry Crockett, and J. Allen Williams (1978: chap. 8) pitch the idea that belief in the devil and religious certainty are ways that people ill-equipped to handle a complex world full of injustice adopt to preserve a sense of the social order (see also Durkheim [1912] 1961).In their fascinating account, only those with less than a high school education increased their belief in the devil from 1953 to 1973 in response to social unrest, and the least tolerant were much more likely to believe in the devil. While some of this relationship was because of status anxiety, not all of it was, and belief in the devil independently contributed to intolerance (see also Gibson 2010; Gibson and Tedin 1988). It seems readily apparent that acknowledging the embodied presence of evil in the world would entail higher stakes for allowing it to act unchecked by government.

On the flip side is the argument about how beliefs about God bear on tolerance judgments. Following Greeley (1995), views of the nature of God analogize to how others should be treated. For instance, Paul Froese, Christopher Bader, and Buster Smith (2008: 33) find that "individuals with harsher and more wrathful images of God will be less forgiving and tolerant of others." In a sense, individuals holding this belief become self-perceived agents of God on earth.

Are Religious Effects a Result of Holding Religious Beliefs Dogmatically?

Far and away the most commonly discussed relationship between beliefs and tolerance is that the particular belief may be less important than the way it is held. Believing there is an absolute, unconditional truth leaves precious little room for disagreement, let alone fundamental disagreement. Moreover, such dogmatism raises the stakes for error, as even slight deviations may entail great peril—from either another group pursuing an errant view or straying from the path oneself. While this dogmatic way of holding beliefs is thought to be distinct from other religious attributes, note the similarity with beliefs in the devil or a vengeful god. As I note below, studies of fundamentalism tend to incorporate all of these dimensions.

Quantifying dogmatism has its roots in the 1950s investigations of authoritarianism (Adorno et al. 1950). Its conceptualization was an attempt to strip out an ideological overlay of the authoritarian "F-scale" that limited its application to conservatives and therefore weakened its analytic value. Interestingly, another attempt to achieve this moved the measurement of authoritarianism into the family by asking about child-rearing practices (Kohn 1977); that approach has been used widely in political science (e.g., Barker and Tinnick 2006; Hetherington and Suhay 2011; Mockabee 2007).

The effect of religious dogmatism is thoroughly documented. Most often, a relationship between a belief in a literal interpretation of the Bible[3] and tolerance is used as evidence for religious dogmatism effects. This relationship holds in national samples (Jelen and Wilcox 1991; Tuntiya 2005; Wilcox and Jelen 1990), among activists (Green et al. 1994; Wilcox and Larson 2006), and over time (Reimer and Park 2001). Literalism is not always pulled out as a distinct item, but it is sometimes used as part of a measure of fundamentalism, which is also closely linked to intolerance (e.g., Ellison and Musick 1993; Tamney and Johnson 1997; but see Wilcox 1987: 287). When these attributes are pulled apart, Nana Tuntiya (2005) finds that literalism is driving intolerance and not a fundamentalist identity. But there are other measures for religious dogmatism; for instance, Ted Jelen and Clyde Wilcox (1991: 35) use an index composed of the existence and importance of clear rights and wrongs.

The battle over the understanding of dogmatism is pitched, however. Dennis Owen, Kenneth Wald, and Samuel Hill (1991) push back against the definition of authoritarianism as a personality trait. Instead, they argue, some religious people are "authority-minded," adopting the teachings of a particular religious tradition as an act of choice—a temporary "state" versus a dispositional "trait." The difference is profound. If religion and politics work has been using religious measures as a proxy for items psychologists claim as predispositions, at least somewhat rooted in biology, then religion is derivative of hard-wired, perhaps genetic traits. The rejection of the trait argument is an attempt to reclaim religion as an independent force in the world. It is a plea for the survival of the subfield itself in some ways.

The problem is that measures of both religious and secular (no religious content) dogmatism have been included in only a few studies. In Marie Eisenstein's (2008: 51–54) analysis, biblical literalism is related to religious commitment, which in turn is related to a less secure personality (dogmatism and self-esteem; see also Eisenstein and Clark 2014). It is more common to find a link between religiosity and dogmatism or a related construct, such as authoritarianism or personality security (Canetti-Nisim 2004; Canetti-Nisim and Beit-Hallahmi 2007; Jelen and Wilcox 1991; Peffley and Sigelman 1990).[4] And some research has assessed how the "big five" personality traits correlate with religious variables (e.g., Francis 2010; Hills et al. 2004). That is, we do not have an answer yet, and no one has deliberately tried to parse out the degree to which authoritarianism differs from authority-mindedness.

What Role Does Social Cloistering by Way of Church Involvement Have?

The third pillar of classic investigations of religious effects on tolerance relates to the first variable investigated—church attendance (Stouffer 1955). By itself, church attendance is a relatively good proxy for more general senses of religiosity (e.g., Layman 2001). Those who attend church more frequently hold more conservative beliefs and attend churches with traditions that encourage more involvement. But once those variables are accounted for, attendance might account for only a few other effects. First, it may entail exposure to a set of information, such as from clergy, that may bear on tolerance. Because researchers rarely have access to this kind of information, they generally ignore that possibility (see Chapters 2 and 3). Instead, attendance has been thought to capture the social structure and the degree to which it is closed to the marketplace of ideas (Green et al. 1994; Smidt and Penning 1982; Sullivan, Piereson, and Marcus 1982). It is assumed that people attending church more regularly therefore socialize with a more homogeneous set of people. Church attendance is thought to indicate a choice in a near zero-sum situation, so that it precludes participation in other social organizations and hence signals a degree of cloistering. Social closure feeds a dogmatic worldview, in which truth is set a priori and deviation is punishable, since individuals do not have to continually wrestle with the value of dissonant arguments. On the other hand, social openness breeds a give-and-take of views that undermines bright boundaries between good and evil (see, e.g., Mill [1869] 1975; Mutz 2006).

While the logic is consistent, it ignores the widely noted link between religion and civic voluntarism and broader political participation (e.g., Musick, Wilson, and Bynum 2000; Verba, Schlozman, and Brady 1995). Moreover, religious groups that differ in their levels of church attendance do not differ substantially in the attributes of members' social networks, including disagreement and political discussion (Djupe and Calfano 2012a). Moreover, churches vary considerably in the amount of diversity within them (Djupe and Gilbert 2009), perhaps outside of race (see, e.g., Scheitle and Dougherty 2010). This does not mean that church attendance is not related to cloistering but instead that it is likely a poor proxy for it when other, better measures may be available.

Criticisms of the Existing Literature

This is not the only criticism of this literature, as Eisenstein (2008) details (see also Gibson 2010). The earliest studies drew on data that had rather weak and idiosyncratic religion batteries about which researchers often expressed regrets. Given the preceding discussion, it is clear that the meaning of each religious variable changes depending on what else is controlled for in the model. Since the model specifications shift around considerably across studies, it becomes almost impossible to compare the effects of church attendance, for instance.

The controls are also important from another perspective. The broader tolerance literature has settled on at least three core features that explain tolerance: the threat posed by a target group, support for democratic norms, and a secure personality (dogmatism, self-esteem, and trust). (For a more complex model, see Marcus et al. 1995.) Until very recently, most studies of religious effects on tolerance have not included these forces. To make matters more complicated, most of those studies have used religious variables as proxies for those forces (especially dogmatism). Again, this is why this section of the chapter is subtitled "A Proxy War." This leaves open the possibility that (1) once those forces are controlled for, religion ceases to matter in tolerance judgments, and we are put out of business; (2) religion works through those forces, which pushes our analyses back to understanding threat, democratic norms, and insecurity (see Eisenstein and Clark 2014; Chapters 5 and 10); or (3) if standard measures of religion no longer matter at the primary or secondary levels, other conceptions of religion do. All three cases are made in this volume, but it is to the last possibility that I now turn by way of concluding this review of the literature.

New Directions in Religious Effects on Tolerance

Until recently, one particular conception of religion has dominated this literature. As Rodney Stark and William Bainbridge (1985) defined it, "religion is a set of beliefs about the divine, humankind's relationship to it, and the consequences of that relationship" (quoted in Kellstedt et al. 1996: 175). This is the logic for capturing religious belief items as they describe the content of divine dictate and presence, while religious behaviors indicate the degree to which individuals are committed to those beliefs. Peter Benson and Dorothy Williams (1982) describe this definition of religion as "vertical" and provide the same definition as Stark and Bainbridge and Lyman Kellstedt and colleagues: "the degree to which religion is understood as a relationship between the individual person and God" (Benson and Williams 1982: 108). However, "vertical" is just one religious theme among eight that Benson and Williams identify. They also name agentic, communal, restricting, releasing, comforting, challenging, and horizontal dimensions. For now, I focus on the last theme: the *horizontal*.

While Benson and Williams define the horizontal theme as "the degree to which religion presses a person to adopt compassionate, caring attitudes and actions" (1982: 108), I would extend and generalize this theme. A better conceptualization would avoid attitudinal content—religion could press people to hold stingy, uncaring attitudes, and that would also be different from a vertical conception. Therefore, I define the horizontal religious theme as *the ways that religion helps individuals structure their social relations*.

Religion might bear on the structure of social relations in a number of ways, one of which has been discussed in the literature through the (negative) effect of church attendance on tolerance. That is, attending church frequently is an immersion in an assumed homogeneous society of believers. But other conceptions are broader, more flexible, and thus more analytically useful. Religious groups are constantly conveying norms of inclusion and exclusion to their members, sometimes at the same time. Inclusion entails reaching out to people who are different from you and accepting them for who they are. This can apply to diversity within the church, community, state, or world. One obvious place to find inclusion is in evangelism outreach, but it is also in mainline "welcoming" churches, which announce their support for gay and lesbian members.

Religious groups are also continually conveying norms of exclusion in multiple senses. Any information that elevates the salience of the ingroup highlights boundaries with the outside world. Therefore, the simple act of gathering sends a message of exclusion, though perhaps not a powerful one. The message "We are different," the encouragement to adopt restrictive dress or diet (Finke and Wittberg 2000), and the call to avoid contamination from the outside world all serve the cause of fostering exclusion.[5] The importance of exclusion is that it raises the stakes for interactions with people outside the ingroup. Such interactions may be dangerous, introducing impurities of thought, values, or disease (see Chapter 6). But exclusion also simply reduces the chances for interactions with outsiders (see Djupe and Calfano 2013b), thus limiting the participation in the marketplace of ideas that breeds tolerance.

Both inclusion and exclusion are elements of the religious economy in which religious firms compete for members. The central force that divides the inclusive from the exclusive is tension with the world. As Rodney Stark and Roger Finke (2000) argue, low-tension groups (historically called "churches") exist consonantly with the world (see also Finke and Stark 2005); they emphasize not distinction but rather integration with the community. On the opposite end of the spectrum lie high-tension groups (often called "sects") that exist embattled in a fallen world filled with peril to one's eternal soul (typically described as fundamentalists). Most, of course, fall in between, but the forces of the religious economy predict a distribution of tension that meets the demand in the marketplace (Stark and Finke 2000).

Brian Calfano and I (Djupe and Calfano 2013a, 2013b) provide a measure of the commitment to inclusion and exclusion conceptualized in terms of values among American Protestant clergy. We use four statements to capture the two value concepts.

Inclusive values

- To be true to your faith, it is important to "love the stranger as yourself."
- To be true to your faith, it is important to invite others to church even if the church begins to change as a result.

Exclusive values

- To be true to my faith, it is important to shop as much as possible at stores owned by other people of my faith.
- To be true to my faith, it is important to keep company with other people of my faith.

Using data from a rather large survey of diverse Protestant clergy, we show that they almost universally present inclusive values and display only a slight variability in exclusive values presentation, with evangelicals more likely to display any commitment to exclusive values. While this version assessed the frequency of clergy presentation of these values, work in this volume assesses the degree to which clergy agree or disagree with these values (see Chapters 1 and 2). Measuring frequency is more appropriate for assessing clergy effects on members of congregations (Djupe and Calfano 2013a), while measuring agreement is more apropos for studying the relationship between values and tolerance among clergy. Chapter 9 assesses the degree to which commitment to inclusive and exclusive values affects threat and tolerance among average citizens.

Another set of religious themes that Benson and Williams (1982) promote is the agentic/communal set of dimensions. In the full discussion in Chapter 7, Stephen Mockabee and I draw on work he did with Kenneth Wald and David Leege (2007) to capture measures of individualism (the agentic dimension) and communitarianism (the communal dimension). As they summarize it, individualism captures the idea that religion demands the perfection of the self through, in part, the avoidance of sin. On the other hand, communitarianism promotes the idea that individuals express their faith best through helping others. Though they appear conceptually related to the inclusive and exclusive values Brian Calfano and I developed, it turns out that they are not especially closely related (and thus surely constitute distinct dimensions of religious values).

I close this section of the chapter with four larger points. First, it is surprising that the religion and politics literature has not, until the past decade, developed measures suitable for framing religious worldviews (for one of the early calls for such measures, see Leege and Kellstedt 1993). Therefore, the classic studies on religion and tolerance have evaded most any measure of the values religious people hold. These values are essential to building a richer vision for religion's influence in the world, as values are specifications of how the world *should* work rather than beliefs about how it *actually* works. That is, values presumably compel particular action; in fact, the classic models of public opinion place values in the driver's seat for dictating a destination. Beliefs interact with values in the sense of directing traffic, suggesting which routes to the destination may work or whether the destination is reachable at all. It is too strong to say that the religion and politics literature has been missing the driver, but the importance of including values should readily present itself.

The second main point is that values (as well as beliefs) are not just dispositions; they are more or less constantly in motion in religious organizations. Conceptualizing religion as simply a vertical relationship between an individual and God misses the organizational setting in which that relationship is shaped and reshaped through time by clergy, fellow congregants, and other sources. Indeed, this is a well-developed thread in the sociology of religion (Bibby 1997; Cavendish, Welch, and Leege 1998; Cornwall 1987; Hadaway and Marler 1993; Welch 1981), but it has also seen development in political science (see, e.g., Djupe and Hunt 2009; Gilbert 1993; Jelen 1992; G. Smith 2008; Wald, Owen, and Hill 1988).

Now, this could be a superfluous step—if congregations help develop and solidify religious beliefs and values, then simply capturing those beliefs and values would be sufficient, and we can ignore the antecedent effects of the congregation. However, there is good reason and some evidence to suggest that the content of the information varies across time, and thus religious organizations are not simply reinforcing beliefs and values. The kind of information conveyed, too, stretches beyond religious beliefs and values to include political and other information that bears on political decisions (Djupe and Gilbert 2009); this is the third major point. Clergy convey arguments on gun control and threats to the nation, members have bumper stickers on their cars, and congregations hold political discussion groups on various topics (see also Wald, Owen, and Hill 1988). None of this is captured in the traditional religious belief or behavior measures, it has not been included in previous tolerance work, and it may bear on the least-liked group that people pick, the threat people may perceive, the democratic norms they hold, and the tolerance they are willing to extend.

There is only one direct piece of evidence for this line of argument thus far. Brian Calfano and I (2013a) variously primed respondents with inclusive or exclusive values before asking them about their political tolerance. Priming is the act of making a consideration (cognition or emotion) salient before the respondents make a decision. Priming exclusion drove up the threat they perceived from their least-liked group and thereby reduced their tolerance for the group's activities. This is important because it moves us away from thinking of religious effects as stable and long-term and highlights again the importance of the social environment in which religious values and beliefs may be communicated and therefore primed—a dynamic that has been found effectual in more and more situations (see also Ben-Nun Bloom and Arikan 2012).

Fourth, while the kind of information presented is important, the way in which it is presented can help develop or undermine tolerance. For instance, clergy can essentially deliberate over policy options, and the more fair the presentation of conflicting sides, the more respect for difference congregants may develop (Djupe and Calfano 2012b; Djupe and Neiheisel 2008; Djupe and Olson 2013). Congregations are surprisingly diverse places, and to deal with this diversity without driving away members, congregations are likely to adopt deliberative norms including mutual respect, diversity of views, and full participation (Neiheisel, Djupe, and Sokhey 2009; see also Chapter 1). The fact of implementing good democratic procedures (for clergy) and experiencing them (for congregants) may help nurture a democratic bent that extends beyond the church walls.

Conclusion

It is an exciting time to be working on religious effects on political tolerance. After a generation of work adopting a vertical definition of religion, a sudden burst of energy has diversified the conceptualizations of religion to come much closer to measuring the list Benson and Williams generated in 1982. Many of the first looks at them are present in this volume. As I reviewed the literature and extended its reach, I made note of where much of this new research falls and organized it into three parts. We begin at the elite level, where I collaborate with Ryan Burge and Brian Calfano in Chapter 1, with Brian Calfano in Chapter 2, and with Jeffrey Kurtz in Chapter 3 to examine for the first time the political tolerance levels of clergy and then clergy effects on congregants' tolerance levels. In Chapter 4, Clyde Wilcox and Christine Kim examine whether and under what conditions political activists extend tolerance to Christian fundamentalists.

Then the floodgates open in the second part, where a variety of social-psychological approaches and methods are employed to study the religion-tolerance connection among average citizens. Marie Eisenstein (Chapters 5 and 10) and April Clark (Chapter 5) back up the causal process and assess how religion affects the antecedents of tolerance. Pazit Ben-Nun Bloom and Marie Courtemanche develop the role of disgust in tolerance judgments (Chapter 6), while Stephen Mockabee and I (Chapter 7) and Joby Schaffer, Anand Sokhey, and I (Chapter 9) further test the role of different conceptions of religious values. In Chapter 8, Dan Cox, Robert Jones, and Juhem Navarro-Rivera draw on new survey data from the Public Religion Research Institute to assess tolerance of atheists, with commentary on the conceptualization of the meaning of "least liked."

The last part turns this formulation around to ask how religious groups respond to intolerance and prejudice. In Chapter 11, Jacob Neiheisel, Laura Olson, and I ask how pleas for tolerance affect associated attempts to persuade, while in Chapter 12, Brian Calfano and I ask how people are responsive to arguments that incorporate calls to restrict the rights of a controversial group. In Chapters 13 and 14, respectively, Christopher Garneau assesses how atheists respond to intolerance and prejudice, and Patrick Schoettmer covers how Muslims respond. In the Conclusion, Ted Jelen achieves the difficult task of pulling these strands together.

Notes

1. The General Social Survey, administered through the National Opinion Research Center (NORC) at the University of Chicago since 1972, is an omnibus survey of several thousand adults gathered every year or so. It is designed to capture in some detail the social life of Americans. More information about the GSS is available at http://www3.norc.org/GSS+Website.

2. Quite a bit of research has subsequently been done to see whether the mode of capturing tolerance bears on our conclusions about its determinants. Essentially all of this work by Jim Gibson (e.g., Gibson 1992; Gibson and Bingham 1985) has found little difference. However, in Chapter 5 of this book, Marie Eisenstein and April Clark suggest that mode does matter for our understanding of religious connections to tolerance.

3. There is some debate in the literature about whether there is a difference between measures of beliefs in biblical literalism and the inerrancy of the Bible. There is little difference in using either one according to Ted Jelen (1989), but Jelen, Clyde Wilcox, and Corwin Smidt (1991) find that respondents distinguish the two items.

4. Secure personality is generally a combination of dogmatism, interpersonal trust, and self-esteem (see Sullivan, Piereson, and Marcus 1982).

5. One good example of exclusive values comes from a hymn commonly sung in church when I was growing up: "They'll Know We Are Christians." While it says, "They will know we are Christians by our love," it is clear that that love is directed toward the ingroup. Each stanza begins with an exclusive message that is repeated several times: "We are one in the spirit; we are one in the Lord," "We will walk with each other; we will walk hand in hand," and "We will work with each other; we will work side by side."

References

Adorno, T. W., Else Frenkel-Brunswik, Daniel J. Levinson, and R. Nevitt Sanford. 1950. *The Authoritarian Personality.* New York: Harper and Brothers.

Barker, David C., and James D. Tinnick III. 2006. "Competing Parental Visions and Ideological Constraint." *American Political Science Review* 100 (2): 249–263.

Beatty, Kathleen M., and Oliver Walter. 1984. "Religious Preference and Practice: Reevaluating Their Impact on Political Tolerance." *Public Opinion Quarterly* 48 (1B): "318–329.

Ben-Nun Bloom, Pazit, and Gizem Arikan. 2012. "A Two-Edged Sword: The Differential Effect of Religious Belief and Religious Social Context on Attitudes towards Democracy." *Political Behavior* 34 (2): 249–276.

Benson, Peter, and Dorothy Williams. 1982. *Religion on Capitol Hill.* New York: Harper and Row.

Bibby, Reginald W. 1997. "Going, Going, Gone: The Impact of Geographical Mobility on Religious Involvement." *Review of Religious Research* 38 (4): 289–307.

Bobo, Lawrence, and Frederick C. Licari. 1989. "Education and Political Tolerance: Testing the Effects of Cognitive Sophistication and Target Group." *Public Opinion Quarterly* 53 (3): 285–308.

Burdette, Amy M., Christopher G. Ellison, and Terrence D. Hill. 2005. "Conservative Protestantism and Tolerance toward Homosexuals: An Examination of Potential Mechanisms." *Sociological Inquiry* 75 (2): 177–196.

Burge, Ryan P. 2013. "Using Matching to Investigate the Relationship between Religion and Tolerance." *Politics and Religion* 6 (2): 264–281.

Canetti-Nisim, Daphna. 2004. "The Effect of Religiosity on Endorsement of Democratic Values: The Mediating Influence of Authoritarianism." *Political Behavior* 26 (4): 377–398.

Canetti-Nisim, Daphna, and Benjamin Beit-Hallahmi. 2007. "The Effects of Authoritarianism, Religiosity, and 'New Age' Beliefs on Support for Democracy: Unraveling the Strands." *Review of Religious Research* 48 (4): 369–384.

Cavendish, James C., Michael R. Welch, and David C. Leege. 1998. "Social Network Theory and Predictors of Religiosity for Black and White Catholics: Evidence of a 'Black Sacred Cosmos'?" *Journal for the Scientific Study of Religion* 37 (3): 397–410.

Cornwall, Marie. 1987. "The Social Bases of Religion: A Study of Factors Influencing Religious Belief and Commitment." *Review of Religious Research* 29 (1): 44–56.

Davis, James A. 1975. "Communism, Conformity, Cohorts, and Categories: American Tolerance in 1954 and 1972–1973." *American Journal of Sociology* 81 (3): 491–513.

Djupe, Paul A., and Brian R. Calfano. 2012a. "American Muslim Investment in Civil Society Political Discussion, Disagreement, and Tolerance." *Political Research Quarterly* 65 (3): 516–528.

———. 2012b. "The Deliberative Pulpit: The Democratic Norms and Practices of the PCUSA." *Journal for the Scientific Study of Religion* 51 (1): 90–109.

———. 2013a. *God Talk: Experimenting with the Religious Causes of Public Opinion.* Philadelphia: Temple University Press.

———. 2013b. "Religious Value Priming, Threat, and Political Tolerance." *Political Research Quarterly* 66 (4): 767–779.

Djupe, Paul A., Brian R. Calfano, and Chelsea Back. 2013. "Why People Will Not Vote for Atheist Candidates." In *God Talk: Experimenting with the Religious Causes of Public Opinion*, edited by Paul A. Djupe and Brian R. Calfano, 74–92. Philadelphia: Temple University Press.

Djupe, Paul A., and Christopher P. Gilbert. 2009. *The Political Influence of Churches*. New York: Cambridge University Press.

Djupe, Paul A., and Patrick K. Hunt. 2009. "Beyond the Lynn White Thesis: Congregational Effects on Environmental Concern." *Journal for the Scientific Study of Religion* 48 (4): 670–686.

Djupe, Paul A., and Jacob R. Neiheisel. 2008. "Clergy Deliberation on Gay Rights and Homosexuality." *Polity* 40 (4): 411–435.

Djupe, Paul A., and Laura Olson. 2013. "Public Deliberation about Gay Rights in Religious Contexts: Commitment to Deliberative Norms and Practice in ELCA Congregations." *Journal of Public Deliberation* 9 (1): Article 1.

Durkheim, Émile. (1912) 1961. *Elementary Forms of Religious Life*. New York: Collier Books.

Edgell, Penny, Joseph Gerteis, and Douglas Hartmann. 2006. "Atheists as 'Other': Moral Boundaries and Cultural Membership in American Society." *American Sociological Review* 71 (2): 211–234.

Eisenstein, Marie A. 2008. *Religion and the Politics of Tolerance: How Christianity Builds Democracy*. Waco, TX: Baylor University Press.

Eisenstein, Marie A., and April K. Clark. 2014. "Political Tolerance, Psychological Security, and Religion: Disaggregating the Mediating Influence of Psychological Security." *Politics and Religion* 7 (3): 1–31.

Ellison, Christopher G., and Marc A. Musick. 1993. "Southern Intolerance: A Fundamentalist Effect?" *Social Forces* 72 (2): 379–398.

Filsinger, Erik. 1976. "Tolerance of Non-believers: A Cross-Tabular and Log Linear Analysis of Some Religious Correlates." *Review of Religious Research* 17 (3): 232–240.

Finke, Roger, and Rodney Stark. 2005. *The Churching of America, 1776–2005: Winners and Losers in Our Religious Economy*. New Brunswick, NJ: Rutgers University Press.

Finke, Roger, and Patricia Wittberg. 2000. "Organizational Revival from Within: Explaining Revivalism and Reform in the Roman Catholic Church." *Journal for the Scientific Study of Religion* 39 (2): 154–170.

Francis, Leslie J. 2010. "Personality and Religious Orientation: Shifting Sands or Firm Foundations?" *Mental Health, Religion, and Culture* 13 (7–8): 793–803.

Froese, Paul, Christopher Bader, and Buster Smith. 2008. "Political Tolerance and God's Wrath in the United States." *Sociology of Religion* 69 (1): 29–44.

Gibson, James L. 1992. "Alternative Measures of Political Tolerance: Must Tolerance Be 'Least Liked'?" *American Journal of Political Science* 36 (2): 560–577.

———. 2010. "The Political Consequences of Religiosity: Does Religion Always Cause Political Intolerance?" In *Religion and Democracy in the United States: Danger or Opportunity?* edited by Alan Wolfe and Ira Katznelson, 147–175. New York: Russell Sage.

Gibson, James L., and Richard D. Bingham. 1985. *Civil Liberties and Nazis: The Skokie Free Speech Controversy*. New York: Praeger.

Gibson, James L., and Kent L. Tedin. 1988. "Etiology of Intolerance of Homosexual Politics." *Social Science Quarterly* 69 (3): 587–604.

Gilbert, Christopher P. 1993. *The Impact of Churches on Political Behavior*. Westport, CT: Greenwood Press.

Greeley, Andrew M. 1995. *Religion as Poetry*. New Brunswick, NJ: Transaction.

Green, John C., James L. Guth, Lyman A. Kellstedt, and Corwin E. Smidt. 1994. "Uncivil Challenges: Support for Civil Liberties among Religious Activists." *Journal of Political Science* 22:25–49.

Hadaway, C. Kirk, and Penny Long Marler. 1993. "All in the Family: Religious Mobility in America." *Review of Religious Research* 35 (2): 97–116.

Hetherington, Marc J., and Elizabeth Suhay. 2011. "Authoritarianism, Threat, and Americans: Support for the War on Terror." *American Journal of Political Science* 55 (3): 546–560.

Hills, Peter, Leslie J. Francis, Michael Argyle, and Chris J. Jackson. 2004. "Primary Personality Trait Correlates of Religious Practice and Orientation." *Personality and Individual Differences* 36 (1): 61–73.

Jelen, Ted G. 1989. "Biblical Literalism and Inerrancy: Does the Difference Make a Difference?" *Sociological Analysis* 49 (4): 421–429.

———. 1992. "Political Christianity: A Contextual Analysis." *American Journal of Political Science* 36 (3): 692–714.

Jelen, Ted G., and Clyde Wilcox. 1990. "Denominational Preference and the Dimensions of Political Tolerance." *Sociological Analysis* 51 (1): 69–81.

———. 1991. "Religious Dogmatism among White Christians: Causes and Effects." *Review of Religious Research* 33 (1): 32–46.

Jelen, Ted G., Clyde Wilcox, and Corwin E. Smidt. 1991. "Biblical Literalism and Inerrancy: A Methodological Investigation." *Sociological Analysis* 51 (3): 307–313.

Kellstedt, Lyman A., John C. Green, James L. Guth, and Corwin E. Smidt. 1996. "Grasping the Essentials: The Social Embodiment of Religion and Political Behavior." In *Religion and the Culture Wars*, edited by John C. Green, James L. Guth, Corwin E. Smidt, and Lyman A. Kellstedt, 174–192. Lanham, MD: Rowman and Littlefield.

Kohn, Melvin L. 1977. *Class and Conformity: A Study in Values*. 2nd ed. Chicago: University of Chicago Press.

Layman, Geoffrey C. 2001. *The Great Divide: Religious and Cultural Conflict in American Party Politics*. New York: Columbia University Press.

Leege, David C., and Lyman A. Kellstedt. 1993. "Religious Worldviews and Political Philosophies: Capturing Theory in the Grand Manner through Empirical Data." In *Rediscovering the Religious Factor in American Politics*, edited by David C. Leege and Lyman A. Kellstedt, 216–234. Armonk, NY: M. E. Sharpe.

Madison, James. (1785) 2000. "Memorial and Remonstrance against Religious Assessments." In *The Founders' Constitution*, edited by Philip B. Kurland and Ralph Lerner, Volume 5, Amendment I (Religion), Document 43. Available at http://press-pubs.uchicago.edu/founders/documents/amendI_religions43.html.

Marcus, George E., John L. Sullivan, Elizabeth Theiss-Morse, and Sandra Wood. 1995. *With Malice toward Some: How People Make Civil Liberties Judgments*. New York: Cambridge University Press.

McClosky, Herbert. 1964. "Consensus and Ideology in American Politics." *American Political Science Review* 58 (2): 361–382.

Mill, John S. (1869) 1975. *On Liberty*. New York: Norton.

Mockabee, Stephen T. 2007. "A Question of Authority: Religion and Cultural Conflict in the 2004 Election." *Political Behavior* 29 (2): 221–248.

Mockabee, Stephen T., Kenneth D. Wald, and David C. Leege. 2007. "Reexamining Religiosity: A Report on the New Religion Items in the 2006 ANES Pilot Study." Available at http://www.electionstudies.org/resources/papers/Pilot2006/nes011907.pdf.

Musick, Marc, John Wilson, and William Bynum, Jr. 2000. "Race and Formal Volunteering: The Differential Effects of Class and Religion." *Social Forces* 78 (4): 1539–1571.

Mutz, Diana C. 2006. *Hearing the Other Side: Deliberative versus Participatory Democracy*. Cambridge: Cambridge University Press.

Neiheisel, Jacob R., Paul A. Djupe, and Anand E. Sokhey. 2009. "Veni, Vidi, Disseri: Churches and the Promise of Democratic Deliberation." *American Politics Research* 37 (4): 614–643.

Nunn, Clyde Z., Harry J. Crockett, Jr., and J. Allen Williams, Jr. 1978. *Tolerance for Nonconformity*. San Francisco: Jossey-Bass.

Owen, Dennis E., Kenneth D. Wald, and Samuel S. Hill. 1991. "Authoritarian or Authority-Minded? The Cognitive Commitments of Fundamentalists and the Christian Right." *Religion and American Culture: A Journal of Interpretation* 1 (1): 73–100.

Peffley, Mark, and Lee Sigelman. 1990. "Intolerance of Communists during the McCarthy Era." *Western Political Quarterly* 43 (1): 93–112.

Reichley, A. James. 1985. *Religion in American Public Life*. Washington, DC: Brookings Institution Press.

Reimer, Sam, and Jerry Z. Park. 2001. "Tolerant Incivility: A Longitudinal Analysis of White Conservative Protestants' Willingness to Grant Civil Liberties." *Journal for the Scientific Study of Religion* 40 (4): 735–745.

Roof, Wade Clark, and William McKinney. 1987. *American Mainline Religion: Its Changing Shape and Future*. New Brunswick, NJ: Rutgers University Press.

Scheitle, Christopher P., and Kevin D. Dougherty. 2010. "Race, Diversity and Membership Duration in Religious Congregations." *Sociological Inquiry* 80 (3): 405–423.

Smidt, Corwin, and James M. Penning. 1982. "Religious Commitment, Political Conservatism, and Political and Social Tolerance in the United States: A Longitudinal Analysis." *Sociological Analysis* 43 (3): 231–246.

Smith, Christian. 2000. *Christian America? What Evangelicals Really Want*. Berkeley: University of California Press.

Smith, Gregory A. 2008. *Politics in the Parish: The Political Influence of Catholic Priests*. Washington, DC: Georgetown University Press.

Stark, Rodney, and William Bainbridge. 1985. *The Future of Religion*. Berkeley: University of California Press.

Stark, Rodney, and Roger Finke. 2000. *Acts of Faith: Explaining the Human Side of Religion*. Berkeley: University of California Press.

Stouffer, Samuel A. 1955. *Communism, Conformity, and Civil Liberties: A Cross Section of the Nation Speaks Its Mind*. New York: Doubleday.

Sullivan, John L., James Piereson, and George E. Marcus. 1979. "An Alternative Conceptualization of Political Tolerance: Illusory Increases 1950s–1970s." *American Political Science Review* 73 (3): 781–794.

———. 1982. *Political Tolerance and American Democracy*. Chicago: University of Chicago Press.

Tamney, Joseph B., and Stephen D. Johnson. 1997. "Christianity and Public Book Banning." *Review of Religious Research* 38 (3): 263–271.

Tuntiya, Nana. 2005. "Fundamentalist Religious Affiliation and Support for Civil Liberties: A Critical Reexamination." *Sociological Inquiry* 75 (2): 153–176.

Verba, Sidney, Kay Lehman Schlozman, and Henry E. Brady. 1995. *Voice and Equality: Civic Voluntarism in American Politics*. Cambridge, MA: Harvard University Press.

Wald, Kenneth D. 2015. "The Choosing People: Interpreting the Puzzling Politics of American Jewry." *Politics and Religion* 8 (1): 4–35.

Wald, Kenneth D., Dennis Owen, and Samuel Hill. 1988. "Churches as Political Communities." *American Political Science Review* 82 (2): 531–548.

Welch, Kevin W. 1981. "An Interpersonal Influence Model of Traditional Religious Commitment." *Sociological Quarterly* 22 (1): 81–92.

Wilcox, Clyde. 1987. "Religious Orientations and Political Attitudes: Variations within the New Christian Right." *American Politics Quarterly* 15:274–296.

Wilcox, Clyde, and Ted G. Jelen. 1990. "Evangelicals and Political Tolerance." *American Politics Quarterly* 18:25–46.

Wilcox, Clyde, and Carin Larson. 2006. *Onward Christian Soldiers? The Religious Right in American Politics*. 3rd ed. Boulder, CO: Westview Press.

I

Religion and the Elitist Theory

1

The Political Tolerance of Clergy and Its Democratic Roots

PAUL A. DJUPE
RYAN P. BURGE
BRIAN R. CALFANO

In the seventy years of the social scientific study of clergy, no one has thought to ask about their political tolerance. Samuel Stouffer did not include clergy in his otherwise comprehensive study of the support for civil liberties among community elites. Later studies of political tolerance likewise elided the clergy. Sociological studies of clergy focused on prejudice, especially against Jews, but did not touch on support for rights and liberties. We are left, then, with the most basic of questions to answer: Are clergy tolerant or intolerant? About whom do they weigh extending rights and liberties? What affects their level of tolerance?

Since tolerance for disliked groups and ideas is at the heart of maintaining a healthy democratic process, it comes as no surprise that some of the key fault lines in clergy's commitment to tolerance are on democratic grounds. Take, for instance, the current debate in primarily evangelical circles about anti-bullying initiatives (e.g., Kersten 2014). While this is not exclusive to clergy, many religious people are concerned with anti-bullying initiatives in the public schools of many states. In their view, proscriptions against bullying lesbian, gay, bisexual, or transgender (LGBT) children will result in rules against the expression of views in opposition to the rights of gays and lesbians (primarily evangelical Christian views). This clash of rights and liberties is at the heart of numerous public policy and legal fights in American politics today, especially gay rights, but also contraception, abortion, and others.

What is particularly interesting about this debate, and about the much larger debate between religion and liberalism discussed in the introduction, is that the true "democratic" position is unclear. In fact, both positions are exclusive to an extent—anti-bullying initiatives will prohibit certain views from being directed toward LGBT students, which is seen by some as essential to protect a minority group and ensure their inclusion in the public sphere. Thus, both sides can lay claim to broader democratic principles to justify their position, or they can take the narrower path regarding the importance of protecting their own citizenship. The democratic process certainly does not impose any particular ideological constraint on citizens, but it does provide a powerful set of symbols and ideas that numerous groups have used across time to support their positions and augment the legitimacy of their group.

In this way, we should not pit religion against democracy a priori and assume that those with positions that conflict with the rights of other groups are less willing to embrace rights or extend rights to others. Their position may simply be a reaction against a perceived impingement on their own rights. Instead, we should look for variable commitment to democratic norms across religious groups. That is not the end of the connection between religion and democracy, however.

Many dimensions to democratic *practice* in houses of worship may be related to the tolerance levels of clergy. We suspect, and have argued as much before, that the exercise of democratic practice in churches matters by analogy (Djupe and Calfano 2012; see also Djupe and Neiheisel 2008; Djupe and Olson 2013; Neiheisel, Djupe, and Sokhey 2009). To the extent that individuals engage in respectful exchange across lines of difference, they will learn essential democratic values that can be exported to the public square (see, e.g., Mutz 2006). Clergy are in a special position to observe the benefits of democratic practice in the often fragile franchises in their charge. That is, they may realize the benefits that fair, respectful processes may have in sustaining a loose confederation of actors. Churches have varying levels of democratic practice in running organizational processes, such as governing boards and adult education/discussion groups (Djupe and Calfano 2012; Djupe and Gilbert 2009; Djupe and Olson 2013; Neiheisel, Djupe, and Sokhey 2009), which are only loosely related to other ways in which democratic practice can be observed.

For instance, clergy can model democratic give-and-take in their public addresses. Engaging with different views is a requisite practice in a democracy, especially, but not solely, from elites. Such engagement helps citizens think through their own positions, builds rich opinions about the direction of government and society, and encourages more nuanced views of groups with different opinions (e.g., Barabas 2004; McClurg 2006; Mutz 2006). Previous work that has examined the deliberative shape of clergy public discourse has arrived at something of a constant—clergy address one argument they disagree with for every four they agree with (Djupe and Calfano 2012; Djupe and Neiheisel 2008). Of course, there is considerable variance in this ratio, but the average does not appear to vary much by issue or population studied. Perhaps one reason is that the forces that affect the diversification of clergy's public dialogue are widely shared. They diversify their speech when they face diversity in the congregation. And diverse speech is more likely when clergy are more interested in the issue, suggesting that their engagement serves to ensnare a broader selection of arguments (Neiheisel and Djupe 2008).

Throughout this body of work, democratic practice in congregations has been linked rhetorically to a political tolerance end game. This association can be undermined in at least two ways. First, while we can draw a logical parallel with democratic practice in the polity, clergy may see the value of democratic norms and practice within the congregation as limited to maintaining the congregational franchise. Diversity may be tolerated in the short run with the eventual aim of opinion convergence, pursuing democratic practice toward antidemocratic ends. Second, clergy may bound their tolerance to the ingroup, limiting the extension of rights beyond the sanctuary doors. This would not be surprising and is supported by the tolerance literature itself. Presumably there are few or no worldview threats within the congregation, but groups in profound disagreement can easily be found in the broader society.

These points of "failure"—where democratic practice in the congregation does not extend to broader democratic norms and practices—may be emphasized in certain portions of the population. For instance, evangelical Protestants are more likely to draw distinctions with the world, promoting a sense of embattlement from the larger culture (Djupe and Calfano 2013b; Smith 1998). Those, too, who are more invested in the political process may feel compelled to draw distinctions about who is deserving of rights protections. However, many clergy are concerned democrats—they value democracy, some even more than religious ends (Djupe and Calfano 2012). Those invested in the democratic process should be more likely to extend rights protections beyond the congregation.

Data and Design

There have been a large number of surveys of clergy in the United States. Surprisingly, none of them have asked about the tolerance levels of clergy. To rectify that, we gathered a sample of clergy from several Christian religious groups, including the Presbyterian Church (USA) (PC[USA]), the Southern Baptist Convention (SBC), the United Methodist Church (UMC), the Greek Orthodox Church, and the Reformed Church in America (RCA).[1] This set includes a variety of American religion, though it is obviously not a systematic snapshot. So far, no systematic national samples of clergy include detailed questions about their politics.[2] The sample does include a wide variety of theological traditions, however, as will become clear, and it will be surprising to note the degree of uniformity across these religious groups in key variables. Still, caution should be exercised in generalizing from any of the descriptions presented below.

Tolerance Levels

Since this is the first investigation of clergy tolerance levels, we might profitably spend a bit of time describing them. We employed the least-liked-group technology to elicit tolerance responses, providing clergy with a list of eight groups that they might select (see Sullivan, Piereson, and Marcus 1982). There was a simple division in how clergy selected groups. The Ku Klux Klan, a racist group, was a much more likely choice by UMC (61 percent), RCA (53 percent), and PC(USA) (68 percent) clergy compared to SBC (27 percent) and Greek Orthodox (29 percent) clergy. Instead, the latter two were several times more likely to choose gay rights groups (23 and 33 percent, respectively) compared to clergy in the other three denominations (0, 10, and, 2 percent respectively). SBC and Greek Orthodox clergy were more likely to choose Islamic fundamentalists by about 7 points on average, while the UMC clergy joined them in their rate of selection of pro-choice activists (10–12 percent). A nonzero amount, though few, of the UMC (3 percent), RCA (6 percent), and PC(USA) (8 percent) clergy picked Christian fundamentalists as their least-liked group, and almost none of the clergy overall picked pro-life activists or atheists.

The content-controlled approach to tolerance was meant to avoid an ideological bias in selecting unpopular groups that may no longer be salient and thus to equalize the amount of prejudice held toward evaluated groups. Thus, it may come as no surprise that tolerance of these groups did not vary much by denomination. Figure 1.1 shows a scatterplot of a tolerance index combining responses to six items described in the online appendix (Cronbach's $\alpha = .83$)—they are nearly the same items used by John Sullivan, James Piereson, and George Marcus (1982).[3] Given the extensive research that has found lower levels of tolerance among evangelicals described in the Introduction, it is surprising that these SBC clergy do not differ from the more mainline denominational clergy. Only the Greek Orthodox priests show a lower tolerance level for their least-liked groups. Still, the variation left to be explained is considerable, as

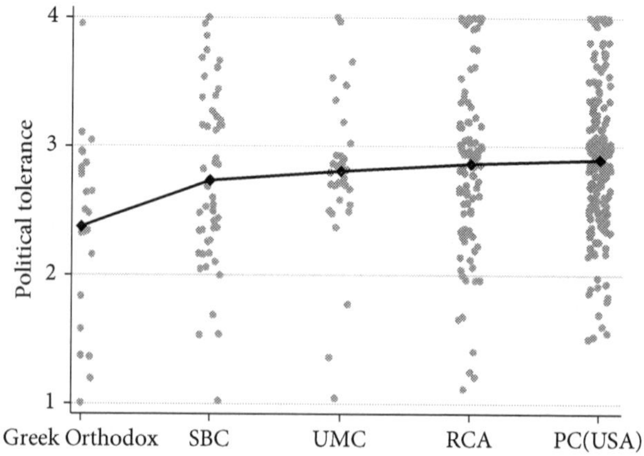

Figure 1.1 Scatterplot of political tolerance levels across surveyed denominations
Note: $F = 4.06$, $p < .01$ for all five denominations; $F = .98$, $p = .40$ for the last four.

each denomination hosts clergy from the intolerant to the very tolerant, though the most intolerant portion of the scale is quite sparsely populated.

Not all of these groups are viewed as threatening. Using a three-item scale (threat to the country, to me, and to my values) ranging from strongly disagree (1) to strongly agree (4), respondent clergy tend to disagree that half of the groups are threatening (they average less than 2.5—the scale midpoint). These groups include the most common group picked, the KKK (2.3), but also the least commonly picked—illegal immigrants, atheists (2.0), and pro-life (1.8) activists. The others drew perceptions of threat, on average. The most threatening were Islamic fundamentalists (2.9), with gay rights activists (2.6) tied with pro-choice activists (2.6), and just ahead of Christian fundamentalists (2.5). We include this measure of threat in our models below in addition to dummy variables for each least-liked group to capture other intangible differences among these groups and the clergy who picked them.

Democratic Norms and Practice

As discussed above, we suspect that one important way in which religion connects to tolerance judgments is through commitment to norms and the practice of democracy in the congregation. We drew on a familiar battery of democratic norms items that highlight the importance of disagreement and debate ($\alpha = .79$; see the online appendix). The final item is perhaps the most bold, asking if respondents agree or disagree that "unless many views are presented, there is little chance that the truth can ever be known." This seems on its face to be quite a strong statement for a clergyperson to agree with given the nature of their enterprise. Yet the sample is overwhelmingly democratic in this way. Only 21 percent disagree and 3 percent strongly disagree; the remaining 75 percent agree (30 percent strongly). Disagreement was stronger among the SBC (34), Greek Orthodox (33), and, perhaps surprisingly, RCA clergy (42), compared to only 14 percent disagreement among PC(USA) and 9 percent among UMC clergy.

Given their strong support for the importance of disagreement and debate, we should not be surprised that these clergy would be committed to democratic practice in their congregations. One place where democratic norms are more likely to be implemented is adult education where it is common to discuss social and political issues. Using a well-established battery (Neiheisel, Djupe, and Sokhey 2009; $\alpha = .73$), we find that these clergy are likewise ready to implement practices that preserve disagreement and debate within the congregation: (1) that members think about and respect the views of others, (2) that all participate, (3) that a range of views are presented, and (4) that participants talk through their differences. The sample mean is "agree" (3) for implementing all four practices; there is some expected variation, but it is not considerable. The least committed to these practices, the Greek Orthodox, average just under agree (2.9), while the most committed in the UMC average over agree (3.4)—the total difference in means is just over a sixth of the scale.

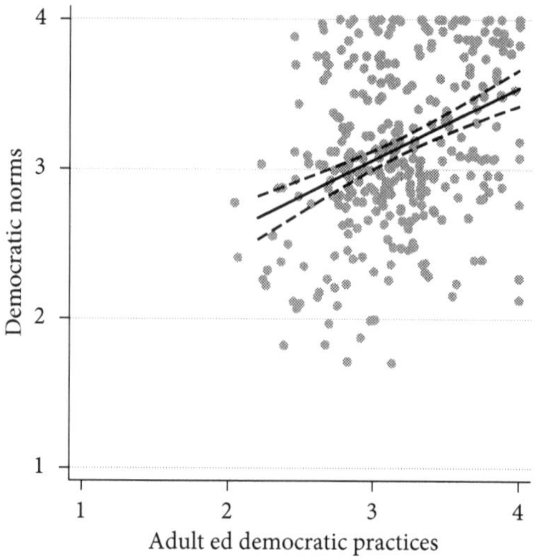

Figure 1.2 Connection between democratic practice in adult education and democratic norm commitment among clergy

Note: $r = .37, p < .01, N = 335$.

The two forms of democratic commitment generally fit together, as the scatterplot in Figure 1.2 shows. The imposed regression line indicates a positive and significant relationship between the two ($r = .37$). However, there is a good degree of slippage here, and the two do not move in lockstep; we can find all combinations of democratic commitment among these clergy. Some are committed to both norms and practice, some to just one, and some to neither. The figure also shows that fundamental disagreement with the value of democratic norms and practice is essentially absent, which is a powerful statement in and of itself.[4]

Model Results: Democratic Norms

At this point, it would be helpful to turn to some models that help us assess the extent to which clergy apply their congregational democratic commitments beyond the church walls.[5] Of course, we are interested in a number of other relationships, including the classic notion that religious conservatism is intimately tied to tolerance judgments. Though religious values have not appeared in the tolerance literature until recently, we are able to test these ideas here—we suspect that clergy's adherence to exclusive religious values would undercut their democratic norms and tolerance and amp up threat. On the other side of that, valuing inclusion should increase democratic norms, decrease threat, and increase tolerance, as inclusion weakens the boundaries between us and them (see also Chapters 7 and 9). We included a series of items that help us contextualize the amount of difference the clergy experience in their community—diversity within the congregation, difference between their own views and their congregation's, and the difference between the congregation and community. If exposure to difference itself is meaningful for these clergy, it should promote the extension of rights to disliked groups.

We begin this investigation with a model of democratic norms (the *y*-axis in Figure 1.2), before turning to models of threat and tolerance regarding their least-liked group. The results for all three dependent variables can be seen in Table 1.1, with the democratic norms estimates in the first set of columns. While we might suspect that tolerance and threat would be "balanced" across religious groups given the content-controlled technology, this logic does not apply to democratic norms. Therefore, it is surprising that religious conservatism has no relationship with democratic norms (or with threat or tolerance for that matter). Instead, democratic norms are tied to a set of values that are common among emergent church clergy, which taps the degree of authority the clergy adopt. After all, the emergent church needs leaders so they can step out of the way—as emergent church thinkers argue (Rollins 2008). For instance, one of the measures is agreement that the Gospel is what the congregation makes of it—a quite organizationally flat notion of theological interpretation. Thus, higher values on the scale indicate opposition to religious authority (of scripture and the pastor). The maximal effect of emergent values is to augment democratic norms by about 0.7 points (about a third of the scale). Here, exclusive value commitments have no effect, but more inclusion is related to higher commitment to democratic norms. Given the effective range of inclusive value commitment, the total effect of inclusion is about 0.4 points (about a fifth of the scale).

Democratic practice in the congregation in adult education sessions is related to the commitment to democratic norms more broadly. That is not surprising, but it is reassuring, given the claims of several earlier articles (e.g., Neiheisel, Djupe, and Sokhey 2009). This also serves to confirm that the relationship we saw in Figure 1.2 holds in the presence of controls. Reinforcing this interpretation is the effect of clergy's view about the connection of the church to democracy. Those who believe that promoting democracy is essential to God's plan are more likely to hold democratic norms, so democratic support is procedural rather than national or patriotic. Interestingly, sample clergy's attitudes are essentially normally distributed about the scale midpoint (which was the most common response with 38 percent)—just about 30 percent agreed that the church should promote democracy, while 33 percent denied at some level that the church had a stake in any form of government. Given the effective range of the variable, the effect of views supportive of a church-democracy relationship is to boost democratic norm commitment by about 0.2 points (a tenth of the scale).

It is notable that the authoritarian tendencies of the clergy have no relationship to their commitment to democratic norms net of everything else. These are the classic child-rearing questions that have been established as an unobtrusive way of capturing authoritarianism (see, e.g., Barker and Tinnick 2006). Given that authoritarianism is at least a close cousin of dogmatism (which is a strong component of the democratic norms dependent variable), we

TABLE 1.1 ORDINARY LEAST SQUARES (OLS) MODELS OF DEMOCRATIC NORMS, THREAT, AND POLITICAL TOLERANCE

		Democratic Norms			*Threat*			*Political Tolerance*		
		β	*SE*	*p*	β	*SE*	*p*	β	*SE*	*p*
	Threat	—			—			–.26	(.05)	.00
Beliefs and values	Religious conservatism	–.01	(.05)	.88	.02	(.07)	.79	.05	(.05)	.37
	Emergent values scale	.14	(.06)	.02	–.19	(.09)	.03	—		
	Inclusive values	.23	(.05)	.00	.37	(.23)	.11	—		
	Exclusive values	–.04	(.04)	.32	.71	(.36)	.05	—		
	Inclusive × exclusive	—			–.14	(.08)	.08	—		
Democracy	Democratic norms	—			.13	(.08)	.13	.15	(.06)	.01
	Adult education norms	.29	(.08)	.00	.08	(.12)	.49	.02	(.08)	.80
	No stake in democracy	–.05	(.02)	.03	.01	(.03)	.78	.02	(.02)	.29
	Authoritarian minded	.00	(.08)	.98	–.04	(.10)	.70	.03	(.08)	.71
Difference	Similarity to community	–.03	(.03)	.23	.03	(.04)	.41	–.01	(.03)	.81
	Difference from congregation	.08	(.06)	.21	.09	(.09)	.29	–.05	(.07)	.42
	Congregational diversity	.00	(.03)	.98	.04	(.04)	.39	.02	(.03)	.63
	New member outreach	–.03	(.03)	.18	.06	(.03)	.08	.02	(.03)	.54
Demographics	Education level	.00	(.05)	.94	–.09	(.06)	.17	.05	(.05)	.28
	Partisanship	.04	(.03)	.11	–.09	(.04)	.02	–.04	(.03)	.16
	Female	.00	(.08)	.96	.05	(.11)	.64	–.07	(.09)	.45
Denomination	SBC	–.02	(.16)	.90	–.05	(.23)	.83	.17	(.17)	.33
	UMC	–.12	(.19)	.53	–.24	(.27)	.36	.29	(.20)	.15
	RCA	–.27	(.15)	.08	–.17	(.21)	.42	.27	(.16)	.09
	PC(USA)	–.06	(.15)	.71	–.17	(.22)	.44	.34	(.16)	.04
Least-liked group	Pro-choice activists	—			.49	(.19)	.01	.82	(.15)	.00
	Pro-life activists	—			–.38	(.41)	.36	.26	(.31)	.42
	Gay rights activists	—			.07	(.17)	.66	.33	(.13)	.01
	Atheists	—			–.54	(.34)	.12	.54	(.25)	.03
	Christian fundamentalists	—			.02	(.17)	.91	.72	(.13)	.00
	Islamic fundamentalists	—			.66	(.12)	.00	–.10	(.10)	.32
	Illegal immigrants	—			–.86	(.50)	.09	.02	(.39)	.96
Constant		1.10	0.52	0.03	0.71	1.22	0.56	2.12	(.50)	.00
Model statistics		$N = 295$, $R^2 = .26$, RMSE = .50			$N = 295$, $R^2 = .22$, RMSE = .68			$N = 297$, $R^2 = .34$, RMSE = .52		

Note: SE = standard error; RMSE = root mean squared error.

expected a stronger relationship. Moreover, the measures of clergy's exposure to difference—in and with the congregation and in the community—have no bearing on their democratic norms. This may make sense since we have behavioral responses to that diversity, at least in the sense of their adult education practices.

The most important finding from this section is the close connection between democracy in the congregation and clergy commitment to democratic norms more broadly. This is important because it may mean the clergy reinforce democratic experiences in the congregation with rhetorical support. Democratic norms are implemented not just to maintain the congregational franchise; or perhaps they are, but then have a longer-term effect on the values clergy hold. Of course, what remains to be tested is whether *members'* democratic experiences in the congregation bear on their commitment to democracy.

Model Results: Threat

As part of the triumvirate of forces that affect tolerance (i.e., insecurity, threat, and democratic norms), threat is perhaps the most closely connected and consistently measured. Until recently, no study of religious effects on tolerance had examined a corollary effect on threat. There is little connection between religiosity and threat (especially given the content-controlled technology) (but see Eisenstein 2006), but there is a connection between threat and the height of boundaries with the world that a religious group may set. It turns out that these are quite malleable—we show in previous work that priming religious values of inclusion or exclusion lowers or raises, respectively, the salience of the ingroup, which affects threat (Djupe and Calfano 2013a). The model results that include the effects of these religious values are presented in the second set of columns of Table 1.1.

Again, religious conservatism has no bearing on threat, but the religious values do. Holding values consistent with those espoused by leaders of the emergent church is linked with reduced levels of threat. Moving from those least committed to emergent church values to the most committed drops threat by a full point. Moreover, inclusive and exclusive values interact sensibly to shape threat given that they should be working in opposite directions (exclusive values to raise threat, inclusive values to lower it). Here, in the absence of a strong commitment to inclusion, holding exclusive values is connected to threat. Then, with inclusion present, the effect of exclusion is weakened considerably. With exclusive value commitment low, inclusive values are linked to low levels of threat perception.

Very little in the rest of the model is linked to threat perceptions. Democratic norms and exposure to diversity itself have no bearing on threat levels. Those who are engaged in more outreach activities for new members perceive more threat and Republicans perceive less threat. And there is some variation among the kinds of least-liked groups—atheists and illegal immigrants, for example, are seen as less threatening relative to the Klan (the excluded reference group).

Across the wide variety of forces represented in this model, little beyond the worldviews of clergy bears directly on how threatened they are by other people.

Therefore, it is no surprise that previous work has found little connection of religion to threat—religion operationalized as religiosity is essentially independent of the kinds of considerations necessary to reshape in-group and out-group boundaries. This chapter helps build on a growing line of work reinforcing the importance of "horizontal" religious values that prescribe appropriate connections to others.

Model Results: Political Tolerance

As we expect from previous work (e.g., Burge 2013) and work in this volume (Chapters 5 and 10), religiosity has no direct bearing on tolerance judgments; nor do the religious values we test here (see the final set of columns of Table 1.1). We included religiosity only because of its long-standing presence in the literature; the others had no effect and were therefore dropped. Instead, the monuments of the broader literature appear important to shaping tolerance. Tolerance drops as the group is perceived as threatening. Tolerance receives a boost with the commitment to democratic norms. There is a fair degree of variation by religious group, with clergy from the mainline Protestant denominations more tolerant than the others (see also Chapter 3). This is no surprise when you consider the place that tolerance holds in the theological and practical approaches of these denominations (though it is by no means uncontested). However, the differences are not large, and the differences largely disappear when we exclude the Greek Orthodox (though the PC[USA] clergy are modestly more tolerant than the SBC). There is also a good deal of variation in the tolerance afforded to different groups, with almost four of the seven groups granted greater levels of rights and liberties than the Klan. Only illegal immigrants, Islamic fundamentalists, and pro-life activists would be treated the same as the Klan.

Conclusion

We conclude this first look at the political tolerance of clergy with a few unambiguous signals. First, clergy are tolerant for the same reasons as other people. The same basic model that has developed over the years in the social sciences applies to clergy without fail. Democratic norms and threat are the most prominent forces structuring the extension of rights and liberties to unpopular groups. Second, clergy are about as tolerant as average Americans. While we do not have access to specific comparisons within these denominations (for that see Chapters 2 and 3), we can compare these results to those from a national sample collected around the 2012 election (see Djupe and Sokhey 2013). Using the same tolerance battery and many of the same least-liked groups (though not the Klan), the average tolerance level was .59 compared to .60 in our clergy sample (collapsed to a 0–1 range). That statistic does not change if we eliminate nonbelievers from the comparison.

Third, while more broadly a tension is pitched between religion and democracy, which is true on the margins, the debate should probably be recast and reversed. In the main, and not just in the mainline, there is a widespread commitment to democratic practice in congregations. These practices are natural strategies clergy may turn to in order to maintain the franchise when they face disagreement in the congregation. Importantly, democratic practice in the congregation is linked to support for broader democratic norms. These norms are important in and of themselves, especially in an era of polarization, but they are also one of the primary forces underpinning political tolerance.

An extension of this notion is that we might reorient the way we think about religious effects to emphasize the structure of relations religion promotes. Democratic values of respecting disagreement are one way to think about this, but they are one subset of a broader category. Relevant dimensions also include where group boundaries are drawn—narrowly or broadly (or as we call them, exclusively or inclusively). But we also added one further dimension especially appropriate to clergy, which is the extent to which they emphasize their role as leader and hierarchy in general or become leaders so they can refuse to lead (see Burge and Djupe 2014, 2015). It is notable that these emergent values are linked to greater democratic norms and reduced threat levels. Though all three of these (democratic norms, inclusiveness, and emergence) constitute different dimensions, they are part and parcel of worldviews that vary along the lines of greater or lesser human differentiation. Traditional measures of religion—group and religiosity—perform poorly in their presence. Given the extent to which these values are linked to a wide range of public opinion and political tolerance in both experimental and observational settings, they are surely worth investigating further.

Notes

1. In February 2014, we e-mailed 16,740 survey invitations. Clergy were contacted to participate via their listed office e-mail address. For the smaller denominations in our study—the Greek Orthodox and RCA—addresses were culled from publicly available parish and denominational websites that listed this individual-level contact information. PC(USA) clergy contact information was provided to the authors from the denomination's in-house research office. For the largest denominations in our study—the UMC and SBC—we relied on a commercially generated e-mail list from the vendor Exact Data, which maintains current congregational lists for a variety of U.S. denominations. Each of the culling methods has drawbacks from the standpoint of representativeness, although it is not possible to determine exact sampling biases a priori. In each denominational case, we endeavored to use the total population of clergy with listed e-mail addresses, which is a subset of the total clergy population in each denomination. Three reminders were sent and the survey closed four weeks later. The sample consists of 456 respondent clergy.

2. There is one exception to this—the United States Congregational Life Study (available at http://www.thearda.com), a portion of which snowball sampled congregations from respondents to the General Social Survey.

3. The appendix, which contains coding notes and additional analyses, is available at http://pauldjupe.com/s/Appendix.docx.

4. Though there appears to be a bit more disagreement with democratic norms than practice, a *t*-test indicates no significant difference.

5. Full variable coding information can be found in the online appendix at http://pauldjupe.com/s/Appendix.docx.

References

Barabas, Jason. 2004. "How Deliberation Affects Policy Opinions." *American Political Science Review* 98 (4): 687–701.

Barker, David C., and James D. Tinnick III. 2006. "Competing Parental Visions and Ideological Constraint." *American Political Science Review* 100 (2): 249–263.

Burge, Ryan P. 2013. "Using Matching to Investigate the Relationship between Religion and Tolerance." *Politics and Religion* 6 (2): 264–281.

Burge, Ryan P., and Paul A. Djupe. 2014. "Truly Inclusive or Uniformly Liberal? An Analysis of the Politics of the Emergent Church." *Journal for the Scientific Study of Religion* 53 (3): 636–651.

———. 2015. "Emergent Church Practices in America: Inclusion and Deliberation in American Congregations." *Review of Religious Research* 57 (1): 1–22.

Djupe, Paul A., and Brian R. Calfano. 2012. "The Deliberative Pulpit: The Democratic Norms and Practices of the PCUSA." *Journal for the Scientific Study of Religion* 51 (1): 90–109.

———. 2013a. "Religious Value Priming, Threat, and Political Tolerance." *Political Research Quarterly* 66 (4): 767–779.

———. 2013b. *God Talk: Experimenting with the Religious Causes of Public Opinion.* Philadelphia: Temple University Press.

Djupe, Paul A., and Christopher P. Gilbert. 2009. *The Political Influence of Churches.* New York: Cambridge University Press.

Djupe, Paul A., and Jacob R. Neiheisel. 2008. "Clergy Deliberation on Gay Rights and Homosexuality." *Polity* 40 (4): 411–435.

Djupe, Paul A., and Laura R. Olson, eds. 2007. *Religious Interests in Community Conflict: Beyond the Culture Wars.* Waco, TX: Baylor University Press.

———. 2013. "Public Deliberation about Gay Rights in Religious Contexts: Commitment to Deliberative Norms and Practice in ELCA Congregations." *Journal of Public Deliberation* 9 (1): Article 1. Available at http://www.publicdeliberation.net/cgi/viewcontent.cgi?article=1214&context=jpd.

Djupe, Paul A., and Anand E. Sokhey. 2013. "Insulated Reasoning: Social Network Access to 'The War on Women.'" Paper presented at the annual meeting of the American Political Science Association, Chicago.

Eisenstein, Marie A. 2006. "Rethinking the Relationship between Religion and Political Tolerance in the U.S." *Political Behavior* 28 (4): 327–348.

Kersten, Katherine. 2014. "Antibullying Bill Raises Troubling Questions." *Minneapolis StarTribune*, February 26. Available at http://www.startribune.com/opinion/commentaries/247368911.html.

McClurg, Scott D. 2006. "Political Disagreement in Context: The Conditional Effect of Neighborhood Context, Disagreement and Political Talk on Electoral Participation." *Political Behavior* 28 (4): 349–366.

Mutz, Diana C. 2006. *Hearing the Other Side: Deliberative versus Participatory Democracy.* Cambridge: Cambridge University Press.

Neiheisel, Jacob R., and Paul A. Djupe. 2008. "Intraorganizational Constraints on Churches' Public Witness." *Journal for the Scientific Study of Religion* 47 (3): 427–441.

Neiheisel, Jacob R., Paul A. Djupe, and Anand E. Sokhey. 2009. "Veni, Vidi, Disseri: Churches and the Promise of Democratic Deliberation." *American Politics Research* 37 (4): 614–643.

Rollins, Peter. 2008. "The Leader Is Needed in Order to Refuse Leadership." *Peter Rollins* (blog), April 4. Available at http://peterrollins.net/2008/04/the-leader-is-needed-in-order-to-refuse-leadership/.

Smith, Christian. 1998. *American Evangelicalism: Embattled and Thriving.* Chicago: University of Chicago Press.

Sullivan, John L., James Piereson, and George E. Marcus. 1982. *Political Tolerance and American Democracy.* Chicago: University of Chicago Press.

2

The Golden Rule Theory

The Nature of Clergy Influence on Congregational Political Tolerance

PAUL A. DJUPE
BRIAN R. CALFANO

As discussed in the Introduction, the literature on religious effects on tolerance has studiously avoided congregational influences. This is a curious omission. Outside of families, congregations are most often where religion is acquired, where communities develop a cognitive infrastructure (beliefs and models of appropriate conduct) that is governed by more or less rigid social enforcement. But congregational influences extend beyond the acquisition of worldviews relevant to tolerance judgments. That is, the relationship between the church experience and tolerance for disliked groups is more complex than clergy merely teaching which groups are sinful. Indeed, given the loose connections many people have with their religious organizations, we argue that tolerance judgments flow from clergy teachings about how people should relate to one other—what we called perspectives on human differentiation in Chapter 1. That is, rather than thinking about tolerance judgments in a vacuum, we see the study of tolerance as a way to think more broadly about the church experience and clergy roles. Assessing clergy influence on the politics of church members should be well integrated into the congregational system.

While we lay out a broader research agenda of congregational influences on political tolerance, we focus on one aspect of that agenda here: the effect of clergy. Clergy, as *fidei defensor*, are perhaps the natural starting point for thinking about congregational effects. From one perspective, clergy are goal oriented, working to transform the world according to theological dictates (Guth et al. 1997: 8; see Jelen 1994 for the theological limitations on political action). They benefit from regular access to the congregation and possess a stature on matters of spirituality and right living that envelop the value conflicts at the root of the question of tolerance. Whether clergy convey their personal predilections or the long-cherished traditions of the religion, we have strong expectations that what clergy communicate will inform congregants' political judgments.

At the same time, a number of features of the congregational context complicate the expected relationship of clergy values and congregant tolerance. Clergy may be less than full-throated in their pursuit of policy goals. Instead, they often prefer processes that maintain social harmony, processes that may challenge attitudes while maintaining peace inside the congregation and in society at large. As we review in this chapter, these complications challenge us to rethink the idea of clergy as valiant defenders of the faith who charge into cultural conflict. Put another way, examining tolerance is useful to help sort out how to think about the role of clergy in public life, continuing the theme from Chapter 1 that examines the determinants of clergy political tolerance.

The Role of Clergy

How should we think about clergy in political life? Here we are discussing not how clergy *should* be engaged in politics but descriptive ideas about how they actually are involved. While there are multiple conceptions of how clergy engage in political life, we might profitably boil them down to three. The first is that they are not. Observers have regularly criticized clergy for not engaging enough to address social problems. They may be essentially bought by powerful community interests (Pope 1942), discouraged from engaging by disagreement in the congregation and community (Campbell and Pettigrew 1959; Djupe and Gilbert 2003; Hadden 1969; Stark et al. 1971), or they may find theological arguments for disengaging from political life to "render unto Caesar" (e.g., Thomas and Dobson 1999) or the necessity for individual rather than collective salvation (Jelen 1994).

Theological conservatives have reenvisioned their role to find support for political engagement over time (Guth 1996), and clergy political activity seems to be higher in recent years than earlier in American history (Djupe and Gilbert 2008). Therefore, a role that makes room for political engagement seems a better candidate. Two tracks to clergy political roles that differ essentially in emphasis are marked in the literature. Everyone we have run across acknowledges the elite status of clergy, recognizing that they often have a well-formed vision of how the world should work and spiritual and vocational imperatives to impart it to the public. One of the tracks emphasizes these imperatives, thinking of clergy as strategic maximizers of policy preferences (Calfano 2009, 2010; Calfano, Oldmixon, and Gray 2013; Guth et al. 1997).

An alternate model starts with clergy as entrepreneurs, responsible for the maintenance of a congregational franchise (Finke and Stark 2005). While we would push past a narrow, purely self-interested conception of entrepreneur here, the predictions of a richer notion are essentially the same. The key difference from the strategic maximizer model is the emphasis on the congregational context—clergy will maintain the congregation even at the expense of their policy goals. Both the thick and the thin version of this track highlight the importance of context, that clergy's ministry is not the same from place to place but changes depending on the congregation, community, and broader environment. The thick version, however, argues that clergy often care deeply for their congregants, cater to their varied needs, and minister to them in place. The fullest and thickest *political* expression of this model is the notion of clergy as representatives of their congregations, as they tend to get involved in politics when their congregations are underrepresented in the community (Djupe and Gilbert 2003), where leadership is scarce (Olson 2000), and at times to challenge their congregation prophetically not to live complacently (Djupe and Gilbert 2003; Hofrenning 1995).

Most of this literature assumes the nature of the goals clergy seek are directional policy goals, though this does not neatly square with at least some of the work on their political activity. There is no doubt that clergy are very active, on balance, engaging a wide range of activities at much higher rates than the average public (Guth et al. 1997). But when it comes to asking the congregation to get involved, many appear to simply invite their congregants to become active rather than push a particular policy direction (Beyerlein and Chaves 2003; Djupe and Gilbert 2003; Djupe and Neiheisel 2012). Moreover, their local activism appears to be congregation- and community-centric, rather than clergy-centric (Olson 2000; Owens 2007). The model does not deny the agency of individual clergy in this process (see, e.g., Cavendish 2001), but it does suggest the contextual incentives are quite powerful in shaping how and to what end clergy engage in politics.

Moreover, clergy may be equally and sometimes more concerned with process compared to policy direction. A theology of inclusion dictates a fundamental concern for fairness and equal treatment (see also Chapter 3, which profiles the promotion of tolerance and inclusion in the Presbyterian Church (USA)). According to Jesse Graham, Jonathan Haidt, and Brian Nosek (2009; see also Chapters 1, 7, and 11), a concern for fairness and equality is universal (additional moral concerns may primarily occupy conservatives). But clergy may promote tolerance for practical reasons—they face an often surprising amount of disagreement within their congregations that can threaten the franchise. That is, people choose to attend a particular church for a host of reasons (e.g., Roof 1999); hence congregations are surprisingly diverse places (Djupe and Gilbert 2009; though not along racial and ethnic lines—Emerson and Smith 2000) that clergy have to learn to navigate and attempt to hold together. One of the resources they can draw on are norms of tolerance that show up in many of their speech patterns and in the small discussion groups they create (Djupe and Calfano 2012; Djupe and Neiheisel 2008; Djupe and Olson 2013; Neiheisel, Djupe, and Sokhey 2009).

While the religion and political behavior literature contains the implicit and sometimes explicit assumption that clergy influence their congregants, the evidence for that is surprisingly sparse and often heavily qualified. Paul Djupe and Christopher Gilbert (2009) document just how tenuous are the lines of communication between clergy and congregation, with widespread misperception of the amount of political speech clergy convey. They find essentially no influence on the opinions of congregants, a null pattern that Gregory Smith (2008) corroborates among Catholics.

But a smattering of studies has found clergy influence on the death penalty among Catholics (Bjarnason and Welch 2004), on matters of peace among Mennonites (Fetzer 2001), and on the environment among Lutherans and Episcopalians (Djupe and Hunt 2009). The dominant reason advanced thus far for why so little clergy influence has been found is the fact of political disagreement that promotes congregants to build defenses over time toward clergy communications (see Djupe and Calfano 2013b; Djupe and Gilbert 2009). If that is true, then continuing to look for direct political pathways of influence is perhaps the wrong route. Instead, we might seek paths to influence that evade congregants' defenses and that emphasize the attributes of clergy that play to their credibility. Among many candidates, one possibility is the communication of religious values that have political implications. Inclusive values attempt to break down barriers between people, while exclusive values reify them, raising the costs of diverse social interaction and social thinking. Experimental exposure to exclusive values has been found to raise threat levels of a least-liked group (Djupe and Calfano 2013a), to reduce support for cooperative foreign intervention by the United States (Djupe and Calfano 2013b), and to reduce support for an expansive immigration policy.

One puzzle that emerged from this research was the nonexistent effects of inclusive value exposure at least in terms of shaping attitudes on foreign intervention policy, which is why the last statement was framed as exposure to exclusive values. We suggested that since inclusive values are much more commonly advanced by clergy, current attitudes already reflect them, or congregants become inured to the message, or both. We have the potential to test those notions here by assessing whether the frequency of exposure, approximated by attendance, interacts with inclusive value presentation. If frequent exposure reduces the effect, then we should see no effect among members who attend church frequently and a greater effect among those who attend infrequently.

We include several other clergy attributes that may bear on the tolerance levels of congregants. As discussed in some detail in Chapter 7, adherence to a communitarian religious worldview should promote greater tolerance than an individualist one in which avoiding sin is paramount. One of the most long-standing findings in the religion and tolerance literature is that fundamentalists are less tolerant for a host of reasons, but primarily drawing on the depth of value conflict and dogmatism (e.g., Jelen and Wilcox 1991; Wilcox and Jelen 1990). We expect clergy holding inerrant views of the Bible to promote more intolerance and threat. Last, clergy also have views about democracy that sometimes trump the dictates of the faith (see Djupe and Calfano 2012). Clergy holding democratic norms should promote less threat and more tolerance. The particular measure we use ("Unless many points of view are presented, there is little chance that the truth can ever be known") doubles as a measure of dogmatism, which is useful in terms of specifying a model though perhaps less useful when trying to test theory.

We include several items to round out the model, including the congregant's political ideology, exposure to political disagreement, and born-again identification—all should correlate with tolerance and feelings of threat. The more highly educated, males, and younger citizens should feel less threat and be more tolerant.

Research Design

The data for this paper are a subset of a larger data set gathered during the winter of 2009–2010. Using computer-assisted telephone interviewing (CATI) technology, we conducted an original phone-based, survey-embedded experiment of a random-digit dialing sample of five thousand landline telephone numbers in Greene County, Missouri.[1] Greene is the county home of Springfield, known as a central location for American evangelicals (it is home to the international headquarters of the Pentecostal Assemblies of God), and it is directly north of Christian County, Missouri, which Dante Chinni and James Gimpel (2010) identify as a quintessential epicenter of evangelical Christianity in the United States. The sample, therefore, contained a significant number of evangelical subjects (56 percent).[2] In the end, 772 subjects agreed to begin participation in the survey experiment, resulting in a response rate of 17.5 percent, though not all finished.[3]

The survey components that were uniform for all respondents included religious identity, belief, and behavior measures, party identification, a political knowledge battery, a political tolerance battery, a social network battery, indicators concerning approval of the pastor, and standard subject demographic measures.[4]

Importantly, interviewers asked for the name and location of the congregation attended by the respondent, and we used these data to build a snowball sample of congregations from which to survey clergy. We faced a number of problems identifying congregations from these responses. Most, but not all, of the attenders provided a church name, though it was not always helpful in identifying a specific congregation. "Assemblies of God" and "Baptist" are hardly useful monikers in the buckle of the Bible Belt. Sometimes the pidgin religio-English of the interviewers was problematic ("Christ Epistaple"), though generally decipherable. Further, we could not locate some of the congregations identified in any online directory or on the web. In the end, we were able to identify eighty congregations. With help from a small (2010) Jack Shand research grant from the Society for the Scientific Study of Religion (SSSR), we conducted a mail survey of these congregations' clergy just a few months after the phone survey was complete (but clearly after the citizen survey). Through multiple follow-up mailings and even a few phone calls in the end to catch congregations with multiple survey respondents, we gathered responses from 44 clergy respondents that we could attach to 114 citizen survey respondents from the initial phone survey. That sample crosses the Christian spectrum with 14 percent Catholic, 23 percent mainline Protestant (mostly UMC), 38 percent Southern Baptist, 9 percent Assemblies of God, and the rest from various evangelical denominations including a handful of nondenominational congregations.

Results

The tolerance battery used the least-liked-group technology, first ascertaining the respondent's prejudices (the "least-liked group") before asking about his or her level of tolerance for the activities of that group in public life. In the phone survey, respondents' group selections were included in the survey questions about tolerance. In the mail survey, clergy were asked to refer to their selection in the previous question when responding to the tolerance questions. In the following analysis, we will follow this empirical trail, first examining the degree to which clergy and congregants share group prejudices, then how clergy shape threat, and then how clergy may shape tolerance judgments.

Group Prejudice

At the heart of the tolerance judgment are the conflicting values between two groups. If there is a tight, direct connection between clergy and congregant, it should be reflected in the mutual selection of a least-liked group—they should share prejudices. Just 18 percent of the congregants selected the same group as their clergyperson did.[5] The punch line is that we find any agreement at all in only three of the group selections. Just over 20 percent of congregants selected Nazis as their least-liked group when their clergy did (compared to 33 percent overall), a quarter selected the Ku Klux Klan (KKK) when their clergy did (compared to 19 percent overall), and less than 10 percent selected atheists when their clergy did (compared to 9 percent overall). No congregant selected Islamic fundamentalists or Christian fundamentalists when their clergy did.

Given that six least-liked groups were listed in the survey, a random distribution of congregant responses would return 17 percent agreement. That does not mean the selections were indeed random, but model results do support the independence of these two responses. Using specifications very close to what is available in Table 2.1, we found that essentially nothing predicts clergy-congregant agreement in selecting a least-liked group (results not shown).[6] Attendance was not a predictor (if anything, it was negative, meaning less agreement with more attendance); nor were communication of particular values, respondent education, exposure to disagreement (though often negative), and political interest. Interestingly, having a strong party identification was the most consistent term and predicted agreement with the clergy.

TABLE 2.1 ESTIMATES OF THREAT PERCEPTIONS AND TOLERANCE OF LEAST-LIKED GROUPS (ORDINARY LEAST SQUARES [OLS] REGRESSION)

		Threat to Country			*Political Tolerance*		
		β	*SE*	*p*	β	*SE*	*p*
Clergy's views	Clergy tolerance level	.10	(.15)		.16	(.09)	*
	Avoid sin	.16	(.25)		−.08	(.22)	
	Inclusive values	−2.43	(1.61)	†	−.67	(.25)	***
	Many points of view needed	.11	(.12)		.23	(.11)	**
	Inerrant belief	−.40	(.20)	*	−.07	(.09)	
	Inclusive × attendance	.43	(.32)	†	.13	(.05)	**
Member variables	Member attendance	−1.64	(1.25)	†	−.92	(.39)	**
	Born again	.41	(.20)	**	−.01	(.21)	
	Age	−.00	(.01)		−.00	(.00)	
	Education	−.00	(.04)		.05	(.03)	†
	Female	.73	(.18)	***	−.25	(.15)	*
	Ideology	−.19	(.07)	***	.01	(.06)	
	Political disagreement	−.20	(.09)	**	.04	(.07)	
Constant		12.01	(6.46)		4.14	(2.04)	**
Model statistics		$N = 76$, $R^2 = .36$, RMSE = .69			$N = 83$, $R^2 = .31$, RMSE = .57		

Source: 2009–2010 Springfield Area Study.

Note: SE = standard error; RMSE = root mean squared error.

***$p < .01$, **$p < .05$, *$p < .10$ (two-tailed tests), † < .10 (one-tailed test)

We own all of the potential problems with the study—responses are not gathered at exactly the same time, and the sample is small. But these results may still not mean that congregants are well out of sync with their clergy. That remains to be determined below. What the results do imply are two things. First, there appears to be little direct connection between clergy and congregants, so while clergy may attempt to be political leaders in their congregations, that role is often unrequited. To the extent that clergy are talking about these unpopular groups (and we have no evidence whether they are), congregants have picked up essentially none of the signals. Second, the results suggest that prejudices that may be gained from the congregation are not locked and loaded. They have to be reminded. Significant questions emanate from that implication: Are those prejudices unstable and subject to priming? Or are they predispositional and at odds with whatever messages are shared in church? We return to this point in the conclusion to the chapter.

Group Threat

One of the dominant explanations of tolerance has been the threat the group is perceived to pose to the country and, to a much lesser degree, to the individual.

Threat has both durable and contemporary components (Marcus et al. 1995). Threat is rooted in value conflict and personal insecurity, but threat value also responds to contemporary information about the activities of a group. From this perspective, there are a number of reasons to think that clergy may be implicated in affecting threat levels. They can do this directly by talking about the danger groups pose to society, though as we have just seen, the selection of a least-liked group by congregants appears to have nothing to do with the clergy's selection. Alternatively, clergy can also shape threat by affecting the cost of social interaction. Essentially, when they preach the value of helping others (a communitarian view) and preach inclusivity, they raise the benefit of diverse social interaction and lower threat (Djupe and Calfano 2013a).

Clergy can also shape threat by raising the price of value conflict, which should increase as a value is more dogmatically held. Another way to put this is that if there are no errors in the Bible, then there is no margin of error in life. Holding an inerrant view of the Bible should be related to higher levels of threat. When aggregated to the congregational level, threat levels cover the full range, though members agree, on average, that their least-liked groups are threatening. Congregations with clergy holding an inerrant view of the Bible tend to be clustered toward the higher end of the threat scale (the correlation at the congregational level is $r = .22$), though inerrantists can be found across the spectrum of threat values.[7] But inerrancy is also strongly related to the promotion of exclusive values ($r = .4$ at the individual level), so we need to model this.

Estimates of the threat posed by least-liked groups can be found in Table 2.1. The degree to which clergy are tolerant and hold an individualist worldview ("avoid sin") have no bearing on member threat levels. Neither does the dogmatic/democratic norms measure ("many points of view"). Instead, clergy believing in biblical inerrancy head congregations with higher threat values (.4 points more threat, on average). The interaction between inclusive values and church attendance is also significant.[8] The pattern of results supports the view that both contact and the frequency of delivery matters. There is little evidence of a defense system in play here. Those exposed to clergy with a high level of commitment to inclusive values exhibit a lower threat level for their least-liked group regardless of their attendance level. Those exposed to what amounts to a slightly lower level of inclusive values (averaging "agree" instead of "strongly agree") have threat levels that depend on attendance—higher attendance means more exposure to inclusive values, which helps reduce threat levels.

Other controls work as expected. Women have a higher level of threat than men, as do conservatives, which is counterbalanced by the reduced level of threat experienced by those identifying as born again in this sample. Moreover, people with less disagreement in their networks experience more threat, ratifying the importance of exposure to a diverse social set to reduce the costs of social exposure. This is just what we found in earlier work (Djupe and Calfano 2013a)—those experimentally exposed to inclusive values reported more disagreement in their networks, suggesting that they were encouraged to broaden their social horizons. Here, the relationship between *clergy's* inclusive value commitment and congregant experience of disagreement is null while it is positive for exposure to exclusive values (as expected); consistent with the experimental evidence, inclusive value commitment among *congregants* is related to more disagreement in their networks. Only over time could we sort out whether actual exposure to inclusive values drives a more diverse social network, but the experimental evidence is highly suggestive.

Political Tolerance

Last, we can evaluate the relationship of clergy political tolerance levels to their congregants'. It is important to remember the caveat that nothing in these data indicates whether clergy have expressed their views about groups in society and whether they should be tolerated—this analysis can merely comment on whether their attitudes are related. Still, given that this is one of the first looks at the political tolerance of clergy and the first to examine their tolerance levels in comparison to congregants, we spend a bit of time describing our analysis.

As Ted Jelen and Clyde Wilcox (1990) argue, tolerance judgments are organized differently depending on the type of activity groups engage in—they find a "Christian consensus on the circumstances in which tolerance may be justified" (Jelen and Wilcox 1990: 69). While we do not ratify that particular message, this is still a fruitful way to begin the investigation, since clergy and congregants do think differently about the various activities they are asked to tolerate. Figure 2.1 shows the distribution of clergy and congregant tolerance (higher is more tolerant) across the six activities we asked about. While there are not tremendous differences, all differences are significant save for making public speeches ($p = .18$) and rallying in public ($p = .79$). Notably, in all cases save teaching in a public school, these clergy are significantly less tolerant than their congregants. An elitist theory of democracy cannot stand on the political tolerance of (these) clergy (though recall the results from Chapter 1).

Now we transition to average tolerance levels (across all activities) by least-liked group. As with Figure 2.1, Figure 2.2 provides a comparison between all clergy and congregants and does not constrain congregants to be in the same congregation (given how few congregants chose the same least-liked group, as seen in Figure 2.A of the online appendix).[9] Figure 2.2 shows wide gaps for all but the most commonly chosen groups (Nazis, KKK, and atheists). Few of either clergy or congregants selected gay rights activists or immigrants, but the tolerance granted to them varies considerably when they did. Congregants are most tolerant of gay rights activists, whereas clergy are the least tolerant of them. The reverse is true of immigrants. At least in Greene County, Missouri, the liberal culture wars groups are the least tolerated by clergy, which is surely a function of the kinds of clergy selecting those groups. The more liberal clergy selecting groups on the right side of the graph are more tolerant of them, ratifying the ideological gaps found among a broader set of elites (Sniderman et al. 1991). To

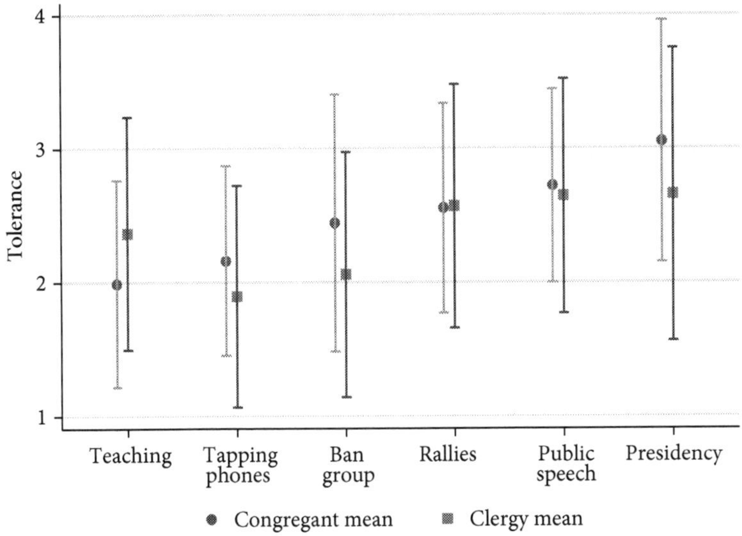

Figure 2.1 Tolerance levels by clergy and congregants by least-liked group activity

Source: 2009–2010 Springfield Area Study.

Note: The capped lines represent ±1 standard deviation.

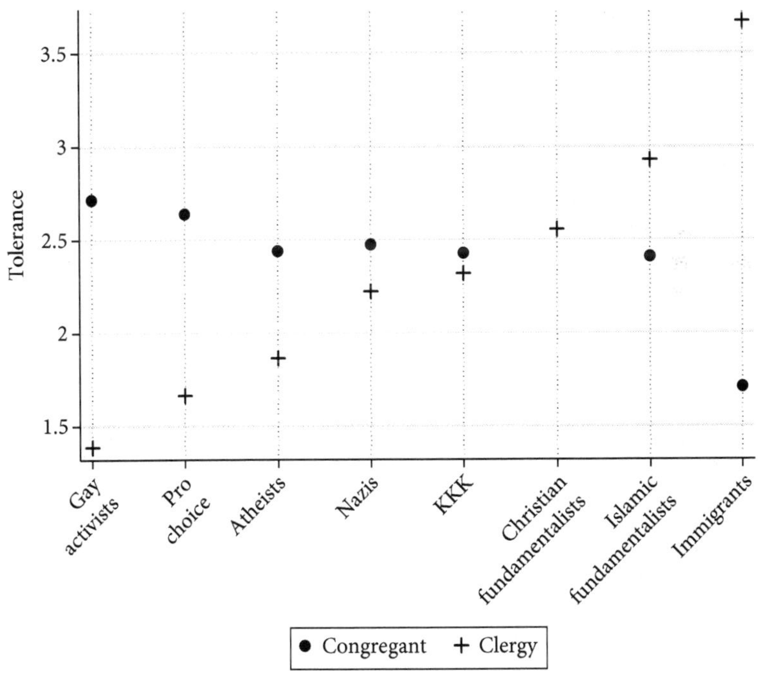

Figure 2.2 Clergy tolerance compared to congregant tolerance levels, by least-liked group

Source: 2009–2010 Springfield Area Study.

Note: No congregant chose Christian fundamentalists as a least-liked group.

ratify the results of Figure 2.1, it is notable that clergy's tolerance levels are, overall, significantly lower (.2, $p = .01$) than the tolerance expressed by their congregants. From this presentation, it is no surprise that clergy tolerance judgments are only very weakly correlated with member tolerance ($r = .05$, $p = .68$, $N = 88$).

Last, we show the specific comparison of clergy's and their congregants' tolerance levels (regardless of least-liked group) in Figure 2.3. Light gray diamonds show the congregants' tolerance in comparison to the clergy's tolerance shown as black dots in the connected line. Thus, each vertical line represents a congregation (sorted from low to high tolerance). The display shows the fairly wide variance in tolerance in congregations, and the generally more moderate responses of congregants. One way to think about the disparity is that it highlights the elite status of clergy, who by dint of their training and sophistication link their values and judgments more tightly, which results in more polar opinions.

Of course, numerous attributes of the clergy and congregants may affect tolerance judgments. Table 2.1 reports estimates of a range of effects, concentrating on those from clergy. All else equal, clergy's tolerance level is positively and significantly related to their congregants', so that congregants with the most tolerant clergy are about half a point more tolerant than those with the least tolerant clergy. It is entirely possible that some portion of this reflects the selection of a congregation, though the previous graphs showing the great range of tolerance views in congregations and the divergent selection of least-liked groups cuts deeply against a selection logic.

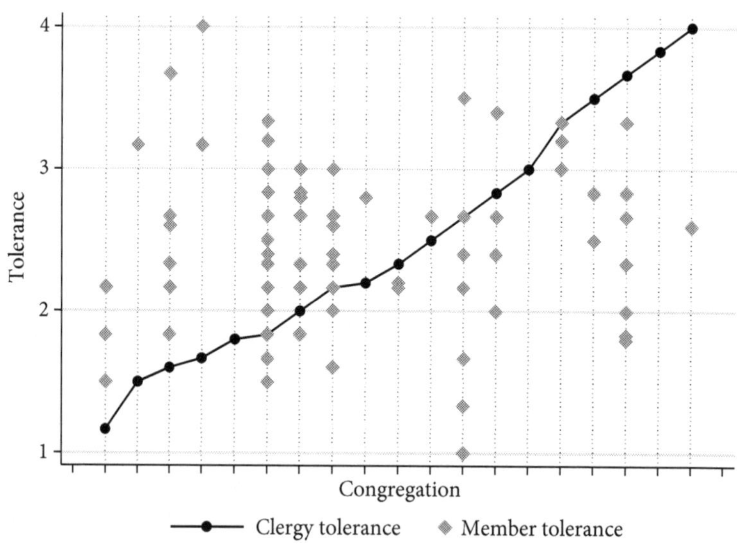

Figure 2.3 Scatter diagram of the clergy's and members' political tolerance by congregation, sorted by the clergy's score

Source: 2009–2010 Springfield Area Study.

Note: $r = .05$, $p = .68$.

Perhaps stronger causal claims can be made with the religious values we investigate. The first is a play on the communitarian-individualism item championed by Stephen Mockabee, Kenneth Wald, and David Leege (2007), asking whether clergy agree that it is essential to avoid sin to be a good Christian (see Chapter 7). The logic is similar to what is developed by Pazit Ben-Nun Bloom and Marie Courtemanche in Chapter 6—the need to avoid sin raises the threat of contamination posed by groups involved in value conflict. The effect is negative, as expected, but it is small and overwhelmed by its standard error (for more on this value, see Chapters 6 and 7).

In a similar style, we asked about whether it was essential to "love the stranger as yourself" and invite others to church even if the church begins to change as a result; we have referred to agreement with these items as elements of inclusive religious values (Djupe and Calfano 2013a; see also Chapters 7 and 9). The logic is that those exposed to inclusive values would expand the boundaries of the ingroup, reduce the threat posed by outsiders, and therefore tolerate least-liked groups more. In these data, the mere attachment of clergy to inclusive values is not linked to tolerance judgments (result not shown). But it is linked to tolerance through congregants' attendance. The results are the mirror image of those in the threat model.[10] The high-attendance congregants show no effect, reflecting defenses to challenging information as well as chronic exposure to inclusive values. Differences are only seen among those attending sporadically. The results suggest that those who attend churches in which clergy push inclusion at a high rate are less tolerant than those who attend lower-inclusion churches at low rates. Several possibilities to interpret these results present themselves. Congregants may participate at reduced rates because of an ill fit with the congregation. Alternatively, clergy may exercise a prophetic role and push inclusion to balance out the congregation. In either case, the conclusion can only be sustained with temporal data.

Last, greater clergy commitment to democratic norms (reduced dogmatism) is linked to greater tolerance in the congregation. Clergy's commitment to democratic process may present in a number of places in the congregation—in the way they address political issues (Djupe and Calfano 2012; Djupe and Neiheisel 2008), the adult education sessions they may organize (Neiheisel, Djupe, and Sokhey 2009), and the few congregational meetings they might hold (Djupe and Olson 2013), not to mention their direct advocacy of democratic norms (Djupe and Calfano 2012). Of course, this relationship is not necessarily causal; it may reflect congregational demands about which clergy serve, but it also may simply reflect the congregational culture. Still, this is the first direct evidence that clergy's personal adherence to democratic norms correlates with such views in the congregation.

Only a few controls work and do so in the expected fashion. The more highly educated are more tolerant, and women are less tolerant. Interestingly, ideology is not linked to tolerance judgments in these data; nor is exposure to disagreement.

Conclusion

It is important to remember that these models are fragile, relying on such a small sample from a highly evangelical community, and obviously the findings need to be replicated in larger, more representative samples. But some results are more robust than others. What seems clear is that the connection between clergy's and congregants' tolerance judgments does not involve politics. That is, the details involved in the tolerance decision are clearly unrelated—they pick disparate least-liked groups, which is the foundation for the value conflict that governs tolerance decisions. Sharing an outgroup is also a foundation for politics beyond the tolerance domain, so the lack of connection here is surprising. It certainly challenges the perspective of clergy as ideologues with an agenda leading their flocks into cultural conflict.

The evidence is probably stronger for the perspective that clergy are more concerned with organizational maintenance and deemphasize or obscure their political attitudes when necessary to avoid further conflict in the congregation. Moreover, congregants erect significant defenses against clergy influence, which pushes us to consider indirect routes to persuasion that play on clergy's strengths. Put most succinctly, clergy can have their most profound effect by shaping the way people treat one another. Are they inclusive? Do they place values above relationships? Do they brook disagreement? We find support for such a conclusion here—we see links between clergy's tolerance-related values and congregants' threat and tolerance levels. Their dogmatism/democratic values, emphasis on inclusion, and theological dogmatism (inerrancy) are all related to congregants' tolerance decisions. Even the seeming direct relationship (calling it an "effect" is premature) between clergy-congregant tolerance levels has to be indirect because it elides the substantive details (the group) of whose activities are being tolerated.

It is important to emphasize that these are some of the first results showing a relationship between the attitudes of the clergy and congregation (in contrast, there is good evidence that clergy can spur political activity). Take Djupe and Gilbert's (2009) conclusion that clergy do not affect congregant attitudes but instead shape what congregants talk about, which activates social influence processes. We might now add to that conclusion that clergy can shape how congregants talk about those issues in the sense that they may have an abiding concern for the rights and liberties of those affected as well as participants in the debate (see also Chapter 3).

We have treated clergy as if they are independently dropped into congregations, which is clearly a problematic assumption. Whether congregations choose clergy is not the only point—clergy also conform to their congregations in important ways. Even Catholic priests shift whether they address abortion given the interests of the congregation (Calfano, Oldmixon, and Gray 2013). But the findings here are consistent with the research showing that how clergy talk about issues shifts depending on the audience. Their argument pattern becomes less strident and more diverse and they mention norms of tolerance and respect too when they face a diverse congregation (see Chapter 11; Djupe and Neiheisel 2008; Neiheisel and Djupe 2008).

While neither probably necessary nor sufficient, the broad pattern forming in the literature suggests the importance of a diverse congregation that provides possibilities for democratic learning and incentives for clergy to instill and install democratic norms governing social interactions. Without diversity, many clergy still indicate that they hold democratic norms, though organizational maintenance is not at stake and there is surely a gap between attitude and behavior. But diversity does not guarantee democratic learning either, as opportunities are needed to experience that diversity. And one strategy clergy engage to deal with diversity in the congregation is to avoid it. While entirely understandable, avoiding stirring the diverse pot undermines a key contribution that churches may provide to the sustenance of democracy.

The tolerance literature, whether on religion or not, has done relatively little with communication effects (though see Marcus et al. 1995; Green et al. 2011). This is curious given the development of an elitist theory of democracy from tolerance work and since elites are continually offering information that would seem to be applicable to attitudes about groups in society. The simple emphasis on value conflict, the mention of the challenge posed by groups, and the practice and promotion of democratic values all would seem to bear on whether a group is tolerated. The work here encourages further exploration of the communicative foundations of political tolerance.

Notes

1. The survey experiments were conducted using a direct-dial protocol with CATI technology in a computer call lab under the authors' supervision during weeknights between 4:00 and 8:00 P.M. between December 2009 and March 2010. The average completion time for the subjects was sixteen minutes and seventeen seconds. The survey was funded by small grants from the Denison University Research Foundation and Missouri State University.

2. Beyond the high percentage of evangelicals in the sample, it is also 59 percent women, overwhelmingly white (96 percent), and reasonably educated (a third have bachelor's degrees or more). The sample figures are a bit more white, female, and educated than Greene County according to the 2010 census, which means it is also more white, female, and educated than the population in Missouri or the nation.

3. This percentage was calculated by excluding the 558 numbers from the sample list that were coded with a "nonworking" disposition.

4. For all variable coding information, please see the online appendix at http://pauldjupe.com/s/Appendix.docx.

5. See Figure 2.A in the online appendix for a more detailed examination of these relationships.

6. In characteristic naked empiricism, we were able to generate model specifications that included a stray significant term, but each was highly unstable and changed markedly with different specifications.

7. See Figure 2.B in the online appendix for a visualization of this relationship.
8. See Figure 2.C in the online appendix for a visualization of this relationship.
9. The online appendix is available at http://pauldjupe.com/s/Appendix.docx.
10. The results of this interaction term can be visualized in Figure 2.D in the online appendix. They can be compared with the results from Figure 2.C from the threat model.

References

Beyerlein, Kraig, and Mark Chaves. 2003. "The Political Activities of Religious Congregations in the United States." *Journal for the Scientific Study of Religion* 42 (2): 229–246.

Bjarnason, Thoroddur, and Michael R. Welch. 2004. "Father Knows Best: Parishes, Priests, and American Catholic Parishioners' Attitudes toward Capital Punishment." *Journal for the Scientific Study of Religion* 43 (1): 103–118.

Calfano, Brian R. 2009. "Choosing Constituent Cues: Reference Group Influence on Clergy Political Speech." *Social Science Quarterly* 90 (1): 88–102.

———. 2010. "Prophetic at Any Price? Clergy Political Behavior and Utility Maximization." *Social Science Quarterly* 91 (3): 649–668.

Calfano, Brian R., Elizabeth A. Oldmixon, and Mark Gray. 2013. "Strategically Prophetic Priests: An Analysis of Competing Principal Influence on Clergy Political Action." *Review of Religious Research* 56 (1): 1–21.

Campbell, Ernest Q., and Thomas F. Pettigrew. 1959. *Christians in Racial Crisis: A Study of Little Rock's Ministry*. Washington, DC: Public Affairs Press.

Cavendish, James C. 2001. "To March or Not to March: Clergy Mobilization Strategies and Grassroots Antidrug Activism." In *Christian Clergy in American Politics*, edited by Sue E. S. Crawford and Laura R. Olson, 203–226. Baltimore: Johns Hopkins University Press.

Chinni, Dante, and James Gimpel. 2010. *Our Patchwork Nation: The Surprising Truth about the "Real" America*. New York: Gotham Books.

Djupe, Paul A., and Brian R. Calfano. 2012. "The Deliberative Pulpit: The Democratic Norms and Practices of the PCUSA." *Journal for the Scientific Study of Religion* 51 (1): 90–109.

———. 2013a. "Religious Value Priming, Threat, and Political Tolerance." *Political Research Quarterly* 66 (4): 767–779.

———. 2013b. *God Talk: Experimenting with the Religious Causes of Public Opinion*. Philadelphia: Temple University Press.

Djupe, Paul A., and Christopher P. Gilbert. 2003. *The Prophetic Pulpit: Clergy, Churches, and Communities in American Politics*. Lanham, MD: Rowman and Littlefield.

———. 2008. "Politics and Church: Byproduct or Central Mission?" *Journal for the Scientific Study of Religion* 47 (1): 45–62.

———. 2009. *The Political Influence of Churches*. New York: Cambridge University Press.

Djupe, Paul A., and Patrick K. Hunt. 2009. "Beyond the Lynn White Thesis: Congregational Effects on Environmental Concern." *Journal for the Scientific Study of Religion* 48 (4): 670–686.

Djupe, Paul A., and Jacob R. Neiheisel. 2008. "Clergy Deliberation on Gay Rights and Homosexuality." *Polity* 40 (4): 411–435.

———. 2012. "How Religious Communities Affect Political Participation among Latinos." *Social Science Quarterly* 93 (2): 333–355.

Djupe, Paul A., and Laura Olson. 2013. "Public Deliberation about Gay Rights in Religious Contexts: Commitment to Deliberative Norms and Practice in ELCA Congregations." *Journal of Public Deliberation* 9 (1): Article 1. Available at http://www.publicdeliberation.net/cgi/viewcontent.cgi?article=1214&context=jpd.

Emerson, Michael O., and Christian Smith. 2000. *Divided by Faith: Evangelical Religion and the Problem of Race in America*. New York: Oxford University Press.

Fetzer, Joel S. 2001. "Shaping Pacifism: The Role of the Local Anabaptist Pastor." In *Christian Clergy in American Politics*, edited by Sue E. S. Crawford and Laura R. Olson, 177–187. Baltimore: Johns Hopkins University Press.

Finke, Roger, and Rodney Stark. 2005. *The Churching of America, 1776–2005: Winners and Losers in Our Religious Economy*. New Brunswick, NJ: Rutgers University Press.

Graham, Jesse, Jonathan Haidt, and Brian A. Nosek. 2009. "Liberals and Conservatives Rely on Different Sets of Moral Foundations." *Journal of Personality and Social Psychology* 96 (5): 1029–1046.

Green, Donald P., Peter M. Aronow, Daniel E. Bergan, Pamela Greene, Celia Paris, and Beth I. Weinberger. 2011. "Does Knowledge of Constitutional Principles Increase Support for Civil Liberties? Results from a Randomized Field Experiment." *Journal of Politics* 73 (2): 463–476.

Guth, James L. 1996. "The Bully Pulpit: Southern Baptist Clergy and Political Activism, 1980–1992." In *Religion and the Culture Wars: Dispatches from the Front*, edited by John C. Green, James L. Guth, Corwin E. Smidt, and Lyman A. Kellstedt, 146–173. Lanham, MD: Rowman and Littlefield.

Guth, James L., John C. Green, Corwin E. Smidt, Lyman A. Kellstedt, and Margaret Poloma. 1997. *The Bully Pulpit: The Politics of Protestant Clergy*. Lawrence: University of Kansas Press.

Hadden, Jeffrey K. 1969. *The Gathering Storm in the Churches*. Garden City, NY: Doubleday.

Hofrenning, Daniel J. B. 1995. *In Washington but Not of It: The Prophetic Politics of Religious Lobbyists*. Philadelphia: Temple University Press.

Jelen, Ted G. 1994. "Protestant Clergy as Political Leaders: Theological Limitations." *Review of Religious Research* 36 (1): 23–42.

Jelen, Ted G., and Clyde Wilcox. 1990. "Denominational Preference and the Dimensions of Political Tolerance." *Sociological Analysis* 51 (1): 69–81.

———. 1991. "Religious Dogmatism among White Christians: Causes and Effects." *Review of Religious Research* 33 (1): 32–46.

Marcus, George E., John L. Sullivan, Elizabeth Theiss-Morse, and Sandra Wood. 1995. *With Malice toward Some: How People Make Civil Liberties Judgments*. New York: Cambridge University Press.

Mockabee, Stephen T., Kenneth D. Wald, and David C. Leege. 2007. "Reexamining Religiosity: A Report on the New Religion Items in the 2006 ANES Pilot Study." Available at http://www.electionstudies.org/resources/papers/Pilot2006/nes011907.pdf.

Neiheisel, Jacob R., and Paul A. Djupe. 2008. "Intraorganizational Constraints on Churches' Public Witness." *Journal for the Scientific Study of Religion* 47 (3): 427–441.

Neiheisel, Jacob R., Paul A. Djupe, and Anand E. Sokhey. 2009. "Veni, Vidi, Disseri: Churches and the Promise of Democratic Deliberation." *American Politics Research* 37 (4): 614–643.

Olson, Laura R. 2000. *Filled with Spirit and Power: Protestant Clergy in Politics*. New York: State University of New York Press.

Owens, Michael Leo. 2007. *God and Government in the Ghetto: The Politics of Church-State Collaboration in Black America*. Chicago: University of Chicago Press.

Pope, Liston. 1942. *Millhands and Preachers: A Study of Gastonia*. New Haven, CT: Yale University Press.

Roof, Wade Clark. 1999. *Spiritual Marketplace: Baby Boomers and the Remaking of American Religion*. Princeton, NJ: Princeton University Press.

Smith, Gregory A. 2008. *Politics in the Parish: The Political Influence of Catholic Priests*. Washington, DC: Georgetown University Press.

Sniderman, Paul M., Joseph F. Fletcher, Peter H. Russell, Philip E. Tetlock, and Brian J. Gaines. 1991. "The Fallacy of Democratic Elitism: Elite Competition and Commitment to Civil Liberties." *British Journal of Political Science* 21 (3): 349–370.

Stark, Rodney, Bruce D. Foster, Charles Y. Glock, and Harold Quinley. 1971. *Wayward Shepherds: Prejudice and the Protestant Clergy*. New York: Harper and Row.

Thomas, Cal, and Ed Dobson. 1999. *Blinded by Might: Can the Religious Right Save America?* Grand Rapids, MI: Zondervan.

Wilcox, Clyde, and Ted G. Jelen. 1990. "Evangelicals and Political Tolerance." *American Politics Quarterly* 18:25–46.

3

Religious Tolerance in the Presbyterian Church (USA)

PAUL A. DJUPE
JEFFREY B. KURTZ

Students of mainline Protestant traditions may know two potential punch lines to the following joke: How many Presbyterians does it take to change a light bulb? One answer, "Change?!," signals well the long, faithful struggle within the Church[1] to live into the opportunities and challenges of our postmodern age. The other punch line may be just as funny: "We'll appoint a committee to answer that question. We should be able to have an answer for you in about two years." As the punch line implies, over the arc of their institutional history, members of the Presbyterian Church (USA) have been willing to deliberate about matters of import. And deliberate. At the core of these deliberations, more often than not, has been a fundamental commitment to tolerance.

As used throughout this volume, *political* tolerance means something very specific: the extension of equal rights and liberties to a group with whom one fundamentally disagrees. Rarely are these preconditions applicable within American religious denominations, though debates over the "intractables" such as recognition of gay clergy, and women clergy before that, suggest that at times they are. And yet tolerance is still employed as a term of art within denominational life, certainly if not especially within the PC(USA). How is it used? On the one hand, the term suggests an elegant simplicity: Ever-mindful of the spectrum of political and religious differences that exist between persons, the word simply means to exercise or demonstrate openness to the facts of these differences and to agree that they be neither embraced nor resolved but merely acknowledged. Potential hostility is deferred and dialogue may transpire. Acceptance is a ready synonym that comes to mind.

On the other hand, while these seem like essential tools for organized life, some may think they have an uneasy fit within religious organizations given their intellectual roots in the enlightenment (see, e.g., Graham 2012). Some question whether tolerance is a precondition for debate or a tool to dictate a bounded set of outcomes. At the heart of the matter, then, is whether tolerance is a norm of accommodation for diverse views, enabling debate, or a wedge to push out some and advantage others. What role does tolerance play in the life of a denomination? These are the questions we confront in this chapter.

Sharon Crowley (2006), for example, underscores the historical roots of tolerance, and especially the ways it emerged out of the intellectual traditions that characterized the Enlightenment. Such traditions typically privileged consensus over contested issues, a consensus that was to be founded on empirically based reason. Chantal Mouffe (2000) likewise maintains that tolerance should be recognized as a primary tool of liberalism. These scholars and others agree that tolerance may function to devalue or altogether exclude arguments which appeal to tradition, authority, or desire (that is, religious faith and emotion). As Michael Sandel has observed in his critique of liberalism, "We are beginning to find that a politics that brackets morality and religion too completely soon generates its own disenchantment. A procedural republic cannot contain the moral energies of a vital democratic life" (1996: 24). Might a similar assertion be made about faith traditions that give too much emphasis to tolerance's banal underpinnings? To borrow from Ezekiel, can such bones live? Where the mainline faithful are concerned, how is tolerance used?

For the Presbyterian Church (USA), the term in fact is fraught with rich ambivalence. Recognizing, on the one hand, what has become the almost urgent necessity to extend tolerance toward different faith traditions, for example, the institutional church has published a variety of resources concerned with articulating justifications and practices for interfaith dialogue. On the other hand, the Church seems all too aware that tolerance is at best a contested term, a kind of stopgap that may be counterproductive to realizing such fundamentally important values as reconciliation, peace, and authentic unity. This awareness is especially evident in reports and other publications around the hotly contested issue of gay ordination.[2]

In the remainder of this discussion we want to survey briefly the PC(USA)'s documented understanding of tolerance. That understanding runs the gamut, from an open-armed embrace to a legitimate skepticism from many angles. Tolerance appears to be affirmed as a necessary precondition to forward movement—discernment. What seems clear is that the Church in recent years has advocated a kind of political and religious engagement that quite tentatively pushes beyond tolerance. And here is the rub that turns on trust about the aims embedded within advocacy of tolerance as well as whether the push beyond tolerance is sufficiently bold. We take the time to recount the contours of that engagement as it specifically concerns interfaith dialogue and the ordination of gays and lesbians. In addition, we reflect on some of the kinds of "everyday practices" demonstrated between and among many of the Presbyterian faithful as they gather for worship, for study, and to do the work of shared governance.

Interfaith Dialogue

Long concerned with building communities among and between different religious traditions, Presbyterian publications that address interfaith dialogue seem both mindful of tolerance and aware of the concept's limitations, especially its demands on participants. That is, documented resources speak of tolerance in addition to "pluralism" where different religious traditions are concerned.[3] The assumption seems to be that, while tolerance may offer initial promises of awareness, what it lacks is a deeper acknowledgment of the intertwined relationships between different faith traditions, whether believers are cognizant of these relationships or not. In the short publication *Presbyterian Principles for Interfaith Dialogue*, for example, the author(s) openly acknowledge the given-ness of diversity within the United States and across global cultures, remarking that "pluralistic U.S. and global societies are the context within which Christians relate to people of other faiths" (PC[USA] 1999). Lest there be confusion about the depth of the extent to which diversity and pluralism are taken as givens, the next sentence amplifies that "Christians live among people grounded in other religions and ideologies, or in none." Significant to these descriptions is their wide-eyed recognition of the pervasiveness of faith traditions and ideologies different from those held by Presbyterians, noted with neither alarm nor disdain. Instead, an obligation tied to recognition is implied: Tolerance for other faiths is the starting point for interfaith dialogue. If such dialogue is to result in authentic encounters and relationships characterized by depth, then some sort of push beyond tolerance, into the possibilities occasioned by pluralism's wider embrace, should inform the ways Presbyterians relate to different faith traditions.

Yet if tolerance is burdened by its limitations, its presence in the published principles certainly is obvious, if not explicitly stated. One way to think of tolerance's benefits, for example, is to circle toward universals it may esteem. These universals find a voice in the Church's understanding of interfaith dialogue, as one of the principles stipulates that believers are "called to work with others in our pluralistic societies for the well-being of our world and for justice, peace, and the sustainability of creation" (PC[USA] 1999). These commitments underscore the appeal if not the very necessity of tolerance: Presbyterians believe that, whatever differences in practice or belief may serve to putatively divide us, they can share with others unshakable commitments to caring for the world's well-being.

The way such tolerance may be achieved is through participating in dialogues that move diverse participants away from lines of division toward common ground, movement inflected by humility, curiosity, openness, and profound acknowledgment (see also Gutmann and Thompson 1996). As one of the Presbyterian principles amplifies, "We need to learn about and understand the religions to which others adhere." Another says, "We need to listen for others' concerns so that we may minister to human needs in our common public life, interreligious families, and shared religious celebrations" (PC[USA] 1999).

These stated commitments leave no room for suspicion or degradation of other traditions. Because Presbyterians explicitly believe in God's affirming presence in the world, this belief propels the faithful toward ends where meaningful dialogue and relationship are made genuinely possible. In this way, then, the necessity of tolerance to such ends cannot be overstated, and therefore tolerance itself may become a point of contention.

Gay Ordination

The Presbyterian Church has been arguing about the ordination of gays and lesbians for nearly three decades. Even a cursory glance at the debate will confirm that tolerance has struggled to find a place at the table. Church members on both sides of the debate are tired, angry, and frustrated. Recognizing in 2006 how contentious the debate had become and with it the growing possibility for schism, the General Assembly (a biennial meeting where significant policy decisions affecting congregations nationwide are discussed and implemented) approved the creation of the Theological Task Force on the Peace, Unity, and Purity of the Church. The group's principal charge was to "lead the Presbyterian Church (U.S.A.) in spiritual discernment of [its] Christian identity in and for the 21st century, using a process which includes conferring with synods, presbyteries, and congregations [levels of institutional governance; congregations are the most local of the three, followed by presbyteries] seeking peace, unity, and purity in the church." Composed of twenty people from diverse backgrounds and theological points of view, the task force undertook as among its most important tasks attempting to discover "ways the church can live more faithfully in the face of deep disagreements" (Theological Task Force on Peace, Unity, and Purity of the Church 2006: 1).

On its face, the creation of such a task force and even the scope of its particular charge may not seem especially novel. Indeed, recent scholars have confirmed the commitment of mainline churches to seize opportunities to debate contentious issues. As Robert Wuthnow and John Evans (2002: 17) have observed, these denominations "focus on keeping a number of issues on the front burner (and a number of others simmering on back burners), fostering debate even when members of the wider public disagree on specific strategies and programs." Such structures and processes, they continue, "function well to draw people into decision-making capacities, to give voice to and resolve significant controversial issues, and to coordinate activities that extend beyond the local level." Wendy Cadge (2002: 279) concurs and amplifies: "Throughout their years of disagreements, the mainline churches have learned, at least thus far, how to disagree without dividing. They have done so by helping opponents focus on their commonalities, including their membership in a common faith tradition, rather than emphasizing their differences." As this scholarship implies, the Church's creation of a task force would seem the very epitome of tolerance and a careful reading of the task force's report indicates a determined attempt to set unimpeachable criteria for coexistence. Their plea for tolerance, without using that word, was characterized by fundamental commitments to biblically informed principles, an explicit concern for (political and theological) authority founded on the exercise of communal discernment, and the insistence, finally, on theological integrity above all else.

The report's reliance on biblically informed principles draws both from the Bible and from the Church's understanding of those principles as they have been recodified in its Book of Order, the governing book of Church polity. Specifically, the report maintains that any foundational claims the Church makes regarding its governance begins with the nonnegotiable acknowledgment that Jesus Christ is the head of the Church. From this acknowledgment stems the conviction that church members and especially those lay leaders charged with the governance and leadership of the Church should not simply "reflect the will of the people, but rather [are] to seek together to find and represent the will of Christ" (Theological Task Force on Peace, Unity, and Purity of the Church 2006: 22). These commitments, derived from Jesus's example and amplified in Paul's various letters, embody an entrenched commitment to embracing the points of view of both majority and minority constituencies (see Allen 2004: 171).

The task force's report explicitly softens the role of authority founded on the exercise of communal discernment. That understanding is achieved through adherence to four pairs of principles: (1) the importance of communal discernment *and* the recognition that "God alone is the Lord of conscience"; (2) adherence by the body of the church to "essential necessary beliefs and practices" *and* respect for "freedom [of choice] in nonessential matters" concerning belief, piety, worship, service, and witness"; (3) maintaining a distinctive Presbyterian identity *and* engaging in mission with Christians of other traditions; and (4) honoring local governing bodies' decisions *and* sustaining the rights of incumbent bodies that have the power of oversight and review (Theological Task Force on Peace, Unity, and Purity of the Church 2006: 21).The parallel with American constitutionalism between rights and liberties on the one hand and democracy on the other is almost unmistakable (in the end, it turns to the tension between states and the federal government). Collectively, these commitments to authority and communal discernment suggest a rationale for deliberation that promotes a depth not accounted for by tolerance. Namely, the rationale seems to impress the conviction that entrenched conflict (in this case, over the very contentious matter of gay ordination) will not be resolved unless communal discernment is established both as a process and a substantive commitment within church polity. The report's authors elaborated on that conviction this way:

> For decisions that have a significant impact on the life of the church, particularly those that are complex or potentially divisive, time is needed for corporate study of Scripture, gathering of information, prayerful reflection, mutual questioning, careful listening, and collective weighing of opinions. For clearer discernment of the mind of Christ, and for the

> sake of the unity of the church, all voices should be heard, including those who may be affected by the potential outcome of a decision. (26)

As may be seen here, the report will not accept a win-at-all costs ethos to hijack contentious deliberations. It also does not hold it acceptable for conflicting parties merely to retreat to neutral concerns (tolerance done poorly). Instead, the authors advance a set of commitments and practices that may spur readers to embrace anew the tenets and practices of faithful interpretation, an interpretive practice that honors tradition and authority. Church members must accept that scripture serves as the foundation from which deliberation must begin. The authority of scripture is not found solely within the text of the Bible, however. The report advances an explicit concern that such authority also is grounded in community; interpretation is corrected, enriched, and strengthened as we move about reasoning together, if we are willing to go about reasoning together. Implied here, finally, is an acknowledgment that difference and disagreement must serve as the foundation on which the very hope of the church may rest. As the report impresses:

> Differences are serious because they revolve around important topics. The differences are difficult to settle, because each of the divergent conclusions attracts substantial numbers of faithful adherents who are persons of sound qualification, good character, and strong faith. Such situations are not uncommon in the history of the church. They require disciplines of patience, mutual forbearance, and dedicated communal discernment to reach faithful resolution as we trust Jesus' promise that the Holy Spirit will ultimately lead the church into all truth. (19)

In thinking about the controversy over gay ordination, then, what may we say about tolerance? A simple answer is not ready available, at least if the depth of the task force's report is considered seriously on its own terms. But perhaps we may acknowledge two things: First, tolerance is an implicit starting point for the contentious back-and-forth over whether the church should ordain gays and lesbians. And second, even if the Church fails to reach discernment on such contentious issues as these, a sort of enhanced tolerance may be a powerful outcome. As they conclude:

> Even as we differ and even as we contend with one another, Jesus prays that we may all be one, that we might love one another despite many differences that threaten to divide us. At a time when people readily kill one another over their differences, a church that lives and works for that kind of witness will capture the attention of a polarized world. What besides the mystery of divine love could give us the capacity to love those whose goals and views differ from, even contradict, our own? (Theological Task Force on Peace, Unity, and Purity of the Church 2006: 39)

Questions for Data Analysis

Given the tense issues for debate in the Church, we investigate two broad concerns: (1) the degree to which tolerance is emphasized and whether there is broad support for a big tent denomination and (2) how tolerance factors into maintenance of the institutional church. Our expectation is that there is considerable variation in support for tolerance and diversity in the church and that the variation parallels the patterns in the broader society. That is, those who see the greatest value in collective engagement and who are the most responsible for maintaining the institutional infrastructure will value tolerance more. Of course, those are clergy, followed by elders (lay leaders), followed by members. As the reports discussed above indicate, tolerance is a necessary precursor to communal deliberation, which is a process that is theorized to maintain satisfaction with a governing system (Gutmann and Thompson 1996), and which perhaps leads to communal discernment. Therefore, we also investigate the extent to which tolerance supported by the member and urged by the clergyperson bears on satisfaction with the denomination.

Data: The Presbyterian Panel

The data for this chapter come from the venerable Presbyterian Panel before it made a crucial switch in its data-gathering practices. In operation since 1973, the Panel includes several thousand members, elders, and clergy in the denomination who respond to four mailed surveys a year for three years (at which time the panel is regenerated). The denomination has generously deposited a large portion of its cache of survey data in the American Religion Data Archive (http://www.thearda.com). Through the time of the survey we use in 2001, the samples of the three groups are largely clustered, thus including clergy, elders, and members of the same congregations.[4] The Presbyterian Panel did not sample a small number of congregations and then sample many people with those congregations. Instead, it maximized the number of congregations involved and did not solely match members and clergy. Of the nearly six hundred members in the data set, just over half could be matched to corresponding clergypersons. On average, three members were surveyed for each congregation, though the full range ran from one to seven. From the other perspective, we kept only the responses of the senior pastor for each congregation, which served to drop about fifty cases. In the end, only 207 in the sample of 939 clergy could be matched to members in the data set. Still, these data are valuable because they allow an assessment of the relationship between clergy and congregants.

In February 2001 in the wake of the highly contentious 2000 presidential election, panelists were asked a series of questions about the kind of congregation and denomination they want to affiliate with; the questions serve to gauge the extent of support for tolerance present in the denomination. What is particularly useful about these questions is that they push past a naïve attachment to tolerance by acknowledging that tolerance is open to disagreement and is related to potential conflict. Therefore, these questions avoid the issue that Americans almost universally agree that First Amendment liberties are important but then apply them rather selectively (Stouffer 1955). In other words, the questions capture tolerance rather than expressions of a potentially weak preference for diversity. Obviously, they capture tolerance in quite a different way than traditional measures in political science or sociology that specify a particular target group. Here, individuals are thinking about the argumentative dimensions of the congregational square. And given the circumstances of their tolerance, it transcends our traditional notions of political tolerance. Those who express a willingness to accept disagreement in the congregation and denomination are also acknowledging that they are willing to engage *directly* with those people in potential conflict over deeply held values.

Results

We begin with a look at tolerance-related judgments by the three levels of actors surveyed within the PC(USA) in 2001. Table 3.1 shows the preferences of clergy, elders, and congregants regarding the kind of congregation they would prefer. Within this denomination, we see evidence of the elitist theory of democracy (McCloskey 1964; Stouffer 1955), with clergy overwhelmingly (74 percent) in favor of people holding different views and openly discussing them. While a majority of congregants (56 percent) also support that view, a strong minority would prefer unanimity in their house of worship; elders lie in between the two. The fact that such a difference is present raises doubts about the connection between clergy and congregants. The bottom portion of Table 3.1 shows essentially the same distribution when asked a bit differently about support for a big-tent

TABLE 3.1 PREFERENCE FOR THE CONGREGATIONAL ENGAGEMENT OF DIFFERENCE AMONG CLERGY, ELDERS, AND MEMBERS

	Clergy	*Elders*	*Members*
Which would you prefer, a congregation wherein . . .			
People all hold more or less the same views	24.1	31.3	38.5
People hold different views but keep them to themselves	2.0	3.3	5.7
People hold different views and openly discuss their disagreements	73.9	65.4	55.8
Which is more important to you?			
A "big-tent" church that tolerates diversity of beliefs and practices	74.9	55.1	52.9
A strict church that requires more uniformity of belief and practice	25.1	44.9	47.1
N	612	599	582

Source: 2001 Presbyterian Panel survey.

congregation. It is surprising that the big-tent pattern is not much different given that conflict in this question is one step removed from the individual (i.e., at the denominational level).

However, the aggregate statistics obscure some underlying relationships. For instance, clergy who say they would prefer a unanimous congregation are more willing (30 percent) to support a big-tent denomination than are clergy who say the reverse—they support a diverse congregation and a unanimous denomination (10 percent). This is not surprising, because they support more diversity away from where they have to accommodate it. Among members, there is more uniformity of answers—about a third value the opposite outcome from the congregation to the denomination. In each case, about 70 percent favor one side (e.g., a diverse congregation) and then just over a quarter to 30 percent turn around and claim to value the other side (e.g., a uniform denomination).

Questions relevant to support for tolerance were asked in other ways as well that focus our attention on explicit conflict (that is, beyond the acknowledgment of difference). Perhaps because of the acknowledgment of conflict, the differences between clergy and laity were smaller. Among clergy, over 80 percent agreed that "I'm willing to tolerate different viewpoints in the church even if it spills over into conflict sometimes," while support was just a bit more tepid among laity (about 70 percent). However, clergy are more likely (than the laity) to agree that they wish there was less conflict, which is what makes their heavy support for difference all the more meaningful. Conversely (and consistently), members are a bit more certain that "if people are no longer willing to fight for their beliefs, the church is in trouble." Support falls off among all three groups in the tension between keeping up the franchise and enforcing agreement, so that all three groups are torn about whether keeping people in church trumps "discipline." Perhaps surprisingly, clergy are the least supportive of prioritizing keeping people in churches, though only by a small amount (less than 10 percent). And this is where the key tension in questions about tolerance and deliberation take hold: everyone wants less conflict, but few seem willing to back down from their positions. The good news for the PC(USA) is that many appear willing to brook disagreement.

The Determinants of Support for Tolerance

Another way of viewing the denominational culture of the PC(USA) is to see to what degree tolerance views are transferred between the clergy and members and to what extent tolerance views are central to Presbyterians' thinking about the denomination.

We begin by examining regression models of two measures of members' tolerance in Table 3.2: the willingness to tolerate difference and the importance of keeping people in the church.[5] The first pits tolerance against social harmony; the second pits tolerance against religious integrity. Combined, the two measures highlight the tough trade-offs required to truly embrace tolerance—one

TABLE 3.2 INFLUENCE OF CLERGY ON MEMBER TOLERANCE FOR DIFFERENT VIEWS AND DIVERSITY OVER DISCIPLINE (ORDERED LOGISTIC REGRESSION)

		Willingness to Tolerate		*Keeping People in Church*	
	Variables	β	p	β	p
Members	Affiliation importance	.20		.11	
	Brand loyalty	−.20		.09	
	Willingness to tolerate	—		.36	**
	Wish for less conflict	−.42	***	.05	
	Keeping people in church	.31	**	—	
	Theological liberalism	.08		−.01	
	Male	.13		−.14	
	Education	.88	***	.75	***
Clergy	Clergy satisfaction index	.59	***	−.07	
	Clergy brand loyalty	.18		.04	
	Clergy willingness to tolerate	−.22		−.03	
	Clergy wish for less conflict	.07		−.01	
	Clergy keeping people in church	.05		.24	**
	Cut point 1	−1.56		.48	
	Cut point 2	1.55		2.97	
	Cut point 3	2.57		4.13	
	Cut point 4	6.68		6.71	
Model statistics		N = 305, Pseudo R^2 = .14		N = 305, Pseudo R^2 = .07	

Source: 2001 Presbyterian Panel survey.

Note: "Cut point" refers to the intercept for the comparison from the category below to the category right above (e.g., picking a 1 versus 2).

***$p < .01$, **$p < .05$, *$p < .10$ (two-tailed tests)

needs to acknowledge that social conflict is likely, even desirable, and that tolerance enables the proliferation of theologies at odds with one's own. The two measures are modestly correlated ($r = .22$, $p < .01$) and we can find all four combinations here—from people willing to tolerate disagreement but wanting to enforce discipline to people who are not tolerant of diversity but want to keep people in the church. Clearly, people envision the social order of the Church in diverse ways.

In an era of weak denominational loyalties, it is not surprising that the importance of a denominational identity has no bearing on either form of tolerance under consideration. While 62 percent of members believe that their denominational affiliation is an important part of their identity, members are not willing to demand Christians remain loyal to their denominations (only 16 percent do), and thus they clearly circumscribe the reach of their denominational identities.

Instead, practical considerations and not principles dominate the models. The desire for less conflict drives down the willingness to tolerate diversity, but drives up the desire to keep people in church. While it is clear that this not a principled stance (for or against tolerance), there are at least two ways to view this effect. Either it is an individualist plea for a safe and functional place to worship, or it is the eminently logical argument that the denomination can only worship effectively with people in the pews who do not fight. How much of general political tolerance operates in the same way, motivated by practical considerations?

Since the two dependent variables are related, we put one in the other's model. The results are telling. The willingness to tolerate diversity is a value statement at a fairly deep level that people are a priority over principle or convenience. That is, the desire to keep people in church promotes a willingness to weather social conflict (i.e., tolerate diversity). We suspect that this pattern implicates the importance of the congregation to some or that the congregation is where thoughts about tolerance are conceived (recall the discussion of congregational practice in Chapter 1). That is, broader commitments in the trade-off between tolerance and conflict are generated, in part, by their desire to keep the congregation together.

It is surprising that theological liberalism is not related to support of these tolerance measures since the way that tolerance tends to be discussed publicly is precisely along the lines dividing liberals from conservatives. That is, liberals want theological innovation, allowing the ordination of people from new groups, for example, while conservatives want to preserve the existing order. The results here suggest that "order" may be defined in more circumscribed ways than we thought, where congregants value (or not) the local *congregational* order, given their particular fit within it. Broader arguments about tolerance, then, may simply reflect a valuation of a church family rather than higher-order ideologies of truth seeking and preservation. However, the fact that higher education is linked to tolerance in both of its guises indicates that individuals are not immune from undertaking principled evaluations.

Clergy's views on these issues have some bearing on how congregants feel, though in different ways. In the first model, congregants are more willing to tolerate disagreement even if it spills over into conflict when the clergyperson is more satisfied with the adequacy of the answers to significant questions the denomination provides.[6] The full effect of the variable is 1.1 points (or over a quarter of the range). Clergy are clearly sharing their satisfaction with the denomination to their congregants, which affects congregants' willingness to put up with disagreement—there must be something valuable to make the discomfort of disagreement worthwhile. No other clergy measure has an effect on congregants' willingness to tolerate disagreement, not even their own attitude on tolerating disagreement.

But it is interesting to note that whether congregants value keeping people in church (model 2) is related to clergy's own valuations—the full effect has about the same size as clergy satisfaction in model 1. Clergy can help set the tone about the value of discipline and the degree to which people should be emphasized over principles—key features of the congregational order. But why is clergy satisfaction not related to these attitudes (as in model 1)? We suspect that satisfaction could lead to ambivalence about both as meaningful outcomes. In further analysis, this is precisely what we find—members with clergy who are more satisfied with the denomination's answers are more likely to run to the middle of the scale, unable or unwilling to choose people over principles they care about.

Does Tolerance Feed Back into Satisfaction?

Given the apparent importance of tolerance in the life of the denomination, we also turned this formulation around to see whether a desire for tolerance is related to satisfaction with the adequacy of the answers the denomination is providing for social, political, and religious life. Tolerance is hardly a directional request—it does not tell that young man to "go West!" but instead to consider all directions on equal grounds (or at least allow those directions to be heard). This is likely to be frustrating to some who want the Church to provide answers or who come to the table strongly committed to a particular direction.

The results are presented in Table 3.3, showing correlates of how clergy, elders, and members feel about the adequacy of the denomination's answers. The first two models just include the responses of clergy and elders, respectively. Models 3 and 5 add clergy responses to the models with elders and members, respectively. The reason for doing this is that the addition of clergy drops the number of elders and members by several hundred, allowing us to compare how the correlates in those two samples function differently (if at all).

Clergy and elders look quite similar in how their denominational satisfaction is ordered. To the extent they value the denomination as part of their identity (affiliation importance) and believe that people should remain loyal to one denomination, the more satisfied they are with the denomination's answers. There is no doubt that the causal arrow may point in both directions here, though this captures elements of "diffuse" rather than "specific" (policy) support for the denomination (Easton 1965). Moreover, for both elders and clergy, the desire to keep people in church rather than enforcing discipline is related to satisfaction.

However, they also differ in crucial ways. Theologically liberal clergy are more satisfied than conservatives, but that distinction carries no weight among elders. The willingness to tolerate diversity is related to satisfaction among clergy but not among elders (until clergy's views are included in model 3). And the desire to reduce conflict is not related to the clergy's satisfaction but drives down that of elders. At least in this initial look, tolerance is related to how clergy think about the denomination.

That conclusion is sustained when we look at the satisfaction levels of members—for them, tolerance of diversity is also implicated, but so is the desire to reduce conflict. Given the similarly sized coefficients, it is tempting to say that they cancel each other out. But the two measures are negatively correlated ($r = -.18$), meaning that those who value tolerance are less desirous of reducing

TABLE 3.3 ROLE OF TOLERANCE IN DENOMINATIONAL CONFLICT: ESTIMATES OF SATISFACTION WITH THE PC(USA)'S ANSWERS REGARDING SOCIAL, POLITICAL, AND RELIGIOUS LIFE (ORDINARY LEAST SQUARES [OLS] REGRESSION)

		Model 1: Clergy		*Model 2: Elders without Clergy*		*Model 3: Elders with Clergy*		*Model 4: Members without Clergy*		*Model 5: Members with Clergy*	
	Variables	*β*	*p*	*β*	*p*	*β*	*p*	*β*	*p*	*β*	*p*
Individuals	Affiliation importance	.08	**	.06	**	.04		.08	***	.05	
	Brand loyalty	.09	***	.10	***	.16	***	.06		.06	
	Willingness to tolerate	.08	**	.03		.09	*	.07	**	.11	**
	Wish for less conflict	–.00		–.12	***	–.06		–.11	***	–.11	***
	Keeping people in church	.07	**	.06	**	.06		.04		.05	
	Theological liberalism	.17	***	.05		.02		.06	*	–.01	
	Male	–.05		–.04		–.04		–.07		–.14	**
	Education	–.02		–.05	***	–.05	*	.01		.02	
Clergy	Satisfaction index					.09	*			.06	
	Brand loyalty					–.02				–.08	**
	Willingness to tolerate					–.02				.04	
	Wish for less conflict					.03				.04	
	Keeping people in church					.04				.00	
Constant		–.54	*	1.10	***	.50		.77	***	.65	
Model statistics		$N = 581$, Adjusted $R^2 = .18$, RMSE = .66		$N = 568$, Adjusted $R^2 = .10$, RMSE = .63		$N = 309$, Adjusted $R^2 = .10$, RMSE = .62		$N = 535$, Adjusted $R^2 = .08$, RMSE = .62		$N = 304$, Adjusted $R^2 = .09$, RMSE = .61	

Source: 2001 Presbyterian Panel survey.

Note: RMSE = root mean squared error.

***$p < .01$, **$p < .05$, *$p < .10$ (two-tailed tests)

conflict. Still, the important point here is that tolerance for disagreement and conflict are important components of how individuals evaluate their denomination, all else equal.

We also assessed whether and how clergy's views on these dimensions were related to member satisfaction. The answers were different for elders and members. For elders, the satisfaction clergy have with the answers the denomination provides is significant and positive. For members, on the other hand, clergy satisfaction has no bearing on their satisfaction. Instead, when they have clergy who believe in brand loyalty, they tend to be less satisfied. There are two possibilities why this might be the case. Clergy brand loyalty may signal that the clergy are disappointed with the direction of the denomination shifting from a traditional path. However, in the clergy model (model 1), we found that more brand loyalty was related to more satisfaction, which belies this interpretation. Instead, we tentatively suggest that increased importance of brand loyalty among the clergy means that they may be less attentive to the demands of the religious marketplace and congregants. One indirect way we might gain some confidence in this interpretation is that clergy were also asked what trends they thought would have the most influence on Presbyterian congregations by 2050. Brand-loyal clergy were much more likely (by more than a factor of 3, $p < .01$) to say "the Internet" and "nontraditional families," both of which imply augmented choice is a threat.

Conclusion

Perhaps it is fitting that we end close to where we began: in tension over the understanding and place of tolerance within the Presbyterian Church (USA). On the one hand, tolerance as a concept is alive and well, recognized implicitly and explicitly in a wide array of institutional documents as a term that must inform deliberations within the Church, particularly when those deliberations involve difficult, challenging issues and questions. On the other hand, it also is clear that the Church has come to recognize tolerance's limitations—namely, that tolerance, taken to its seemingly logical end, results in a respect from which no further substantive engagement may be genuinely possible. What may result is a kind of benign acceptance but not an authentic reconciliation. In underscoring this tension we do not mean to minimize or dismiss how significant tolerance is to various mainline traditions. Indeed, the results confirmed that tolerance is significant and thoroughly present as one important component of satisfaction with the adequacy of the denomination's answers on questions from spiritual needs to social problems. But it was not the only force, and the somewhat abstract commitment to tolerance is counterbalanced by practical considerations that arise simultaneously. Tolerance implies the presence of disagreement and, perhaps, conflict, which impedes the essential delivery of a wide variety of benefits. It may be that the process of working through conflict is a valuable end, but it also means maintaining a diverse membership, both of which are important to sustaining the denomination.

What we hope to accomplish in this chapter, however briefly, is to offer a snapshot of one mainline denomination's efforts to wrestle meaningfully with profound differences within the denomination that have led to the emphasis on tolerance as a de facto organizing principle, even a theological tenet. While tolerance is meant to be a means by which groups maintain society in the face of disagreement, the fact that tolerance has replaced hard answers is profoundly troubling to some on both sides, though more so among conservatives. Therefore, although disagreement creates a need for participants to practice tolerance and deliberation to interact in a way that respects all, that move creates its own flash point of conflict. In organizations created on principle, perhaps schism is the only viable solution to the fact of disagreement. Clearly, the weight of American religious history suggests that this is so.

This chapter also helps document the influence that the social and organizational setting has on how people evaluate tolerance. The attitudes and, we presume, information conveyed by elites bear on members' attitudes. Aside from work that documents the effect of events in the broader environment (such as the attacks of September 11, 2001, or a march in the neighborhood), very little literature outside this volume documents the effects of elite communication on tolerance judgments (but see Green et al. 2011). Given the links found here that emphasize that those relationships may not be direct ones (i.e., clergy tolerance → member tolerance), we need to pay careful attention to how members think about their quality of life and how that translates into the social and personal discomfort they are willing to endure.

Notes

1. We capitalize "Church" when we refer to the specific denomination, the PC(USA), and use the lowercase "church" when referring to a particular church organization.

2. After allowing the ordination of gay clergy in 2011, in June 2014 the PC(USA) General Assembly voted overwhelmingly (429–175) to amend their definition of marriage to be "between two people," thereby allowing same-sex marriage. The body also voted 371–238 to allow clergy to perform same-sex marriages in states where they are legal. Those decisions will now proceed to a vote in the 172 regional presbyteries.

3. "Pluralism" means different things to different disciplines. In political science, pluralism most often refers to a politics of contention between groups with different interests that promotes stability in the polity. The idea is associated with James Madison, Arthur Bentley, David Truman, and Robert Dahl. There is a related strand of pluralism in political philosophy, most prominently associated with Isaiah Berlin and William Connolly, that, in very broad brush, shifts to the individual level and calls for dialogue and the embrace of ambiguity and moderation. That second meaning is what we intend here.

4. We had to contact the Research Services agency to acquire the congregational identifier code to link the three data sets. We thank Jack Marcum and Ida Smith-Williams for their help in supplying these data with an appropriate linking ID. In the

panel following 2001, they randomly sampled within each group, thus severing the congregational tie.

5. For information about how the variables are coded, please see the online appendix at http://pauldjupe.com/s/Appendix.docx.

6. Clergy are asked to rate the adequacy of their denomination's answers to "the moral problems and needs of the individual," "the problems of family life," "people's spiritual needs," "the problems of society," and "the problems of local communities." The response options are no (0), not sure (1), and yes (2). The index has an α value of .85. It is troubling for the denomination to note that the clergy sample average is .92 (SD = .73), or close to "not sure" and leaning toward "no."

References

Allen, Danielle. 2004. *Talking to Strangers: Anxieties of Citizenship since Brown v. Board of Education*. Chicago: University of Chicago Press.

Cadge, Wendy. 2002. "Vital Conflicts: The Mainline Denominations Debate Homosexuality." In *The Quiet Hand of God: Faith-Based Activism and the Public Role of Mainline Protestantism*, edited by Robert Wuthnow and John H. Evans, 265–286. Berkeley: University of California Press.

Crowley, Sharon. 2006. *Toward a Civil Discourse: Rhetoric and Fundamentalism*. Pittsburgh: University of Pittsburgh Press.

Easton, David. 1965. *A Systems Analysis of Political Life*. New York: Wiley.

Graham, Billy. 2012. "The Sin of Tolerance." Billy Graham Evangelistic Association, October 3. Available at http://billygraham.org/story/the-sin-of-tolerance/.

Green, Donald P., Peter M. Aronow, Daniel E. Bergan, Pamela Greene, Celia Paris, and Beth I. Weinberger. 2011. "Does Knowledge of Constitutional Principles Increase Support for Civil Liberties? Results from a Randomized Field Experiment." *Journal of Politics* 73 (2): 463–476.

Gutmann, Amy, and Dennis Thompson. 1996. *Democracy and Disagreement: Why Moral Conflict Cannot Be Avoided in Politics, and What Should Be Done about It*. Cambridge, MA: Harvard University Press.

McClosky, Herbert. 1964. "Consensus and Ideology in American Politics." *American Political Science Review* 58 (2): 361–382.

Mouffe, Chantal. 2000. *The Democratic Paradox*. London: Verso.

PC(USA) (Presbyterian Church [USA]). 1999. *Presbyterian Principles for Interfaith Dialogue*. Available at http://www.pcusa.org/site_media/media/uploads/interfaith relations/pdf/principlesforinterfaithdialogue.pdf.

Sandel, Michael J. 1996. *Democracy's Discontent: America in Search of a Public Philosophy*. Cambridge, MA: Harvard University Press.

Stouffer, Samuel A. 1955. *Communism, Conformity, and Civil Liberties: A Cross Section of the Nation Speaks Its Mind*. New York: Doubleday.

Theological Task Force on Peace, Unity, and Purity of the Church. 2006. *A Season of Discernment: The Final Report of the Theological Task Force on Peace, Unity, and Purity of the Church*. Available at http://faithfulness.com/finalreport.pdf.

Wuthnow, Robert, and John H. Evans, eds. 2002. *The Quiet Hand of God: Faith-Based Activism and the Public Role of Mainline Protestantism*. Berkeley: University of California Press.

4

Fearful Asymmetry

Tolerance of Christian Fundamentalists among Political Elites

CLYDE WILCOX
CHRISTINE KIM

Political tolerance is a fundamental principle of a religiously pluralistic liberal democracy. James Gibson notes, "Tolerance is one of the few viable solutions to the tensions and conflict brought about by multiculturalism and political heterogeneity; tolerance is an essential endorphin of a democratic body" (2006: 21). Political elites are generally more committed to civil liberties than the general public, but elites are not universally tolerant of groups they dislike or fear. Moreover, not all sets of elites are equally tolerant (Stouffer 1955; McClosky 1964; Nunn, Crockett, and Williams 1978; Sullivan, Piereson, and Marcus 1979, 1982). For example, on the basis of samples of Canadian and U.S. political elites, Paul Sniderman and colleagues (1991) found that liberal and conservative elites had markedly different levels of tolerance; indeed, conservative elites were not only less tolerant than liberal elites, but they were also markedly less tolerant than the average liberal citizen.

One set of conservative political elites who have demonstrated substantial levels of political intolerance are leaders of the Christian Right. Although some movement leaders have promoted tolerant messages in training sessions (Rozell and Wilcox 1996; Shields 2007), the movement is best known for a series of intolerant statements about religious and political liberals; feminists; environmentalists; lesbian, gay, bisexual, or transgender (LGBT) citizens; and even television and fictional characters (Wilcox 2010). Studies of members of Christian Right groups who contribute money to politics have reported remarkably low levels of support for basic democratic freedoms (Guth and Green 1991; Rozell and Wilcox 1996; Wilcox 2010).

These studies have identified several distinct sources of intolerance among the Christian Right, including apocalyptic views of politics that lead to fear and distrust of those they see as opposing God's plan. In addition, Christian Right elites are found to be intolerant because of their fundamentalist religious theology. A long line of research has shown that religious fundamentalism is associated with lower levels of political tolerance (Beatty and Walter 1984; Wilcox and Jelen 1990). For those who believe in a single truth and an infallible document, the utility of a marketplace of ideas is substantially reduced. In addition, those who believe in a literal devil are more likely to want to limit the spread of ideas that they perceive to be dangerous (Gibson 2010; Nunn, Crockett, and Williams 1978).

Conservative media and bloggers frequently charge that liberals are at least as intolerant of Christian conservatives as the reverse, an observation that some liberal commentators have made as well (Douthat 2014; Linker 2014; Nazworth 2014; and Saletan 2014).[1] They point to multiple examples of this perceived liberal intolerance, citing, for example, requirements in the Affordable Care Act that employers provide contraceptive coverage to employees as limiting religious freedom and court rulings that commercial vendors who offer wedding services must be available for same-sex couples. They argue that the Democratic Party is intolerant of religious Americans and that American elites are waging a "war on Christmas."[2]

Although there has been little research on intolerance toward fundamentalists, studies have shown that the general public holds negative views of fundamentalists, with liberals voicing intensely negative evaluations. Using the 1988–1996 American National Election Study (ANES), Louis Bolce and Gerald De Maio (1999b), for example, found that about one-fifth of the nonfundamentalist public intensely disliked fundamentalist Christians, and that this was especially true among the highly educated and secular. After 1992 and the first Clinton presidential election, the antagonism assumed a more partisan, ideological cast, with cultural progressivism, political liberalism, and Democratic partisanship becoming more important predictors of negative affect toward fundamentalist Christians. Feelings toward fundamentalist Christians predict party assessment, presidential vote choice, and policy preferences (Bolce and De Maio 1999a, 2006, 2007). The authors concluded, "Christian fundamentalists have become important to the political thinking of American voters" (Bolce and De Maio 1999a: 509).

The mass media frequently depicts fundamentalists as intolerant, racist, and sometimes even violent (Bolce and De Maio 2006). Moreover, media frames focus on the politicization of religious conservatives and its threat to democratic pluralism (Kerr 2003; Kerr and Moy 2002). For many Americans who have little interaction with fundamentalists and other evangelical groups, these media frames may stoke fears that fundamentalists might soon press for limits on civil rights. That fear may also lead liberals to be intolerant toward fundamentalists.

Yet Bolce and De Maio demonstrated not that liberals were *intolerant* of fundamentalists but merely that they held negative evaluations. It is normal to dislike, distrust, and fear those on the other side of the political spectrum. The true test of tolerance is allowing those whom you dislike, distrust, or fear to have access to the public square. To date, there is limited empirical evidence about the tolerance of liberal religious and secular elites toward fundamentalists and other conservative Christians.

In this chapter, we seek to answer several questions about political tolerance for fundamentalists. We choose fundamentalists rather than broader categories of "conservative Christian" first because fundamentalists are the best known and most controversial evangelical group; therefore, attitudes toward them are likely to be stronger and more stable. Second, we focus on fundamentalists because past literature suggests antipathy toward this specific religious community. Finally, we choose fundamentalists because they are explicitly identified in our survey data as a target of tolerance. We explore first the extent of intolerance toward fundamentalists and compare that to fundamentalist intolerance of liberal outgroups. Next, we seek to explain intolerance toward fundamentalists using religious, political, and intervening variables.

Data and Measures

Data for the present analysis came from a mail survey of a stratified random sample of donors to presidential primary campaigns in 2000. Contributing cash is an atypical form of political participation (Verba, Schlozman and Brady 1995), and donors in this and past studies were more broadly active in politics and had generally high levels of education and income. The sample included donors who gave to one or more of the several GOP candidates and those who gave to Democrats Bill Bradley and Al Gore and Green Party candidate Ralph Nader. The survey was mailed to significant donors, who gave more than $200, drawn from the Federal Election Commission (FEC) disclosure record, as well as small donors drawn from FEC matching fund requests and George W. Bush's campaign website. The first wave of the survey was mailed in the summer of 2001, and nonrespondents received four additional mailings. Excluding undeliverable questionnaires, the response rate was 50 percent. The final sample consisted of 1,538 donors who gave less than $200 and 1,330 donors who gave more than that amount. The survey was stratified to obtain equal numbers of donors to each candidate, although response rates varied across candidates. In this analysis we present unweighted data but have checked our results using data that weighted each candidate to his total share of the donor pool.

Fundamentalist Christians constituted 11 percent of respondents, and 18 percent of nonfundamentalists listed at least one related religious identity, including evangelical, born again, Pentecostal, or charismatic. But the sample also contained significant numbers of those with religious identities expected to be more negative toward fundamentalists, including liberal Christians, ethical humanists, reformed and conservative Jews, and atheists/agnostics. Many donors were strong liberals, who took progressive positions on issues such as abortion and LGBT rights and are expected to hold negative views of fundamentalists.

Tolerance was measured by pairs of questions asking (1) whether members of various groups should be allowed to demonstrate "assuming that there is no threat of violence" and (2) whether respondents would allow members of these groups to teach in the local public schools "assuming professional conduct." These questions therefore removed the most common objections to tolerance of public demonstrations and hiring teachers with diverse views. The groups referenced in these questions included Christian fundamentalists, feminists, homosexuals, atheists, environmentalists, white power advocates, black nationalists, and militia members. Although the survey did not allow respondents to choose their least-liked group, we do have access to feeling thermometers toward many of these groups that allow us to control for the degree of negative affect.

We begin by exploring affect toward and tolerance for Christian fundamentalists among various groups of elites and compare them with Christian fundamentalists' tolerance of liberal groups. We then explore the sources of tolerance of Christian fundamentalists among nonfundamentalist donors. We have estimated a series of models controlling for various religious variables (including affiliation, identity, and behavior) and general demographic variables (including education, gender, race, region, and income). We also control for partisanship and ideology.

Threat perception is operationalized by a question asking for respondents' perceptions of how active fundamentalist Christians were in their community and state. Moreover, we control for respondents' thermometer ratings toward fundamentalist Christians as well as two traits that have been linked to tolerance: support for the democratic process and social trust (see Gibson 2010; Sullivan and Transue 1999).

Fearful Asymmetry: Affect, Threat, and Tolerance

Table 4.1 shows attitudes toward fundamentalist Christians by various groups of nonfundamentalist elites. We first show affect with an average feeling thermometer and the percentage of respondents in the category who rated fundamentalists at zero. Then we show perceived threat as the percentage of each group who said that Christian conservatives were very active in their community or state. Finally, we show the percentage of each group willing to extend the right to demonstrate and to teach in public schools to fundamentalists.

We first show all nonfundamentalist respondents and then break out other evangelicals (i.e., those who did not identify as fundamentalists but did identify as one or more of the following: evangelical Christian, born-again Christian, Pentecostal Christian, and charismatic Christian). The rest of the table shows the attitudes of nonevangelicals, or those who did not choose one of these orthodox religious identities. Here, we first present groups with different religious identities and then those with political identities that might lead them to be hostile, or friendly, to fundamentalists. In Table 4.2, for comparison, we show the affect, threat perception, and tolerance of fundamentalists toward three key outgroups:

TABLE 4.1 AFFECT, THREAT, AND TOLERANCE TOWARD FUNDAMENTALISTS BY NONFUNDAMENTALISTS

Nonfundamentalist Respondent Group	*Mean Thermometer Rating of Fundamentalists by Listed Group*	*"0" Degrees (%)*	*Christian Conservatives "Very Active" in Community (%)*	*Christian Conservatives "Very Active" in State (%)*	*Tolerant of Demonstrating in Public (%)*	*Tolerant of Teaching in Public Schools (%)*	*N*
All nonfundamentalists	33	29	20	32	89	68	2,445
Other evangelicals	65	5	27	38	89	79	722
All nonevangelicals	25	35	18	30	89	66	2,146
Traditional Catholic	47	13	16	29	86	66	328
Progressive Catholic	22	31	21	35	95	74	161
Liberal Christians	17	39	23	34	89	66	309
Ethical humanists	9	58	21	39	92	69	223
Atheists/agnostics	10	58	16	26	94	64	318
Jews	10	53	15	25	89	53	148
Strong Democrats	5	71	24	37	87	62	279
Strong Republicans	47	12	19	27	84	61	571
Strongly support LGBT rights	10	57	22	35	92	69	832
Member feminist group	7	65	24	38	94	69	158

TABLE 4.2 AFFECT, THREAT, AND TOLERANCE OF FUNDAMENTALISTS TOWARD LIBERAL GROUPS

Liberal Outgroup	*Mean Thermometer Rating of Listed Group by Fundamentalists*	*"0" Degrees (%)*	*Liberals "Very Active" in Community (%)*	*Liberals "Very Active" in State (%)*	*Tolerant of Demonstrating in Public (%)*	*Tolerant of Teaching in Public Schools (%)*
Environmentalists	33	22	19	37	82	67
Gays and lesbians	14	56	14	33	55	22
Atheists	n/a	n/a	n/a	n/a	68	38
Feminists	13	52	8	20	76	44

Note: $N = 296$. The survey did not ask respondents to rate their feelings toward atheists; thus, mean thermometer scores for this group are not available.

feminists, atheists, and gays and lesbians. For comparison, we also provide similar data on fundamentalist attitudes toward environmentalists, for whom fundamentalists have no obvious theological animus (but see Guth et al. 1995).

The results in the first column of Table 4.1 show that even evangelicals who are not fundamentalists were somewhat ambivalent toward fundamentalists, rating them on average at 65 degrees and with a surprising 5 percent (primarily Pentecostals) rating them at 0 degrees. Among nonevangelicals, feelings were far more negative. More than one-third of all nonevangelical elites rated Christian fundamentalists at 0 degrees, as did more than 70 percent of strong Democrats and nearly two-thirds of feminist group members. Strong Republicans and traditional Catholics were more positive toward fundamentalists, but even among these political and cultural allies, the average thermometer score fell below 50. Perceptions of fundamentalist activism were less variable, although it is striking that strong Republicans were significantly less likely to see fundamentalists as very active in their state than were strong Democrats.[3]

A comparison with the results in the first column of Table 4.2 shows that negative affect is somewhat symmetrical, with fundamentalists slightly warmer toward their cultural opponents than vice versa. But fundamentalists were cool toward environmentalists, giving them an average thermometer score of 33 degrees, and more than one-half rated gays and lesbians and feminists at 0. The results on the left side of Tables 4.1 and 4.2, therefore, suggest reciprocal dislike by cultural and political opponents, with liberal groups somewhat cooler toward fundamentalists.

The results on the right side of Tables 4.1 and 4.2, however, indicate a strong asymmetry in the application of tolerance. Among each respondent group in Table 4.1, approximately 90 percent of evangelicals and nonevangelicals supported the right of fundamentalists to demonstrate in their community. But here the story is quite different than affect, for the limited variation is not explained by political and cultural alliances. Indeed, members of feminist groups and atheists/agnostics were *more* supportive than were nonfundamentalist evangelicals, progressive Catholics were more supportive than traditional Catholics, and strong Democrats were slightly more supportive than strong Republicans. In contrast, only 82 percent of fundamentalists would allow environmentalists to demonstrate in their community, and only 55 percent would allow gays and lesbians the rights of public protest.

Approximately two-thirds of nonfundamentalists would allow fundamentalists to teach in public schools, with support highest among other evangelicals and progressive Catholics and lowest among Jews. Somewhat surprisingly, nearly 20 percent of nonfundamentalist evangelicals would not allow fundamentalists to teach in the public schools, suggesting nervousness even among those who may share broad curricular preferences. Again, tolerance is asymmetrical: Although two-thirds of fundamentalists would allow environmentalists to teach in public schools "assuming professional conduct," less than half would allow feminists to teach, and only one-fifth would allow gays and lesbians to teach. These low levels of tolerance are striking in a population of political activists of whom nearly two-thirds have a college degree or higher.

Intolerance of fundamentalists in the classroom is not as centered on the culture wars as Fox News might have us believe. Progressive Catholics were *more* likely to allow fundamentalists into the classroom than were traditional Catholics (74 percent versus 66 percent). And among those who did not hold any evangelical religious identities, strong Democrats and strong Republicans were equally likely to oppose allowing fundamentalists to teach in local public schools. The correlation between attitudes on gay rights and tolerance toward fundamentalists in the classroom was .07, but those who strongly *favored* LGBT rights were also *more* supportive of fundamentalists in the classroom.

The asymmetry in tolerance is more striking since fundamentalists were, if anything, slightly warmer toward their cultural opponents. The correlation between affect, as measured with a feeling thermometer, and tolerance was higher for fundamentalists toward liberal groups than vice versa. Among fundamentalists, the correlation between their feeling thermometer for gays and lesbians and opposition to GLBT teachers was .32, whereas among nonevangelicals, the correlation between feeling thermometer scores for fundamentalists and opposition to fundamentalists in the classroom was .18.

Among nonevangelicals, more than one-half of those who rated fundamentalists at zero in a feeling thermometer would allow them to teach in public schools, as would 70 percent of those who rated fundamentalists at or below 50 degrees. Among fundamentalists, in contrast, only 11 percent of those who rated gays and lesbians at 0 degrees would allow them to teach in public schools, and the same was true of a majority of those who rated gays and lesbians at 50 degrees. Thus, fundamentalists were intolerant even when they had neutral affect, but nonfundamentalists were tolerant even when they were hostile.

This asymmetry suggests that liberal elites were more willing to extend civil liberties to Christian fundamentalists than the latter were to reciprocate. Moreover, intolerance toward fundamentalists in the classroom was as widespread among nonevangelical conservatives as it was among liberals and as common among nonevangelical strong Republicans as among strong Democrats.

Nevertheless, fully one-third of highly educated nonevangelical elites would not allow members of a large mainstream religious movement to teach in public schools. It is possible that, despite the caveat of "assuming professional conduct," respondents worried that fundamentalists might subtly inject creationism (or at least doubts about the theory of evolution) into the biology curriculum or skew sex education lessons to include moral judgments of sexual minorities and admonitions for abstinence. Of course, fundamentalists may have similar fears about the role of environmentalists, feminists, and LGBT teachers in subtly shaping curricula. However, the level of intolerance among Pentecostals and other evangelicals for fundamentalists is surprising, since sizable numbers of these religious groups would share fundamentalists' curricular preferences. We turn now to explaining the variation in tolerance of fundamentalists.

Sources of Intolerance of Fundamentalists

We estimated logistic regression models predicting support for allowing fundamentalists to demonstrate in one's community and teach in the public schools. We identified a number of models and present here ones that include key religious, political, and psychological variables and the critical demographic predictors.[4] We estimated models with all nonfundamentalists and dummies for those identifying with other evangelical groups, as well as models that included only nonevangelicals. The results were substantively identical, with evangelicals more tolerant in both larger models. Here, we present only the models for nonevangelicals in Table 4.3. The key test is whether these elites, who were

TABLE 4.3 SOURCES OF TOLERANCE TOWARD FUNDAMENTALISTS AMONG NONEVANGELICAL ELITES

	Demonstrate			*Teach*		
	β	*Odds Ratio*	*Wald*	*β*	*Odds Ratio*	*Wald*
Feeling thermometer toward fundamentalists	.03	1.03	25.00**	.03	1.03	52.7**
Religious Variables						
Attendance	.02	1.02	.04	.94	.91	2.36
Bible views	.22	1.25	1.84	.18	1.19	2.55
Liberal Christian	−.14	.65	.11	−.12	.89	.34
Ethical humanist	.44	.87	1.93	.21	1.23	.78
Atheist/agnostic	.41	1.51	1.07	.00	.98	.00
Jew	−.99	.37	5.99*	−.93	.39	13.36**
Religion out of politics	−.91	.40	8.58**	−.37	.69	2.80
Political Variables						
Partisanship	.18	1.20	6.41*	.04	1.05	1.07
Support LGBT	.24	.79	4.28*	.20	.82	9.20**
Fundamentalists active in community	−.45	.64	7.20**	.03	1.03	.11
Intervening Variables						
Democratic norms	.61	1.85	21.82**	.27	1.30	1.09**
Social trust	.06	1.07	.29	.18	1.19	6.19*
Demographics						
Age	−.04	1.04	19.41**	−.02	1.02	17.47**
Women	−.50	.61	3.95*	−.11	.90	.49
Education	.28	1.32	9.05**	.17	1.19	8.42**
Nagelkerke R^2		.24			.17	
Percent predicted correctly		92			71	

Note: Additional models included controls for traditional and progressive Catholic identification, religious affiliation and subjective religious salience, ideology, membership in a feminist organization, region, and income. In no model were any of these variables significant predictors. Please see the online appendix for specific variable coding.
$*p \leq .05$; $**p \leq .01$

antagonistic to the religious right's political agenda, were significantly different in their tolerance level.

The first model explained variation in support for allowing fundamentalists to demonstrate in the community. Not surprisingly, affect toward fundamentalists as measured by the feeling thermometer is the most powerful predictor. Frequency of church attendance and Bible views did not predict tolerance of fundamentalists among elites who did not have an evangelical identity, and those who identified as liberal Christians, ethical humanists, atheists, or agnostics were not significantly more or less willing to allow fundamentalists to protest. In our expanded models, subjective religious salience, identity as a traditional or progressive Catholic, and denominational dummies also failed to predict tolerance of fundamentalists. However, Jews were significantly less supportive of fundamentalists holding demonstrations, as were those who believed that religion was a private matter best kept out of politics.

Political variables better predicted support for fundamentalists' right to demonstrate, but the direction of these coefficients was inconsistent with culture war explanations. Partisanship predicts tolerance, but it was Democrats who were more likely to support fundamentalist rights rather than nonevangelical Republicans. Support for LGBT equality also predicted support for demonstrating, but again, it was those who were most supportive of LGBT rights who also wanted to protect fundamentalists' rights. Those who reported that Christian conservatives were especially active in their community were less supportive of demonstrations, perhaps because they perceived a heightened threat that Christian conservatives might win local elections and affect public policy.

Those who were more supportive of democratic norms of compromise and deliberation were much more likely to support fundamentalist demonstrations, but social trust was not a predictor. Finally, younger respondents, men, and better-educated respondents were more supportive of fundamentalist rights to demonstrate.

The results for the model predicting support for fundamentalists teaching were especially dominated by affect. Jews were also less supportive of fundamentalists in the classroom, but here, political secularism was not a factor, perhaps because teaching is more related to employment than political protest.[5] Neither partisanship nor perceived fundamentalist activity in the community was a predictor of support for fundamentalists in the classroom, but supporters of LGBT equality were more supportive of fundamentalists teaching.

Support for democratic norms and more social trust both predicted more support for fundamentalist teachers. Trust may matter here because monitoring public school teachers is difficult. Demonstrations are frequently marked by heightened police presence, but teachers are typically alone in the classroom with students for most of the day. Thus, a lack of trust could translate into support for barring from the classroom those with objectionable ideas. Finally, youth and education, but not gender, predicted support for fundamentalist teachers.

Conclusion

The results show that among presidential donors in 2000, there was substantial and generally symmetrical polarization in affect toward social and religious groups. Many donors who were members of various liberal groups held very negative evaluations of fundamentalists, and fundamentalist donors held very negative views of feminists, atheists, gays and lesbians, and, to a lesser extent, environmentalists. That conservative nonevangelicals were also lukewarm toward fundamentalists suggests that this religious group has a more widespread image problem.[6]

However, contrary to the claims of conservative activists, *intolerance* was not symmetrical, at least in 2000. Many Christian fundamentalists were willing to deny the right to demonstrate to members of liberal groups, and majorities would bar atheists, feminists, and gays and lesbians from teaching in the public schools. The relationship between affect and tolerance was different in the two sets of elites: Fundamentalists were willing to deny civil rights even when they rated groups neutrally, but liberals were frequently willing to extend civil rights even when they rated fundamentalists at zero degrees.

Indeed, in the bivariate and multivariate models, it was political *liberals* who were more supportive of allowing fundamentalists to demonstrate and teach. Those who strongly supported LGBT equality were more likely to support fundamentalists teaching in the classroom than those who were strongly opposed to LGBT equality, even though fundamentalists had worked hard in many states and communities to condemn homosexuality in the classroom. Democrats were also more likely to support fundamentalists teaching in local public schools than Republicans. Moreover, in the bivariate data, even nonfundamentalist evangelicals were somewhat divided about allowing fundamentalists to teach.

Although the two models predicting tolerance of demonstrations and teaching were quite similar, there were some differences that made sense as well. Politically secular respondents—that is, those who thought that religion should remain a private matter—were more likely to oppose political demonstrations by fundamentalists but not more likely to oppose them teaching in the classroom. Similarly, those who perceived that Christian conservatives were very active in their communities were less likely to support demonstrations but again were not opposed to fundamentalists teaching in public schools. In contrast, social trust was a predictor of allowing fundamentalists to teach, but not to demonstrate. With police surrounding contentious demonstrations, trust is not needed to extend civil liberties, but in an unmonitored setting with children exposed to ideas, trust may be more essential in supporting teachers with potentially different curricular preferences.

Education was predictably a positive predictor of tolerance, but younger respondents were also more tolerant than older elites. The age range among donors was somewhat truncated, with few donors younger than middle age. Younger donors lived a bigger portion of their lives with fundamentalist political activity; as a result, perhaps they were less threatened by what they perceived as normal political mobilization.

Strikingly, American Jews were less supportive of allowing fundamentalists to teach and demonstrate in their local communities, as the multivariate model results suggest. Jews may perceive a far greater threat to the maintenance of religion and state in a liberal democracy from fundamentalist hegemony than other religious liberals and have access to collective memory of what happens when intolerant groups gain power (Wald 2015). Moreover, fundamentalist Christian preferentialism may be more of a threat to non-Christians. Our data here, however, do not permit us to see if Muslims, Buddhists, and others might be equally opposed to fundamentalist mobilization.

This study has explored affect, threat, and tolerance of fundamentalists, but there are the inevitable caveats. Donors are a special class of political activists, and although many of these donors are active in many political groups and in other forms of participation, it may be that other elite samples would provide different results. The composition of the donor pool is affected by the candidates who chose to run, and the Democratic presidential field in 2000 provided a truncated range of ideology, although Ralph Nader appealed to many secular liberals. Perhaps most importantly, the study was conducted in 2000; the years since have moved the debate on LGBT rights, and the collapse of the Christian Right may have lessened liberal fears of fundamentalist victory.

The current political debate frequently depicts liberals as intolerant of those with whom they disagree, especially on the extension of gay rights. While our results show the antagonism liberals held toward Christian fundamentalists, many appeared to take a sober second thought before calling for a restriction of fundamentalists' rights to advocate for their interests or to participate in civil society through the public schools. Many more liberals than fundamentalists were able to disconnect their antipathy from the equal extension of rights, which enables disagreements to remain within the confines of politics, where peaceful processes exist for dispute resolution.

Notes

Acknowledgment: We thank Paul Djupe, Ken Wald, and Napp Nazworth for their review of the chapter and helpful comments.

1. Some conservative commentators who write about liberal intolerance describe it as a recent phenomenon, occurring after the majority of public opinion shifted to support same-sex marriage.

2. For a comic review of Fox News's coverage of the war on Christmas, see the clip of an episode of *The Colbert Report* at http://www.patheos.com/blogs/friendlyatheist/2013/12/12/stephen-colbert-mocks-fox-news-coverage-of-the-war-on-christmas/.

3. In general, perceptions of fundamentalist activity were closely related to state of residence.

4. All variable coding can be found in the online appendix associated with this chapter available at http://pauldjupe.com/s/Appendix.docx.

5. The coefficient was significant at 0.09, however.

6. It is worth noting that among Democratic donors there was ambivalence toward feminists also.

References

Beatty, Kathleen M., and Oliver Walter. 1984. "Religious Preference and Practice: Reevaluating Their Impact on Political Tolerance." *Public Opinion Quarterly* 48 (1B): 318–329.

Bolce, Louis, and Gerald De Maio. 1999a. "The Anti-Christian Fundamentalist Factor in Contemporary Politics." *Public Opinion Quarterly* 63 (4): 508–542.

———. 1999b. "Religious Outlook, Culture War Politics, and Antipathy toward Christian Fundamentalists." *Public Opinion Quarterly* 63 (1): 29–61.

———. 2006. "The Divisiveness Rationale and Negative Reference Group Association in Church-State Controversies." In *Religion, Politics, and American Identity*, edited by David S. Gutterman and Andrew R. Murphy, 101–127. Lanham, MD: Lexington Books.

———. 2007. "Secularists, Anti-Christian Fundamentalists, and the New Religious Divide in the American Electorate." In *From Pews to Polling Places: Faith and the Politics in the American Religious Mosaic*, edited by J. Matthew Wilson, 251–276. Washington, DC: Georgetown University Press.

Douthat, Ross. 2014. "Diversity and Dishonesty." *New York Times*, April 12. Available at http://www.nytimes.com/2014/04/13/opinion/sunday/douthat-diversity-and-dishonesty.html.

Gibson, James L. 2006. "Enigmas of Intolerance: Fifty Years after Stouffer's Communism, Conformity, and Civil Liberties." *Perspectives on Politics* 4 (1): 21–34.

———. 2010. "The Political Consequences of Religiosity: Does Religion Always Cause Political Intolerance?" In *Religion and Democracy in the United States: Danger or Opportunity?* edited by Alan Wolfe and Ira Katznelson, 147–175. New York: Russell Sage.

Guth, James, and John Green. 1991. "An Ideology of Rights: Support for Civil Liberties among Political Activists." *Political Behavior* 13 (4): 321–344.

Guth, James, John Green, Lyman Kellstedt, and Corwin Smidt. 1995. "Faith and the Environment: Religious Beliefs and Attitudes on Environmental Policy." *American Journal of Political Science* 39 (2): 364–382.

Kerr, Peter A. 2003. "The Framing of Fundamentalist Christians: Network Television News, 1980–2000." *Journal of Media and Religion* 2 (4): 203–235.

Kerr, Peter A., and Patricia Moy. 2002. "Newspaper Coverage of Fundamentalist Christians, 1980–2000." *Journalism and Mass Communication Quarterly* 79 (1): 54–72.

Linker, Damon. 2014. "How Liberalism Became an Intolerant Dogma." *The Week*, July 11. Available at http://theweek.com/article/index/264546/how-liberalism-became-an-intolerant-dogma.

McClosky, Herbert. 1964. "Consensus and Ideology in American Politics." *American Political Science Review* 58 (2): 361–382.

Nazworth, Napp. 2014. "8 Recent Examples of Liberals Behaving Illiberally." *Christian Post*, April 7. Available at http://www.christianpost.com/news/8-recent-examples-of-liberals-behaving-illiberally-117439/.

Nunn, Clyde Z., Harry J. Crockett, Jr., and J. Allen Williams, Jr. 1978. *Tolerance for Nonconformity.* San Francisco: Jossey-Bass.

Rozell, Mark and Clyde Wilcox. 1996. "Second Coming: The Strategies of the New Christian Right." *Political Science Quarterly* 111 (2): 271–294.

Saletan, William. 2014. "Brendan Eich and the New Moral Majority." *Slate*, April 7. Available at http://www.slate.com/blogs/saletan/2014/04/07/brendan_eich_homophobia_and_corporate_values_the_left_is_the_new_moral_majority.html.

Shields, Jon. 2007. "Between Passion and Deliberation: The Christian Right and Democratic Ideals." *Political Science Quarterly* 122 (1): 89–113.

Sniderman, Paul M., Joseph F. Fletcher, Peter H. Russell, Philip E. Tetlock, and Brian J. Gaines. 1991. "The Fallacy of Democratic Elitism: Elite Competition and Commitment to Civil Liberties." *British Journal of Political Science* 21 (3): 349–370.

Stouffer, Samuel A. 1955. *Communism, Conformity, and Civil Liberties: A Cross Section of the Nation Speaks Its Mind.* New York: Doubleday.

Sullivan, John L., James Piereson, and George E. Marcus. 1979. "An Alternative Conceptualization of Political Tolerance: Illusory Increases, 1950s–1970s." *American Political Science Review* 73 (3): 781–794.

———. 1982. *Political Tolerance and American Democracy.* Chicago: University of Chicago Press.

Sullivan, John L., and John E. Transue. 1999. "The Psychological Underpinnings of Democracy: A Selective Review of Research on Political Tolerance, Interpersonal Trust, and Social Capital." *Annual Review of Psychology* 50:625–650.

Verba, Sidney, Kay Lehman Schlozman, and Henry E. Brady. 1995. *Voice and Equality: Civic Voluntarism in American Politics.* Cambridge, MA: Harvard University Press.

Wald, Kenneth D. 2015. "The Choosing People: Interpreting the Puzzling Politics of American Jewry." *Politics and Religion* 8 (1): 4–35.

Wilcox, Clyde. 2010. "The Christian Right and Civic Virtue." In *Religion and Democracy in the United States: Danger or Opportunity*, edited by Alan Wolfe and Ira Katznelson, 176–211. Princeton, NJ: Princeton University Press.

Wilcox, Clyde, and Ted G. Jelen. 1990. "Evangelicals and Political Tolerance." *American Politics Quarterly* 18:25–46.

II

Social Psychology of Religion and Citizen Political Tolerance

5

Heterogeneous Religion Measures and Political Tolerance Outcomes

MARIE A. EISENSTEIN
APRIL K. CLARK

Given the theoretical importance of political tolerance, it is hardly surprising that scholars have tried to understand the levels and sources of political tolerance and support for democratic values (Bobo and Licari 1989; Gibson 1992; Golebiowska 1995; Marcus et al. 1995; Mondak and Sanders 2003; Nunn, Crockett, and Williams 1978; Stouffer 1955; Sullivan, Piereson, and Marcus 1979, 1982). Among the many variables that have been suggested as determinants of political tolerance, religion has emerged as a key factor.

It is often argued that religion is an obstacle to the development of democratic values and support for civil liberties. The overwhelming evidence confirms that the absence of religion, or "secular detachment," is an important source of tolerance (Nunn, Crockett, and Williams 1978; Stouffer [1955] 1992; Sullivan, Piereson, and Marcus 1982). In addition, it is often claimed that denominational differences in tolerance reflect divergent theological beliefs[1]—so that members of conservative religious traditions (evangelicals, fundamentalists, etc.) are more intolerant than members of other Christian traditions (Beatty and Walter 1984; Green et al. 1994; Nunn, Crockett, and Williams 1978; Stouffer [1955] 1992; Wilcox and Jelen 1990). Some emphasize the importance to the individual of religious involvement, finding that higher levels of religious salience, commitment, or service attendance undermine support for political tolerance (Beatty and Walter 1984; Jelen and Wilcox 1991; Wilcox and Jelen 1990).

Despite considerable attention devoted to the linkage between religion and tolerance (Beatty and Walter 1984; Eisenstein 2006; Eisenstein and Clark 2014; Gibson 1989; Green et al. 1994; Layman 1997; McClosky and Brill 1983; Nunn, Crockett, and Williams 1978; Stouffer [1955] 1992; Sullivan et al. 1982; Wilcox and Jelen 1990), there is disagreement about the exact nature of the relationship.

While religion variables are clearly important, there are reservations about the extent to which religion influences tolerance or if the religious-tolerance link is mediated by some other factor that fosters the inverse association between religiosity and democratic values. For example, using a modeling approach able to distinguish between direct and indirect effects, we (Eisenstein and Clark 2014) found little evidence in support of a direct influence of religion on political tolerance (see also Burge 2013; Canetti-Nisim 2004; Eisenstein 2006; Gaddy 2003). However, the direct religion-intolerance link persists, as prominently indicated by James Gibson (2010: 166–167).

We argue that there are three main reasons for the conflicting views on the relationship between religion and tolerance. First, researchers disagree on the correct way to assess religion and often rely on a single-item measure (such as religious tradition or a measure of belief) or a composite religion measure that prevents separating out the specific effects of denominational preference, theological beliefs, and/or strength of religious commitment. Therefore, we analyze the interrelated, yet separate, components of religion as measured in the extant literature. Our purpose is to understand how the alternative measurement strategies affect variations in values, such as political tolerance, that are important for the existence of a healthy and strong civil society. Second, scholars have raised concerns about the conceptualization and measurement of political tolerance. Studies that measure tolerance by offering specifically named outgroups preselected by the interviewer (known as the Stouffer method) display a more optimistic picture of tolerance than questions about least-liked groups chosen by the respondent (known as the content-controlled method—see Sullivan, Piereson, and Marcus 1979, 1982; also Gaddy 2003). Therefore, we consider the possibility that alterations in the religion-tolerance nexus may reflect how political tolerance is conceptualized and measured rather than signaling changes in tolerance attitudes. Previous research estimating the variation in tolerance has typically relied on either a predetermined list of target groups (the Stouffer method) or the "least-liked group" modeling approach. In considering these practices, we empirically test the role of religion on both the General Social Survey (GSS) tolerance measures, which are based on a modified version of the Stouffer indicators, and the content-controlled technique developed by John Sullivan, James Piereson, and George Marcus (1979). Our purpose is to determine whether religion-based differences in tolerance established in previous studies occur regardless of the "objection precondition" (Sullivan, Piereson, and Marcus, 1979, 1982).[2] Finally, there are concerns about the common analytical approaches employed in the tolerance literature, as only some allow direct and indirect linkages between religion and political tolerance. Therefore, a final contribution of this study is to employ two different modeling techniques (ordinary least squares [OLS] regression and structural equation modeling [SEM]) that are common in the tolerance literature to evaluate the adequacy of the models for examining the link between religion and political tolerance. While it is generally believed that religion leads to intolerance, numerous empirical works utilizing causal modeling have failed to establish a direct link from religious belief, belonging, and behavior to political tolerance. Rather, any negative influence has been indirect, working through psychological or political variables (such as a secure personality or support for democratic norms).

Conceptualizing and Measuring Religion and Political Tolerance

Researchers have generated a vast literature showing that religion influences individuals' willingness to extend rights to objectionable groups (tolerance). In studies of political tolerance, the "religion variables" have been conceptualized and operationalized as consisting of religious belonging, behavior, beliefs, or a combination of these. The empirical study of religion has long argued that these three Bs of religion constitute interrelated, yet distinct, dimensions that must be accounted for simultaneously and separately. In spite of the fact that these distinct aspects of religion predict different, and sometimes countervailing, influences on one's decision to tolerate others, scholars often rely on a single-item measure such as religious involvement (i.e., behavior) or a composite scale consisting of variations of the different dimensions. Gibson (2010), as well as others, argues that compiling a "potpourri" of religious questions, which include measures of both belief and behavior, into a single construct constitutes an effective measure of religiosity.[3] In short, Gibson contends that in creating a single index (comprising a blend of traditional and less traditional religion measures), no methodological precision was lost, because religiosity is a single dimension. Gibson's measurement of religion thus differs from the belief, belonging, and behavior trichotomy advocated by the three-B measurement strategy even though compelling evidence suggests that the different dimensions of religion have a differential influence on tolerance attitudes (Ben-Nun Bloom and Arikan 2012; Eisenstein 2006; Wald and Smidt 1993). At the same time, there is reason to believe that measures constituting theological conservatism as a moral framework are differentiated from the traditional belief, belonging, and behavior trichotomy of measuring religion (Hempel, Matthews, and Bartkowski 2012). Theological conservatism as a moral framework is reflected in a belief system about scripture (the authoritativeness of the Bible), sin (beliefs in human depravity and the existence of hell), and salvation (the need for a born-again experience to be saved as well as the desire to impart this information to others).

Accordingly, one objective of this study is to highlight and contrast alternate measurement strategies employed in the literature to investigate which model best captures the effects of religion on political tolerance. The head-to-head matchup should also reveal if the composite measurement approach produces estimates consistent with the independent effects of the separate dimensions of religion. We compare estimates from models using both the least-liked-group and Stouffer methods of measuring political tolerance, which aid us in understanding whether tolerance must be measured for a least-liked group (Gibson 1992), particularly in relationship to religion.

Modeling Religion and Tolerance

Our objective is to evaluate analytical strategies used in the literature for examining the relationship between religion and political tolerance. The common modeling technique of employing OLS multivariate regression in previous studies may not satisfactorily assess the religion and political tolerance relationship. Admittedly, standard regression models were widely used in early studies to address the development of political tolerance, so we do not mean to imply that these researchers committed an error in judgment by using this technique. However, advances in statistical methods provide a clear basis for reconsidering the practice of relying on standard regression models when claiming that an individual characteristic (such as religion) influences political tolerance.

Likewise, we argue that the differing views on the relationship between religion and tolerance found in previous studies are, in part, a result of shortcomings associated with standard regression methods. Specifically, OLS regression cannot distinguish between *direct* and *indirect* effects the way that path analysis or structured equation modeling can.[4] It may be, as suggested elsewhere, that the negative effect of religion on political tolerance is indirect via psychological insecurity predictors such as dogmatism and self-esteem (on this point see Canetti-Nisim 2004; Eisenstein 2006; Eisenstein and Clark 2014; Gibson 2010). The implication of these studies is that religion is not a direct influence on tolerance; instead religion conditions the psychological attributes that are determinants of tolerance.

Data and Measures

To facilitate direct comparisons and to speak confidently about the significance of results, the data for this analysis were taken from the General Social Survey (GSS) and the 1987 *Freedom and Tolerance* survey (Gibson [1987] 1991).[5]

Preselected Reference Groups: 2008 General Social Survey (GSS)

The data adopting the Stouffer method are from the 2008 General Social Survey (GSS),[6] which is a nationally representative survey of noninstitutionalized U.S. adults. The standard tolerance battery contained in the GSS includes fifteen questions gauging political tolerance for allowing members of five reference groups to make a public speech, teach at a college, and keep a book expressing their beliefs in the local library.[7] Unlike the original Stouffer items, which focused exclusively on actors on the political left (Communists, socialists, and atheists), the modified battery asks about an array of ideologically diverse groups: racists, militarists, atheists, homosexuals, and Communists. Since respondents are asked three dichotomous items per group, scores on the composite tolerance scale range from 0 to 15.[8] The mean score for the scale is 10.29, and the standard deviation is 4.41; the coefficient α, an estimate of the lower bound of reliability, is .90.

Measures of Tolerance for Least-Liked Groups: 1987 Freedom and Tolerance Data Merged with the 1987 GSS

To correct for the potential problems inherent in the General Social Surveys (GSS) tolerance measure, we also draw on data from the 1987 *Freedom and Tolerance* survey. According to the least-liked-group protocol introduced by Sullivan, Piereson, and Marcus (1979), it is essential to ask respondents to specify target groups they most strongly oppose followed by a series of statements in an agree/disagree format that elicit their views about a range of activities in which members of that group might have participated. The *Freedom and Tolerance* survey merged with the 1987 GSS enables the use of a national sample that brings together a least-liked-group measure of political tolerance, the important predictor variables—measures of dogmatism, self-esteem, and trust—as well as measures of religious belief and religious behavior.[9] Scores on the GSS composite tolerance scale range from 0 to 15. The mean score for the fifteen-item Stouffer scale is 8.90, with a standard deviation of 4.99 ($\alpha = .92$). The mean tolerance score for the *Freedom and Tolerance* six-item scale ranging from 0 to 24 is 9.56; the standard deviation is 5.22 ($\alpha = .79$).

Religion

To assess the effectiveness with which religion has been conceptualized in previous studies on tolerance, we employ several different measurement models of religion. To investigate the claim that among the various properties of religion, religious beliefs are the dimension with the greatest impact, we construct a theological conservatism measurement model. Following Lynn Hempel, Todd Matthews, and John Bartkowski (2012), we design the theological conservatism measure to address whether human sinfulness (belief in the existence of hell, HELL), scripture (a belief in the Bible as the inerrant word of God, BIBLE), and salvation (as reflected in two items: had born-again experience, REBORN, and ever tried to encourage someone to believe in or accept Jesus Christ as his or her savior, SAVESOUL) influence political tolerance.[10] In sum, the theological conservatism measure consists of four items that characterize core beliefs identified as consistent with a religious worldview (Bartkowski 2001; Hempel and Bartkowski 2008).[11] All items have been coded so that higher scores correspond to a stronger level of theological conservatism ($\alpha = .71$).

Previous applications have conceived of religion as a single, unifying dimension for which distinguishing between the different dimensions is unnecessary (on this point see Gibson 2010). In line with this viewpoint, we create a multi-item index consisting of a belief in the existence of God (GOD), religious involvement (based on frequency of religious attendance, ATTEND), and strength of religious affiliation (RELITEN).[12] All items have been coded so that higher scores reflect a greater degree of religiosity. Gibson (2010) constructed a similar measurement model of religiosity in his religious traditionalism construct.[13] We therefore refer to this measure of religion as the religious traditionalism scale ($\alpha = .65$).

Finally, we make use of religion measures designed to capture multiple religious dimensions (the three Bs). This model considers the potential that belief, belonging, and behavior are empirically distinct elements of religion. The religious questions consist of: belief in the Bible question (BIBLE), items designed to assess religious behavior including frequency of attendance (ATTEND) and measuring how often respondents pray (PRAY), and strength of religious affiliation (a measure of belonging) (RELITEN). The correlations between the four religion variables used for the three-B measurement strategy range from .39 to .58 in the 2008 data and from .23 to .50 in the 1987 data, lending support to the contention that a single measurement scale has the potential to mask differences related to these variables.

It is clear that the operationalization of religion varies within the tolerance literature. To sum up, in measurement models 1 and 2, religion is conceived of as a multi-item index; model 1 features religious beliefs and model 2 is a single scale of the three Bs. The final measurement approach examines the three dimensions separately—taking into consideration that a single measurement scale may "hide" substantively important differences in the phenomenon being measured.

Control Variables

Also included in the model predicting political tolerance are a number of control variables identified in the literature as important antecedents of tolerance such as age, education, income, and ideology. When we analyze the 1987 *Freedom and Tolerance* and GSS merged data, we are also able to include controls for psychological and political predictors of political tolerance.

Findings

We start by considering the suggestion that the diverging views on the relationship between religion and tolerance result from differences in how the influence of religion is conceptualized. We also test for modeling effects (OLS versus SEM) in estimating the influence of religion on political tolerance. Table 5.1 presents the regression results based on a comparison of different formulations of religion and the tolerance items contained in the 2008 GSS. In model 1, the measurement of religion is captured in the theological conservatism construct—reflecting beliefs about the Bible, hell, and belief in salvation associated with a born-again experience and spreading the conviction of Jesus Christ as one's personal savior. This model also contains a multivariable scale of religious involvement

TABLE 5.1 DIFFERENT CONCEPTUALIZATIONS OF RELIGION ON POLITICAL TOLERANCE OUTCOMES USING THE GSS 2008 (ORDINARY LEAST SQUARES [OLS] REGRESSION)

	Model 1: Hempel, Matthews, Bartkowski 2012			*Model 2: Gibson 2010*			*Model 3: Belief and Behavior*		
	β	*SE*	*p*	*β*	*SE*	*p*	*β*	*SE*	*p*
Religious involvement	–.04	(.04)		—			—		
Theological conservatism	–.28	(.10)	***	—			—		
Religious traditionalism	—			–.21	(.03)	***	—		
Religious behavior	—			—			–.03	(.04)	
Religious belief	—			—			–.28	(.15)	***
Age	–.10	(.01)	**	–.09	(.00)	***	–.10	(.00)	***
Education	.30	(.06)	***	.34	(.04)	***	.28	(.04)	***
Income	.12	(.08)	***	.11	(.06)	***	0.1	(.06)	***
Ideology	–.04	(.15)		–.08	(.10)	**	–.07	(.10)	**
Party	.00	(.09)		.02	(.07)		.03	(.07)	
Intercept	8.30	(1.50)		5.62	(.91)		8.96	(1.01)	
Adjusted R^2		.268			.233			.274	
N		492			967			959	

Note: See the online appendix for information on the specific content of the political tolerance scales and religion measures. Differences in sample sizes are a consequence of variations in the measurement of religion.

$^{**}p \leq .05$, $^{***}p \leq .01$

containing two items that assess frequency of religious attendance and congregational involvement. In model 2, we include a religious traditionalism scale that combines beliefs about God's existence, worship service attendance, and an indicator for strength of religious commitment.[14] Finally, in model 3, the religious dimensions are disaggregated using the conventional three-Bs approach to measuring religious belief and religious behavior. Thus, models 1 and 3 allow us to take into account the separate, and potentially distinctive, effects of religious beliefs and behavior on political tolerance, albeit with slightly different measurement strategies (as composite measures of belief and behavior in M1 or using a single indicator as in M3) for the religious concepts.

The results demonstrate that the negative association between religion and tolerance remains despite differences in the measurement of religion (Table 5.1). The estimated effects, aside from a slight reduction in the coefficient for religious traditionalism, are quite similar. Since the religious behavior results (in models 1 and 3) demonstrate that active involvement is unimportant in the decision to tolerate, we suspect that religious beliefs are the critical source of religious-based differences in tolerance. Separate analyses (not shown but available upon request) partly confirm our suspicion. We find that when the items of the religious traditionalism scale are considered separately, the strongest negative influence comes from religious beliefs (–.16), and while the influence of religious involvement on intolerance is statistically significant, the effect is rather weak

(−0.08). There is no support for an association between the intensity of religious commitment and intolerance. What is more, the goodness-of-fit statistics indicate that the models that take into account the separate effects of religious beliefs, as a composite measure (model 1) or an individual indicator (model 3), yield higher values, indicating better-fitting models.[15]

Results of the structural equation models (SEM) for these three different conceptualizations of religion are largely consistent with those in Table 5.1 based on the OLS regression models (results not shown but available upon request).[16] Theological conservatism (−.32), religious traditionalism (−.26), and doctrinal orthodoxy (−.31) all have a statistically significant *direct* negative influence on political tolerance. However, the coefficients for religious involvement (−.05) in model 1 and behavior (−.05) in model 3 (Hempel, Matthews, and Bartkowski 2012 and three Bs, respectively) achieve significance within conventionally acceptable levels ($p < 0.10$). More importantly, the results indicate a *direct* path relating religion to political intolerance. Taken together, these results suggest there is sufficient reason to argue that the tendency toward greater intolerance among the religious is largely a product of their theological belief systems. Likewise, the results demonstrate that regardless of differences in modeling and measurement, the effect of religious beliefs remains relatively constant.

The OLS regression estimates for the predetermined list of out-groups in the GSS and the least-liked-group measures in the *Freedom and Tolerance* survey appear in Table 5.2 in a different set of models. With a quick glance at the results, it becomes clear that the impact of religion is contingent on the conceptualization and measurement of tolerance.[17] Religious differences in tolerance are observed in the GSS measurement strategy (models 1 and 2), but the results for the least-liked-group approach in models 3 and 4 reveal no significant variation in tolerance that can be attributed to religion. These results are unchanged regardless of differences in the religion measurement that combine beliefs about God's existence and religious involvement (models 1 and 3) and the models that consider the separate influence of a range of religious orientations (models 2 and 4). It is worth noting that the influence of a number of the tolerance predictors also changes depending on the tolerance measure employed. In particular, we find that the psychological predictors (namely, dogmatism) and political variables (e.g., support for the norms of democracy and perceived threat) have by far the strongest negative effect on the willingness to extend civil liberties and rights to groups that are disliked in the content-controlled method (models 3 and 4). A different picture emerges when the GSS-modified rendering of the Stouffer tolerance battery is considered. The negative influence of religion dominates in affecting tolerance, the dogmatism effect is radically reduced, and the effects of democratic norm support and threat perception are no longer statistically significant (models 1 and 2).

To test for modeling effects, we compared the OLS results in Table 5.2 with estimates obtained using SEM (results not shown but available upon request). Generally speaking, the estimated effects across the different models are

TABLE 5.2 RELIGION AND POLITICAL TOLERANCE OUTCOMES USING THE 1987 GSS AND 1987 *FREEDOM AND TOLERANCE* SURVEY (OLS REGRESSION)

	Predetermined List of Groups						*Least-Liked Groups*					
	Model 1			*Model 2*			*Model 3*			*Model 4*		
	β	*SE*	*p*	*β*	*SE*	*p*	*β*	*SE*	*p*	*β*	*SE*	*p*
Religious traditionalism	–.21	(.04)	***	—			.01	(.04)		—		
Attendance	—			–.13	(.09)	***	—			–.03	(.09)	
Prayer frequency	—			.02	(.15)		—			.06	(.15)	
Strength of affiliation	—			–.07	(.23)	*	—			.03	(.23)	
Inerrant Bible	—			–.14	(.29)	***	—			–.06	(.29)	
Age	–.16	(.01)	***	–.17	(.01)	***	.00	(.01)		–.01	(.01)	
Education	.36	(.06)	***	.33	(.07)	***	.07	(.06)	*	.06	(.07)	
Ideology	.01	(.14)		.01	(.14)		.03	(.14)		.04	(.14)	
Dogmatism scale	–.08	(.05)	*	–.08	(.05)	*	–.25	(.05)	***	–.25	(.05)	***
Self-esteem scale	–.04	(.07)		–.05	(.07)		.00	(.06)		–.01	(.06)	
Trust scale	.11	(.08)	**	.11	(.08)	***	–.06	(.08)		–.06	(.08)	
Norms (general)	–.02	(.14)		–.01	(.14)		–.24	(.14)	***	–.24	(.14)	***
Norms (procedural)	–.05	(.09)		–.05	(.09)		.21	(.09)	***	.21	(.09)	***
Threat scale	–.05	(.03)		–.06	(.03)		–.15	(.03)	***	–.15	(.03)	***
Intercept	10.31	(2.47)		11.97	(2.60)		16.90	(2.46)		17.24	(2.60)	
Adjusted R^2		.277			.286			.270			.271	
N		548			548			637			637	

Note: See the online appendix for information on the specific content of the political tolerance scales, religion measures, and all political and psychological scales. Differences in sample sizes are a consequence of variations in the measurement of religion.

$*p \leq .10$; $**p \leq .05$; $***p \leq .01$

consistent. Aside from a few minor adjustments, the association between religion and tolerance remains intact. In this way, we find a moderate increase in the effect of religious traditionalism from −.21 in the OLS estimate (model 1 in Table 5.2) to −.34 in the SEM results. Additionally, the contribution of beliefs about the Bible to tolerance is twice as large in the SEM results as in the regression results found in model 2 in Table 5.2 (−.28 and −.14, respectively). It is worth mentioning that while model 2 in Table 5.2 considers the religious behavior association in the separate variables of prayer and church attendance frequency, the SEM results combine these involvement items under a single dimension of religious behavior. Yet the results—regardless of differences in measurement—are quite consistent across the modeling techniques (−.13 attendance and .02 prayer frequency in Table 5.2 as compared to an estimated −.11 effect of religious behavior on political tolerance from SEM results). The consistency of these results lends support to the contention that this subdimension of religion can be captured by combining involvement indicators into a religious behavior scale. However, we advise caution in the use of a composite measure of religious behavior as the results indicate that the distributions and specific consequences of the involvement measures vary. More specifically, the effect of prayer frequency is largely inconsequential for tolerance whereas attendance has a modest but statistically significant effect, and these observed differences are hidden in the combined religious behavior measure.[18]

We also see consistency when comparing the OLS results for models 3 and 4 in Table 5.2 with the SEM results (not shown) for the same models. The influence of religion on political tolerance is completely eliminated when conceptualizing and measuring tolerance using the least-liked-group strategy. Further, the SEM results for models 3 and 4 also demonstrate that religion has no influence on the psychological predictors of political tolerance—namely, dogmatism (we are unable to compare the religion-dogmatism connection in the analyses employing the 2008 GSS data as the dogmatism item does not appear in that survey year). Regardless of the religion measurement strategy employed, the relationship between religion and dogmatism was nonexistent. Thus, the role of religion—both to political tolerance and to other predictors of political tolerance—is entirely dependent on the measurement of political tolerance.

Conclusion

Our research deviates from previous work by attempting to address three concerns that plague tolerance and religion studies. The results support several important conclusions concerning the religion-intolerance relationship. First, as far as explaining differences in tolerance outcomes is concerned, it may be appropriate to conceive of religion as a unidimensional concept, as argued by Gibson (2010)—but not precisely in the manner he conceptualized. Rather, the results here suggest that the effect of religion is quite well embodied in items that capture expressions of religious beliefs. More specifically, measures that tap into a commitment to religious truths that address beliefs about human sinfulness, scripture, and salvation provide a reliable conceptualization of religion. The results make clear that among the religious orientations, diverging theological beliefs are the accelerant that promotes intolerance. This finding is confirmed in the different strategies for measuring religion and modeling approaches. The one major caveat is that the religion-tolerance connection appears to be entirely contingent on whether the least-liked-group or Stouffer tolerance approach is employed.

This brings us to the second contribution of this study. The effect of religion virtually vanishes once we take advantage of the least-liked-group measurement strategy (see models 3 and 4 in Table 5.2). The most obvious explanation is that this approach offers an equivalence of the stimulus across respondents where every individual is provided an objection precondition.[19] Once faced with groups identified as disliked by the respondent, religion in any formulation (e.g., a multi-item religious traditionalism scale or consideration of the separate dimensions of belief, behavior, and belonging) becomes largely inconsequential either directly or indirectly as a source of political tolerance. The contention is that since the religious are distinctive in the groups they choose as their most disliked groups (Gibson 2010: 164) and the fixed list contained in the GSS contains several of their most disliked groups (while also excluding groups they do not find objectionable), the religion-intolerance link is overstated. Thus, the findings suggest that the GSS measures fail to capture the objection precondition for the irreligious. However, once we provide the opportunity for everyone to dislike under a least-liked-group approach, the religious are no more likely to express intolerance.

The important implication is that while tolerance among the religious and the irreligious is indistinguishable when antipathy toward the target group is comparable across respondents, one could argue that the groups identified in the Stouffer-modified GSS questions symbolize representative out-groups. As a result, the likelihood of political repression in American society is quite high. The underlying assumption is that the religious find politically salient groups highly objectionable and, as a consequence, are unwilling to support the legitimate democratic rights of these unpopular groups (i.e., to promote intolerance), posing a significant threat to freedom in the United States.

At the same time, we find that dogmatic tendencies play a significant role and far outweigh the influence of the remaining tolerance predictors. The direct, negative influence of dogmatism is hardly surprising given the extant literature (Canetti-Nisim 2004; Eisenstein 2006; Eisenstein and Clark 2014; Gibson 1987, 2010; Sullivan et al. 1981; Sullivan, Piereson, and Marcus 1982). Finally, while it is clear that the broad outlines of the relationship between religion and political tolerance are attainable employing an OLS regression, the results here suggest that a modeling approach that distinguishes between the direct and indirect effects of political tolerance determinants is clearly preferred. In essence, a more nuanced assessment is available by using a more sophisticated modeling technique.

While this study has accomplished much in the way of advancing theoretical, empirical, and modeling insights into the religion-intolerance link, it is not without its limitations. The two most notable limitations are that we did not control for religious tradition and we did not have access to a least-liked-group or content-controlled measure of tolerance in more recent years. The first limitation is remedied by further research, and we think that a logical extension of this research is an undertaking that incorporates religious tradition into the models. The second limitation is much more problematic. In terms of a national sample using a least-liked-group political tolerance measure, we know of only one, which was the basis of Gibson's (2010) chapter on religion and tolerance. Our analysis identifies deficiencies that exist in the available tolerance data sets and certainly justifies the need for a major national survey containing the least-liked-group measures of political tolerance, all the predictor variables related to political tolerance, and the multidimensionality of religion (belief, belonging, and behavior).

Nevertheless, a word of caution is needed. In Gibson's work (2010), two variables not commonly used to measure religion were employed: a measure about moving away from God as problematic and a measure regarding belief in the devil. In order to truly assess whether or not those different religion measures lead to different political tolerance outcomes, a head-to-head comparison is needed. That is, would our results have been different if we were able to include those same two measures in our religious traditionalism scale? We cannot know the answer to that question, but it is an extremely important consideration as Gibson (2010) maintains that religion—even using the least-liked-group measurement strategy—*directly* influences political tolerance.

That result runs contrary to our findings using the 1987 least-liked-group tolerance survey and, while we cannot think of any reason in the years since that data became available that relationships between the variables of interest have changed, we are unable to empirically verify that this is so. Specifically, there is no basis to expect the relationship of religion to tolerance (or religion-dogmatism) to have modified with time. In fact, a number of tolerance studies confirm that the important role played by individual characteristics—such as psychological security and the various dimensions of religion—has remained constant (e.g., Davis and Silver 2004; Eisenstein 2006; Gibson 2010; Sullivan and Hendriks 2009). So while we may expect the selection of target groups to be different today than in the past, the relationships of the key predictors of tolerance are not expected to change. As a consequence, we expect results based on current observations would imitate those uncovered in the 1987 survey.

Taken as a whole the results indicate that as a predictor of intolerance, religion is not the chief culprit. We also encourage greater caution in the tolerance measurement strategy to ensure confidence in the expected relationships. While substantial evidence exists in the extant literature that tolerance may vary with the nature of religious convictions, practice, and denomination, nonetheless, a variety of studies have found that when other factors are controlled, religion is either unrelated to, or actually fosters support for, civil liberties (Burge 2013; Canetti-Nisim 2004; Eisenstein 2006; Gaddy 2003). The evidence presented in this study suggests that, collectively, religious variables as a source of political tolerance are minimally important.

In fact, the models containing the GSS tolerance items indicate the importance of the belief subdimension. Each model in this approach suggests that tolerance is influenced by religion, but the indicator with the strongest link is religious beliefs encompassed in a theological worldview about the scripture, the existence of hell, and salvation as well as a single measure of belief in the Bible as the inerrant word of God. We argue, therefore, that since the GSS approach is still the most widely used measurement strategy, efforts to understand variations in tolerance will continue to regard the religious as more politically intolerant—a view that may not be completely deserved. So, in response to Gibson (1992), the results here suggest "yes"—tolerance must be measured for "least-liked group" at least as far as the relationship (or the lack thereof) between religion and tolerance is concerned.

Notes

1. Clyde Nunn, Harry Crocket, and Allen Williams (1978) show that belief in the devil, rather than God, is a particularly strong predictor of intolerance, whereas James Gibson (2010: 167) demonstrates that the "active ingredient" in his religious traditionalism index contributing to intolerance is the belief that people are "moving away from God."

2. Debate exists about how much these two measurement approaches differ. In fact, in a comparison of the least-liked-group measures of intolerance to the Stouffer-based measures employed in the General Social Survey, Gibson (1992) argues that the approaches perform equally well (see also Mondak and Sanders 2003). Nonetheless, there is good reason to believe that the influence of religion may be contingent on the tolerance measures used. After all, one of the important findings of Sullivan, Piereson, and Marcus (1982) is that when using a least-liked-group method versus the GSS method of measuring political tolerance, a number of social-demographic variables such as age and education become unimportant in explaining political tolerance (this is supported by Gaddy 2003; Eisenstein 2006).

3. For example, some of the proponents of the three-B method of measuring the multidimensionality of religion have also employed a single construct of religion incorporating elements of belief, belonging, and behavior (Kellstedt et al. 1996; Layman 2001).

4. This is also true of other measurement techniques not considered here. Specifically, a technique called "matching" was recently employed to assess the linkage between religion and political tolerance, and consistent with results using the SEM approach, the negative association between religion and political tolerance failed to materialize (Burge 2013).

5. The *Freedom and Tolerance* study was a re-interview of the 1987 GSS respondents. The GSS study was conducted in the spring, and the *Freedom and Tolerance* study was conducted in June and July of that same year. Of the 1,459 subjects eligible for re-interview, interviews were completed with 1,267 respondents (approximately 87 percent of the original GSS sample). The 1987 GSS survey also included an oversample of

353 black respondents beyond the 191 blacks in the main sample (for a total of 544); 436 black respondents (approximately 80 percent) were re-interviewed in the summer survey.

6. The 2008 GSS was used because that particular year contains the most religion variables and permits us to model religion as operationalized by Lynn Hempel, Todd Matthews, and John Bartkowski (2012) and the three-B trichotomy of belief, belonging, and behavior (Kellstedt 1993; Kellstedt et al.1996; Layman and Green 1998). For example, Hempel, Matthews, and Bartkowski (2012) use a variable about belief in the existence of hell (HELL), which is not available in more recent GSS years. However, no GSS year allows us to completely re-create Gibson's (2010) religious traditionalism scale; Gibson (2010) had six items and the GSS asks only three of them.

7. Please see the online appendix at http://pauldjupe.com/s/Appendix.docx for a list of all items associated with the measurement for all variables discussed in this section.

8. We code each of the fifteen items as 1 if the respondent agreed that the act should be permitted and 0 if not. We code "don't know" responses as missing, meaning that a response counts only if respondents explicitly indicate that an act should or should not be permitted.

9. The 1987 *Freedom and Tolerance* survey merged with the GSS of the same year also allows for the use of a sophisticated coding scheme as it relates to religious belonging (i.e., the coding scheme for religious affiliation outlined in Steensland et al. 2000).

10. Coding for all available measures is in the online appendix at http://pauldjupe.com/s/Appendix.docx.

11. This model also contains a multivariable scale of religious behavior containing two items measuring frequency of religious attendance (ATTEND) and congregational involvement (RELACTIV). However, considering the underlying presupposition that among the various religion dimensions divergent theological values are central to understanding the relationship between intolerance and religiosity, we test but do not expect religious behavior to be robustly associated with political tolerance.

12. In a strict sense, this item is an insufficient measure of religious belonging since it fails to account for differences across the traditions, but rather it measures whether one holds a denominational preference and the intensity of that attachment.

13. While the GSS and *Freedom and Tolerance* survey include measures that capture the multidimensionality of religion (belief, belonging, and behavior), we are unable to replicate exactly the "religious traditionalism" construct created by Gibson (2010: 161). In that study, some of the religion predictors employed are not commonplace within the broad scope of the tolerance literature. In particular, we are unable to incorporate items that tap into religious beliefs concerning the existence of the Devil and distance to God in society and a dichotomous nonbeliever question. Given these constraints on comparability, a word of caution is offered. In particular, earlier research has found that a belief in the Devil is a strong predictor of intolerance (Nunn, Crockett, and Williams 1978), and as a consequence, any conclusions reached from these analyses may be more suggestive than definitive.

14. Again, this is the model based on Gibson's (2010) religious traditionalism scale. As indicated previously, we employed three of the six items used by Gibson for this scale (the other items are not available in the GSS).

15. For comparison purposes, we ran similar regression models on the 2012 GSS data. The results indicate that religious belief is the more potent source of variation in political tolerance and that religious behavior and involvement are not. A cautionary note is in order however, as the 2012 GSS data did not have available all the same religious

variables as the 2008 data. Most notably, we were unable to include all the religious belief indicators used in model 1 (as presented in Table 5.1) in 2012.

16. All SEM results provided here are based on a comprehensive model of political tolerance (see Gibson 2006, 2010), which incorporates all primary determinants of political tolerance, such as dogmatism, support for norms of democracy, and threat perception in addition to the control variables of age, education, income, and ideology.

17. For this analysis, we could not assess the Hempel, Matthews, and Bartkowski (2012) religious measurements because the 1987 GSS did not have those religious items.

18. The correlation between the PRAY and ATTEND variable in the 1987 GSS is .50.

19. Separate analyses (not shown but available upon request) demonstrate differences between the religious and nonreligious in naming disliked groups that may, in part, account for the lack of association between religion and tolerance. That is, once respondents are provided the opportunity to define their "outgroup," the religious are no more intolerant.

References

Bartkowski, John P. 2001. *Remaking the Godly Marriage: Gender Negotiation in Evangelical Communities.* New Brunswick, NJ: Rutgers University Press.

Beatty, Kathleen M., and Oliver Walter. 1984. "Religious Preference and Practice: Reevaluating Their Impact on Political Tolerance." *Public Opinion Quarterly* 48 (1B): 318–329.

Ben-Nun Bloom, Pazit, and Gizem Arikan. 2012. "A Two-Edged Sword: The Differential Effect of Religious Belief and Religious Social Context on Attitudes towards Democracy." *Political Behavior* 34 (2): 249–276.

Bobo, Lawrence, and Frederick C. Licari. 1989. "Education and Political Tolerance: Testing the Effects of Cognitive Sophistication and Target Group." *Public Opinion Quarterly* 53 (3): 285–308.

Burge, Ryan P. 2013. "Using Matching to Investigate the Relationship between Religion and Tolerance." *Politics and Religion* 6 (2): 264–281.

Canetti-Nisim, Daphna. 2004. "The Effect of Religiosity on Endorsement of Democratic Values: The Mediating Influence of Authoritarianism." *Political Behavior* 26 (4): 377–398.

Davis, Darren W., and Brian D. Silver. 2004. "Civil Liberties vs. Security: Public Opinion in the Context of the Terrorist Attacks on America." *American Journal of Political Science* 48 (1): 28–46.

Eisenstein, Marie A. 2006. "Rethinking the Relationship between Religion and Political Tolerance in the U.S." *Political Behavior* 28 (4): 327–348.

Eisenstein, Marie A., and April K. Clark. 2014. "Political Tolerance, Psychological Security, and Religion: Disaggregating the Mediating Influence of Psychological Security." *Politics and Religion* 7 (3): 1–31.

Gaddy, Beverly. 2003. "Faith, Tolerance, and Civil Society." In *Faith, Morality, and Civil Society,* edited by Dale McConkey and Peter Augustine Lawler, 159–195. Lanham, MD: Lexington Books.

Gibson, James L. (1987) 1991. *Freedom and Tolerance in the United States, 1987.* Ann Arbor, MI: Inter-university Consortium for Political and Social Research. Available at http://doi.org/10.3886/ICPSR09454.v2.

———. 1987. "Homosexuals and the Ku Klux Klan: A Contextual Analysis of Political Intolerance." *Western Political Quarterly* 40 (3): 427–448.

———. 1989. "The Structure of Attitudinal Tolerance in the United States." *British Journal of Political Science* 19 (4): 562–570.

———. 1992. "Alternative Measures of Political Tolerance: Must Tolerance Be 'Least Liked'?" *American Journal of Political Science* 36 (2): 560–577.

———. 2006. "Enigmas of Intolerance: Fifty Years after Stouffer's Communism, Conformity, and Civil Liberties." *Perspectives on Politics* 4 (1): 21–34.

———. 2010. "The Political Consequences of Religiosity: Does Religion Always Cause Political Intolerance?" In *Religion and Democracy in the United States: Danger or Opportunity?* edited by Alan Wolfe and Ira Katznelson, 147–175. New York: Russell Sage.

Golebiowska, Ewa A. 1995. "Individual Value Priorities, Education, and Political Tolerance." *Political Behavior* 17 (1): 23–48.

Green, John C., James L. Guth, Lyman A. Kellstedt, and Corwin E. Smidt. 1994. "Uncivil Challenges: Support for Civil Liberties among Religious Activists." *Journal of Political Science* 22:25–49.

Hempel, Lynn M., and John P. Bartkowski. 2008. "Scripture, Sin, and Salvation: Theological Conservatism Reconsidered." *Social Forces* 86 (4): 1647–1674.

Hempel, Lynn M., Todd Matthews, and John P. Bartkowski. 2012. "Trust in a 'Fallen World': The Case of Protestant Theological Conservatism." *Journal for the Scientific Study of Religion* 51 (3): 522–541.

Jelen, Ted G., and Clyde Wilcox. 1991. "Religious Dogmatism among White Christians: Causes and Effects." *Review of Religious Research* 33 (1): 32–46.

Kellstedt, Lyman A. 1993. "Religion, the Neglected Variable: An Agenda for Future Research on Religion and Political Behavior." In *Rediscovering the Religious Factor in American Politics*, edited by David C. Leege and Lyman A. Kellstedt, 273–303. Armonk, NY: M. E. Sharpe.

Kellstedt, Lyman A., John C. Green, James L. Guth, and Corwin E. Smidt. 1996. "Grasping the Essentials: The Social Embodiment of Religion and Political Behavior." In *Religion and the Culture Wars*, edited by John C. Green, James L. Guth, Corwin E. Smidt, and Lyman A. Kellstedt, 174–192. Lanham, MD: Rowman and Littlefield.

Layman, Geoffrey C. 1997. "Religion and Political Behavior in the United States: The Impact of Beliefs, Affiliation, and Commitment from 1980 to 1994." *Public Opinion Quarterly* 61 (2): 288–316.

———. 2001. *The Great Divide: Religious and Cultural Conflict in American Party Politics*. New York: Columbia University Press.

Layman, Geoffrey C., and John C. Green. 1998. "The Changing Religious Voter: The Political Impact of Belonging, Believing, and Behaving." Paper presented at the annual meeting of the Midwest Political Science Association, Chicago.

Marcus, George E., John L. Sullivan, Elizabeth Theiss-Morse, and Sandra Wood. 1995. *With Malice toward Some: How People Make Civil Liberties Judgments*. New York: Cambridge University Press.

McClosky, Herbert, and Alida Brill. 1983. *Dimensions of Tolerance*. New York: Russell Sage.

Mondak, Jeffery J., and Mitchell S. Sanders. 2003. "Tolerance and Intolerance, 1976–1998." *American Journal of Political Science* 47 (3): 492–502.

Nunn, Clyde Z., Harry J. Crockett, Jr., and J. Allen Williams, Jr. 1978. *Tolerance for Nonconformity*. San Francisco: Jossey-Bass.

Steensland, Brian, Jerry Z. Park, Mark D. Regnerus, Lynn D. Robinson, W. Bradford Wilcox, and Robert D. Woodberry. 2000. "The Measure of American Religion: Toward Improving the State of the Art." *Social Forces* 79 (1): 291–318.

Stouffer, Samuel. (1955) 1992. *Communism, Conformity and Civil Liberties: A Cross-Section of the Nation Speaks Its Mind.* New Brunswick, NJ: Transaction.

Sullivan, John L., and Henriët Hendriks. 2009. "Public Support for Civil Liberties Pre- and Post-9/11." *Annual Review of Law and Social Science* 5:375–391.

Sullivan, John L., George E. Marcus, Stanley Feldman, and James E. Piereson. 1981. "The Sources of Political Tolerance: A Multivariate Analysis." *American Political Science Review* 75 (1): 92–106.

Sullivan, John L., James Piereson, and George E. Marcus. 1979. "An Alternative Conceptualization of Political Tolerance: Illusory Increases, 1950s–1970s." *American Political Science Review* 73 (3): 781–794.

———. 1982. *Political Tolerance and American Democracy.* Chicago: University of Chicago Press.

Wald, Kenneth D., and Corwin E. Smidt. 1993. "Measurement Strategies in the Study of Religion and Politics." In *Rediscovering the Religious Factor in American Politics,* edited by David C. Leege and Lyman A. Kellstedt, 26–49. Armonk, NY: M. E. Sharpe.

Wilcox, Clyde, and Ted G. Jelen. 1990. "Evangelicals and Political Tolerance." *American Politics Quarterly* 18:25–46.

6

Religion, Morality, and Tolerance

The Role of Disgust

PAZIT BEN-NUN BLOOM
MARIE COURTEMANCHE

Across numerous cultures, religion has worked to emphasize the moral quest for purity, manifested in the notion that one's body, soul, and community constitute a temple that can be contaminated by immoral individuals, groups, and acts. An extreme anecdote that illuminates the possible connection between religion, moral purity, and intolerance is the Westboro Baptist Church's warning against the moral turpitude of gay people, fallen soldiers, and even Taylor Swift for the role model she constitutes for many young Americans. Some Haredi (ultra-Orthodox) Jewish leaders similarly have called little girls not wearing Orthodox styles of dress "prostitutes," called the Israeli security forces "Nazis," and referred to their struggle against the Israeli Higher Court as a war between the holy and the impure. While these are cases of great controversy, the belief that some groups, individuals, or institutions are responsible for a societal moral degradation is shared by other religious leaders who frame political issues in terms of morals and values (Djupe and Neiheisel 2008; Price, Nir, and Capella 2005). This highlights the fact that religion can be a potent force in fostering outgroup animus with moral reasoning the driving mechanism.

Current literature in moral psychology argues that the emotion of disgust underlies the purification schema (Ritter and Preston 2011; Rozin et al. 1999; Tek and Ulug 2001). It is believed that this emotional reaction is evolutionarily adaptive by nature, with individuals employing disgust as a means of protecting both their body and their environment from potentially threatening substances (Haidt and Joseph 2007; Rozin, Haidt, and McCauley 2000; Schaller and Duncan 2007). These reactions apply to both ingestible toxins as well as groups thought to pose a threat to a community's well-being. Indeed, current research in moral psychology reports that the religious are more sensitive to disgust (Olatunji et al. 2005; Terrizzi, Shook, and Ventis 2010) and are more likely to express disgust from contact with outgroup religious beliefs (Ritter and Preston 2011).

Using this literature as a guide, we hypothesize that disgust underlies intolerance toward religious outgroups. Both an informational environment where this emotion is evoked (state disgust) and an individual propensity to disgust sensitivity (trait disgust) should increase expressed antipathy toward the religiously dissimilar. It is also believed that disgust provides the connection between religion and such social attitudes, above and beyond a particular denomination and context. We tested these hypotheses using an experimental design that primed state disgust among American Catholics and Israeli Jews and captured trait proclivities. We demonstrate that individuals with easily triggered repulsions as well as those in whom repugnance was evoked were more likely to articulate religious intolerance. The findings also suggest that disgust sensitivity mediates the relationship between religion and distaste for the religiously dissimilar. Our research indicates that religious intolerance is at least partly an attempt to protect the moral purity of the self and community. The results are compelling for a variety of reasons. Because they replicate across two divergent political and cultural landscapes, they suggest that while some may be more sensitive to disgust, the emotion itself functions in a similar manner across religious groups. The results further demonstrate the relevance of moral emotions as a mediator of religion and attitudes toward social groups.

The Link between Religion and Morality

Religion is often viewed as the origin, or at least a key source, of morality. As such, religion-based morality is thought to play an important role in human evolution by facilitating cooperation in large-scale societies (Bloom 2012; Graham and Haidt 2010; Roes and Raymond 2003). Indeed, religious rituals have been shown to decrease selfishness (Norenzayan and Shariff 2008) while increasing the occurrence of oath adherence between individuals (Boyer 2001), moral awareness (Mazar, Amir, and Ariely 2008), and a host of moral and prosocial behaviors, including honesty, generosity, and philanthropy (Brooks 2003; Forbes and Zampelli 1997; Hoge and Yang 1994; Pichon, Boccato, and Saroglou 2007; Randolph-Seng and Nielsen 2007; Shariff and Norenzayan 2007; Torgler 2006). It has also been suggested that a decline of religion underlies both more permissive and self-interested behaviors, and ultimately leads to moral breakdown (Ter Voert, Felling, and Peters 1994).

To understand the link between religion and morality, some conceptualization of morality is necessary. Psychological approaches to the concept of morality can be roughly divided into predominantly cognitive versus emotive approaches, with the current literature lending support to both views (Ben-Nun Bloom 2013, 2014). While the two schools focus on different aspects of the phenomenon, both view religion as tied to moral judgment.

The social-cognitive domain theory advanced by Elliot Turiel (1983) builds on the classical models of morality as rational, advanced by Jean Piaget and Lawrence Kohlberg. Domain theory postulates a distinction between moral and conventional rules. In the moral domain, judgments of acts pertain to the welfare of others, including matters of harm, justice, and rights, which remain absolutely right or wrong unconditional on, and even when in conflict with, self-interest, political or cultural institutions, or the majority opinion in the country (following the philosophies of Gerald Dworkin and John Rawls). In the conventional domain, by contrast, judgments follow arbitrary social rules (Nucci and Turiel 1993; Turiel 1983). According to this theory, children acquire the distinction between moral and other rules by experiencing the consequences of, and responses to, harm and welfare matters in their early years (Turiel 1983). In turn, consequences and responses are based on informational assumptions about what is harmful (Turiel, Hildebrandt, and Wainryb 1991). Religion is a particularly important source of informational assumptions, shaping beliefs about welfare, justice, and harm (Turiel and Neff 2000). For instance, assumptions about the moment when a fetus becomes a person and is thus subject to harm are at the heart of political discussions of abortion and stem-cell research.

While cognitivist approaches to morality emphasize universal criteria like the denunciation of individual rights violations and harm to the individual, the cultural approach proposed by Richard Shweder, from which the emotive approach derives, demonstrates cross-cultural peculiarities in morality, with mundane behaviors for one culture viewed as extremely immoral for another (Shweder, Mahapatra, and Miller 1987). Shweder argues as a result that morality is broader in scope than argued by cognitivist domain theory and that it encompasses three types of ethics, with each focusing on specific moral goals: the Ethic of Autonomy, the Ethic of Community, and the Ethic of Divinity. The Ethic of Autonomy is concerned with individual autonomy, including aspects of freedom, welfare, rights, and harm. The Ethic of Community puts the social group at the foundation of moral authority, such that morality is defined in terms of obedience, duty, loyalty, and respect. Finally, the Ethic of Divinity is concerned with attaining purity and striving for the divine. Religion guides the individual in attaining virtue and purity and avoiding moral degradation and thereby constitutes an important source of morality (Shweder et al. 1998).

Expanding Shweder's conceptualization of morality, Jonathan Haidt and Jesse Graham (2007) propose five foundations of evolved moral intuitions, including harm, fairness, loyalty, authority, and purity, and argue that these moral intuitions are related to ideology, such that liberals value and employ the first two, while conservatives value and employ all five. While they agree that religion undergirds all five foundations, they suggest that religious narratives and teachings are often aimed at the three "binding" foundations, instructing the devout to develop loyalty to their group, give respect to authority figures, and protect the purity of their body and soul (Graham and Haidt 2010). Specifically, as in Shweder's Ethic of Divinity, the rules in the purity and sanctity foundation regulate food, clothing, behavior, and social interactions so that one may remain clean and chaste.

Disgust as a Vehicle for Moral Purity

The emotion of disgust plays a leading role in the process of converting the conventional into the moral, as a mechanism differentiating between the pure and the degraded. The view that disgust is associated with appraisals of impurity and contamination—that is, with the moral domain of purity (Horberg et al. 2009)—derives from the appraisal perspective, according to which emotions influence judgments in domains that are thematically related to the specific appraisals they elicit (Lerner and Keltner 2000). If a noxious substance, such as feces or vomit, is encountered, disgust provokes the individual to retreat. The emotional reaction ultimately serves to protect the body from potential environmental harm and oral contamination (Rozin, Haidt, and McCauley; 2000; Schaller and Duncan 2007). In this role disgust has worked to promote the evolutionary survival of individuals through the creation of an automatic alert system. While originally related to the evolutionary challenges of avoiding contamination of one's body, the emotion of disgust is suggested to extend to the rejection of contaminants of one's soul, lifestyle, and social environment (Haidt and Joseph 2007; Rozin et al. 1999). Thus, disgust also functions as a means of ensuring the maintenance of spiritual purity.

Disgust is associated with purity-related political positions like opposition to abortion and gay rights (Inbar, Pizarro, and Bloom 2009) as well as negative beliefs about tabooed sexual behavior (Horberg et al. 2009). Much research has in fact demonstrated that moral beliefs are driven by environments *evoking disgust*, as well as *trait disgust*—that is, individual-level disgust sensitivity. Consequently all individuals, even those low in trait disgust sensitivity, have the potential to respond to disturbing stimuli within the environment, although some may more readily respond to the evocative stimuli. Indeed, Jonathan Haidt, Silvia Koller, and Maria Dias (1993) found that after being exposed to disgust-evoking scenarios, such as having sex with a chicken, participants engaged in moralizing. Inducing disgust through a variety of means has been shown to increase the tendency of individuals to dole out harsh moral judgments (Ben-Nun Bloom 2014; Eskine, Kacinik, and Prinz 2011; Wheatley and Haidt 2005). For instance, presenting descriptions and colorful pictures of delicacies from around the world that many in the West perceive as disgusting, such as Vietnamese raw blood soup, fertilized duck eggs, and snake wine, was found to increase the tendency to perceive a political issue as a moral one (Ben-Nun Bloom 2014).

As highlighted with some of the previous examples, disgust is not confined merely to concerns regarding bodily functions; it extends to broader contexts involving social and religious phenomena (Bloom 2004; Nussbaum 2001). To protect the local environment from contamination, individuals have learned over time to dislike outsiders, to obey individuals in position of power, and to regularly engage in cleansing rituals. Individuals react emotionally to stimuli in a manner that is intended to protect both their community and their local environment. The overarching argument is similar to that for avoiding ingestible toxins. Thus, the arrival of outsiders brings with it the potential introduction of new hazardous diseases, as well as new destructive, potentially contagious values and norms, causing individuals to build an aversion toward groups of dissimilar people (Schaller and Duncan 2007).

Religion, Disgust, and Intolerance

Much research has connected disgust and the maintenance of purity within the general population. For instance, having individuals recall past transgressions increased the likelihood that they would feel morally sullied as well as express a desire to take part in a self-cleansing activity (compared to the reaction of a control group) (Zhong and Liljenquist 2006). Similarly, participants in an experimental study who were induced to experience disgust and then exposed to a cleansing exercise were less judgmental of certain immoral actions than those who were prevented from engaging in acts of purification (Schnall, Benton, and Harvey 2008). While these results tentatively suggest that reactions involving disgust are likely universal, researchers have established connections between disgust sensitivity and certain belief orientations, specifically conservatism and religiosity.

With disgust functioning as a means of ensuring the maintenance of spiritual purity, religions across the world maintain moral codes that link disgust to notions of purity with rituals functioning to purify and cleanse the body of moral pollution (Rozin et al. 1999). Indeed, numerous researchers have made connections between sin, ablutions, and disgust among the religious. Ryan Ritter and Jesse Preston (2011) found that Christians allowed to engage in a cleansing activity (hand washing) after being asked to copy a Qur'an verse exhibited less disgust than those not permitted to engage in the same cleansing activity. Additional work has demonstrated strong associations between religiosity and anxiety involving contamination and cleanliness (Tek and Ulug 2001), with purity concerns mediating the relationship between disgust and religious cleansing rituals (Greenberg and Witzum 1994). Thus, emotional disgust manifests through the fear of contact with objects of an impure and contaminating nature.

In the same vein, even though all people may react with disgust to, and tend to moralize about, certain stimuli, there appear to be systematic differences in disgust sensitivity and in their tendency to moralize. Specifically, research has found meaningful differences in the visceral reactions people have toward disturbing stimuli. Yoel Inbar, David Pizarro, and Paul Bloom (2009), for example, found conservative identifiers more likely to express intolerance toward disgusting acts than self-identifying liberals, an effect that held across samples, demographic differences, and personality types. Disgust sensitivities have further been linked to socially conservative values (Terrizzi, Shook, and Ventis 2010), voting behaviors (Inbar et al. 2012), and authoritarian personality predispositions (Hodson and Costello 2007).

Religiosity is similarly tied to trait disgust. Thus, individuals with tendencies toward religious fundamentalism (Terrizzi, Shook, and Ventis 2010) and religious obsessions (Olatunji et al. 2005) are more likely to experience disgust. Similarly, religious principles, like the principle that one should try to avoid having immoral thoughts, have been associated with concerns about purity related to fear of contamination (Olatunji 2008). However, in at least one study, religious affiliation does not appear to influence self-reported disgust sensitivity (Inbar, Pizarro, and Bloom 2009); for example, Catholics are not more likely to express low levels of disgust sensitivity than Protestants or the nonaffiliated.

While morality and disgust are intimately related to religion, moral reasoning and its underpinnings, in turn, facilitate outgroup aversions. Thus, disgust governs the contraction of one's moral circle; repulsion is frequently felt in response to members of disliked social groups and people who have come into contact with them (Pizarro, Detweiler-Bedell, and Bloom 2006). Therefore, disgust should be associated with social and political intolerance. In correlational work, Jason Faulkner and colleagues (2004) found that individuals naturally more inclined to fear vulnerability to disease were more likely to associate foreign outgroups with danger. Additional work by Faulkner and colleagues (2004) manipulating disease salience established a connection between exposure and negative attitudes toward foreign immigrants. These findings were extended by researchers who demonstrated that experimentally manipulating disgust caused not only outgroup denigration but also greater ingroup amiability (Navarrete and Fessler 2006). On a related note, Gordon Hodson and Kimberly Costello (2007) established a connection between interpersonal disgust sensitivity and outgroup antipathy. Individuals who expressed greater discomfort at the thought of wearing clean, used clothing, for instance, were more likely to express dislike for immigrants. Similarly, a survey of undergraduate students found that individuals scoring high in trait disgust had an increased tendency to express dislike toward homosexuals (Olatunji 2008). Individuals exposed to malodorous smells were more likely to evince negative sentiments toward gay men but not toward other groups like the elderly or African Americans (Inbar, Pizarro, and Bloom 2012),[1] and disgust sensitivity was associated with more conservative attitudes particularly on purity-related issues, such as abortion and gay marriage (Inbar, Pizarro, and Bloom 2009). These findings extend to religious outgroups as well. Religious individuals asked to write out passages from the sacred text of a divergent religion were more likely to harshly rate soda than were individuals in a control group (Ritter and Preston 2011). Given the expansive research within the field of moral psychology on the relationship between disgust and rejection of dissimilar others, we expect that experimentally manipulating disgust will cause greater intolerance toward those who are dissimilar. Specifically, we posit:

H_1: Disgust induction (evoked disgust) should lead to religious intolerance.

Relatedly, because work has demonstrated a connection between the ease with which disgust is evoked and moral reasoning pertaining to outgroup antipathy, we expect that those sensitive to disgust will be more intolerant. Specifically:

H_2: Disgust sensitivity (trait disgust) is related to religious intolerance.

Further, since theories of morality suggest that religion is an important source of assumptions and guidelines as to what is pure and what is disgusting, we expect that disgust mediates the relationship between religion and outgroup antipathy.[2] The assumption that emotions of disgust are subordinate to religiosity is based on the fact that most adherents were born and raised religious. Their religious environment, in turn, governed their belief system about purity, and their view of what is disgusting. Indeed, both Shweder's Ethic of Divinity and Turiel's idea of informational assumptions suggest that religion spiritually guides the individual by illuminating what is pure and what is morally decayed. Graham and Haidt similarly posit that religious narratives and laws instruct individuals in matters of purity of the body and soul, and often govern what is viewed as disgusting. For instance, because of the kosher and hallal laws, Jews and Muslims—but not Christians—view bacon as disgusting. There is less reason to expect that sensitivity to disgust will draw most religious adherents toward religion. As purity is a mechanism that invokes religious intolerance, we expect that disgust mediates the relationship between religion and outgroup antipathy. That is:

H_3: The relationship between religion and religious outgroup aversion is mediated by disgust, such that dislike for outgroup members will be felt through the emotion of disgust for religious group members.

Data and Design

We conducted two original web-based survey-embedded experiments of a largely religious adult sample during the summer of 2013. To ensure a religious sample, we used local web-surveying services with a large number of active panel members (Qualtrics in the United States, $N = 109$; iPanel in Israel, $N = 132$), and we defined strata sampling by level of religiosity, limiting the samples to Catholics and Jews.[3]

Participants were randomly assigned to one of three between-subjects experimental conditions, where two different treatments were employed to prime incidental disgust and the third group was a no-prime control group. In the first experimental group, we used a questions-as-treatments framework (Ben-Nun Bloom and Arikan 2013; Ben-Nun Bloom, Arikan, and Courtemanche 2015; Chong, Citrin, and Conley 2001; Transue 2007). Participants were first presented with a prompt that read, "How disgusting would you find each of the following experiences? Please mark how disgusted you would be, with 1 indicating not disgusted at all and 5 indicating extremely disgusted," after which they answered a battery of three disgust sensitivity questions adopted from the DS-R (Disgust Scale—Revised; see Haidt, McCauley, and Rozin 1994; Olatunji et al. 2007). They then immediately answered items on religious intolerance, and finally were presented with a battery of control variables. The disgust sensitivity items were: "You see a man with his intestines exposed after an accident"; "You are about to drink a glass of milk when you smell that it is spoiled"; "You discover that a friend of yours changes underwear only once a week."

In the second experimental group, participants were presented with a short paragraph about disgusting delicacies and were asked to recall a situation in which they encountered a relevant experience (a brief form of the disgust induction manipulation in Ben-Nun Bloom 2014). The essay read, "Most people have encountered at least one dish from a different culinary tradition they found truly disgusting. For instance, escamoles is made from the eggs of black ants, often eaten in tacos. Vietnamese raw blood soup is made with the raw blood of ducks or geese (and sometimes pigs), with peanuts and herbs on top. During the aging process, a fly called piophila casei deposits its eggs on Italian maggot-infested Casu Frazigu cheese, excreting enzymes that give it an overwhelmingly pungent smell, a rotten taste, and a soft, creamy texture. Please recall a situation in which you have seen, smelled, and/or tasted nauseating food, and write the name of the dish below: ____________________." Religious intolerance was measured immediately after the priming manipulation, following by control variables.

The dependent variable, religious intolerance, is a scale of three items, measured as follows: "Now we would like to ask you a few questions about different types of contact with people from a different religion from you—for instance, if you're Christian [Jewish], non-Christian [Jewish] people. In each situation please state how willing you would be to engage in the following activity. (1) Occasionally spending social time with a person from a different religion; (2) Living next door to a person from a different religion; (3) Being best friends with a person from a different religion." Response scales originally varied from 1 (I would definitely do this) to 4 (I would definitely not do this).[4]

The models control for religiosity, ideology (conservatism), authoritarianism, education, income, gender (male), age, and the political context (Israel versus United States).[5] All measures are coded to vary between 0 and 1, except for age, which is measured in years.[6]

Results

The Effect of Disgust Induction

The multivariate analysis presented in Table 6.1 tests the effect of the primes on religious intolerance, when holding constant background variables, including

TABLE 6.1 EFFECT OF DISGUST PRIMES ON RELIGIOUS INTOLERANCE (ORDINARY LEAST SQUARES [OLS] REGRESSION)

	Model I (Pooled)			*Model II (United States)*			*Model III (Israel)*		
	β	*SE*	*p*	*β*	*SE*	*p*	*β*	*SE*	*p*
Disgust prime 1	.09	(.03)	***	.08	(.04)	**	.11	(.06)	**
Disgust prime 2	.02	(.04)		.04	(.03)	*	.01	(.06)	
Religiosity	.16	(.08)	**	.06	(.07)		.19	(.17)	
Ideology (conservative)	.13	(.06)	**	.07	(.04)	*	.21	(.12)	*
Authoritarianism	.12	(.05)	**	.07	(.05)		.13	(.09)	
Education	.12	(.11)		.13	(.10)		.07	(.16)	
Income	–.28	(.10)	***	–.13	(.09)		–.55	(.23)	**
Male	–.03	(.03)		–.05	(.03)	*	–.03	(.05)	
Age	.00	(.00)		.00	(.00)	**	.00	(.00)	
Israel (vs. United States)	.33	(.03)	***	—			—		
Constant	–.13	(.08)		.01	(.10)		.10	(.15)	
N		236			104			132	
R^2		.48			.10			.19	

Note: One-tailed significance tests (two-tailed 90%) were more appropriate where hypotheses were directional.
*$p < .10$, **$p < .05$, ***$p < .01$

ideology, level of religiosity, authoritarianism, education, income, gender, age, and the political context. Starting with the pooled sample (model I), the questions-as-treatment disgust induction (disgust prime 1) was found to increase religious intolerance. Thus, exposure to this experimental treatment was associated with a 9 percent increase in religious intolerance compared to the control group, all else constant. The alternative disgust manipulation (disgust prime 2), based on a disgust-inducing paragraph, did not have a statistically significant effect in the pooled model, though it did in the U.S. portion of the sample.

Moving to the control variables, religiosity, conservatism, authoritarianism, and a low income were all related to religious intolerance. In addition, the Israeli sample shows an overall stronger religious intolerance compared to the American sample. This is in line with the current literature, which suggests that the United States shows greater tolerance of religious diversity, while most other countries tend to support cultural homogeneity (Citrin and Sides 2008). Finally, the effects of education, gender, and age were insignificant.

Next, we carved up the sample so as to test the effect of the two disgust induction manipulations separately for the two countries. First, as can be seen in models II and III of Table 6.1, the effect of the questions-as-treatment disgust induction (prime 1) was consistent across the two countries. Exposure to this experimental manipulation was associated with an 8 percent and an 11 percent increase in religious intolerance compared to the control group among American Catholics (model II) and Israeli Jews (model III), respectively. Second, the disgusting paragraph manipulation (prime 2) had a marginally significant effect among American Catholics (model II) but not among Israeli Jews (model III). Thus, exposure to the disgusting paragraph treatment was associated with a 4 percent increase in religious intolerance compared to the control group among Catholics, all else constant.

Overall, we find that disgust increases religious intolerance, in accord with H_1. However, while one manipulation was effective in both samples, it seems that the alternative manipulation was effective in only one of the two samples. Perhaps the paragraph was too short, or some of the participants skipped reading it, while the questions-as-treatments manipulation forced respondents to process it, as it required answering the questions on the disgust scale.[7] Future research using a disgusting essay manipulation should consider offering a longer essay, accompanying it with vivid pictures and verifying that the participants have encountered it (as in Ben-Nun Bloom 2014).

As a robustness check, we examined potential interactive effects of the primes with political ideology, level of religiosity, authoritarianism, education, and gender. In each case, the potential moderation was examined by entering two interactive terms into the pooled regression from Table 6.1 (e.g., disgust prime 1 × political ideology and disgust prime 2 × political ideology). None of the interactions of the two primes with ideology, religiosity, authoritarianism, education, or gender returned results of statistical significance.

The Mediational Role of Disgust Sensitivity

To test H_2, according to which disgust sensitivity is related to religious intolerance, and H_3, according to which purity mediates the effect of religiosity on religious intolerance, we ran a mediation analysis, presented in Table 6.2. Model I in Table 6.2 presents the pooled analysis from Table 6.1. In model IV we integrated the disgust sensitivity scale into the regression. The results of the mediation analysis, based on Sobel and Goodman-2 tests, are presented in model IV in Table 6.2.

As can be seen in model IV, disgust sensitivity is related to religious intolerance, in accord with H_2. Thus, moving from the minimum to the maximum on the disgust sensitivity scale is associated with a 15 percent increase in religious intolerance, all else constant. Also note that the effect of the disgust prime remains intact when controlling for disgust sensitivity (cf. model I).

We then submitted the religiosity and disgust sensitivity scales to a mediation analysis. Supporting H_3, results indicated that the variance in disgust sensitivity accounts for about a fifth of the effect of religiosity on religious intolerance (cf. the coefficients of religiosity in models I and IV). The mediation by disgust sensitivity is marginally significant using both the Sobel and Goodman-2 mediation tests. This finding suggests that the effect of religiosity on religious intolerance among the devout is at least partly governed by personal preference for moral purity.[8]

TABLE 6.2 MEDIATIONAL ROLE OF DISGUST SENSITIVITY ON RELIGIOUS TOLERANCE (OLS REGRESSION)

	Model I			Model IV		
	β	*SE*	*p*	β	*SE*	*p*
Disgust prime 1	.09	(.03)	***	.09	(.03)	***
Disgust prime 2	.02	(.04)		.03	(.04)	
Disgust sensitivity	—			.15	(.07)	**
Religiosity	.16	(.08)	**	.13	(.08)	*
Ideology (conservative)	.13	(.06)	**	.14	(.06)	**
Authoritarianism	.12	(.05)	**	.13	(.05)	***
Education	.12	(.11)		.13	(.11)	
Income	−.28	(.10)	***	−.26	(.10)	***
Male	−.03	(.03)		−.01	(.03)	
Age	.00	(.00)		.00	(.00)	
Israel (vs. United States)	.33	(.03)	***	.34	(.03)	***
Constant	−.13	(.08)		−.25	(.10)	**
Mediation: religiosity → disgust sensitivity		—			$p_{Sobel} = .09$ $p_{Goodman2} = .08$	
N		236			231	
R^2		.48			.49	

Note: The significance test for the mediation analysis results from a Sobel test and a Goodman-2 test.
$^*p < .10$, $^{**}p < .05$, $^{***}p < .01$

Conclusion

While much research suggests that religion has played an important role in the successful growth of large-scale societies through the fostering of moral norms such as cooperation and generosity (Bloom 2012; Boyer 2001; Norenzayan and Shariff 2008), its effects on intolerance and prejudice are well documented (Adorno et al. 1950; Ginges, Hansen, and Norenzayan 2009; Johnson, Rowatt, and LaBouff 2010). Accordingly, scholars and pundits often point to a "values divide" between traditionalists and progressives, characterized by the return of religion to the public sphere and the emergence of an impassioned debate over religious and moral issues (e.g., Hunter 1991; White 2002).

Such morally induced discourse has important political implications. It is not amenable to compromise (Mooney and Schuldt 2008), transgressions may be viewed as sins (Meier 1999), and the debate is accompanied by resentment, extremism, and aggression (Ben-Nun Bloom 2010, 2013). In fact, the current "cultural conflict" in the United States is often defined as a "political and social hostility rooted in different systems of moral understanding" (Hunter 1991: 42). Indeed, there is empirical evidence that morality is related to preference for social distance, such that some individuals are decreasingly willing to maintain social, private, and economic relationships with, or even sit next to, people who do not share a stance that the individual reports as a moral conviction (Skitka, Bauman, and Sargis 2005). Evidence also points to a relationship between morality and a decreased level of political tolerance in the sense of respect for the political and civil rights of those holding contrasting views, such as freedom of organization and speech (Ben-Nun Bloom 2010).

This study posited that morality, and specifically the moral emotion of disgust, underlies the connection between religion and intolerance. Taking a cue from the recent literature in psychology, we focused on emotions that motivate moral cognition. Specifically, individuals react with disgust to environmental stimuli in a way that is evolutionarily adaptive. As a means of protecting themselves from contaminants to their body, soul, and community, disgust is a signal of avoidance and withdrawal. Current literature demonstrates that the religious are more sensitive to disgust (Olatunji et al. 2005; Terrizzi, Shook, and Ventis 2010) and are more likely to experience disgust from contact with outgroup religious beliefs (Ritter and Preston 2011).

Using this line of reasoning as a guide, we posited that disgust operates as a mechanism linking religion to antipathy for outgroups. We tested our suppositions using an experimental design that primed incidental disgust among American Catholics and Israeli Jews and captured trait proclivities. Results confirm that both trait and state disgust underlie intolerance of those who are religiously different.

Our findings are compelling for a number of reasons. First, they suggest that disgust can have a powerful effect on multiple social phenomena. More importantly, we are able to make strong assertions regarding the nature of the relationship as a result of our experimental design. Because we successfully demonstrated that primed incidental disgust leads to greater intolerance, we are more confident that emotion drives the relationship, rather than the other way around (animus causing disgust). Consequently, our findings improve on much of the literature, which is largely correlational in form.

Moreover, because this study was conducted across environmental contexts with generally robust findings, our work suggests not only that emotional reactions are universal in nature but also that they can be easily manipulated. This has important real-world implications. Political and religious leaders who wish to instill and foster intolerance need only prime disgust as a means of doing so.

Future research should focus on how the effects of disgust can be neutralized, potentially by relying on the emotion regulation paradigm (Gross 2007). In addition, other mechanisms underlying the moralization tendencies of the devout in general and religious intolerance more specifically should be investigated, primarily nonemotional mechanisms such as a nonconsequentialist (insensitivity to outcomes, deontological) thinking style (Piazza and Sousa 2013) but also other negative moral emotions, such as shame and contempt, and positive moral emotions, such as compassion, solidarity, awe, and elevation.

Notes

Acknowledgment: Pazit Ben-Nun Bloom gratefully acknowledges the generous financial support from the Marie Curie Grant of the 7th European Community Framework Programme (CIG grant 293769).

1. Interestingly, conservatives and liberals were equally affected, suggesting that while conservatives may be more susceptible to disgust in general, the emotion affects all equally.

2. Mediation is said to occur when the effect of some variable X (in this case, religion) on the outcome Y (intolerance) is at least partly explained by some intervening variable M (disgust), such that $X \rightarrow M \rightarrow Y$.

3. The filter questions were church attendance and ethnicity in the United States, and religious group (ultra-Orthodox, religious, traditional, or secular) and ethnicity in Israel.

4. There was sufficient variance on this variable: About 53 percent of the distribution was in the lower third and 12 percent in the upper third of the religious intolerance scale.

5. The randomization was successful in that individuals associated with theoretically relevant variables were dispersed throughout the manipulations and control group. For example, there were 34 males, 50 conservatives and 46 authoritarians in prime 1, compared to 40, 50 and 56 in prime 2 and 36, 42 and 42 in the control condition, respectively. Still, given the relatively small sample and our theoretical interest in these variables, we integrated them in the analysis.

6. Descriptive statistics for included variables (Table 6.A) as well as coding information can be found in the online appendix at http://pauldjupe.com/s/Appendix.docx.

7. Indeed, the interaction of the disgust essay prime (but not the questions-as-treatment manipulation) with disgust sensitivity yielded statistically significant evidence that induced disgust increases religious intolerance when disgust sensitivity is low but not when it is high. This finding may strengthen the view that those sensitive to disgust have quickly skipped the manipulation upon the first clue of disgust induction and thus that the prime was effective only for respondents lower on disgust sensitivity, which would explain the null result in the overall sample.

8. Note that the sampling scheme filtered for religiosity (allowing only individuals who did not answer "never" on the religious attendance item to take the survey), which may have limited the variance in the disgust sensitivity scale. Future research should further investigate the mediational role of disgust sensitivity in the general population.

References

Adorno, T. W., Else Frenkel-Brunswik, Daniel J. Levinson, and R. Nevitt Sanford. 1950. *The Authoritarian Personality.* New York: Harper.

Ben-Nun Bloom, Pazit. 2010. "The Moral Public: Moral Judgment and Political Attitudes." Ph.D. diss., Stony Brook University.

———. 2013. "The Public's Compass: Moral Conviction and Political Attitudes." *American Politics Research* 41 (6): 937–964.

———. 2014. "Disgust, Harm, and Morality in Politics." *Political Psychology* 35 (4): 495–513.

Ben-Nun Bloom, Pazit, and Gizem Arikan. 2013. "Priming Religious Belief and Religious Social Behavior Affects Support for Democracy." *International Journal of Public Opinion Research* 25 (3): 368–382.

Ben-Nun Bloom, Pazit, Gizem Arikan, and Marie Courtemanche. 2015. "Religious Social Identity, Religious Belief, and Anti-Immigration Sentiment." *American Political Science Review* (forthcoming).

Bloom, Paul. 2004. *Descartes' Baby: How the Science of Child Development Explains What Makes Us Human*. New York: Basic Books.

———. 2012. "Religion, Morality, Evolution." *Annual Review of Psychology* 63:179–199.

Boyer, Pascal. 2001. *Religion Explained: The Evolutionary Foundations of Religious Belief*. New York: Basic Books.

Brooks, Arthur. C. 2003. "Religious Faith and Charitable Giving." *Policy Review* 121:39–48.

Chong, Dennis, Jack Citrin, and Patricia Conley. 2001. "When Self-Interest Matters." *Political Psychology* 22 (3): 541–570.

Citrin, Jack, and John Sides. 2008. "Immigration and the Imagined Community in Europe and the United States." *Political Studies* 56:33–56.

Djupe, Paul A., and Jacob R. Neiheisel. 2008. "Clergy Deliberation on Gay Rights and Homosexuality." *Polity* 40 (4): 411–435.

Eskine, Kendall J., Natalie A. Kacinik, and Jesse J. Prinz. 2011. "A Bad Taste in the Mouth: Gustatory Disgust Influences Moral Judgment." *Psychological Science* 22 (3): 295–299.

Faulkner, Jason, Mark Schaller, Justin H. Park, and Lesley A. Duncan. 2004. "Evolved Disease-Avoidance Mechanisms and Contemporary Xenophobic Attitudes." *Group Processes and Intergroup Relations* 7 (4): 333–353.

Forbes, Kevin F., and Ernest M. Zampelli. 1997. "Religious Giving by Individuals: A Cross Denominational Study." *American Journal of Economics and Sociology* 56 (1): 17–30.

Ginges, Jeremy, Ian Hansen, and Ara Norenzayan. 2009. "Religion and Support for Suicide Attacks." *Psychological Science* 20 (2): 224–230.

Graham, Jesse, and Jonathan Haidt. 2010. "Beyond Beliefs: Religion Binds Individuals into Moral Communities." *Personality and Social Psychology Review* 14:140–150.

Greenberg, David, and Eliezer Witzum. 1994. "The Influence of Cultural Factors on Obsessive Compulsive Disorder: Religious Symptoms in a Religious Society." *Israel Journal of Psychiatry and Related Sciences* 31:211–220.

Gross, James J. 2007. *Handbook of Emotion Regulation*. New York: Guilford Press.

Haidt, Jonathan, and Jesse Graham. 2007. "When Morality Opposes Justice: Conservatives Have Moral Intuitions That Liberals May Not Recognize." *Social Justice Research* 20 (1): 98–116.

Haidt, Jonathan, and Craig Joseph. 2007. "The Moral Mind: How 5 Sets of Innate Moral Intuitions Guide the Development of Many Culture-Specific Virtues, and Perhaps Even Modules." In *The Innate Mind*, vol. 3, *Foundations and the Future*, edited by Peter Carruthers, Stephen Laurence, and Stephen P. Stich, 367–392. New York: Oxford University Press.

Haidt, Jonathan, Silvia Helena Koller, and Maria G. Dias. 1993. "Affect, Culture, and Morality, or Is It Wrong to Eat Your Dog?" *Journal of Personality and Social Psychology* 65 (4): 613–628.

Haidt, Jonathan, Clark McCauley, and Paul Rozin. 1994. "Individual Differences in Sensitivity to Disgust: A Scale Sampling Seven Domains of Disgust Elicitors." *Personality and Individual Differences* 16 (5): 701–713.

Hodson, Gordon, and Kimberly Costello. 2007. "Interpersonal Disgust, Ideological Orientations, and Dehumanization as Predictors of Intergroup Attitudes." *Psychological Science* 18 (8): 691–698.

Hoge, Dean R., and Fenggang Yang. 1994. "Determinants of Religious Giving in American Denominations: Data from Two Nationwide Surveys." *Review of Religious Research* 36 (2): 123–148.

Horberg, E. J., Christopher Oveis, Dacher Keltner, and Adam B. Cohen. 2009. "Disgust and the Moralization of Purity." *Journal of Personality and Social Psychology* 97 (6): 963–976.

Hunter, James D. 1991. *Culture Wars: The Struggle to Define America*. New York: Basic Books.

Inbar, Yoel, David A. Pizarro, and Paul Bloom. 2009. "Conservatives Are More Easily Disgusted than Liberals." *Cognition and Emotion* 23 (4): 714–725.

———. 2012. "Disgusting Smells Cause Decreased Liking of Gay Men." *Emotion* 12 (1): 23–27.

Inbar, Yoel, David A. Pizarro, Ravi Iyer, and Jonathan Haidt. 2012. "Disgust Sensitivity, Political Conservatism, and Voting." *Social Psychological and Personality Science* 3 (5): 537–544.

Johnson, Megan K., Wade C. Rowatt, and Jordan LaBouff. 2010. "Priming Christian Religious Concepts Increases Racial Prejudice." *Social Psychological and Personality Science* 1 (2): 119–126.

Lerner, Jennifer S., and Dachner Keltner. 2000. "Beyond Valence: Toward a Model of Emotion Specific Influences on Judgment and Choice." *Cognition and Emotion* 14 (4): 473–493.

Mazar, Nina, On Amir, and Dan Ariely. 2008. "The Dishonesty of Honest People: A Theory of Self-Concept Maintenance." *Journal of Marketing Research* 45 (6): 633–644.

Meier, Kenneth J. 1999. "Drugs, Sex, Rock, and Roll: A Theory of Morality Politics." *Policy Studies Journal* 27 (4): 681–695.

Mooney, Christopher Z., and Richard G. Schuldt. 2008. "Does Morality Policy Exist? Testing a Basic Assumption." *Policy Studies Journal* 36 (2): 199–218.

Navarrete, Carlos David, and Daniel M. T. Fessler. 2006. "Disease Avoidance and Ethnocentrism: The Effects of Disease Vulnerability and Disgust Sensitivity on Intergroup Attitudes." *Evolution and Human Behavior* 27 (4): 270–282.

Norenzayan, Ara, and Azim F. Shariff. 2008. "The Origin and Evolution of Religious Prosociality." *Science* 322:58–62.

Nucci, Larry, and Elliot Turiel. 1993. "God's Word, Religious Rules, and Their Relation to Christian and Jewish Children's Concepts of Morality." *Child Development* 64 (5): 1475–1491.

Nussbaum, Martha C. 2001. *Upheavals of Thought: The Intelligence of Emotions*. New York: Cambridge University Press.

Olatunji, Bunmi O. 2008. "Disgust, Scrupulosity and Conservative Attitudes about Sex: Evidence for a Mediational Model of Homophobia." *Journal of Research in Personality* 42 (5): 1364–1369.

Olatunji, Bunmi O., David F. Tolin, Jonathan D. Huppert, and Jeffrey M. Lohra. 2005. "The Relation between Fearfulness, Disgust Sensitivity and Religious Obsessions in a Non-Clinical Sample." *Personality and Individual Differences* 38 (4): 891–902.

Olatunji, Bunmi O., Nathan L. Williams, David F. Tolin, Jonathan S. Abramowitz, Craig N. Sawchuck, Jeffrey M. Lohr, and Lisa S. Elwood. 2007. "The Disgust Scale: Item Analysis, Factor Structure, and Suggestions for Refinement." *Psychological Assessment* 19 (3): 281–297.

Piazza, Jared, and Paulo Sousa. 2013. "Religiosity, Political Orientation, and Consequentialist Moral Thinking." *Social Psychological and Personality Science* 5 (3): 334–342.

Pichon, Isabelle, Guilio Boccato, and Vassilis Saroglou. 2007. "Nonconscious Influence of Religion on Prosociality: A Priming Study." *European Journal of Social Psychology* 37 (5): 1–6.

Pizarro, David A., Brian Detweiler-Bedell, and Paul Bloom. 2006. "The Creativity of Everyday Moral Reasoning: Empathy, Disgust, and Moral Persuasion." In *Creativity and Reason in Cognitive Development*, edited by James C. Kaufman and John Baer, 81–98. New York: Cambridge University Press.

Price, Vincent, Lilach Nir, and Joseph N. Capella. 2005. "Framing Public Discussion of Gay Civil Unions." *Public Opinion Quarterly* 69 (2): 179–212.

Randolph-Seng, Brandon, and Michael E. Nielsen. 2007. "Honesty: One Effect of Primed Religious Representations." *International Journal for the Psychology of Religion* 17 (4): 303–315.

Ritter, Ryan S., and Jesse Lee Preston. 2011. "Gross Gods and Icky Atheism: Disgust Responses to Rejected Religious Beliefs." *Journal of Experimental Social Psychology* 47 (6): 1225–1230.

Roes, Frans L., and Michel Raymond. 2003. "Belief in Moralizing Gods." *Evolution and Human Behavior* 24 (2): 126–135.

Rozin, Paul, Jonathan Haidt, and Clark McCauley. 2000. "Disgust." In *Handbook of Emotions*, 2nd ed., edited by Michael Lewis, Jeannette Haviland-Jones, and Lisa Feldman Barrett, 637–652. New York: Guilford Press.

Rozin, Paul, Laura Lowery, Sumio Imada, and Jonathan Haidt. 1999. "The CAD Triad Hypothesis: A Mapping between Three Moral Emotions (Contempt, Anger, Disgust) and Three Moral Codes (Community, Autonomy, Divinity)." *Journal of Personality and Social Psychology* 76 (4): 574–586.

Schaller, Mark, and Lesley A. Duncan. 2007. "The Behavioral Immune System: Its Evolution and Social Psychological Implications." In *Evolution and the Social Mind: Evolutionary Psychology and Social Cognitions*, edited by Joseph P. Forgas, Martie G. Haselton, and William von Hippel, 293–307. New York: Psychology Press.

Schnall, Simone, Jennifer Benton, and Sophie Harvey. 2008. "With a Clean Conscience: Cleanliness Reduces the Severity of Moral Judgments." *Psychological Science* 19 (12): 1219–1222.

Shariff, Azim F. and Ara Norenzayan. 2007. "God Is Watching You: Supernatural Agent Concepts Increase Prosocial Behavior in an Anonymous Economic Game." *Psychological Science* 18 (9): 803–809.

Shweder, Richard A., Jacqueline J. Goodnow, Giyoo Hatano, Robert A. Le Vine, Hazel R. Markus, and Peggy J. Miller. 1998. "The Cultural Psychology of Development: One Mind, Many Mentalities." In *Handbook of Child Development*, edited by William Damon, 865–937. New York: Wiley.

Shweder, Richard A., Manamohan Mahapatra, and Joan G. Miller. 1987. "Culture and Moral Development." In *The Emergence of Morality in Young Children*, edited by Jerome Kagan and Sharon Lamb, 1–83. Chicago: University of Chicago Press.

Skitka, Linda J., Christopher W. Bauman, and Edward G. Sargis. 2005. "Moral Conviction: Another Contributor to Attitude Strength or Something More?" *Journal of Personality and Social Psychology* 88 (6): 895–917.

Tek, Cenk, and Berna Ulug. 2001. "Religiosity and Religious Obsessions in Obsessive-Compulsive Disorder." *Psychiatry Research* 104:99–108.

Terrizzi, John A., Jr., Natalie J. Shook, and W. Larry Ventis. 2010. "Disgust: A Predictor of Social Conservatism and Prejudicial Attitudes toward Homosexuals." *Personality and Individual Differences* 49 (6): 587–592.

Ter Voert, Marijke, Albert Felling, and Jan Peters. 1994. "The Effect of Religion on Self-Interest Morality." *Review of Religious Research* 35 (4): 302–323.

Torgler, Benno. 2006. "The Importance of Faith: Tax Morale and Religiosity." *Journal of Economic Behavior and Organization* 61:81–109.

Transue, John. E. 2007. "Identity Salience, Identity Acceptance, and Racial Policy Attitudes: American National Identity as a Uniting Force." *American Journal of Political Science* 51 (1): 78–91.

Turiel, Elliot. 1983. *The Development of Social Knowledge: Morality and Convention*. Cambridge: Cambridge University Press.

Turiel, Elliot, Carolyn Hildebrandt, and Cecilia Wainryb. 1991. "Judging Social Issues: Difficulties, Inconsistencies, and Consistencies." *Monographs of the Society for Research in Child Development* 56 (2): 1–103.

Turiel, Elliot, and Kristin Neff. 2000. "Religion, Culture, and Beliefs about Reality in Moral Reasoning." In *Imagining the Impossible: The Development of Magical, Scientific, and Religious Thinking in Contemporary Society*, edited by Karl S. Rosengren, Carl N. Johnson, and Paul L. Harris, 269–304. Cambridge: Cambridge University Press.

Wheatley, Thalia, and Jonathan Haidt. 2005. "Hypnotic Disgust Makes Moral Judgments More Severe." *Psychological Science* 16 (10): 780–784.

White, John Kenneth. 2002. *The Values Divide*. New York: Chatham House Press.

Zhong, Chen-Bo, and Katie Liljenquist. 2006. "Washing Away Your Sins: Threatened Morality and Physical Cleansing." *Science* 313:1451–1452.

7

Religious Worldviews and Political Tolerance

Communitarianism, Inclusiveness, and Moral Foundations

PAUL A. DJUPE
STEPHEN T. MOCKABEE

Fueled by a standardization of measures in the 1989 National Election Studies (NES) pilot study (Leege and Kellstedt 1993a), research on religion and public opinion in political science has largely come to embrace the "three-B" approach to conceptualizing and measuring religion (see Smidt, Kellstedt, and Guth 2009). More belief, behavior, and belonging (the three Bs) promotes exposure to some unmeasured set of information that has historically been correlated with conservative views. The three-B approach has been especially persistent in studies of political tolerance. Our critique of prior research on the relationship between religion and tolerance begins with the assertion, common in religious studies, that it matters less *how religious a person is* than *how a person is religious* (Yinger 1969; see also Geertz 1973). We explore three different conceptions of religious values, or worldviews, that map out how a person is religious. These values should bear on individuals' political judgments generally and their political tolerance judgments in particular.

Two of the three perspectives we explore in this paper have long roots in the social sciences while the third, moral foundations theory (e.g., Haidt 2007), is a newcomer. However, all three draw on the idea that how people wish the world to be ordered is (1) shaped by religious sources, (2) a powerful force shaping how opinions are formed, and (3) more proximate to opinion holding than abstract religious beliefs devoid of value content.

Notably, a sense of the values people hold has been missing from the tolerance literature, especially the religion and tolerance literature, with one significant exception: democratic values (e.g., Gibson 2010; Marcus et al. 1995). Our investigation is motivated by the discussion in the Introduction that lays out clearly the gaps in the literature—the conveyance of information in congregations or from other religious sources (especially clergy) that may bear on tolerance judgments, the social networks of believers, and their more or less democratic experiences in the work, study, and play of congregational life. Last, while there are surely other missing elements from the study of the connection between religion and tolerance, one important missing ingredient is the content of how religion is to be lived—religious values. It is to this that we turn our attention now, developing three promising approaches to value dimensions and effects.

Religious Communitarianism

Scholars have long recognized the complex, multidimensional nature of religion. A rich tradition of research in the psychology of religion dating back to Gordon Allport and Michael Ross (1967) has made a distinction between "intrinsic" and "extrinsic" religiousness. The former is a "sincere" religious commitment characterized by adherence to normative motives and practices, while the latter refers to the use of religion for instrumental purposes such as to gain social connectedness and security. In a careful review of the beliefs and practices of major American religious traditions, Adam Cohen and colleagues (2005) find considerable differences between Protestant traditions, other "catholic" Christian traditions (described shortly), and the Jewish tradition in the extent to which social motives and ritual practices, in contrast to individual motives, are considered normative. Cohen and colleagues summarize the implications of their findings for the measurement of religiosity by noting that most existing scales "reflect a distinctly American Protestant emphasis on individual and emotionally laden motivations for religious practice while at the same time, they devalue the social- and ritual-based motivations for religious practice" (2005: 58).

The devaluing of the social and communal aspects of religion leads to tradition-specific measurement bias. Previous empirical examinations of standard religiosity items confirm this bias, finding significant differences across religious traditions both in the proportion of respondents identifying particular religious practices as important for a person in their religion and in the percentage who self-reported engaging in those practices (Mockabee, Monson, and Grant 2001; see also Cohen, Siegel, and Rozin 2003 on differences in the importance of religious beliefs across traditions). A one-size-fits-all approach to measuring religious attachment will result in bias.

Religious adherents in the *catholic* traditions (Roman Catholics, Episcopalians, most Lutherans, and even some United Church of Christ and Presbyterian Church [USA] members) use liturgies and prayers that are collective. Like Jews, Catholics recognize that each worshipping *community* unites with similar *communities* throughout the world and across time in these rituals. Confession and intercession, even by individuals praying alone, are done in virtual community. Individual social responsibility exists as part of collective action. For the most part, that *is not* what a standard survey battery measures as religion.

On the other hand, norms among conservative Protestants derive from *individual choice*, and that is why conversion and public testimony, strict doctrinal adherence, frequent private prayer and Bible reading, and public worship attendance are so essential. For the most part, that *is* what surveys like the American National Election Studies (ANES) measure as religion and why, therefore, it is likely that religiosity appears to encourage conservative political choices and lower levels of political tolerance.

Past research suggests that the communitarian-individualist distinction is relevant for understanding political behavior. For example, in a series of studies of Catholic data sets, David Leege (1988), Leege and Thomas Trozzolo (1989), and Leege and Michael Welch (1989) have shown that individualistic religious norms that approximate American evangelical practice are associated with political conservatism and personal responsibility for ameliorating social ills, while communitarian religious norms like those of historic Catholicism are associated with political liberalism and collective responsibility for overcoming social ills. Paralleling this, the individualists were more apt to seek military solutions to international conflict, and the communitarians to seek political solutions. Robert Wuthnow (1993) perceives an emerging "two camp" situation within church bodies in the United States as best characterized by the individualism-communitarianism gap, not the church attendance gap. Each has different norms for religious practice, different patterns for religious socialization (assent versus descent), and different consequences for moral and political behavior. Like the studies cited previously, empirical data analyzed by Wuthnow bear witness to these politically consequential religious dimensions.

Recent evidence of the political importance of the communitarian-individualist distinction is found in the work of Stephen Mockabee, Kenneth Wald, and David Leege (2007, 2009, 2012), who developed new survey items that appeared on the 2006 ANES pilot study and 2008 ANES surveys. The two-question sequence measuring communitarian religiosity began with a filter asking, "Have there been times in your life when you tried to be a good Christian, or is that not something you have tried to do?" The next question asked, "When you have tried to be a good Christian, which did you try to do more: avoid doing sinful things yourself, or help other people?" This is a new question that has no exact match in the literature. The nearest thing to it is found in Peter Benson and Dorothy Williams's (1982) and David Leege and Lyman Kellstedt's (1993b) discussions of individualism and communitarianism. Analysis by Mockabee, Wald, and Leege (2009, 2012) shows that those answering "avoid sin" are more likely to hold politically conservative views on so-called culture war issues such as abortion and gay rights, while those answering "help other people" are more likely to hold moderate to liberal views on social welfare issues such as government provision of health insurance and government aid to disadvantaged groups.

In sum, prior research finds strong evidence that the individualist-communitarian distinction is politically consequential. Therefore it seems reasonable to expect that communitarian religious values may be related to political tolerance. Specifically, we expect that those with a communitarian religious outlook will be more tolerant of unpopular groups than will those who hold an individual piety perspective. A horizontal orientation focused on helping others would seem to be more compatible with tolerating differences than would a vertically oriented desire for individual piety. To test this expectation, we employ a slightly modified version of the ANES questions studied by Mockabee and colleagues. The question wording replaces "a good Christian" with "a good person of your faith" to apply to both Christian and non-Christian groups.

The Religious Economic Roots of Inclusion

The second dimension of religious worldviews we explore takes a cue from the religious economy approach in the sociology of religion as well as the intergroup relations literature in psychology (see Djupe and Calfano 2013a, 2013b). This conception of religious values follows the classic distinction among religious organizations of churches and sects first identified by Ernst Troeltsch (1931; see also Niebuhr 1951). Church and sect lie at the end points of a scale marking the degree of tension between the group and society (Finke and Stark 2005; Johnson 1963): Churches are coincident with society, and sects live in tension (Stark and Finke 2000). Put simply, tension is the engine driving the religious economy, the essential variable shaping religious growth and decline (Finke and Stark 2005; Stark and Finke 2000). Congregations differentiate themselves along this dimension in order to appeal to the various religious demands in the population. This suggests that one is highly likely to encounter values in the local religious context that vary between assimilation and distinctiveness, barriers and bridges, or what we refer to as inclusive and exclusive values.[1]

Regarding religious exclusivity, Scott Appleby suggests, "Enclave builders portray their religion's truths, 'rights,' and responsibilities as inherently superior to those of their rivals. . . . The strength of a religious community's claim to the loyalty of its adherents rests on the community's ability to present itself as the exclusive bearer of specific moral and/or material benefits" (2003: 181–182). It is no surprise then that more exclusive, sectlike religious organizations host much more dense social networks (Stark and Finke 2000; Stark and Glock 1968; but see Djupe and Gilbert 2009; Djupe and Calfano 2012). The presentation of exclusive values should encourage people to pit their group's interests against those of a broader world—the outgroup.[2]

In contrast, religious values relating to inclusion seek openness and communion with others, including and especially those not already part of the particular community (Sowle Cahill 1994). The landmark transition in the Catholic Church known as Vatican II was a way to embrace inclusion and a measure of diversity. This shift had real implications for church activity—those with an inclusive, post-Vatican II vision for the church were much more engaged in social outreach and activism than those with a more exclusive, pre-Vatican II vision (Leege and Trozzolo [1989] 2006). Thus, we expect that those exposed to inclusive values will evince more concern for the interests of others beyond their group.

There is little doubt that these values live in tension. Miroslav Volf, for instance, while advocating for inclusion, defines sin itself "as the practice of exclusion" (1996: 72). In broad brush, whether religious bodies take more inclusive or exclusive directions is the essence of ongoing denominational battles, most recently in the Evangelical Lutheran Church in America (ELCA), Episcopal Church, and Presbyterian Church (USA) over the acceptance of gay clergy and among Latter-Day Saints regarding immigration. At the same time, aspects of both inclusive and exclusive values appear to be reflected in the seven heavenly virtues (Cairns 1996), suggesting that both value sets should be equally recognizable to religious adherents across a variety of communities.[3]

These values recognize varying degrees of intergroup tension in the role of religious communities in society—whether the constituted aim is to reach out and be inclusive of people or to reinforce boundaries with the world and focus inward to the exclusion of outsiders. On this basis, inclusive and exclusive values should bear a close connection with threat and tolerance judgments. In particular, higher adoption of exclusive values should raise the stakes of interacting with outsiders, in part by simply emphasizing the inherent goodness of the ingroup. Inclusive values, on the other hand, deemphasize the risk of interacting with the outgroup. Taken together, exclusive values should augment threat posed by a least-liked group while inclusive values should reduce threat perceptions. The connection to tolerance is more tenuous because these values do not convey any particular content about groups. At the same time, our expectations dovetail with expectations about threat—inclusive values should reduce intolerance by broadening a sense of the ingroup, while exclusive values should boost intolerance by reinforcing close boundaries to the world.

Moral Foundations

The last dimension of religious worldviews we explore is moral foundations. Building from previous work (e.g., Shweder et al. 1997; Kohlberg 1969), Jonathan Haidt and colleagues (Haidt and Graham 2007; Haidt and Joseph 2004) have reacted to common narrow uses of morality and built a more inclusive and complex conception of the concept. In their formulation, moral reasoning has five components that tend to be adopted at systematically different rates by political liberals and conservatives. The five include harm, fairness, loyalty, authority, and purity. *Harm* consists of disliking pain in others and liking those who reduce or prevent pain in others and is seen in the virtues of compassion and kindness. *Fairness* is at essence a commitment to procedural justice, in which all individuals are treated equally. *Loyalty* is perhaps the opposite of fairness in its valuation of ingroup members over outgroup members, which finds expression in patriotism and anger at attempts to question the ingroup (nation), particularly when the ingroup is threatened. The value of *authority* acknowledges that deference (whether voluntarily adopted or imposed) is essential to an ordered society and that attempts to question authority are dangerous. Last, Haidt and Jesse Graham (2007) suggest that *purity*, as it evolved with humans' use of a meat-heavy diet, serves to protect the body from disease. Purity has shifted to take on social dimensions and can be evoked by a nonconforming appearance or occupation with nonconforming, diseased, disgusting, or dirty objects (see also Chapter 6).

The application of these different value dimensions to threat and tolerance is fairly straightforward. *Fairness* and *harm* go hand in hand to promote the worth of individuals. Given that tolerance is a key virtue of liberal democracies, which are also highly individualistic, adherence to the drives to avoid harm to others and to promote fairness in their treatment should be linked to greater tolerance. We suspect they also are linked to reduced threat since these approaches seek to place everyone on the same moral plane. On the other hand, *purity*, *loyalty*, and *authority* see the individual as something less than a sense of order in the whole. Therefore, it seems logical to expect that employers of these moral dimensions would see a least-liked group as more threatening and would grant them fewer political freedoms.

Data and Design

To assess the connections between these value systems, we draw on survey data from a nationally representative sample of 631 Americans collected in 2011.[4] The survey included a content-controlled tolerance battery (Sullivan, Piereson, and Marcus 1982), the religious communitarianism items, the inclusive/exclusive values items, the moral foundations batteries obtained from the Moral Foundations Theory website, as well as three-B religiosity items and other important controls including democratic norms and threat. It is important to note that the tolerance battery came first in the survey and thus suffers from no effects of question order.

The most commonly chosen least-liked group, by far, was the Ku Klux Klan (46 percent), followed by illegal immigrants (18 percent) and Islamic fundamentalists (15 percent), while the remaining five groups were in the single digits. Respondents granted the three most commonly chosen the fewest political liberties, which highlights the sense that collective threat is shared.

The communitarianism questions began with a filter asking if the respondent had tried to be a good person of his or her faith (compared to being a "good Christian" in the ANES) (Mockabee, Wald, and Leege 2007, 2009, 2012). In the Qualtrics sample, 88 percent of respondents said they had tried to be good people of their respective faiths. This is in line with the ANES results—94 percent of respondents in 2006 and 91 percent of respondents in 2008 said there had been times when they tried to be good Christians. Likewise, the distribution of the communitarianism item reflects previous results of the ANES, as about 35 percent of respondents chose the individual piety option of avoiding sinful personal behavior, while 65 percent chose the more communitarian option of helping others. In the 2006 ANES, 36 percent chose "avoid sin," and in the 2008 ANES, 47 percent did so.

The items capturing the value of inclusion and exclusion follow the well-used language developed by Paul Djupe and Brian Calfano (2013b) and listed in the Introduction. Respondents were asked if they agreed that each activity was important to being a "good person of your faith": love the stranger as yourself (inclusive, 77 percent agree), invite others to their house of worship even if it changes as a result (inclusive, 38 percent agree), keep company with others of my faith (exclusive, 45 percent agree), and shop as much as possible at stores owned by people of my faith (exclusive, 12 percent agree). For the remainder of the chapter, we combine the two questions for each dimension.

Figure 7.1 shows how communitarianism varies across support for inclusive and exclusive values. There is very slight movement across the inclusive values, suggesting that they are almost purely orthogonal (since there is nearly universal support for inclusion). But there is significant movement across commitment to exclusive values ($r = -.13$, $p < .01$)—the more value that respondents see in exclusion, the more they tried to avoid sin when trying to be good people of their faith. Given the correlations between communitarianism, which tends to be inclusive in its treatment of people, and political liberalism, it is not surprising to see this relationship. Still, it is a weak relationship, which suggests that inclusive/exclusive values and communitarianism are capturing distinct concepts.

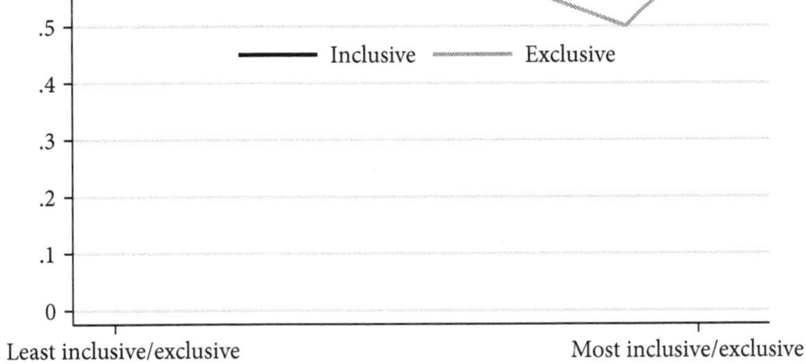

Figure 7.1 Mean communitarianism scores across the ranges of religious inclusivism and exclusivism

Note: $N = 621$. The correlation between inclusion and communitarianism is $r = -.04$, $p = .36$; the correlation between exclusion and communitarianism is $r = -.13$, $p < .01$.

Turning to the moral foundations items, we find that they behave largely as we would expect based on the work of Haidt and colleagues, who found that fairness tends to be heavily used as a moral foundation by both liberals and conservatives. This is the case in our data as well; the mean for fairness is the highest of the moral foundations dimensions across all categories of political ideology. As expected, liberals score highly on harm, with lower scores on authority, loyalty, and purity. Conversely, conservatives value all of the dimensions at essentially the same rate, though authority, loyalty, and purity all rank a bit higher than harm. Among moderates, fairness gets the highest score on average, and the means for the other moral foundations cluster closely together. Put differently, all people rank harm and fairness essentially equivalently, but they vary in how they evaluate the importance of the other three. The importance ascribed to authority, loyalty, and purity increases as conservatism grows, and the differences by ideology are statistically significant.

The interplay between the moral foundations and inclusive/exclusive religious values largely comport with reasonable expectations. Scores on the inclusive values measure have positive, statistically significant correlations with each of the five moral foundations. The strongest of these correlations is with the harm dimension ($r = .17$). In contrast, the exclusive values scale is *not* correlated with either the harm or fairness foundations (since harm and fairness are valued equally among liberals and conservatives). The strongest correlation with exclusive values is the purity dimension ($r = .22$), and there are also statistically significant correlations with loyalty and authority—the moral foundations that we would expect to be associated with valuing ingroup exclusivity. However, it should be noted that these relationships are modest in size, so it seems clear that the moral foundations items and the inclusive/exclusive values measures are tapping distinct concepts.

We also assessed how individualism and communitarianism overlap with the moral foundations. Those who indicated that they would try to be a good person of their faith by helping others, rather than by avoiding sin, are classified as communitarians. Communitarians score higher on the harm and fairness dimensions, while individualists score higher on the purity dimension. The direction of these differences is as expected, given what we know about the tendency of communitarians to support left-leaning positions on issues related to social justice and social welfare, though there is a deep irony, even a contradiction, in the logic as harm and fairness are primarily about protecting the individual. No statistically significant differences were found on the authority and loyalty commitments.

To sum up, the measures of the three types of values we wish to examine—religious communitarianism, inclusive and exclusive religious values, and moral foundations—display patterns that at a minimum do not suggest validity problems and in many instances provide evidence of construct validity. Having examined the data on these key variables, we turn next to multivariate models of threat perceptions and political tolerance that test the influence of these religious and moral values.

Threat Analysis

As noted previously, we view the lack of attention paid to threat perceptions as one of the primary deficiencies in the literature on religion and tolerance. Therefore our analytical approach affords a prominent place to respondents' perceptions of the threat posed by their least-liked group. After identifying the group they most disliked, respondents were asked how strongly they agreed or disagreed that this group presents "a grave threat to the country as a whole." This four-point agree/disagree scale serves as the dependent variable in our model of threat in Table 7.1, and as an independent variable in the model of tolerance presented on the right side of Table 7.2. Some key predictors in our models have already been previewed in earlier sections of the chapter: communitarianism,

TABLE 7.1 ESTIMATES OF THREAT PERCEPTIONS OF LEAST-LIKED GROUPS (OLS REGRESSION)

	B	*SE*	*p*	*β*
Communitarianism	.04	(.08)		
Inclusive values	–.08	(.06)		
Exclusive values	.09	(.05)	†	.09
Harm	–.11	(.06)	*	–.12
Fairness	.06	(.07)		
Loyalty	.06	(.07)		
Authority	.02	(.06)		
Purity	.13	(.06)	**	.14
Democratic norms	–.02	(.01)		
Religious attendance	.01	(.03)		
Mainline Protestant	.06	(.11)		
Catholic	–.05	(.11)		
Jewish	–.11	(.34)		
Mormon	.30	(.25)		
Other religions	.10	(.28)		
Devil exists	.08	(.04)	**	.11
Female	.00	(.08)		
Age under 40	–.17	(.11)	†	–.07
Age over 60	.00	(.09)		
Education	–.09	(.03)	***	–.13
Political ideology	.04	(.02)	†	.08
Constant	2.36	(.42)	***	
Model statistics	N = 490, Adjusted R^2 = .08, RMSE = .84			

Note: RMSE = root mean squared error.

***$p < .01$, **$p < .05$, *$p < .10$, †$p < .10$ (one-tailed test)

TABLE 7.2 ESTIMATES OF POLITICAL TOLERANCE OF LEAST-LIKED GROUPS (OLS REGRESSION)

	Tolerance Model 1				*Tolerance Model 2*			
	B	*SE*	*p*	*β*	*B*	*SE*	*p*	*β*
Threat perception	—				−.49	(.03)	***	−.56
Communitarianism	−.01	(.07)			.01	(.06)		
Inclusive values	.17	(.05)	***	.17	.14	(.04)	***	.13
Exclusive values	−.10	(.05)	**	−.13	−.06	(.04)	†	−.07
Harm	.03	(.05)			−.02	(.04)		
Fairness	−.04	(.06)			−.01	(.05)		
Loyalty	−.08	(.06)			−.04	(.05)		
Authority	−.03	(.05)	†	−.08	−.02	(.04)		
Purity	−.07	(.05)	†	−.09	−.01	(.04)		
Democratic norms	.00	(.01)			−.01	(.01)		
Religious attendance	.03	(.02)			.03	(.02)	†	.06
Mainline Protestant	−.21	(.09)	**	−.13	−.18	(.08)	**	−.11
Catholic	−.06	(.10)			−.07	(.08)		
Jewish	.39	(.28)			.34	(.23)	†	.05
Mormon	.05	(.21)	†	.06	.20	(.17)		
Other religions	.00	(.23)			.03	(.19)		
Devil exists	−.02	(.03)			.02	(.03)		
Female	−.12	(.07)	*	−.08	−.11	(.05)	**	−.07
Age under 40	.01	(.09)			−.07	(.07)		
Age over 60	.05	(.08)			.05	(.06)		
Education	.14	(.03)	***	.23	.09	(.02)	***	.15
Political ideology	.00	(.02)			.02	(.02)		
Constant	2.20	(.35)	***		3.34	(.30)	***	
Model statistics	N = 492, Adjusted R^2 = .13, RMSE = .71				N = 490, Adjusted R^2 = .42, RMSE = .58			

Note: RMSE = root mean squared error.
***$p < .01$, **$p < .05$, *$p < .10$, †$p < .10$ (one-tailed test)

inclusive/exclusive values, and moral foundations. In addition, the model contains several religion variables that have been used in previous research on tolerance, including frequency of church attendance (a standard measure ranging from never to more than once a week), doctrinal orthodoxy (the respondent's level of agreement that the devil really exists), and religious tradition (as constructed from items on religious preference and born-again/evangelical identity, with evangelical Protestant as the excluded reference category). We also include controls for adherence to democratic norms (measured by agreement that it is important for differences of opinion to be expressed in politics), educational attainment, gender, age, and liberal-conservative ideology.[5] Thus the models provide a stringent test of our expectations that religious values will influence threat perception and political tolerance.

In the model of threat perceptions, two of the moral foundations variables emerge as significant predictors: harm and purity. As one would expect, there are opposite signs on these two coefficients. A commitment to purity, which is associated with maintaining conformity, has the expected positive relationship with perceiving threat from a disliked group (see also Chapter 6). In contrast, a commitment to reducing the harm done to others has a negative influence on threat perception. With respect to inclusive and exclusive religious values, the signs on the coefficients are in the expected directions, but only the exclusive values variable approaches statistical significance, and its effect is as strong as political ideology. No effect is found for communitarian religiosity, church attendance, or religious tradition. A significant effect does emerge for the lone religious belief item—believing that the devil exists has a positive relationship with perceived threat. Educational attainment works to mitigate threat perception, while political conservatism has a modest effect in the other direction.

It is noteworthy that the most potent predictor of threat in the model is the purity variable, which has an effect similar in magnitude to that of education. The moral foundations of purity and harm influence threat, while most of the religiosity variables have no effect; only the doctrinal orthodoxy variable about the devil is statistically significant. Taken together, these results support our theoretical expectation that the core values forming religious worldviews will be more proximate to opinion holding than the typically used religiosity measures that are largely devoid of value content.

Tolerance Analysis

Turning to political tolerance as the dependent variable, we present two models in Table 7.2. Both models include the same set of independent variables used in the model of threat perception in Table 7.1, but model 2 adds the threat variable to the right-hand side of the equation predicting tolerance. Multiple considerations lead us to estimate these two versions of tolerance models. As noted earlier, the previous literature on religion and tolerance has, until recently, largely overlooked the role of threat perceptions in explaining tolerance, so we want to be able to compare models with and without this predictor to assess its influence. At the same time, threat has been the dominant influence in the literature, so models excluding it are easily misspecified. Model 1 does not include threat, permitting a test of the influence of the values variables on tolerance without the threat variable in the equation, and model 2 includes it.

Of particular note in the models of tolerance is the influence of inclusive religious values. As expected, but in a departure from the literature thus far, inclusive values promote greater tolerance. This effect is similar in magnitude to the effect of educational attainment, and it is the largest effect of any religion variable in the model. The negative effect of exclusive religious values on tolerance is also in the expected direction, albeit less potent than was the case for inclusive values. The difference is that prior research primed these values, and in that context they affected threat but did not affect tolerance directly (Djupe and Calfano 2013b). These results may indicate that over time more inclusive and less exclusive value commitments work their way through threat to be linked to tolerance. Some evidence for that interpretation is that the effects of these values decline somewhat when threat is introduced (model 2), but their effects do not disappear.

Other results with respect to the religion variables are of note for what we did *not* find. Prior research has found evangelicals to be less tolerant, yet in this model with an array of controls there were few differences based on religious tradition; the only sizable effect was actually in the opposite direction, with nonevangelical Protestants less tolerant than their evangelical brethren. Similarly, the previous finding that church attendance is associated with lower political tolerance is not replicated here. To the contrary, a very modest *positive* effect on tolerance is found for church attendance. In sum, several variables that have been used to measure "religion" in prior studies of tolerance—religiosity, religious tradition, doctrinal orthodoxy—do not emerge as important predictors, but the inclusive and exclusive values dimensions do.

In model 2 we find that, as expected, perceived threat is a powerful predictor. Threat is by far the most potent independent variable, as evidenced by the standardized coefficients. Our expectations were not confirmed, however, with respect to the communitarianism variable—no effect was found. We expected that communitarians would be more tolerant than individualists, but this difference did not occur.[6] We also did not find any statistically significant effects on tolerance for the moral foundations variables in model 2. However, a key point to be taken from the models in Tables 7.1 and 7.2 is that the moral foundations variables of harm and purity had *indirect* effects on tolerance via their influence on threat perceptions. Similarly, belief that the devil exists and political conservatism have indirect negative influence on tolerance through increasing threat perceptions. Two variables, educational attainment and exclusive religious values, had both indirect and direct effects on tolerance.

Overall the findings in Tables 7.1 and 7.2 support the notion that religious values, particularly inclusive and exclusive values, play important roles in forming individuals' judgments about threat and tolerance. The usual three-B measures of religious affiliation and commitment had some, but little, explanatory power in our models.

Conclusion

Although the literature on the religious roots of intolerance spans over five decades, the operationalizations of religion have been surprisingly limited to religious beliefs and behaviors or to blunt measures of religious affiliation. In this chapter, we expand the conceptualization of religion to include what we regard as a serious omission: religious worldviews, the value systems that individuals hold. These value systems are likely to be featured in messages transmitted from religious elites to parishioners and are therefore likely to be more proximate to opinion formation than specific doctrinal beliefs or denominational affiliations.

We tested the influence of three values systems that have been examined in recent scholarship: religious communitarianism, inclusive/exclusive religious values, and Haidt's moral foundations. In models with a host of controls, we found that inclusive and exclusive religious values are significant predictors of tolerance. We also found that moral foundation dimensions of harm and purity are important predictors of threat perception, thereby having indirect effects on tolerance. Only with regard to the communitarianism variable were our expectations unmet; we found no effects of communitarianism on threat perceptions or tolerance.

Commonly used measures of religion such as religious tradition, church attendance, and doctrinal orthodoxy rarely exerted significant influence in the models, and any influence was weak. Thus, it appears that conclusions about the relationship between religion and political tolerance made in previous research may well have been misinterpretations. Our findings suggest that the influence of religion on political tolerance operates primarily through the transmission and reception of values related to inclusiveness and exclusiveness, rather than via religiosity as it has been most commonly conceptualized and measured in the literature.

Notes

A previous version of this chapter was presented at the seventy-first annual meeting of the Midwest Political Science Association, Chicago, Illinois, April 11–14, 2013.

1. These values bear at least a superficial resemblance to what Allport and Ross (1967) labeled extrinsic and intrinsic religious orientations, where the extrinsic is self-centered and the intrinsic is compassionate to others. Though Allport and Ross's definitions may comport generally with this perspective, these orientations have come to be considered personality traits, not values presented variably in religious communities (for recent applications, see Ford et al. 2009; Mavor and Gallois 2008; Whitley 2009).

2. There is evidence from a recent study that exclusive values encourage people to think about the ingroup and inclusive values encourage thinking about the outgroup. People who were primed with exclusive values reported social networks that were more insular (more discussion partners knew each other) than when an equivalent group was primed with inclusive values (Djupe and Calfano 2013b).

3. Former U.S. Supreme Court Justice David Souter offered examples of the universality of exclusivist commandments across religious traditions in his dissent in *Zelman v. Simmons-Harris* (536 U.S. at 713–714n24):

> See, *e.g.*, Christian New Testament (2 Corinthians 6:14) (King James Version) ("Be ye not unequally yoked together with unbelievers: for what fellowship hath righteousness with unrighteousness? and what communion hath light with darkness?"); The Book of Mormon (2 Nephi 9:24) ("And if they will not repent and believe in his name, and be baptized in his name, and endure to the end, they must be damned; for the Lord God, the Holy One of Israel, has spoken it"); Pentateuch (Deut. 29:19) (The New Jewish Publication Society Translation) (for one who converts to another faith, "[t]he Lord will never forgive him; rather will the Lord's anger and passion rage against that man, till every sanction recorded in this book comes down upon him, and the Lord blots out his name from under heaven"); The Koran 334 (The Cow Ch. 2:1) (N. Dawood transl. 4th rev. ed. 1974)

("As for the unbelievers, whether you forewarn them or not, they will not have faith. Allah has set a seal upon their hearts and ears; their sight is dimmed and a grievous punishment awaits them").

4. The survey was funded by a Jack Shand Research Grant awarded by the Society for the Scientific Study of Religion to Paul Djupe and Laura Olson. We purchased a sample from the Qualtrics panel, which administered the survey October 21–27, 2011. These are the same data used in Chapter 11. The sample is 38 percent Democratic, 40.8 percent Republican, 21 percent independent (thus it has too many pure independents); 51.5 percent female (which fits 2010 Census figures); 29 percent identifying as "born again or evangelical," which is perhaps a few points too high (see the Pew Religious Landscape Survey); and 33 percent have a bachelor's degree or more education, which is just a few points above the 2010 Census figures (28 percent have a bachelor's or higher degree).

5. For full coding details, please see the online appendix at http://pauldjupe.com/s/Appendix.docx.

6. We tested a wide array of interactions to see if there were contingent effects of communitarianism and found no support for those.

References

Allport, Gordon W., and J. Michael Ross. 1967. "Personal Religious Orientation and Prejudice." *Journal of Personality and Social Psychology* 5 (4): 432–443.

Appleby, R. Scott. 2003. "Serving Two Masters? Affirming Religious Belief and Human Rights in a Pluralistic World." In *The Sacred and the Sovereign: Religion and International Politics*, edited by John D. Carlson and Erik C. Owens, 170–195. Washington, DC: Georgetown University Press.

Benson, Peter, and Dorothy Williams. 1982. *Religion on Capitol Hill.* New York: Harper and Row.

Cairns, Earle E. 1996. *Christianity through the Centuries: A History of the Christian Church.* 3rd ed. Grand Rapids, MI: Zondervan.

Cohen, Adam B., Daniel E. Hall, Harold G. Koenig, and Keith G. Meador. 2005. "Social versus Individual Motivation: Implications for Normative Definitions of Religious Orientation." *Personality and Social Psychology Review* 9:48–61.

Cohen, Adam B., Joel I. Siegel, and Paul Rozin. 2003. "Faith versus Practice: Different Bases for Religiosity Judgments by Jews and Protestants." *European Journal of Social Psychology* 33 (2): 287–295.

Djupe, Paul A., and Brian R. Calfano. 2012. "American Muslim Investment in Civil Society Political Discussion, Disagreement, and Tolerance." *Political Research Quarterly* 65 (3): 516–528.

———. 2013a. *God Talk: Experimenting with the Religious Causes of Public Opinion.* Philadelphia: Temple University Press.

———. 2013b. "Religious Value Priming, Threat, and Political Tolerance." *Political Research Quarterly* 66 (4): 767–779.

Djupe, Paul A., and Christopher P. Gilbert. 2009. *The Political Influence of Churches.* New York: Cambridge University Press.

Finke, Roger, and Rodney Stark. 2005. *The Churching of America, 1776–2005: Winners and Losers in Our Religious Economy.* New Brunswick, NJ: Rutgers University Press.

Ford, Thomas E., Thomas Brignall, Thomas L. VanValey, and Michael J. Macaluso. 2009. "The Unmaking of Prejudice: How Christian Beliefs Relate to Attitudes toward Homosexuals." *Journal for the Scientific Study of Religion* 48 (1): 146–160.

Geertz, Clifford. 1973. *The Interpretation of Culture*. New York: Basic Books.

Gibson, James L. 2010. "The Political Consequences of Religiosity: Does Religion Always Cause Political Intolerance?" In *Religion and Democracy in the United States: Danger or Opportunity?* edited by Alan Wolfe and Ira Katznelson, 147–175. New York: Russell Sage.

Haidt, Jonathan. 2007. "The New Synthesis in Moral Psychology." *Science* 316:998–1002.

Haidt, Jonathan, and Jesse Graham. 2007. "When Morality Opposes Justice: Conservatives Have Moral Intuitions That Liberals May Not Recognize." *Social Justice Research* 20 (1): 98–116.

Haidt, Jonathan, and Craig Joseph. 2004. "Intuitive Ethics: How Innately Prepared Intuitions Generate Culturally Variable Virtues." *Daedalus* 133 (4): 55–66.

Johnson, Benton. 1963. "On Church and Sect." *American Sociological Review* 28 (4): 539–554.

Kohlberg, Lawrence. 1969. *Stage and Sequence: The Cognitive-Developmental Approach to Socialization*. Chicago: Rand McNally.

Leege, David C. 1988. "Catholics and the Civic Order: Parish Participation, Politics, and Civic Participation." *Review of Politics* 50:704–736.

Leege, David C., and Lyman A. Kellstedt, eds. 1993a. *Rediscovering the Religious Factor in American Politics*. Armonk, NY: M. E. Sharpe.

———. 1993b. "Religious Worldviews and Political Philosophies: Capturing Theory in the Grand Manner through Empirical Data." In *Rediscovering the Religious Factor in American Politics*, edited by David C. Leege and Lyman A. Kellstedt, 216–234. Armonk, NY: M. E. Sharpe.

Leege, David C., and Thomas A. Trozzolo. (1989) 2006. "Religious Values and Parish Participation: The Paradox of Individual Needs in a Communitarian Church." Notre Dame Study of Catholic Parish Life, Report No. 4. Available at https://icl.nd.edu/assets/39489/report4.pdf.

Leege, David C., and Michael R. Welch. 1989. "The Roots of Political Orientations: Examining the Relationship between Religion and Politics among American Catholics." *Journal of Politics* 51 (1): 137–162.

Marcus, George E., John L. Sullivan, Elizabeth Theiss-Morse, and Sandra Wood. 1995. *With Malice toward Some: How People Make Civil Liberties Judgments*. New York: Cambridge University Press.

Mavor, Kenneth I., and Cindy Gallois. 2008. "Social Group and Moral Orientation Factors as Mediators of Religiosity and Multiple Attitude Targets." *Journal for the Scientific Study of Religion* 47 (3): 361–377.

Mockabee, Stephen T., Joseph Quin Monson, and J. Tobin Grant. 2001. "Measuring Religious Commitment among Catholics and Protestants: A New Approach." *Journal for the Scientific Study of Religion* 40 (4): 675–690.

Mockabee, Stephen T., Kenneth D. Wald, and David C. Leege. 2007. *Reexamining Religiosity: A Report on the New Religion Items in the 2006 ANES Pilot Study*. Available at http://www.electionstudies.org/resources/papers/Pilot2006/nes011907.pdf.

———. 2009. "Is There a Religious Left? Evidence from the 2006 and 2008 ANES." Paper presented at the annual meeting of the American Political Science Association, Toronto.

———. 2012. "In Search of a Religious Left: Re-examining Religiosity." In *Improving Public Opinion Surveys: Interdisciplinary Innovation and the American National Election Studies*, edited by John Aldrich and Kathleen M. McGraw, 278–298. Princeton, NJ: Princeton University Press.

Niebuhr, H. Richard. 1951. *Christ and Culture*. New York: Harper.
Shweder, Richard A., Nancy C. Much, Manamohan Mahapatra, and Lawrence Park. 1997. "The 'Big Three' of Morality (Autonomy, Community, and Divinity) and the 'Big Three' Explanations of Suffering." In *Morality and Health*, edited by Allan M. Brandt and Paul Rozin, 119–169. New York: Routledge.
Smidt, Corwin, Lyman A. Kellstedt, and James L. Guth. 2009. "The Role of Religion in American Politics: Explanatory Theories and Associated Analytical and Measurement Issues." In *The Oxford Handbook of Religion and American Politics*, edited by Corwin Smidt, Lyman Kellstedt, and James Guth, 3–42. New York: Oxford University Press.
Sowle Cahill, Lisa. 1994. *Love Your Enemies: Discipleship, Pacifism, and Just War Theory*. Minneapolis, MN: Augsburg Fortress.
Stark, Rodney, and Roger Finke. 2000. *Acts of Faith: Explaining the Human Side of Religion*. Berkeley: University of California Press.
Stark, Rodney, and Charles Y. Glock. 1968. *American Piety: The Nature of Religious Commitment*. Berkeley: University of California Press.
Sullivan, John L., James Piereson, and George E. Marcus. 1982. *Political Tolerance and American Democracy*. Chicago: University of Chicago Press.
Troeltsch, Ernst. 1931. *The Social Teachings of the Christian Churches*. Vol. 1. New York: Macmillan.
Volf, Miroslav. 1996. *Exclusion and Embrace: A Theological Exploration of Identity, Otherness, and Reconciliation*. Nashville, TN: Abingdon Press.
Whitley, Bernard E. 2009. "Religiosity and Attitudes toward Lesbians and Gay Men: A Meta-analysis." *International Journal for the Psychology of Religion* 19 (1): 21–38.
Wuthnow, Robert. 1993. *Christianity in the 21st Century: Reflections on the Challenges Ahead*. New York: Oxford University Press.
Yinger, Milton. 1969. "A Structural Examination of Religion." *Journal for the Scientific Study of Religion* 8 (1): 88–99.

8

Nonreligious Tolerance

American Attitudes toward Atheists, America's Most Unpopular Religious Group

DANIEL COX
ROBERT P. JONES
JUHEM NAVARRO-RIVERA

The rise of Americans with no formal religious identity has been one of the most important demographic developments of the twenty-first century. Although self-identified atheists make up a minority of all religiously unaffiliated Americans, most public opinion surveys find that they now rival the size of other culturally important religious communities, such as Jews.[1] Atheist groups have also become much more visible in recent years, in part by conducting more aggressive public outreach campaigns. Despite these recent developments, atheists remain a relatively small part of the overall population and less organized than established religious communities. Yet in the United States atheists have frequently been maligned, often characterized as immoral or embracing values well outside the mainstream. This chapter seeks to provide a better understanding about the nature of intolerance toward atheists and to identify the sources of intolerant feelings. We also attempt to more fully explore the relationship between negative affect and political tolerance.

In the United States, few groups provoke more animosity than atheists. Even as Americans become increasingly tolerant of a whole range of different behaviors, value systems, and beliefs, atheists remain poorly regarded by wide swaths of the country, and not just among the most religiously devout. In the United States, six states have constitutional provisions that effectively bar nonbelievers from holding public office, although these provisions have not been enforced (Bulger 2012). The Boy Scouts of America, which recently changed its policy banning gay scouts, still denies atheists membership (Winston 2013). Military culture in the United States has evolved with a "God and country" ethos that has made open expressions of nonbelief a risky proposition for atheist soldiers. The Air Force Academy has been the site of ongoing controversy for its mandatory chapel service and fostering an explicitly evangelical Christian atmosphere. A current Marine Corps training document suggests that a potential warning sign indicating whether a marine poses a risk to others is "lack or loss of spiritual faith" (Liebelson 2013).

Americans generally hold negative views of atheists—a pattern that has been surprisingly stable since at least the mid-twentieth century. Recent surveys have shown that atheists continue to rank toward the bottom of affinity scales among most social and religious groups in the United States. On a feeling thermometer scale, which allows respondents to rank different groups from 0 to 100 where 0 represents cold feelings and 100 represents warm feelings, a majority (51 percent) of the public express a negative view of atheists, ranking them from 0 to 49. Thirty-seven percent of the public holds generally favorable views (51–100), and 10 percent express a neutral opinion (50). No other group, with the exception of Muslims, engenders such strong negative sentiment.[2]

Americans also generally believe that atheists are a negative social influence. The public is four times more likely to say that atheists are changing American society for the worse than it is to say they are changing it for the better (39 percent versus 10 percent). In contrast, fewer than three in ten Americans believe that Muslims (27 percent) or gay and lesbian people (29 percent) are changing the United States for the worse.[3]

Americans are also reluctant to support atheist candidates for public office. In 1958, only 18 percent of Americans reported they would vote for "a generally well-qualified" atheist for president. That same year, 54 percent of the public said they would vote for a woman, 63 percent said they would vote for someone who is Jewish, and two-thirds (67 percent) reported that they would be willing to support a Catholic for president—two years before John F. Kennedy became the first Catholic president.[4] By the end of the twentieth century, more than nine in ten Americans reported that they would support a well-qualified female, Catholic, or Jewish candidate for president, but less than half (49 percent) indicated that they would support a well-qualified atheist for president. As Figure 8.1 shows, while Americans are increasingly more likely to cast a ballot for an atheist today than in the past, the changes have been tepid when compared to willingness to vote for candidates from other groups. Currently, only 54 percent of the public say they would vote for an atheist presidential candidate.[5]

Reflecting these findings, a recent survey showed that two-thirds (67 percent) of Americans reported that they are somewhat or very uncomfortable with an atheist serving as president of the United States. Less than one-third (31 percent) reported that they would be comfortable with an atheist president. In comparison, a majority of Americans say they would be comfortable with an evangelical Christian or a Mormon serving as president. Americans expressed similar levels of discomfort with the idea of a Muslim president, with more than six in ten (63 percent) reporting that this would make them uncomfortable and 33 percent reporting they would be comfortable with a Muslim president.[6]

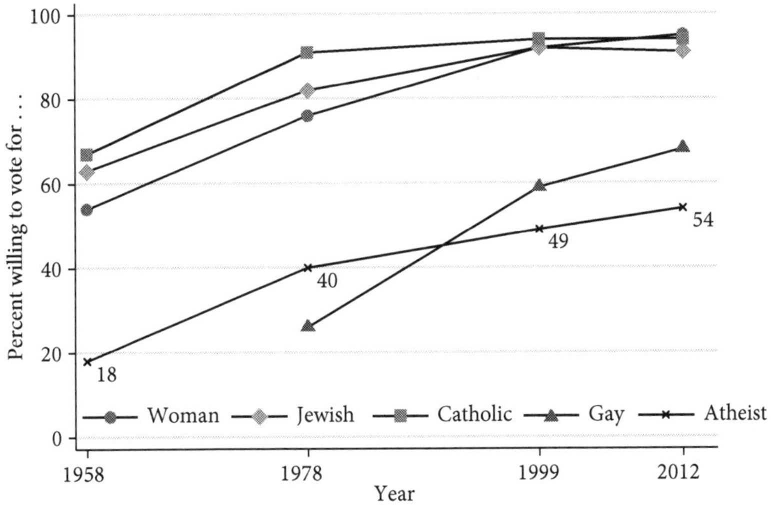

Figure 8.1 Willingness to support candidates from various groups for president
Source: Gallup surveys, 1958–2012.

Despite the persistence of discriminatory practices and the low regard in which atheists are generally held, it is notable that relatively few Americans believe that atheists face significant discrimination in society, particularly when compared to other minority groups. Fewer than one-third (31 percent) of Americans believe that atheists face a lot of discrimination in the United States. On the other hand, at least twice as many Americans believe gay and lesbian people (68 percent) and Muslims (65 percent) face a lot of discrimination in society. Not surprisingly, Americans who self-identify as atheist are more likely to believe that atheists experience significant discrimination in the United States today. Nearly half (49 percent) of Americans who identify as either atheist or agnostic believe that atheists face a lot of discrimination.[7]

Atheists versus Nonreligious People

As recent research has shown, despite being the most visible representatives of the religiously unaffiliated, atheists actually make up only a minority of the growing group of religious "nones." A 2012 study conducted by the Public Religion Research Institute found that the religiously unaffiliated include three different subgroups: unattached believers, seculars, and atheists and agnostics (Jones, Cox, and Navarro-Rivera 2012). At 29 percent, atheists account for a minority of all unaffiliated Americans. Moreover, atheists differ from other Americans who make up the unaffiliated both demographically and religiously.[8] They are more likely to be white and male, tend to be more highly educated, and have sharply different views about religion and its role in public life.

Given the unique profile of atheists and the more visible place they occupy in American public life, it is perhaps not surprising that they are viewed differently from Americans who express no religious preference. Whereas a majority of the public holds an overall negative impression of atheists, only 29 percent express negative views about nonreligious people, and 51 percent hold generally positive feelings about this group. Americans are also less likely to believe that nonreligious people versus atheists are changing society for the worse (31 percent versus 39 percent), although here the differences are more modest.[9]

Beyond Protestant, Catholic, Jew: Atheists in an Increasingly Pluralistic America

In the mid-twentieth century, sociologist Will Herberg ([1955] 1983) summarized the American religious landscape with the phrase "Protestant, Catholic, Jew." In the second half of the twentieth century, religious diversity in the United States has grown well beyond these boundaries (Eck 2001). In part, the new pattern of immigration was the result of the passage of the 1965 Immigration and Nationality Act, which overturned restrictive measures enacted several decades earlier. José Casanova (2007) notes that unlike previous waves of immigrants who came primarily from western Europe, the new immigrants were mostly coming from the Americas and Asia. The most recent wave of immigrants differed racially, ethnically, culturally, linguistically, and religiously in a way that set them apart from their European predecessors. These differences affected the religious landscape in the United States in two important ways. First, non-European Christians, who constituted the majority of these new immigrants, have been remaking American Christianity. For instance, American Catholics, once primarily European, increasingly hail from Latin America and Asia, bringing different cultural perspectives with them (Warner 1997). Second, and perhaps more importantly, many of the newcomers were not part of a Judeo-Christian faith tradition. As Casanova notes, "The most striking new development with extraordinary potential repercussions, both national and global, is the arrival of increasing numbers of Muslims, Hindus, and Buddhists" (2007: 71).

Although non-Christian immigrants like Buddhists, Hindus, and Muslims remain small in actual numbers, they are having a significant influence on American culture as they are increasingly integrated into American society. Despite their different cultural heritage, most of these immigrants "are middle class, college-educated professionals who live in the same kinds of neighborhoods as other Americans, send their children to the same schools, vote in the same elections, shop at the same stores, and watch the same programs on television" (Wuthnow 2005: 37). A recent survey of American Muslims supports this assessment (Pew Research Center 2007). Robert Putnam and David Campbell note similarly that religious segregation and ghettoization is occurring with less frequency than in the past: "Rather than cocooning into isolated religious communities, Americans have become increasingly likely to work with, live alongside, and marry people of other religions" (2010: 10).

Rising religious diversity in the United States has led to a reimagining and a broadening of American identity to include members of other religious traditions. However, even as the notion of what counts as American has changed, it remains deeply connected to a belief in God. This integration of pluralism and theism was articulated by Rick Warren, part of a new generation of evangelical pastors, who recently stated, "I think God likes variety. There's value in that. We should enjoy our differences" (quoted in Djupe and Calfano 2013: 768). Despite these fundamental changes in how Americans approach their religious identity and how they relate to other faiths over the last century, theistic belief has remained remarkably stable. Over the last sixty years, Gallup has found that belief in God has never slipped below nine in ten. In 1944, the first year Gallup measured belief in God among the public, 96 percent responded affirmatively. In 2011, 92 percent reported belief in God.

Emerging Fault Lines: Religious versus Nonreligious Americans

There are at least three reasons why rising religious pluralism in the United States has not translated into widespread acceptance of atheists. First, increasing acceptance and incorporation of new religious communities does not necessarily translate into broader acceptance of nonreligious people. In fact, broader acceptance of religious differences might actually serve to draw brighter lines between the religious and the nonreligious (Edgell, Gerteis, and Hartmann 2006). The preference for religious beliefs, regardless of type, was perhaps most bluntly expressed by President Dwight Eisenhower, who claimed, "Our form of government has no sense unless it is founded in a deeply-felt religious faith, and I don't care what it is. With us, of course, it is the Judeo-Christian concept, but it must be a religion with 'all men are created equal'" (quoted in Schultz 2011: 73).

These views are still present in distinctions Americans make today. For example, about two-thirds (66 percent) of Americans say it is important for a candidate for president to have strong religious beliefs,[10] but only 42 percent say it is important that a candidate shares their particular religious beliefs.[11] Moreover, 48 percent of Americans deem belief in God necessary to be moral and have good values.[12] Thus, while Americans appear more open to a variety of different religious beliefs, the acknowledgment of some type of religious belief is still an important cultural signifier.

Second, the rise of the New Atheist movement, with its growing assertive public face, is providing more occasions for open conflict between religious and nonreligious Americans. Although it lacks a centralized structure or organizing principle, the movement, which includes prominent atheist writers and secular organizations, is adopting a much more assertive position in defense of secularism and nonbelief. Atheist thought-leaders such as Richard Dawkins, author of *The God Delusion* (2006), and Christopher Hitchens, author of *God Is Not Great* (2007), have staked out uncompromising and often combative positions toward religion and religious people. Atheist and secular organizations are also making a more concerted effort to attract nonbelievers and to change public perceptions of atheists. In 2009, the New York Chapter of the Coalition of Reason launched a public campaign by running banners on city buses that read, "A million New Yorkers are good without God. Are you?" (Lee 2009). Meanwhile, on college campuses, secular student groups have witnessed dramatic growth over the last decade. According to the Secular Student Alliance, an organization that aims to "organize and empower nonreligious students around the country," the number of student affiliate groups on college campuses has increased from 42 in 2003 to more than 300 in 2011 (Boorstein 2011).

A final reason why growing religious pluralism might not necessarily mitigate negative feelings about atheists is that many atheists are not "out of the closet," something that prevents more Americans from knowing that they have atheists in their social circles. In part, this is a result of atheists refusing to identify as such for fear of experiencing social isolation or mistreatment. In a recent article, Peter Foster details the challenges faced by young atheists in rural Virginia. One young atheist summarized his experience as follows:

> A lot of my friends have difficulty talking publicly about their atheism because there is a lot of societal pressure against atheists. They have the risk of losing their friends, they have the risk of being kicked out of the house by their family and when your biggest social group is the church, the instant you come out as atheist you lose all of that. Certainly most Christians will accommodate your beliefs, but there is a big aspect of the community that you're no longer involved in. (Quoted in Foster 2014)

Previous work has shown that the development of interpersonal relationships is key to increasing religious tolerance and understanding (Allport 1954). More recently, in *American Grace* Robert Putnam and David Campbell (2010) find that as Americans' religious networks become more diverse to include members of other religious groups, feelings toward these groups become warmer. Putnam and Campbell argue that it is only because so many "Americans are intimately acquainted with people of other faiths" that intense religious devotion and significant religious diversity do not lead to mass interreligious conflict in society (526). With regard to atheists, however, this dynamic will continue to be hampered to the extent that atheists feel considerable social stigma attached to their identity, and to the extent that social contact includes mostly disagreeable discussions. Recent evidence suggests that social interaction between groups with fundamental disagreements can actually increase group insularity and heighten feelings of otherness (Djupe and Calfano 2012).

The Relationship between Religion and Intolerance

The earliest studies of political tolerance found that religious behavior and affiliation were important determinants of intolerant attitudes (Stouffer 1955). Stouffer concluded that lower levels of religious attendance were associated with increased levels of tolerance, and that Protestants exhibited more intolerant attitudes than either Catholics or Jews. Subsequent work built on Stouffer's classic study to include more sophisticated measures of religious affiliation, such as denominational identity (Beatty and Walter 1984; Smidt and Penning 1982; Wilcox and Jelen 1990) and doctrinal belief (Nunn, Crockett, and Williams 1978), but these studies largely came to the same conclusions—commitment to religion and orthodox beliefs are negatively correlated with politically tolerant attitudes (but see Eisenstein 2006).

The rise of the Christian Right in the late 1970s and the strident rhetoric employed by some conservative Christian leaders led many commentators to worry that religious-based intolerance was increasing. Scholars have noted that certain religious traditions might be more prone to intolerant behavior. If religious groups consider their beliefs to be based on inerrant sacred texts, for example, they often see little room for compromise. To the extent that conservative Christians believe that the behavior of some social or religious groups challenges deeply held religious ideals or undermines traditional notions of American society, they are unlikely to exhibit tolerant attitudes. Further, intolerance among these communities may be exacerbated by lack of exposure to differing viewpoints, the result of insular social networks (Green et al. 1994; Wilcox and Jelen 1990).

Measuring Tolerance toward Atheists: A New Approach

In measuring political tolerance, this analysis differs from previous work in how it treats those with favorable or ambivalent views of atheists. Unlike previous scholarship (Sullivan, Piereson, and Marcus 1979) that operationalized tolerance by first identifying groups toward which Americans feel negatively, this analysis is not limited only to respondents who report negative feelings about atheists. There are both theoretical and practical grounds for not removing those who report positive or neutral views. First, we argue that affect—the degree to which Americans like or dislike atheists—and disagreement, on which tolerance is theoretically predicated, are different concepts. Second, measuring group affect based on self-reports with live interviewers is subject to considerable measurement error because of social desirability effects. Previous research has demonstrated that public opinion surveys consistently underestimate the extent of negative feelings Americans have about social, political, and religious groups (Hartman, Newman, and Bell 2014). For these reasons, those with neutral or even positive self-reported views of atheists are included in the analysis. The only group excluded from the analysis below was self-identified atheists themselves.

Extending the work of John Sullivan, James Piereson, and George Marcus (1979), the current study introduces four measures of political tolerance that include fundamental civil liberties such as freedom of expression and assembly, as well as more general opportunities to participate in both the political process and civil society. Importantly, many of these measures focus on providing opportunities for atheists to engage in persuasion activities and to compete for cultural and political influence, ideas at the heart of democratic theory (Dahl 1971). Unlike other measures of tolerance, such as those found in the General Social Survey that treat the concept dichotomously, these measures provide a fuller range of opinion. Each statement includes four response options, ranging from completely agree to completely disagree, allowing us to measure the strength of agreement for each item. Further, tolerance statements explicitly identified atheists as the subject, who were defined as "people who do not believe in God." This approach also differs from the General Social Survey, which asks about people who are "against all religion," which is a less clearly defined group.

The items were included in a short battery as part of a follow-up to the Public Religion Research Institute's 2013 American Values Survey, which was conducted among a nationally representative random sample of 2,317 adults (age eighteen and up) living in the United States and who are part of GfK's Knowledge Panel. The follow-up survey was conducted among a subset of 1,839 respondents from the original survey, representing a 79 percent recontact rate. Interviews were conducted online and completed in both English and Spanish.

The Impact of Belief, Belonging, and Behavior

In general, Americans' disposition toward atheists is marked more by tolerance than intolerance, although a significant minority of the public display intolerant feelings on all measures—see Table 8.1. More than six in ten Americans agree that atheists should be allowed to teach in public schools (63 percent) and should be allowed to hold public rallies (61 percent). Nearly two-thirds (64 percent) reject the idea that atheists should be banned from becoming president of the United States. By contrast, however, half (51 percent) of Americans say atheists should be banned from putting up displays about their beliefs on public property, compared to 47 percent who disagree.

There are notable divisions between different religious traditions, although two traditions stand out for their intolerant dispositions. White evangelical Protestants and black Protestants demonstrate the most intolerant feelings about atheists. Nearly half of white evangelical Protestants (46 percent) and black Protestants (46 percent) believe atheists should be banned from serving as president. Six in ten (60 percent) white evangelical Protestants and nearly seven in ten (69 percent) black Protestants believe atheists should not be allowed to put up public displays celebrating their beliefs. Nearly six in ten black Protestants say that atheists should be banned both from holding public rallies

TABLE 8.1 INTOLERANCE TOWARD ATHEISTS BY RELIGIOUS AFFILIATION, RELIGIOUS BELIEF, AND RELIGIOUS BEHAVIOR AMONG AMERICANS WHO DO NOT SELF-IDENTIFY AS ATHEIST

	Atheists Should Be Banned from Becoming President (%)	*Atheists Should Not Be Allowed to Teach in Public Schools (%)*	*Atheists Should Not Be Allowed to Put Up Public Displays (%)*	*Atheists Should Not Be Allowed to Hold Rallies (%)*
All Americans[a]	34	36	51	37
Religious Affiliation				
White evangelical Protestant	46	48	60	43
White mainline Protestant	37	30	51	34
Black Protestant	46	57	69	57
Catholic	34	38	54	41
Non-Christian religions	19	25	37	21
Unaffiliated	10	17	29	18
View of Scripture				
Bible is literal word of God	55	57	60	55
Bible is book written by men	12	19	37	20
Frequency of Worship				
Attend weekly or more	41	46	59	45
Attend seldom or never	24	27	42	29

Source: Public Religion Research Institute, American Values Survey, 2014 Supplement, March 2014.
[a]Excluding self-identified atheists.

(57 percent) and from teaching in public schools (57 percent). Not surprisingly, non-atheist, religiously unaffiliated Americans demonstrate the lowest feelings of intolerance, followed by members of non-Christian religions such as Judaism, Islam, and Hinduism.

Views about scripture—a measure of conservative doctrinal orthodoxy—appear to be even more strongly related to intolerance. Majorities of Americans who hold a literal view of the Bible agree that atheists should be banned from every activity measure: putting up public displays celebrating their beliefs (60 percent), becoming president (55 percent), teaching in public schools (57 percent), and holding public rallies (55 percent). Conversely, Americans who believe that the Bible is a book written by men and not the word of God exhibit much lower levels of intolerance. Only 12 percent would support banning atheists from serving as president, although it is notable that 37 percent of even this group support banning atheists from putting up public displays celebrating their beliefs.

Religious behavior is also associated with increased feelings of intolerance toward atheists, although the relationship is somewhat weaker than with views of scripture. Forty-one percent of Americans who attend religious services weekly or more often say atheists should be banned from becoming president, while 46 percent would ban them from teaching in public schools and 45 percent would not allow them to hold public rallies. Among Americans who report attending religious services seldom or never, levels of intolerance are much lower. Roughly one-quarter would support banning atheists from serving as president (24 percent), and 29 percent would not allow them to hold public rallies.

Discussion: The Atheist Tolerance Scale

To provide a more composite measure of tolerance, all four political tolerance measures were combined using an additive scale. The 13-point scale (scores ranged from 4 to 16) was collapsed into four discrete categories: very tolerant (4–6), mostly tolerant (7–9), mostly intolerant (10–12), and very intolerant (13–16). All four tolerance measures are highly correlated, suggesting that they are suitable candidates to create a scale. A reliability analysis for the scale produced a Cronbach's alpha score of .79.

The overall portrait provided by the scale reinforces the analysis of the individual questions above. As we show in Table 8.2, a majority of Americans express either very tolerant (23 percent) or mostly tolerant (31 percent) attitudes toward atheists. However, nearly half of Americans hold intolerant views of atheists, including 29 percent who hold mostly intolerant views and 18 percent who hold very intolerant views. As above, religious identity, behavior, and beliefs are strongly associated with tolerance toward atheists as measured by the composite scale.

There are striking differences in levels of tolerance toward atheists by religious affiliation, religious attendance levels, and beliefs about the Bible. White evangelical Protestants and black Protestants report among the lowest levels of tolerance toward atheists (41 percent and 32 percent hold mostly or very tolerant views, respectively). At the other end of the spectrum, religiously unaffiliated Americans rank as the most tolerant religious group, with 80 percent holding very or mostly tolerant views. There is a notable gap between Americans who attend religious services often and those who attend rarely or not at all. Forty-four percent of those who attend worship services at least weekly hold tolerant attitudes toward atheists, compared to 64 percent of those who report attending services seldom or never. There is an even larger tolerance gap evident between those who adhere to literalist interpretations of scripture and those who do not. Only one-third (33 percent) of Americans who believe the Bible is the literal word of God hold tolerant views toward atheists; in stark contrast, 77 percent of those who believe it is a book written by men and not the word of God hold tolerant views toward atheists.

Additionally, there are notable differences in tolerance toward atheists by political ideology, educational attainment, region, and age. Americans of different political stripes express very distinct views of atheists. Sixty-eight percent

TABLE 8.2 ATHEIST TOLERANCE SCALE AMONG AMERICANS WHO DO NOT SELF-IDENTIFY AS ATHEIST

	Very Tolerant	*Mostly Tolerant*	*Mostly Intolerant*	*Very Intolerant*
All Americans[a]	23	31	29	18
Religious Affiliation				
White evangelical	12	29	31	28
White mainline	25	31	27	16
Black Protestant	5	27	38	30
Catholic	16	33	35	16
Unaffiliated	55	25	15	5
Non-Christian	35	34	24	8
Frequency of Worship				
Attend weekly+	14	30	33	23
Attend seldom/never	34	30	25	11
View of Scripture				
Bible is literal word of God	6	27	33	34
Bible was written by men	47	30	18	5
Political Affiliation				
Liberal	41	27	23	8
Conservative	15	28	31	26
Age Group				
18–29	33	23	30	14
65+	14	30	36	19
Education				
College	37	33	21	10
High school or less	13	25	36	26
View of Atheists				
Positive	42	31	20	6
Neutral	38	35	23	4
Negative	10	27	34	29

Note: Feelings toward atheists were measured using a feeling thermometer scale (0–100). Respondents who rated atheists from 0 to 49 were defined as having a negative view of atheists, those who scored them at 50 were identified as having a neutral view, and those who rated them from 51 to 100 were defined as having a positive view.

[a]Excluding self-identified atheists.

of liberals hold very tolerant or somewhat tolerant attitudes toward atheists, compared to only 43 percent of conservatives. The education gap is similarly large. Seven in ten (70 percent) Americans with a college degree hold somewhat or very tolerant views toward atheists, compared to only 38 percent of those with a high school education or less. Southerners also exhibit lower levels of tolerance toward atheists than Americans living in any other region of the country, but particularly compared to Americans living in the western United States (45 percent versus 65 percent hold somewhat or very tolerant attitudes toward atheists; regional results are not shown in Table 8.2). Young adults (age 18–29) are significantly more likely than seniors (age 65 and older) to hold tolerant views of atheists (56 percent versus 44 percent).

The Relationship between Affect and Tolerance

Americans' affective disposition toward atheists—the degree of warm or cold feeling—is also strongly associated with feelings of tolerance. The atheist tolerance scale and atheist feeling thermometer scale are positively correlated ($r = .52$),[13] indicating that the more favorable the disposition Americans exhibit toward atheists, the greater their propensity to express tolerance toward atheists.

Americans who view atheists positively express higher levels of tolerance toward atheists than those who do not, but a significant number hold intolerant views. Nearly three-quarters (73 percent) of Americans who rate atheists favorably—defined as those scoring the group between 51 and 100 on a feeling thermometer scale—have generally tolerant views. But only 42 percent express very tolerant views, and more than one-quarter (26 percent) of Americans who have warm feelings about atheists nonetheless hold somewhat or very intolerant attitudes toward atheists. Americans who express neutral views closely resemble those who view atheists positively, with 73 percent expressing generally tolerant views and 27 percent expressing generally intolerant views. In contrast, nearly two-thirds (63 percent) of Americans who view atheists negatively report intolerant attitudes, but only 29 percent express very intolerant attitudes.

Predictors of Intolerance

To sort out the role that affect plays in structuring attitudes toward atheists, two models were constructed: a basic model that excluded affective disposition toward atheists and another that included it as an independent control variable. Both models included a range of other important characteristics as controls, such as evangelical Protestant affiliation, view of scripture, frequency of worship attendance, and other demographic and political variables.

In the basic model in Table 8.3, which excluded a measure of affect, religious characteristics were strongly associated with intolerant views toward atheists, but not all religious factors were equally influential. Identifying as an evangelical Protestant and Catholic were the strongest predictors of embracing intolerant attitudes. Both evangelical Protestants and Catholics are approximately three times more likely than religiously unaffiliated Americans to express intolerance toward atheists. Biblical literalists are 1.7 times as likely as non–biblical literalists to hold intolerant views of atheists. When controlling for religious identity and biblical literalism, frequency of worship attendance has no significant effect on expressing intolerant views of atheists.

Age, gender, and educational attainment are also predictors of holding intolerant views of atheists. Seniors (those age 65 or older) are more likely than

TABLE 8.3 LOGISTIC REGRESSION PREDICTING INTOLERANT VIEWS OF ATHEISTS

	Basic Model		*Affect Model*	
	β	*p*	*β*	*p*
Evangelical Protestant	1.17	.00	.93	.00
Non-Christian religious	.74	.00	.29	.32
Catholic	1.11	.00	.83	.00
Other Christian	.99	.00	.67	.00
Biblical literalist	.55	.00	.41	.01
Attend weekly or more	.11	.42	−.03	.86
Female	.21	.05	.32	.01
Black	.86	.00	.51	.02
Latino	.60	.00	.26	.21
Liberal	−.41	.01	−.23	.19
Conservative	.42	.00	.16	.29
Young adult (age 18–29)	.07	.66	.12	.51
Senior (age 65+)	.34	.02	.44	.01
College graduate	−.38	.01	−.39	.02
High school education	.74	.00	.69	.00
Southerner	.22	.06	.18	.19
Negative view of atheists	—		1.13	.00
Constant	−1.96	.00	−2.10	.00
N	1,788		1,382	

Source: Public Religion Research Institute, American Values Survey Supplement, 2013.
Note: Other Christian category includes mainline Protestants, Mormons, and Orthodox Christians.

younger Americans to hold intolerant views of atheists. Women hold more intolerant views toward atheists than men, even after controlling for a number of different religious characteristics. Educational attainment has a strong relationship to intolerant attitudes toward atheists. In fact, after religious affiliation and race (black), no single characteristic more strongly predicts holding intolerant attitudes toward atheists than educational attainment. Americans with a high school education or less are more than twice as likely as those with at least some college education to have intolerant attitudes toward atheists. Being politically liberal predicts more tolerant views toward atheists, while being conservative predicts greater intolerance.

Consistent with the descriptive analyses, the second model demonstrates that affective disposition has a significant effect on expressions of intolerance. Compared to those with positive or ambivalent feelings, Americans with negative feelings toward atheists are three times more likely to exhibit intolerance. Although affect remains the strongest predictor when included in the model, the effect size is only slightly greater than religious affiliation, specifically identifying as evangelical Protestants. Even after controlling for affect, evangelical Protestants are much more likely to demonstrate intolerance than other religious groups, particularly the religiously unaffiliated. White evangelical Protestants are about two and a half times more likely to express intolerance toward atheists than the unaffiliated. In fact, controlling for affect had only a modest mitigating effect on the strength of evangelical Protestant identity. Having a literal view of scripture also remained a significant predictor of intolerance, although the predictive power declined somewhat after controlling for affect.

Several characteristics that were significant in the first model were no longer significant in the second model once a control was introduced for affect. Ethnicity (identifying as Latino), which had a modest influence on intolerance, is not a significant predictor in the second model. Similarly, political ideology—identifying as conservative or liberal—is no longer a significant predictor of intolerance when controlling for feelings toward atheists.

Three characteristics stand out in this analysis: education, gender, and age. The effect of education was constant across both models, indicating that the way in which education influences intolerance is independent from overall views of atheists. Gender, which had a modest effect in the first model, exhibited a more substantial effect in the second model, indicating that factors beyond affect play a stronger role among women than among men. While the inclusion of affective orientation in the model reduces the effect size for nearly every measure, it actually increases the effect size of gender. This might suggest that for older Americans and for women, intolerance is not rooted in negative feelings toward atheists. Given that women demonstrate much higher levels of religious commitment than men and tend to have stronger ties to religious institutions,[14] perhaps women are more concerned about the effect atheists are having on society. The pattern was similar for older Americans, for whom controlling for affective disposition actually increased the size of the effect. Older Americans also retain closer connections to religious institutions than younger Americans and are more heavily invested in the current religious order, thus making the specter of increasing atheist influence on society more salient to them.

Conclusion

These findings suggest that expressions of intolerance by religious Americans are not entirely—or even primarily—driven by negative feelings about atheists. Evangelical Protestants and Catholics exhibit intolerant attitudes that cannot be fully explained by their levels of antipathy toward atheists. Rather these results may reflect two new features of the American religious landscape: the emergence of a more organized secular coalition that is actively seeking converts and challenging the historically hegemonic position of established religious communities, and the rise of religious disaffiliation, particularly among young adults. If religious groups in the United States believe that atheists are actively and successfully promoting nonbelief and disaffiliation from traditional religious groups, it is not difficult to understand why established religious communities might want to limit the political freedoms of atheists. Moreover, this sentiment may be somewhat independent from feelings about atheists.

That the effect of education level operates independently from feelings about atheists suggests that college experience might serve to mitigate feelings of threat by exposing graduates to atheists or secular viewpoints. A college education might also serve to emphasize the importance of the free expression of ideas, particularly of minority viewpoints, in a democratic society. This would mean that education level has a positive effect on tolerance generally and tolerance of atheists in particular.

Although we might expect conservatives to adopt more intolerant positions when it comes to atheists, after controlling for feelings toward atheists and religious characteristics, conservatives do not demonstrate greater intolerance than political moderates or liberals. Similarly, liberals are not any more likely to exhibit tolerant attitudes once feelings about atheists are included in the model. Political ideology only influences tolerance indirectly by influencing affective views of atheists, which then structure tolerance. This suggests that intolerance of atheists is less about prevailing political differences than a conflict over the basic conception of American culture. For instance, two-thirds (67 percent) of white evangelical Protestants believe that atheists are changing American culture and way of life for the worse.[15] This view has also been a common refrain among some prominent conservative Christian leaders. Pat Robertson, founder and host of the *700 Club*, warned in his show that the United States is under assault by "militant atheists, secularists, those who want to destroy all of the fabric of faith in our society" (2014).

Finally, these results also suggest that intolerance toward atheists will likely decrease over time. The two factors most strongly related to holding intolerant views, lower education levels and a belief in biblical literalism, are represented at higher levels among older Americans than among younger Americans. The higher levels of educational attainment and lower levels of religious affiliation associated with the millennial generation, for example, dampen intolerant attitudes.

The current study also makes a contribution to the conceptualization of tolerance, particularly with regard to how affect and disagreement are measured and operationalized. Central to the concept of tolerance is the belief that members of every group in society—particularly those who challenge the values or influence of others—should be allowed the same opportunities to participate in public life and compete for influence in the public square. Tolerance has been traditionally understood as a willingness to afford the same basic freedoms and rights to all members of society, especially to those who espouse beliefs or engage in activities that others find disagreeable. Sullivan, Piereson, and Marcus define tolerance as a "willingness to 'put up with' those things that one rejects. Politically it implies a willingness to permit the expression of those ideas or interests that one opposes" (1979: 784). The crucial component of tolerance is not the degree to which groups are disliked but the existence of a fundamental disagreement between them.

These results confirm the distinction between affect and disagreement. Atheists are among the least-liked religious groups in the United States, but tolerance for atheists is not confined only to those who view them negatively. More than one-quarter (27 percent) of Americans who hold neutral or positive views demonstrate at least somewhat intolerant views of atheists. Affect is a powerful predictor of political tolerance of atheists, but it is only one among many factors. The perception that atheists aim to fundamentally alter American culture, in a way that is hostile to the values of religious Americans, also likely fuels feelings of intolerance among certain religious communities.

Future work in tolerance should understand the limitations of using affect as part of a measurement scheme to define target groups by identifying those with whom the respondent expresses the greatest disagreement or, alternatively, the group whose values or beliefs are most diametrically opposed. This type of measure has the benefit of being conceptually closer to the idea of tolerance and is likely to induce less measurement error attributable to social desirability effects. It is probably easier to report to a stranger that you have a significant disagreement with another social, political, or religious group than to say that you simply do not like any member of this group.

Notes

1. Most surveys find that self-identified atheists make up roughly 2–3 percent of the adult population.
2. Public Religion Research Institute, American Values Survey, October 2013, http://publicreligion.org/research/2013/10/2013-american-values-survey/.
3. Public Religion Research Institute, Religion, Values and Immigration Reform Survey, March 2013, http://publicreligion.org/research/2013/03/2013-religion-values-immigration-survey/.
4. Gallup Poll, September 1958.
5. Gallup Poll, June 2012.
6. Public Religion Research Institute, American Values Survey, November 2011, http://publicreligion.org/research/2011/11/2011-american-values-survey/.
7. Public Religion Research Institute, LGBT Issues and Trends Survey, February 2014, http://publicreligion.org/research/2014/02/2014-lgbt-survey/.
8. Public Religion Research Institute, American Values Survey, October 2013.
9. Public Religion Research Institute, Religion, Values and Immigration Reform Survey, March 2013, http://publicreligion.org/research/2013/03/2013-religion-values-immigration-survey/.
10. Public Religion Research Institute, American Values Survey, November 2011, http://publicreligion.org/research/2011/11/2011-american-values-survey/.
11. Public Religion Research Institute, PRRI/RNS Religion News Survey, May 2012, http://publicreligion.org/research/2012/05/may-rns-2012-research/.
12. Public Religion Research Institute, American Values Survey, October 2013, http://publicreligion.org/research/2013/10/2013-american-values-survey/.
13. The correlation score was computed between the feeling thermometer scale (0–100) and the original tolerance scale (4–16), in which a score of 4 indicated the most tolerant position and 16 indicated the most intolerant position.
14. According to a Gallup survey (June 2012), 65 percent of women report being a member of a church, synagogue, or mosque, compared to 53 percent of men.

15. Public Religion Research Institute, Religion, Values and Immigration Reform Survey, March 2013, http://publicreligion.org/research/2013/03/2013-religion-values-immigration-survey/.

References

Allport, Gordon W. 1954. *The Nature of Prejudice*. Cambridge, MA: Addison-Wesley.

Beatty, Kathleen M., and Oliver Walter. 1984. "Religious Preference and Practice: Reevaluating Their Impact on Political Tolerance." *Public Opinion Quarterly* 48 (1B): 318–329.

Boorstein, Michelle. 2011. "Delving into the Study of Secularism." *Washington Post*, December 17. Available at http://www.highbeam.com/doc/1P2-30333841.html.

Bulger, Matthew. 2012. "Unelectable Atheists: U.S. States That Prohibit Godless Americans from Holding Public Office." *Humanist Network News*, May. Available at http://americanhumanist.org/HNN/details/2012-05-unelectable-atheists-us-states-that-prohibit-godless.

Casanova, José. 2007. "Immigration and the New Religious Pluralism: A European/United States Comparison." In *Democracy and the New Religious Pluralism*, edited by Thomas Banchoff, 59–84. New York: Oxford University Press.

Dahl, Robert. 1971. *Polyarchy: Participation and Opposition*. New Haven, CT: Yale University Press.

Dawkins, Richard. 2006. *The God Delusion*. Boston: Houghton Mifflin.

Djupe, Paul A., and Brian R. Calfano. 2012. "American Muslim Investment in Civil Society Political Discussion, Disagreement, and Tolerance." *Political Research Quarterly* 65 (3): 516–528.

———. 2013. "Religious Value Priming, Threat, and Political Tolerance." *Political Research Quarterly* 66 (4): 767–779.

Eck, Diana L. 2001. *A New Religious America: How a "Christian Country" Has Become the World's Most Religiously Diverse Nation*. New York: HarperCollins.

Edgell, Penny, Joseph Gerteis, and Douglas Hartmann. 2006. "Atheists as 'Other': Moral Boundaries and Cultural Membership in American Society." *American Sociological Review* 71 (2): 211–234.

Eisenstein, Marie A. 2006. "Rethinking the Relationship between Religion and Political Tolerance in the U.S." *Political Behavior* 28 (4): 327–348.

Foster, Peter. 2014. "Is America Losing Faith? Atheism on the Rise but Still in the Shadows." *The Telegraph*, March 25. Available at http://www.telegraph.co.uk/news/worldnews/northamerica/usa/10626076/Is-America-losing-faith-Atheism-on-the-rise-but-still-in-the-shadows.html.

Green, John C., James L. Guth, Lyman A. Kellstedt, and Corwin E. Smidt. 1994. "Uncivil Challenges: Support for Civil Liberties among Religious Activists." *Journal of Political Science* 22:25–49.

Hartman, Todd K., Benjamin J. Newman, and C. Scott Bell. 2014. "Decoding Prejudice toward Hispanics: Group Cues and Public Reactions to Threatening Immigrant Behavior." *Political Behavior* 36 (1): 143–163.

Herberg, Will. (1955) 1983. *Protestant-Catholic-Jew: An Essay in American Religious Sociology*. Chicago: University of Chicago Press.

Hitchens, Christopher. 2007. *God Is Not Great: How Religion Poisons Everything*. New York: Hachette.

Jones, Robert P., Daniel Cox, and Juhem Navarro-Rivera. 2012. *2012 Pre-Election American Values Survey: How Catholics and the Religiously Unaffiliated Will Shape the 2012 Election and Beyond*. Available at http://publicreligion.org/site/wp-content/uploads/2012/10/AVS-2012-Pre-election-Report-for-Web.pdf.

Lee, Jennifer. 2009. "'Good without God,' Atheist Subway Ads Proclaim." *City Room* (blog) *New York Times*, October 19. Available at http://cityroom.blogs.nytimes.com/2009/10/19/good-without-god-atheist-subway-ads-proclaim.

Liebelson, Dana. 2013. "The U.S. Military Has a Problem with Atheists." *The Week*, August 7. Available at http://theweek.com/article/index/247830/the-us-military-has-a-problem-with-atheists.

Nunn, Clyde Z., Harry J. Crockett, Jr., and J. Allen Williams, Jr. 1978. *Tolerance for Nonconformity*. San Francisco: Jossey-Bass.

Pew Research Center. 2007. *Muslim Americans: Middle Class and Mostly Mainstream*. Available at http://www.pewresearch.org/2007/05/22/muslim-americans-middle-class-and-mostly-mainstream/.

Putnam, Robert D., and David E. Campbell. 2010. *American Grace: How Religion Divides and Unites Us*. New York: Simon and Schuster.

Robertson, Pat. 2014. *700 Club*, CBN, April 24. Available at http://www.cbn.com/tv/3503645169001.

Schultz, Kevin M. 2011. *Tri-faith America: How Catholics and Jews Held Postwar America to Its Protestant Promise*. New York: Oxford University Press.

Smidt, Corwin, and James M. Penning. 1982. "Religious Commitment, Political Conservatism, and Political and Social Tolerance in the United States: A Longitudinal Analysis." *Sociological Analysis* 43 (3): 231–246.

Stouffer, Samuel A. 1955. *Communism, Conformity and Civil Liberties: A Cross Section of the Nation Speaks Its Mind*. New York: Doubleday.

Sullivan, John L., James Piereson, and George E. Marcus. 1979. "An Alternative Conceptualization of Political Tolerance: Illusory Increases, 1950s–1970s." *American Political Science Review* 73 (3): 781–794.

Warner, R. Stephen. 1997. "Religion, Boundaries, and Bridges." *Sociology of Religion* 58 (3): 217–238.

Wilcox, Clyde, and Ted G. Jelen. 1990. "Evangelicals and Political Tolerance." *American Politics Quarterly* 18:25–46.

Winston, Kimberly. 2013. "One Scouts Ban Remains Intact: Atheists." *Religion News Service*, May 30. Available at http://www.religionnews.com/2013/05/30/one-scouts-ban-remains-intact-atheists/.

Wuthnow, Robert. 2005. *America and the Challenges of Religious Diversity*. Princeton, NJ: Princeton University Press.

9

The Religious Economy of Political Tolerance

JOBY SCHAFFER
ANAND E. SOKHEY
PAUL A. DJUPE

Since Samuel Stouffer's (1955) pioneering analysis of the American public, much scholarly effort has been spent untangling the causes of intolerant attitudes (for a summary, see Gibson 2006). Within this broader research agenda, a small but important body of literature has sought to explain the religious roots of intolerance. Alongside education, religious variables are some of the most consistent predictors of political intolerance (e.g., Burdette, Ellison, and Hill 2005). Yet achieving a consensus on the conditions and mechanisms that underlie these associations has proven difficult. For instance, the finding that evangelical Protestants tend to be more politically intolerant has been variously attributed to factors such as attendance and salience, dogmatism, and specific beliefs like cosmic conflict and the nature of God (e.g., Beatty and Walter 1984; Eisenstein 2006; Ellison and Musick 1993; Froese, Bader, and Smith 2008; Reimer and Park 2001; Wilcox and Jelen 1990; exceptions include Smith 2000).[1] At their conceptual core, these explanations focus on religion in "vertical" terms—a human's relationship to the divine. Typifying this approach, Paul Froese, Christopher Bader, and Buster Smith note, "The most obvious [explanation of intolerance] supposes that certain religious beliefs lead individuals to diminish the importance of individual freedom in appeasement of a higher religious authority" (2008: 30). In other words, all of these examinations reflect a psychological orientation to the study of religion and politics that is largely grounded in measurements of religiosity (e.g., Kellstedt et al. 1996; Layman 2001; Putnam and Campbell 2010).

In this chapter, we seek to both complement and challenge vertical conceptions of the religious mechanisms driving political intolerance. We do so by advancing a more "horizontal" perspective, invigorating the *social* component of a social-psychological approach (e.g., Djupe and Gilbert 2009; Huckfeldt, Plutzer, and Sprague 1993). This hangs on taking into account more politicized church environments (e.g., Wald, Owen, and Hill 1988) and on capturing how people understand and live out their *religious social values* (Djupe and Calfano 2013a, 2013b)—something we define as people's beliefs about how they should engage with co-religionists and those outside their faith (for related arguments in the context of religious elites, see Djupe and Sokhey 2003). In psychological terms, these values relate to the normative boundaries that people erect between their ingroups and their outgroups. Those who hold *exclusive values* believe that ingroup solidarity is important, and in turn, ingroup solidarity works through antipathy and threat perception to increase levels of political intolerance (Gibson and Gouws 2000). Those who hold *inclusive values* believe that a welcoming orientation toward those who belong to outgroups is important, thereby diminishing hostility toward outgroups and promoting tolerance. Measures gauging inclusive and exclusive values—as well as the level of politicization in congregations—capture important local variation in how people interact with and experience the broader political world.

Our focus derives, in part, from the idea that inclusive and exclusive values are not mutually exclusive (see Finke and Stark 2005). Indeed, everyone holds varying levels of support for each. In different spheres of religious life, exclusivity or inclusivity is more or less privileged. For instance, it may seem rare for a strong believer to marry a nonbeliever or maintain her closest friendships with those of different faiths (in actuality, this is not rare; for a recent examination, see Putnam and Campbell 2010). However, the same person may believe that developing good relationships with nonbelievers is a fundamental component of her religious duty. Our task is to examine the balance between exclusive and inclusive religious social values, to evaluate their respective effects on political tolerance, and to consider whether any such effects hold in the presence of measures tapping the more vertically oriented aspects of religious experience (i.e., attendance and salience).

In doing so, we are able to shed some perspective on why scholars have pitched sometimes diametrically opposing assessments of evangelicals' support for civil liberties (for example, some suggest that evangelicals actually have a strong commitment to liberal ideas like political tolerance—Hunter 1983, 1987; Kraynak 2001; Smith 2000). Focusing on the horizontal aspects of church points to the fact that America's religious economy permits tremendous variance in churches both across and within religious traditions (Stark and Finke 2000). Thus, it is entirely possible that while evangelicals share a common core of beliefs and a strong commitment to making religion central to their lives, these other elements of religious experience differ markedly across congregations.

The rest of the chapter is organized as follows: In the first section, we examine how including the concept of religious social values enhances and clarifies existing explanations that stress religiosity (whether looked at in terms of dogmatism, specific religious beliefs, simple measures of attendance and salience, or a combination of these). In our view, relying exclusively on vertical notions of religion leads scholars to miss other dimensions of religious experience that bear on threat and tolerance judgments. In the second section, we illustrate the merits of our horizontal, values-based explanation, analyzing data from an original study conducted in 2010 in Colorado Springs, Colorado—a city that has been called "a Mecca for Evangelical Christians" (Brady 2005).

Tolerance as a Social Judgment

Political intolerance, at its base, is a social judgment, which is to say that it involves an assessment of whether those with whom one disagrees should be allowed to take actions to advocate their beliefs or interests. As has become customary in the literature, when we refer to political intolerance, we are referring to the willingness to put up with these group-action pairings—for example, should members of the KKK (group) be allowed to teach in public schools (action)?

As a social judgment, political intolerance taps a number of cognitive considerations. Largely sidestepping the issue of affective concerns,[2] the central question in the scholarly literature has focused on the elements making up the deliberative judgment, finding explanatory power in factors such as threat perception, commitments to democratic values, and education. Each force illuminates a different feature of the tolerance evaluation. The primary relevance of threat perception indicates that people consider the costs to both public morality and public safety when assessing a group-action pair, and research that primes people to deliberate indicates that this cost assessment is an overriding concern (Kuklinski et al. 1991). The importance of having a commitment to democratic values suggests that, in addition to assessing the costs of potentially losing their own freedoms (especially those groups in the minority), people recognize the inherent need to allow others the right to voice their interests and opinions. The effect of education suggests that when people are exposed to a broader range of ideas—or possess the ability to engage with alternative ideas (cognitive capacity)—they grow more receptive to those with whom they disagree.

A key theme that emerges when examining different features of the tolerance judgment is that political intolerance is fundamentally about how a person relates to other groups in society (this is the *social* in social judgment). Groups are only threatening when considered in juxtaposition to the goals and identities of one's own group; democratic values are only relevant when a society's pluralism is recognized. Education rescues tolerance when someone is able to put themselves in other people's shoes—that is, to imagine the thought processes of those with whom they disagree. It is no wonder, then, that recent research has begun to apply concepts and theories from intergroup-relations theory to consider why some people develop intolerant attitudes (e.g., Gibson and Gouws 2000, 2003). The key hypothesis follows from a simple piece of logic: Those committed to ingroup solidarity—which often but not always follows from holding a strong identity—are more likely to see higher costs in permitting political acts by their foes (i.e., to have higher threat perception). The social space that separates ingroups from outgroups is thus a crucial feature of the tolerance judgment. When this space is large and clearly demarcated, the potential for political intolerance is high.

Unfortunately, the socially rooted explanation has only marginally entered research on the religious roots of political intolerance; it is worth reiterating that this literature gauges notions of social separation at best indirectly (and at worst, not at all). Clyde Nunn, Harry Crockett, and Allen Williams (1978) yielded the forerunner of a standard religiosity-based explanation—they argued that the rigidity of certain religious beliefs combines with high levels of church involvement (measured by attendance) to produce intolerance. John Sullivan, James Piereson, and George Marcus (1982), the first adopters of the least-liked-group measurement strategy, found that beliefs were less important than simple measures of religiosity. John Green and colleagues (1994) attached varying propensities of separation to specific beliefs—namely, the tendency among conservative Protestants to believe that the world was coming to an end soon (pre-millennialism). Sam Reimer and Jerry Park come closer to a social perspective—they suggest (but do not test) the idea that because of higher levels of attendance, evangelicals are "more likely to have a shared sense of ingroups and outgroups, and maintain a distinctive identity that allows them to draw symbolic boundaries, thus maintaining tension with outgroups" (2001: 743).[3]

The Horizontal Church: Inclusive/Exclusive Religious Social Values and Politicization

At base, we argue that religious social values are the tangible expression of religious intent (see also Djupe and Calfano 2013a). While certain beliefs likely have some degree of reciprocity with religious social values,[4] the latter are largely distinct from the vertical (i.e., religiosity-driven) approaches that are commonplace in the literature. Put differently, while examining *how religious a person is* (i.e., religiosity) matters for tolerance assessments, so does understanding *how a person is religious* (i.e., how a person lives out her faith in the context of her congregation and community). Work on America's religious economy gives reason to pause before imputing a degree of homogeneity in religious experience. While churches within a tradition adhere to a set of shared teachings, there is considerable range in everything from which teachings are stressed, to how congregants relate to each other, to how they relate to the community and broader world (Djupe and Gilbert 2009). In no small part, this diversity reflects the fact that churches from the same tradition often operate in different social circumstances (e.g., urban or rural, heterogeneous or homogeneous religious demographics). The people who attend these churches bring their social and personal experiences (and networks) with them (Djupe, Sokhey, and Gilbert 2007) and expect their religious leaders to address the challenges they face (Djupe and Gilbert 2003).

To reiterate, we draw on the idea of "exclusive" and "inclusive" religious social values. Those who hold exclusive religious social values believe that members of the social group should strive to intermingle with each other and avoid interaction with members of other groups. In contrast, inclusive religious values are similar to Peter Benson and Dorothy Williams's (1982) description of community-centered values. Rather than being internally focused, those who hold inclusive religious values are associated with low ingroup boundaries and are characterized by a welcoming orientation toward members of outgroups.

As a complement to this, we also focus on another horizontal measure—the extent to which a congregation or church context is reported to be political (e.g., Calhoun-Brown 1996; see Djupe and Gilbert [2009] and Djupe and Olson [2007] for discussions).The political church links the religious and the public explicitly; such an organizational environment presents the potential for not only top-down (elite-driven) and bottom-up (network-based) patterns of political communication (e.g., Djupe and Gilbert 2003, 2009) but also requests for mobilization or activity (e.g., Djupe, Sokhey, and Gilbert 2007; Putnam and Campbell 2010; Verba, Schlozman, and Brady 1995) and the abundant provision of ambient information (Wald, Owen, and Hill 1988). We include the political church measure to examine the consequences of conceptualizing religious experience in terms of political commitment. If a congregation sends the message that living one's faith is about engaging in politics, does that condition the relationship between religiosity and tolerance?

Hypotheses

Tying values and the politicization of the church to political intolerance is straightforward. Among those who most highly value ingroup solidarity, antipathy for outgroups is high. As a consequence, the intrinsic value of hearing alternative perspectives is diminished, and more stringent ingroup boundaries expand the set of actions and groups that pose a threat to the ingroup. *Through both channels, ingroup solidarity leads to threat and political intolerance. In contrast, inclusive values are likely to warm feelings and dissipate threat, leading to lower levels of political intolerance.* With respect to the church environment, we expect that more exposure to information and communication—whether from clergy, small groups, social networks, or the context as a whole (Djupe and Gilbert 2009)—should serve to highlight notions of social separation. Accordingly, being in *a more political congregation should increase threat while decreasing tolerance.*

Data and Design: The 2010 Colorado Springs Survey

To examine these hypotheses, we draw on an original mail survey conducted by the authors in El Paso County (Colorado Springs), Colorado, in March 2010. Colorado Springs is home to Christian leaders such as James Dobson and the organization he founded, Focus on the Family, as well as a number of other Christian organizations. Given its evangelical presence and reputation, it is a site well suited for examining the relative contributions of vertical versus horizontal models of religion.

Of course, reflecting the variety associated with America's religious economy, Colorado Springs also contains a rich diversity of church congregational sizes and structures, ranging from megachurches like the New Life Church to small, intimate congregations like the Church at the Springs (which consists of a group of home-based churches). In the end, 247 registered voters completed the survey—descriptively, the sample is in many ways roughly similar to the 2000 census. However, the sample is not representative of the population by race (aside from including some Hispanics), necessitating the use of a collapsed categorical variable for all nonwhite respondents. Another sample characteristic that warrants mention is the higher response rate from older individuals—whereas the 2010 census reported the median adult age of forty-seven years, our sample had a reported age of fifty-four.[5]

In addition to standard demographic questions, we asked respondents to report their religious preference, along with whether they consider themselves to be "born-again or evangelical Christians." Because the survey did not contain measures for denomination or other questions about specific theological beliefs, we use these categorical labels as a proxy for any systematic differences that may stem from different religious traditions. Comparing the self-identifications of the sample to the 2008 American Religious Identification Survey (ARIS) indicates that the distribution is roughly similar to the national distribution. Moreover, the high concentration of "other Christians" is in line with what the ARIS found for cities throughout the West to Midwest (Kosmin and Keysar 2009).[6] Of course, the survey also included batteries tapping tolerance and religious social values; it is to these items that we now turn our attention.

Results

We begin with a brief exploration of typical ways in which religion and tolerance are discussed—that is, as organized by religious tradition, for which we used standard categorizations (e.g., Steensland et al. 2000). Given the central importance of threat in shaping tolerance judgments, we included several items to assess whether there are different dimensions of threat beyond individual and socio-tropic threat. That is, we asked whether the group was threatening to "American values," whether the group was "likely to engage in violent activities," whether the group is a threat to "other people's freedom," and whether the group is "threatening to me personally." An index of all four measures (on a five-point scale from strongly disagree to strongly agree, so more threatening is higher) had a Cronbach's α value of .88, indicating high reliability. The tolerance items were chosen from John Sullivan, James Piereson, and George Marcus's (1982) content-controlled battery, asking about members of the least-liked group giving a speech, teaching, running for office, having their phones tapped, holding public rallies, and placing a book in the library ($\alpha = .92$).

Examining the mean threat and tolerance scores, we observe that *there is essentially no variance across the religious traditions* (results not shown).[7] The sample, almost uniformly across these categories, believes their least-liked group to be threatening and holds a reasonable degree of tolerance for them. This is the intent of the content-controlled approach—to provide equal opportunity for malice. Of course, membership in a religious tradition is correlated with particular religious beliefs and practices, but these results leave open three possibilities. First, variance in the sample can be explained by still unmeasured religious beliefs; second, the variance can be seen as a function of congregational orientations toward the community as seen in their value and political commitments; or third, the variance can be explained by other salient differences that have been identified in the literature (our set of controls).

Following Paul Djupe and Brian Calfano (2013b), we operationalize inclusive and exclusive values starting with the introduction "There are many values that make a person a good person of faith. Think seriously about them, and then please tell us if the following values are important to being a good person of your faith." The statements are:

Inclusive

- To be true to my faith, it is important to "love the stranger as yourself."
- To be true to my faith, it is important to invite others to church even if the church begins to change as a result.

Exclusive

- To be true to my faith, it is important to shop as much as possible at stores owned by other people of my faith.
- To be true to my faith, it is important to keep company with other people of my faith.

Correlations between the items are fairly high, though higher among the exclusive value items ($r = .61$) than the inclusive (.40). It is also interesting to note that there are significant correlations between the two indices (created by averaging the two relevant items, $r = .23$). In accord with Rodney Stark and Roger Finke (2000), our sample suggests that most all congregations are implicated in the religious economy and face an ongoing tension over the right balance of inclusive and exclusive orientations, which results in public expressions of both.

As one would expect, there is more commitment to inclusive values than exclusive ones. The sample averages "agree" with the two inclusive items and "disagree" with the two exclusive items. The balance is a bit different across religious traditions and in the expected ways: First, all traditions espouse a greater commitment to inclusive than exclusive values. Second, evangelicals are more exclusive than other religious tradition members, though not by much. Notably, they also indicate a stronger agreement with inclusive values, which attests to their ascribed label "Evangelical" (results not shown).

Before turning to the multivariate results, we briefly describe our operationalization of the horizontal notion of a "political church." A long line of research—drawn largely from work on black churches—assesses the degree to which a congregation can be deemed "political" (e.g., Calhoun-Brown 1996; McDaniel 2008). These analyses often use a single measure asking whether the congregation has held "political meetings," or whether the clergy have talked about political topics (see Djupe and Gilbert 2009 for a discussion). We follow in this vein, asking, "How politically active is your place of worship?" The responses among those who reported include not at all (28 percent), not very (41 percent), somewhat (24 percent), and very active (7 percent). There are no differences between evangelicals and nonevangelicals in this sample in reporting the politicization of their church—both average just above "not very," and about 30 percent of both groups report a somewhat or very active political church. For purposes of analysis, we append to this 1–4 scale a category of 0 for those who did not respond to this question (since they do not attend church).

Threat Model Results

In the first set of columns in Table 9.1, we present results of our estimation of the threat index (higher is more threatening). The key tests of our theory are presented in the second and third rows. As expected, the more individuals cling to exclusive values, which emphasize ingroup boundaries, the more they see their least-liked group as threatening. Moving from one standard deviation below the mean to one above the mean shifts the threat index .41 points (about a half standard deviation in the threat index and one-tenth of the scale range). Holding more inclusive values has no estimated effect on threat.

The exclusive values effect holds in the presence of a large number of controls, most notably religious tradition, attendance, and religious guidance. Believing religion to be a greater guide to life has about the same estimated effect as exclusive values; attendance has no effect. Catholics do not believe their least-liked groups are more or less threatening, but the evangelical indicator does have a significant interaction with belonging to a more political church. In panel A of Figure 9.1, we plot the marginal effect of being evangelical on threat perception, conditioned on the full range of church politicization. The results suggest that a more politicized church mobilizes evangelicals to report higher levels of threat—in a completely nonpoliticized environment (i.e., among those who do not attend church), being evangelical predicts lower levels of threat (statistically significant at $p = .08$); the effect becomes positive in the most political congregations and falls just outside conventional levels of statistical significance ($p = .11$).

TABLE 9.1 ESTIMATES OF THREAT AND TOLERANCE (ORDINARY LEAST SQUARES REGRESSION)

	Threat Model				*Tolerance Model*			
	β	*SE*	*p*	Δ	β	*SE*	*p*	Δ
Threat	—				–.16	(.02)	***	–.34
Exclusive values	.33	(.13)	***	.41	–.13	(.05)	***	–.16
Inclusive values	–.11	(.14)			.10	(.05)	**	.12
Political church	–.19	(.09)	**		.02	(.03)		
Evangelical	–.62	(.36)	*		.10	(.13)		
Evangelical × political church	.30	(.15)	**		–.08	(.05)	.13	
Catholic	.02	(.22)			–.09	(.08)		
Religious attendance	–.11	(.08)			.02	(.03)		
Religious guidance	.22	(.11)	**	.43	.03	(.04)		
Political participation index	.01	(.03)			.00	(.01)		
Community groups	.04	(.07)			–.03	(.02)		
Year born	–.01	(.00)	**	–.03	.00	(.00)		
Gender	.09	(.15)			.06	(.05)		
Income	.02	(.05)			.04	(.02)	**	.12
Education	–.03	(.06)			.01	(.02)		
Lost job	–.04	(.22)			–.07	(.08)		
Ideology	–.15	(.08)	*	–.33	.01	(.03)		
White	–.20	(.24)			.00	(.09)		
Constant	–17.32	(9.25)	*		1.47	(3.30)		
Model statistics	$N = 234$, Adjusted $R^2 = .05$, RMSE = 1.05				$N = 234$, Adjusted $R^2 = .24$, RMSE = .37			

Source: 2010 Colorado Springs Study.

Note: Δ refers to the effects from moving from one standard deviation below the mean to one above, which are not shown for variables involved in an interaction (see Figure 9.1). RMSE = root mean squared error.

$^{***}p < .01$, $^{**}p < .05$, $^{*}p < .10$

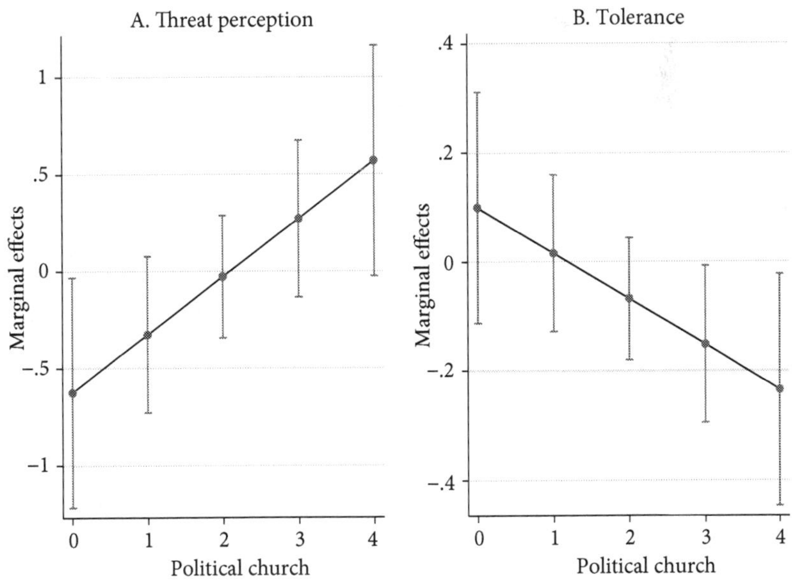

Figure 9.1 Predicting threat and tolerance: the marginal effects of being evangelical conditional on church politicization

Note: Estimates come from Table 9.1; 90 percent confidence intervals presented.

Perhaps fewer controls than expected emerge as significant predictors of threat. Only age (younger citizens see their least-liked group as less threatening) and ideology (liberals see their least-liked group as less threatening) bear on threat judgments in this sample, and no significant differences are generated by gender, education, community and political participation, or economic insecurity.

Tolerance Model Results

The second set of columns in Table 9.1 displays the tolerance results, and again the crucial tests appear at the top of the table. Historically, tolerance models have been dominated by the perceived threat of the target group. That remains true here, as threat exercises more than twice the effect of the other significant variables. Consistent with prior work, none of the traditional religiosity-based ("vertical") variables find purchase in the model. However, the next strongest effect comes from commitment to exclusive values, which draws down tolerance judgments by .16 on average. This highlights the importance of orientations to exclusive values, as they underpin threat perceptions as well (as seen in the threat model). At the same time, we see that inclusive values predict increases in tolerance (by .12 points, on average).

Aside from a similarly sized effect for income (in which higher income is related to greater tolerance), we also see a borderline-significant effect on the interaction term between the evangelical indicator and political church membership ($p = .13$). In panel B of Figure 9.1, we plot the marginal effect of being evangelical on tolerance judgments, conditioning across the full range of church politicization. Being evangelical predicts higher levels of tolerance when the respondent resides in a wholly nonpolitical church environment (though the effect is not statistically significant, $p = .4$). However, evangelicals' tolerance drops when they attend more politically engaged churches ($p = .07$). The obvious inference to make is that the communication within evangelical political churches tips toward intolerance, though we hasten to add that the source of the communication is by no means clear (it could include clergy, congregants, denominational sources, or a combination of these).

Conclusion

Our community study of Colorado Springs has some obvious limitations in terms of its generalizability. However, we chose this area as the site for our study to demonstrate a point—diversity often exists in places where reputation (and more aggregate approaches) might suggest otherwise (Djupe and Olson 2007). Looking within a famously evangelical county, we have found evidence that horizontal—that is, social and contextual—forces vary meaningfully across the members of this community and are at work in structuring threat and tolerance assessments. The effects of inclusive/exclusive social religious values and of political commitment in congregations (i.e., political churches) are robust to the inclusion of standard social-psychological variables (e.g., Burdette, Ellison, and Hill 2005; Reimer and Park 2001) and are not a function of power or specification.

To be clear, we do not argue that religiosity-based approaches hold no promise; we do not advocate their removal from model specifications. However, our examination of the religious economy of political tolerance provides yet another example of why we must look to the social to complement the psychological and why we should use explicit operationalizations of key concepts rather than general proxies. As an expression of religious intent, a values framework holds great promise for helping scholars link religion to action. Clearly, people develop and hold a mix of both inclusive and exclusive values, and they reside in organizations that vary in expressed political commitments. Understanding this variance, and acknowledging that both factors can be primed by clergy and other social sources (Djupe and Calfano 2013a, 2013b), may provide a way forward for studies of religion and tolerance and for studies of tolerance more generally.

Notes

1. Although Sam Reimer and Jerry Park (2001) refer to this group as "conservative Protestants," they rely on Brian Steensland and colleagues' (2000) technique for grouping observations in the General Social Survey (GSS), which refers to this group as "evangelical Protestants."

2. This sidestepping of affective concerns occurs largely because the approach of measuring tolerance for the respondent's least-liked group assumes that each respondent has an equal level of antipathy toward his or her outgroup. An important exception is the work of James Kuklinski and colleagues (1991), who examine both affective and deliberative aspects of the evaluation.

3. They use the label "Conservative Protestants."

4. Consider studies that privilege particular beliefs. In our view, these beliefs may be important insofar as they serve to shape how someone understands the legitimacy of another person's political and social actions. For example, a belief in a cosmic conflict between God and the devil leads people to view those with whom they disagree as instruments of evil (Ellison and Musick 1993); a belief in a wrathful God that punishes sinners for their misdeeds leads people to see others as sinners worthy of punishment (Froese, Bader, and Smith 2008); a belief that the world is going to end soon leads people to devalue social connections with non-like-minded strangers (Green et al. 1994); and a belief in original sin motivates people to support institutions and laws that control those who have not been saved (Tamney and Johnson 1997). A similar rationale applies to dogmatism, wherein the idea that one has "truth" leads to a devaluing of those who spread alternative notions (Burdette, Ellison, and Hill 2005; Ellison and Musick 1993; Jelen and Chandler 1996; Tuntiya 2005; Wilcox and Jelen 1990).

5. Other key comparisons with the 2010 census include gender (52 percent male; 48 percent female in the survey versus 48.8 percent male; 50.2 percent female in the census) and race (92 percent white in the survey versus 84.2 percent white, alone or in combination, in the census).

6. Comparisons with the 2008 ARIS: Catholic (15 percent in the sample versus 25 percent in the 2008 ARIS); other Christian (64 percent in the sample versus 51 percent in the 2008 ARIS); other Religion (8 percent in the sample versus 3 percent in the 2008

ARIS); no religion (8 percent in the sample versus 15 percent in the 2008 ARIS); evangelical (29 percent in the sample versus 34 percent in the 2008 ARIS).

7. Additional results and coding information are available in the online appendix at http://pauldjupe.com/s/Appendix.docx.

References

Beatty, Kathleen M., and Oliver Walter. 1984. "Religious Preference and Practice: Reevaluating Their Impact on Political Tolerance." *Public Opinion Quarterly* 48 (1B): 318–329.

Benson, Peter, and Dorothy Williams. 1982. *Religion on Capitol Hill.* New York: Harper and Row.

Brady, Jeff. 2005. "Colorado Springs a Mecca for Evangelical Christians." *National Public Radio,* January 17. Available at http://www.npr.org/templates/story/story.php?storyId=4287106.

Burdette, Amy M., Christopher G. Ellison, and Terrence D. Hill. 2005. "Conservative Protestantism and Tolerance toward Homosexuals: An Examination of Potential Mechanisms." *Sociological Inquiry* 75 (2): 177–196.

Calhoun-Brown, Allison. 1996. "African-American Churches and Political Mobilization: The Psychological Impact of Organizational Resources." *Journal of Politics* 58 (4): 935–953.

Djupe, Paul A., and Brian R. Calfano. 2013a. *God Talk: Experimenting with the Religious Causes of Public Opinion.* Philadelphia: Temple University Press.

——. 2013b. "Religious Value Priming, Threat, and Political Tolerance." *Political Research Quarterly* 66 (4): 767–779.

Djupe, Paul A., and Christopher P. Gilbert. 2003. *The Prophetic Pulpit: Clergy, Churches, and Communities in American Politics.* Lanham, MD: Rowman and Littlefield.

——. 2009. *The Political Influence of Churches.* New York: Cambridge University Press.

Djupe, Paul A., and Laura R. Olson, eds. 2007. *Religious Interests in Community Conflict: Beyond the Culture Wars.* Waco, TX: Baylor University Press.

Djupe, Paul A., and Anand E. Sokhey. 2003. "The Mobilization of Elite Opinion: Rabbi Perceptions of and Responses to Anti-Semitism." *Journal for the Scientific Study of Religion* 42 (3): 443–454.

Djupe, Paul A., Anand E. Sokhey, and Christopher P. Gilbert. 2007. "Present but Not Accounted For? Gender Differences in Civic Resource Acquisition." *American Journal of Political Science* 51 (4): 906–920.

Eisenstein, Marie A. 2006. "Rethinking the Relationship between Religion and Political Tolerance in the U.S." *Political Behavior* 28 (4): 327–348.

Ellison, Christopher G., and Marc A. Musick. 1993. "Southern Intolerance: A Fundamentalist Effect?" *Social Forces* 72 (2): 379–398.

Finke, Roger, and Rodney Stark. 2005. *The Churching of America, 1776–2005: Winners and Losers in Our Religious Economy.* New Brunswick, NJ: Rutgers University Press.

Froese, Paul, Christopher Bader, and Buster Smith. 2008. "Political Tolerance and God's Wrath in the United States." *Sociology of Religion* 69 (1): 29–44.

Gibson, James L. 2006. "Enigmas of Intolerance: Fifty Years after Stouffer's *Communism, Conformity, and Civil Liberties.*" *Perspectives on Politics* 4 (1): 21–34.

Gibson, James L., and Amanda Gouws. 2000. "Social Identities and Political Intolerance: Linkages within the South African Mass Public." *American Journal of Political Science* 44 (2): 278–292.

———. 2003. *Overcoming Intolerance in South Africa: Experiments in Democratic Persuasion*. New York: Cambridge University Press.

Green, John C., James L. Guth, Lyman A. Kellstedt, and Corwin E. Smidt. 1994. "Uncivil Challenges: Support for Civil Liberties among Religious Activists." *Journal of Political Science* 22:25–49.

Huckfeldt, Robert, Eric Plutzer, and John Sprague. 1993. "Alternative Contexts of Political Behavior: Churches, Neighborhoods, and Individuals." *Journal of Politics* 55 (2): 365–381.

Hunter, James D. 1983. *American Evangelicalism: Religion and the Quandary of Modernity*. New Brunswick, NJ: Rutgers University Press.

———. 1987. *Evangelicalism: The Coming Generation*. Chicago: University of Chicago Press.

Jelen, Ted G., and Marthe A. Chandler. 1996. "Patterns of Religious Socialization: Communalism, Associationalism, and the Politics of Lifestyle." *Review of Religious Research* 38 (2): 142–158.

Kellstedt, Lyman A., John C. Green, James L. Guth, and Corwin E. Smidt. 1996. "Grasping the Essentials: The Social Embodiment of Religion and Political Behavior." In *Religion and the Culture Wars*, edited by John C. Green, James L. Guth, Corwin E. Smidt, and Lyman A. Kellstedt, 174–192. Lanham, MD: Rowman and Littlefield.

Kosmin, Barry A., and Ariela Keysar. 2009. *American Religious Identification Survey Summary Report*. Hartford, CT: Institute for the Study of Secularism in Society and Culture.

Kraynak, Robert P. 2001. *Christian Faith and Modern Democracy: God and Politics in a Fallen World*. Notre Dame, IN: University of Notre Dame.

Kuklinski, James H., Ellen Riggle, Victor Ottati, Norbert Schwarz, and Robert S. Wyer, Jr. 1991. "The Cognitive and Affective Bases of Political Tolerance Judgments." *American Journal of Political Science* 35 (1): 1–27.

Layman, Geoffrey C. 2001. *The Great Divide: Religious and Cultural Conflict in American Party Politics*. New York: Columbia University Press.

McDaniel, Eric L. 2008. *Politics in the Pews: The Mobilization of Black Churches*. Ann Arbor: University of Michigan Press.

Nunn, Clyde Z., Harry J. Crockett, Jr., and J. Allen Williams, Jr. 1978. *Tolerance for Nonconformity*. San Francisco: Jossey-Bass.

Putnam, Robert D., and David E. Campbell. 2010. *American Grace: How Religion Divides and Unites Us*. New York: Simon and Schuster.

Reimer, Sam, and Jerry Z. Park. 2001. "Tolerant Incivility: A Longitudinal Analysis of White Conservative Protestants' Willingness to Grant Civil Liberties." *Journal for the Scientific Study of Religion* 40 (4): 735–745.

Smith, Christian. 2000. *Christian America? What Evangelicals Really Want*. Berkeley: University of California Press.

Stark, Rodney, and Roger Finke. 2000. *Acts of Faith: Explaining the Human Side of Religion*. Berkeley: University of California Press.

Steensland, Brian, Jerry Z. Park, Mark D. Regnerus, Lynn D. Robinson, W. Bradford Wilcox, and Robert D. Woodberry. 2000. "The Measure of American Religion: Toward Improving the State of the Art." *Social Forces* 79 (1): 291–318.

Stouffer, Samuel A. 1955. *Communism, Conformity and Civil Liberties: A Cross Section of the Nation Speaks Its Mind*. New York: Doubleday.

Sullivan, John L., James Piereson, and George E. Marcus. 1982. *Political Tolerance and American Democracy*. Chicago: University of Chicago Press.

Tamney, Joseph B., and Stephen D. Johnson. 1997. "Christianity and Public Book Banning." *Review of Religious Research* 38 (3): 263–271.

Tuntiya, Nana. 2005. "Fundamentalist Religious Affiliation and Support for Civil Liberties: A Critical Reexamination." *Sociological Inquiry* 75 (2): 153–176.

Verba, Sidney, Kay Lehman Schlozman, and Henry E. Brady. 1995. *Voice and Equality: Civic Voluntarism in American Politics.* Cambridge, MA: Harvard University Press.

Wald, Kenneth D., Dennis Owen, and Samuel Hill. 1988. "Churches as Political Communities." *American Political Science Review* 82 (2): 531–548.

Wilcox, Clyde, and Ted G. Jelen. 1990. "Evangelicals and Political Tolerance." *American Politics Quarterly* 18:25–46.

10

Predispositions, Standing Decisions, Political Tolerance, and the Role of Religion

An Exploratory Model

MARIE A. EISENSTEIN

In *With Malice toward Some*, George Marcus, John Sullivan, Elizabeth Theiss-Morse, and Sandra Wood (1995) effectively argue that political tolerance judgments are the result of three major influences: predispositions (such as personality or gender), standing decisions (long-term strongly held attitudes such as attitudes toward democratic principles), and contemporary information (as it relates to particular situations). They call the first two influences (predispositions and standing decisions) "antecedent considerations." However, in their analysis of these two "antecedent considerations," religion was not included despite the fact that religious beliefs, like all worldviews, have the potential to influence both types of considerations:

> Since religious beliefs, like other worldviews, structure or organize other attitudes and information by accommodating only those constructs that are consistent with it, information or attitudes inconsistent with them are rejected, ignored, altered, or adjusted to fit. Thus religion *can* have a significant influence on other antecedent considerations. (Gaddy 2003: 165)

Because the work of Marcus and colleagues (1995) represents the seminal and foundational work shifting the explanation of variation in political tolerance from a purely cognitive perspective to an integrated emotional-cognitive one, the exclusion of religion from such analyses and models is problematic.[1] Indeed, if religion is to remain relevant to studies of political tolerance, it should (and deserves) to play a role in the newest and most cutting-edge models for explaining political tolerance. In this chapter, I analyze the influence of religion[2] in conjunction with various predispositions and standing decisions on political tolerance. I do not attempt either a broad-based defense or critique of the theoretical rationale employed by Marcus and colleagues (1995); instead I embrace the assumptions and results of that scholarship and use it as a benchmark for this chapter.

Antecedent Considerations: Predispositions and Standing Decisions

Antecedent considerations are "the entire class of long-term influences that have long-lived effects . . . on the judgments people make" (Marcus et al. 1995: 19). Predispositions and standing decisions are two types of antecedent considerations (Kuklinski et al. 1991; Marcus et al. 1995; Marcus et al. 2005). Predispositions are "deeply rooted and stable individual characteristics . . . that result in generalized predilections to think, feel, and behave in certain ways" (Marcus et al. 1995: 19). Standing decisions are "established attitudes and beliefs applied to a specific domain" (Marcus et al. 1995: 20). While Marcus and colleagues (1995) conceptualize predispositions as distinct and separate from standing decisions, they nevertheless argue that standing decisions (as a direct effect) will encapsulate the influence of predispositions (an indirect effect). In select cases a variable can be both a predisposition and a standing decision.[3]

The argument regarding standing decisions and predispositions in relationship to political tolerance is that individuals do not re-create their political tolerance every time they are faced with an opportunity to practice it; some individuals are simply more politically tolerant than others. That is, individuals have a "standing decision" regarding political tolerance, which can be captured by measuring that person's support for democratic norms. In addition, some personality types[4]—a predisposition—are more inclined toward political tolerance than others; nonetheless personality predispositions should be "encapsulated" in measures of standing decisions, such as support for democratic norms (Marcus et al. 1995: 164). In addition to gender and threat perception as a predisposition, Marcus et al. (1995) tested three different personality dimensions: neuroticism, openness to experience, and extraversion[5] in relationship to political tolerance. In general, those with high levels of neuroticism, higher levels of extraversion, and low levels of openness are expected to have lower levels of political tolerance.[6]

The Antecedent Model of Political Tolerance—with Religion

Within political tolerance research, there is a standard and accepted cross-sectional model of political tolerance, which can be seen in Figure 10.1. Although Marcus and colleagues (1995: 38) paid deference to that model, their comprehensive analyses did not detail explicitly how the aforementioned personality variables (neuroticism, extraversion, and openness) fit into it. For example, in the

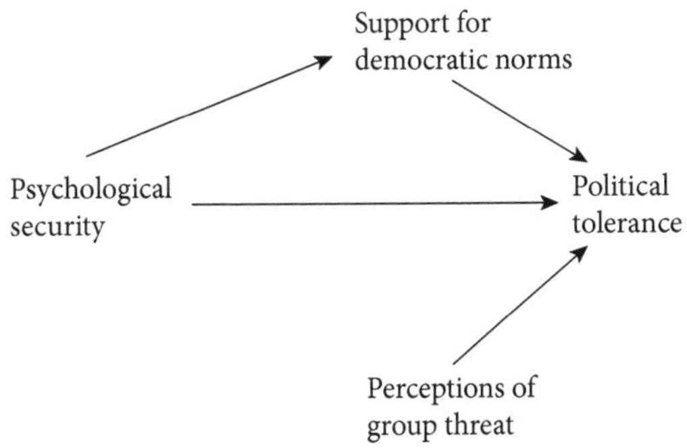

Figure 10.1 Conventional, cross-sectional model of the origins of political tolerance
Note: This is the basic model of political tolerance (see Sullivan, Piereson, and Marcus 1982; Marcus et al. 1995; Gibson 2006).

standard model of political tolerance, psychological security is both a direct and an indirect influence on political tolerance. Psychological security is typically operationalized as a multi-item construct measuring dogmatism, self-esteem, and trust (or some combination thereof) (Eisenstein 2006; Sullivan, Piereson, and Marcus 1982). These various items—dogmatism, self-esteem, and trust—are all aspects of personality (Sullivan et al. 1981; Sullivan, Piereson, and Marcus 1982); and dogmatism and trust are proxy measures for authoritarianism.[7] In short, dogmatism, self-esteem, and trust would all be considered predispositions by the standards employed by Marcus and colleagues (1995). Should the three newer personality variables—neuroticism, extraversion, and openness—replace or be measured alongside of these other personality dimensions? We do not know. Marcus and colleagues (1995) entirely sidestep this issue; the traditional measures of psychological security (e.g., dogmatism, self-esteem, and trust) are not part of that study. They also do not explicitly detail, for example, how they would model threat perception as a standing decision versus threat perception as a disposition[8] or how they would incorporate gender into the standard cross-sectional model of political tolerance.[9] These are all important issues to explore.

In Figure 10.2 is an antecedent model of tolerance that incorporates religion. Within political science, religion has predominantly been modeled as influencing personality (Canetti-Nisim 2004; Eisenstein 2006; Eisenstein and Clark 2014; Gaddy 2003; Jelen and Wilcox 1991; Sullivan, Piereson, and Marcus 1982). Thus, religious beliefs and religious behavior are each modeled as having a distinct influence on various personality constructs.[10] Understandably, the direction of the linkage between personality and religion is disputed particularly within the psychology of religion and sociology of religion.[11] While I assess the influence of religion on the antecedent considerations of political tolerance put forth by Marcus and colleagues (1995), other research considers religion as shaping other aspects, such as the contemporary information individuals have.

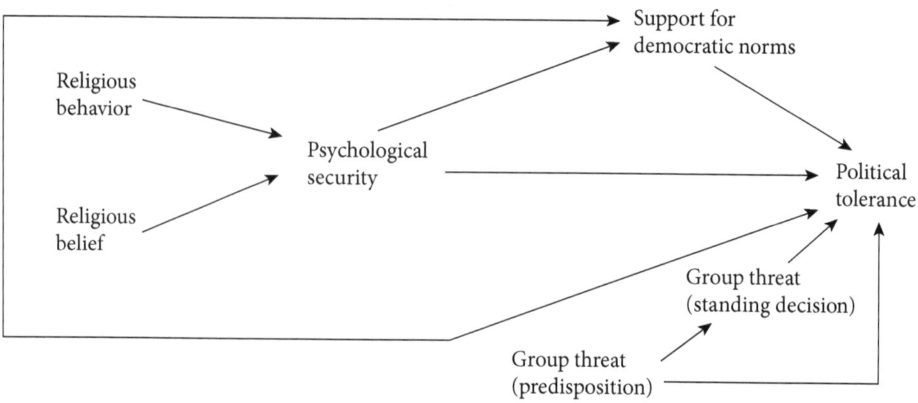

Figure 10.2 Antecedent model of political tolerance with religion
Note: To accommodate the arguments of Marcus and colleagues (1995), I modify the conventional model in two ways: (1) for psychological security, I use the neuroticism, extraversion, and openness variables alongside a measure of dogmatism, which is also a standard measure of psychological security in previous tolerance studies, and (2) I include religion. Psychological security is measured by neuroticism, extraversion, openness, and dogmatism variables.

The expectations regarding the influence of religion on the personality constructs are various. First, increases in religious belief and religious behavior are expected to lead to increased dogmatism (Gibson 2010; Green et al. 1994; Jelen and Wilcox 1991; Wilcox and Jelen 1990). Increased religious belief is also expected to correspond to lower levels of openness (Saroglou 2002), while religious behavior in relationship to openness has not been determined. On the basis of previous results wherein religious belief and not religious behavior is the active ingredient in the religion-personality-tolerance linkage (Eisenstein 2006; Eisenstein and Clark 2014; Gibson 2010), I expect that religious behavior will exhibit minimal to no influence on openness. However, the relationship between religious belief and neuroticism depends on how religious belief is measured (Francis 2010; Saroglou 2002) as well as by level of religious behavior (Francis 2010). Vassilis Saroglou (2002) and Leslie Francis (2010) suggest that increased religious belief (as measured in this study) is likely to lead to increased neuroticism, while Saroglou (2002), Francis (2010), and Peter Hills and colleagues (2004) suggest that religious behavior will have minimal to no influence on neuroticism. The relationship between both religious belief and behavior to extraversion is expected to be weak (Beit-Hallahmi and Argyle 1997; Francis 2010; Saroglou 2002).

I also expect gender to affect the relationship among religion, personality, and political tolerance. While gender is not part of the standard cross-sectional model of political tolerance (see Figure 10.1), gender is important in understanding the influence of religion and thus is an important component here. After all, robust findings show that women more so than men identify with a

Christian religious orientation (Stark 2001, 2002); are religiously devout (Stark 2002; Stouffer 1955; Sullivan, Piereson, and Marcus 1982); are more likely to offer religion-based objections to target groups, while men oppose these same groups on ideological grounds (Sullivan, Piereson, and Marcus 1982); and possess a greater reluctance to allow unpopular groups to exercise their constitutional rights (Bobo and Licari 1989; Gibson 1992; Golebiowska 1995; Marcus et al. 1995; Nunn, Crockett, and Williams 1978). In short, given the important influence of gender on level of religious belief and behavior, it is expected that the influence of religion on personality will differ by gender.

Consistent with the theory as well as the causal paths argued for by Marcus and colleagues (1995), the models also incorporate threat as both a predisposition and a standing decision. Because personality dimensions are appropriately thought of as elements of psychological security, all personality dimensions[12] are modeled as having a direct influence on political tolerance as well as an indirect influence on support for norms of democracy.[13] As is typical in political tolerance models, support for democratic norms and threat perception (as a standing decision) have a direct influence on political tolerance.

Data and Measures

The data for this study come from an anonymous survey of 282 college students enrolled in introductory social sciences courses (American government, sociology, and psychology). The surveys were conducted during the summer and fall sessions of 2008 at a regional campus of a large state-funded university in Lake County, Indiana. The basic demographics of this sample reflect the diversity represented in Lake County, Indiana, and the commuter nature of the campus.[14] While these data are not ideal for generalizability (see Sears 1986), they are nonetheless adequate for an exploratory analysis of the various arguments and constructs presented by Marcus and colleagues (1995; see also Druckman and Kam 2011). Specifically, I replicate all the antecedent measures (personality and threat) employed by Marcus and colleagues (1995), and I model the relationships between these variables consistent with their research while also expanding on their work to incorporate religion. In short, these results should not be dismissed simply on the basis of the "college sophomore" problem specifically (Sears 1986; but see Druckman and Kam 2011) or the issues with generalizability generally, but rather the results are suggestive that further work is worth pursuing.

A considerable number of items are employed in this study. Because the role of religion is my focus here, I discuss the religion measures.[15] In general, all measures employed in this chapter (excluding religion) are consistent with the measurement strategies employed by Marcus and colleagues (1995). This includes using the content-controlled measurement approach for political tolerance. Two religion measures are used in this chapter: religious belief and religious behavior.

Religious Belief

The focus is on the substance of religious beliefs, and it is measured by biblical literalism and biblical inerrancy.[16] Both questions have a three-point scale so that the combined answers from both questions create a scale ranging from 1 to 6. The items have been coded so that 1 corresponds to low doctrinal orthodoxy and 6 corresponds to high doctrinal orthodoxy. The alpha reliability coefficient for this scale is .67.

Religious Behavior

Religious behavior is also referred to as a measure of religious commitment. It is measured by frequency of attendance (at a religious institution), frequency of personal prayer, and religious salience (Kellstedt et al. 1996; Layman and Green 1998). Although religious salience is an attitudinal variable, in the empirical measurement of religious commitment, scholars typically also include the subjective question of salience of religion (Guth and Green 1993; Kellstedt 1993). The scale ranges from 3 to 20, and the items have been coded such that 3 corresponds to low levels of religious commitment and 20 corresponds to high levels of religious commitment. The alpha reliability coefficient for this scale is .72.

Results

Before moving into an analysis of the model presented in Figure 10.2, I begin with ordinary least squares (OLS) regression so that we can more readily assess the differences between the influence of predispositions, standing decisions, and religious belief as well as religious behavior. The OLS regression analyses in Table 10.1 allow us to examine each of these variables in relationship to each other in terms of influence on political tolerance before we examine the results of our causal model presented in Figure 10.2. In essence, the analyses in Table 10.1 provides a baseline for expectations as we move from the less-defined OLS models into causal structural models.

A brief review of models 1 through 3 in Table 10.1 will highlight the relationship between religion and political tolerance. Consistent with research that posits religion is a multidimensional variable consisting of belief, behavior, and belonging (Kellstedt 1993; Kellstedt et al. 1996; Layman and Green 1998), as well as research arguing that religious belief influences tolerance positively while religious behavior influences tolerance negatively (Ben-Nun Bloom and Arikan 2012), I begin with a focus on the two religion variables of religious belief and religious behavior. When controlling for religious behavior or religious belief exclusively, each one has an important negative and statistically significant influence on political tolerance (–.26 and –.30, respectively). However, when both of these religion variables are included in model 3 (Table 10.1), we see that religious belief maintains an important and statistically significant negative

TABLE 10.1 INFLUENCE OF RELIGION AND PSYCHOLOGICAL ANTECEDENT CONSIDERATIONS ON POLITICAL TOLERANCE

	Model 1		*Model 2*		*Model 3*		*Model 4*		*Model 5*		*Model 6*	
	β	p	β	p	β	p	β	p	β	p	β	p
Intercept	22.76	***	24.67	***	24.66	***	28.75	***	24.10	***	31.77	***
Religious Determinants												
Religious behavior	–.26	***			–.08		–.10		–.10		–.09	
Religious belief			–.30	***	–.23	**	–.22	**	–.15		–.13	
Psychological Determinants												
Dogmatism							–.23	***			–.19	***
Neuroticism									–.12		–.11	
Extraversion									–.20	***	–.19	***
Openness									.24	***	.21	***
Political Determinants												
Norms of democracy							.20	***	.20	***	.16	**
Standing decision—threat							–.32	***	–.27	***	–.29	***
Age	–.01		–.03		–.03		–.05		–.12	*	–.13	
Income	–.06		–.02		–.04		.00		.04		.01	
Ideology	–.07		–.06		–.05		.04		.03		.03	
Gender	.21	***	.21	***	.21	***	.18	***	.13	*	.14	**
Adjusted R^2	.10		.13		.12		.36		.37		.40	
N	244		244		243		230		230		230	

$^*p \leq .10$, $^{**}p \leq .05$, $^{***}p \leq .01$

relationship to political tolerance (–.23) while religious behavior does not. These findings contradict the work of Pazit Ben-Nun Bloom and Gizem Arikan (2012), but they are consistent with other research that has differentiated between religious belief and religious behavior (Eisenstein 2006; Eisenstein and Clark 2014; Gibson 2010). In addition, for these first three models in Table 10.1, gender is the only sociodemographic variable consistently exerting a significant influence on political tolerance.

In models 4 through 6 (Table 10.1), I include both support for norms of democracy and threat perception (as a standing decision),[17] as these are the two primary determinants of political tolerance, and then I add in the personality constructs with an eye toward comparing dogmatism to neuroticism, extraversion, and openness particularly in relationship to the religion variables. While the influence of religious behavior across models 4 through 6 (Table 10.1) remains consistent and inconsequential, the influence of religious belief on political tolerance changes depending on the psychological determinants included in models 4 through 6. Specifically, as can be seen in model 4, when the only psychological determinant in the model is dogmatism, religious belief maintains a strong negative influence on political tolerance (–.22, consistent with results from models 1 through 3), and dogmatism has a considerable and significant (–.23) influence on political tolerance as well. When all psychological determinants are included (model 6 in Table 10.1), the influence of dogmatism remains statistically significant at –.19, but the influence of religious belief falls (–.13) and is no longer statistically significant. The results in model 5 are similar; when dogmatism is not one of the psychological determinants but neuroticism, extraversion, and openness are included as psychological determinants, the influence of religious belief becomes an insignificant –.15. In short, a most interesting finding is the fact that in models 5 and 6 (Table 10.1), which include the personality constructs employed by Marcus and colleagues (1995), religious belief fails to attain any substantive or statistical influence on political tolerance. Nevertheless, gender continues to exert an influence on political tolerance even in these comprehensive models.

To better understand the pathways between these relationships, I now turn to a data presentation based on the diagram in Figure 10.2, using path analysis with maximum likelihood estimation. As seen in Figure 10.3, religious behavior continues to have an inconsequential influence on political tolerance, directly or indirectly.[18] In contrast, religious belief does influence political tolerance both directly and indirectly. Religious belief attains nominal statistical significance with a minimal direct influence on political tolerance (–.10); and, as expected, it also exerts a substantial influence (statistically significant) on openness (–.32) and a moderate influence (with nominal statistical significance) on neuroticism (.16). Likewise, consistent with expected results, religious behavior did not have any substantive influence on openness, neuroticism, or extraversion. Contrary to expectations, neither religious belief nor behavior had a substantive negative influence on dogmatism. Thus, the traditional link between religious belief and

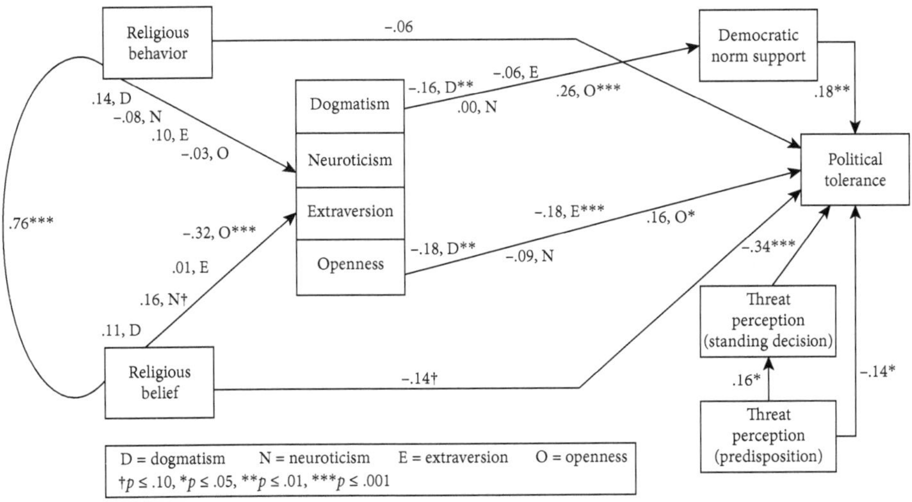

Figure 10.3 Estimates for the antecedent model of political tolerance

Note: Control variables are income and age. Because the sample is of college students exclusively, education is not included.

dogmatism is washed out in this model and the most important link between religious belief and the personality dimensions is its negative influence on openness. In terms of both direct and indirect influences on political tolerance, dogmatism, extraversion, and openness are the variables of interest. And given the strong influence of openness on support for democratic norms, it is arguably a more important predictor of political tolerance than dogmatism (e.g., it has more direct and indirect influence, combined, on political tolerance than does dogmatism). Neuroticism has no apparent influence on political tolerance.

Because of the importance afforded gender by Marcus and colleagues (1995) and the substantial influence of gender demonstrated across all models in Table 10.1, as well as the importance of gender to religion, I also conduct path analyses controlling for gender focusing exclusively on the religion-personality-tolerance linkages.[19] When comparing the results of females versus males in Figure 10.4, the intersection of gender and religion showed different patterns. For women, religious belief is an active ingredient for three of the four personality constructs. Religious belief influences dogmatism (.23), neuroticism (.27), and openness (–.37), whereas for men, religious belief had no statistically significant influences on personality. However, religious behavior did have an immense influence on dogmatism (.47) for men, whereas religious behavior had no influence on personality for women. Furthermore, religious belief had a direct negative influence on political tolerance (–.26) for women but only a nominal influence on it (–.14) for men, while religious behavior did not register any statistically significant relationship to political tolerance for either men or women.

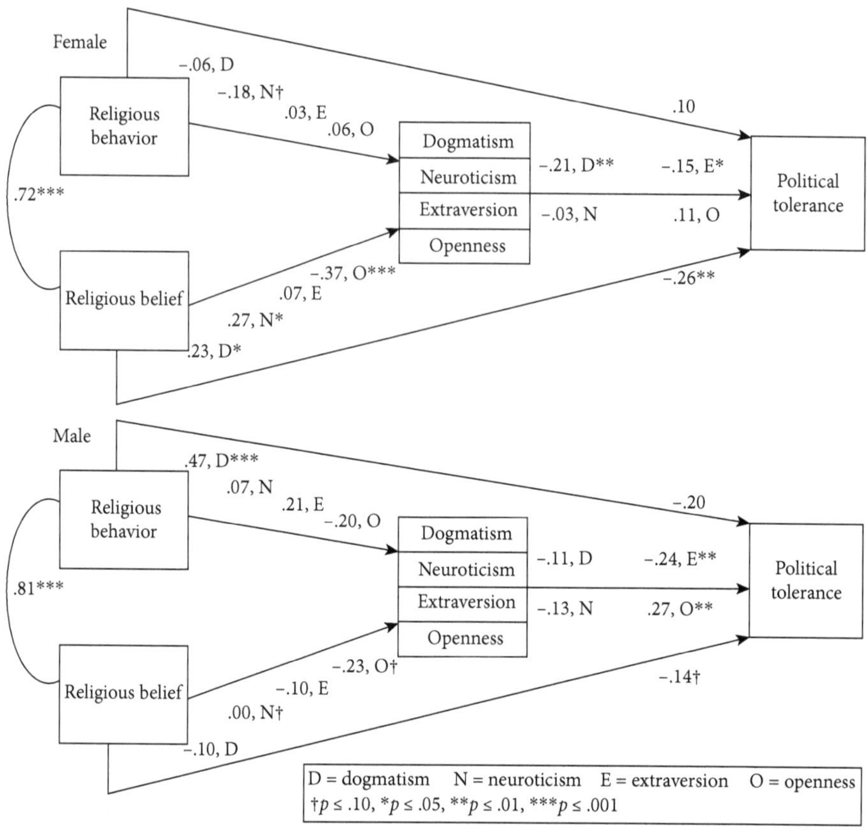

Figure 10.4 Religion, personality, political tolerance linkages by gender
Note: Control variables are income and age. Because the sample is of college students exclusively, education is not included.

The personality variables also suggest a different pattern for men versus women. For women, both dogmatism (–.21) and extraversion (–.15) influence political tolerance directly, and dogmatism (–.16) and openness (.16) also indirectly influence political tolerance via support for democratic norms (data not shown). Thus dogmatism, both in its influence on political tolerance directly and in its influence on democratic norm support, is an important predictor for women. In contrast, for men, the influence of dogmatism wanes. Dogmatism attains nominal statistical significance for its influence on support for democratic norms (–.15) (data not shown) and fails to register a statistically significant relationship to political tolerance (–.11). The openness construct emerges as the most important personality predictor of political tolerance both directly (.27) and indirectly (.41) via support for democratic norms (data not shown) for men. For both men and women, extraversion exerted a significant negative influence on political tolerance (–.24 and –.15, respectively).

Discussion and Conclusions

These general findings present some interesting issues for continued studies at the intersection of religion and political tolerance. First, the established link between religion and dogmatism does not manifest when other personality variables are included in the model of political tolerance. A cursory look at the results (Table 10.1 and Figure 10.3) suggests that the personality variables (most notably openness and extraversion) are more potent influences on political tolerance than dogmatism even though dogmatism is one of the standard means of measuring psychological influences particularly for the linkage between religion and political tolerance. This raises the question as to which of these variables are better positioned for use in religion–political tolerance studies. If there is to be one comprehensive model detailing the determinants of political tolerance, the appropriate mix of personality variables needs to be ascertained. Although the growing literature on personality–political behavior linkages (Mondak 2010; Mondak and Halperin 2008) does not focus on political tolerance or the role of religion in the personality-tolerance chain, it offers insight into an effective personality measurement strategy by drawing on the five-factor personality taxonomy from the psychology literature.

Nonetheless, the results from this chapter support past research that suggests religious behavior is not a variable of interest in terms of understanding the linkages among religion, personality, and political tolerance. Instead, religious belief is the active ingredient important in understanding the influence of religion within a comprehensive model of political tolerance (Eisenstein 2006; Eisenstein and Clark 2014; Gibson 2010; but see Ben-Nun Bloom and Arikan 2012). In short, religious belief is most linked to the personality variables (dogmatism, openness), and religious behavior is not. Within political science we have argued that we need the three Bs of religion (belief, belonging, and behavior) to capture religion in all its dimensions, but research using the content-controlled measure of political tolerance suggests that religious behavior is not necessary to understanding political tolerance. Also important in understanding the linkage among religion, personality, and political tolerance is gender. Gender affects the influence of religion on the personality determinants of political tolerance. Thus, gender needs to play an important role in continued studies investigating the influence of religion on political tolerance. In fact, the differences between men and women are dramatic; while the data here are merely exploratory, this aspect of the results should not be underemphasized.

Nevertheless, in discussing where religion fits into a comprehensive model of political tolerance, the causal chain requires greater focus. Given the dispute as to where religion is positioned in relationship to personality constructs, more research is needed to better understand whether religion precedes personality or personality precedes religion, or if the relationship is dependent on the specific measure of religion (religious belief, religious belonging, religious behavior) as well as the specific personality construct under review. Within political science,

I give weight and preference to Daphna Canetti-Nisim (2004), who effectively argued that religion precedes personality. While her study dealt with how religion influences authoritarianism (a personality construct), it is solely one study within the discipline of political science, and other disciplines (such as the psychology of religion and sociology of religion) argue for personality preceding religion. Given the complexity of the relationships between religion and personality, as well as the importance of understanding how religion influences such a major determinant of political tolerance, this is something that merits further attention. Until there is a critical mass of empirically driven research within political science, this issue of causal ordering will plague religion and tolerance studies.

Notes

1. Following Marcus and colleagues (1995), subsequent works also left religion out of their analyses (e.g., Marcus, Neuman, and MacKuen 2000; Skitka, Bauman, and Mullen 2004; Marcus et al. 2005; Halperin, Canetti-Nisim, and Hirsch-Hoefler 2009).

2. Religion is conceptualized as having three distinct yet interrelated dimensions: religious belief (doctrinal orthodoxy), religious belonging (also called religious tradition), and religious behavior (religious commitment) (Kellstedt 1993; Kellstedt et al. 1996; Layman and Green 1998).

3. For example, threat perception can be both a predisposition (a base level or generic sense of threat perception) and a standing decision (the threat one perceives from his or her most disliked group). Thus, threat perception is conceptualized—and measured—in two ways.

4. For Marcus and colleagues (1995), demographic variables as well as personality constructs are considered predispositions. This is consistent with the work of previous political tolerance scholarship, wherein age, income, and education (demographics) were modeled as indirect influences on political tolerance (Sullivan, Piereson, and Marcus 1982). It diverges from previous scholarship insofar as "psychological security" (which can also be thought of as a measure of secure personality combining dogmatism, trust, and self-esteem) is one of the three primary (direct) determinants in the standard political tolerance model (Sullivan, Piereson, and Marcus 1982; Marcus et al. 1995: 38; Gibson 2006).

5. Neuroticism is "the general orientation to be nervous, worried and anxious on the one hand, or to be calm and secure on the other" (Marcus et al. 1995: 162). Openness to experience is contrasted with a lack of openness, which is signified by being "constrained, conservative, and likely to cling to the familiar" (Marcus et al. 1995: 164). Extraversion (an extraversion/introversion measure) is the "general orientation to be sociable, lively, and venturesome (extraversion), or withdrawn, passive, and shy (introversion)" (Marcus et al. 1995: 162).

6. These three traits (neuroticism, extraversion, and openness) are defined in the measurements section. It seems intuitive that increased neuroticism (increased anxiety versus more calmness and security) would correspond to increased intolerance. Likewise for openness, it is intuitive that increased openness versus being constrained (or clinging to the familiar) would correspond to decreased intolerance. However, extraversion has a less intuitive association. Marcus and colleagues (1995) argue that increased extraversion

leads to increased intolerance, but they acknowledge that the influence of extraversion, theoretically, is mixed.

7. Essentially, dogmatism is considered an alternative measure to authoritarianism because it assesses open-mindedness and flexibility without regard to ideological content, which was a major criticism of the F-scale as a traditional measure of authoritarianism. And trust is argued for as an indirect measure that taps a central component of authoritarianism (Sullivan et al. 1981; Sullivan, Piereson, and Marcus 1982).

8. Marcus and colleagues (1995) conceptually distinguished between threat perception as a standing decision and as a predisposition. While these are two different measurements, they are nonetheless similar. These distinctions will be highlighted when data and measures are discussed.

9. Gender was not one of the "indirect" influences included in the comprehensive model of political tolerance developed by John Sullivan, James Piereson, and George Marcus (1982) and on which the standard model of political tolerance is based.

10. To test for the direct and indirect influence of religion on political tolerance, religion is also modeled as influencing support for democratic norms and political tolerance.

11. Some literature suggests that psychological attributes precede religion (for example, Koenig and Bouchard 2006; Bradshaw and Ellison 2008; Vance, Maes, and Kendler 2010). Other research suggests there are arguments both for religion preceding psychological traits and for the reverse (Leak and Randall 1995; Francis 2010). Then there is the argument that both psychological traits and religion might be the outcome of a third factor (Altemeyer 1996).

12. These include dogmatism, neuroticism, extraversion, and openness. Dogmatism is the only one of the traditional personality measures of psychological security included in this study because in previous religion and political tolerance work, dogmatism is the only construct that influences political tolerance (Eisenstein and Clark 2014).

13. These relationships are consistent with previous research (Sullivan et al. 1981; Sullivan, Piereson, and Marcus 1982; Gibson 2006; Eisenstein 2006).

14. The racial breakdown is 64 percent white, 12.6 percent Hispanic, 18.7 percent African American, 1.8 percent Asian, and 2.9 percent other. Gender distribution is 57.5 percent women and 42.5 percent men. The religious tradition breakdown is 28.9 percent Catholic, 42.9 percent Protestant (all), 0.7 percent Jewish, 12.9 percent none, and 11.1 percent other (3.5 percent did not answer the question).

15. For coding information on the remaining variables, see the online appendix at http://pauldjupe.com/s/Appendix.docx.

16. Biblical literalism and biblical inerrancy are the two doctrinal orthodoxy measures most used by the National Election Study (NES) since 1980 (Kellstedt and Smidt 1993).

17. Marcus and colleagues (1995) argue that threat as a standing decision would encapsulate the effects of threat as a predisposition. Indeed, in analyses not shown here, when threat as a predisposition is added to the model of political tolerance alongside threat as a standing decision, the influence of threat as a predisposition drops dramatically. Thus, I retain only threat as a standing decision.

18. I did not display the path from the religion variables to support for democratic norms, but I did test for this indirect influence on political tolerance, which failed to manifest for either religious behavior or religious belief.

19. Using the model presented in Figure 10.2, I analyze each gender separately—essentially controlling for gender. There are two different ways in which gender can be

included in the analysis. It can be either included as a dummy variable or modeled so each gender is analyzed separately. This second option is the more interesting analysis, since I can assess the independent contributions of each variable and whether the effect changes across gender. This cannot be accomplished when gender is included as a separate dummy variable, as this procedure assumes the only variable that changes across gender is the dependent variable, political tolerance. While I report findings only for the religion-personality-tolerance linkages by gender, I obtained the data using the comprehensive model shown in Figure 10.2.

References

Altemeyer, Bob. 1996. *The Authoritarian Specter.* Cambridge, MA: Harvard University Press.

Beit-Hallahmi, Benjamin, and Michael Argyle. 1997. *The Psychology of Religious Belief and Experience.* London: Routledge.

Ben-Nun Bloom, Pazit, and Gizem Arikan. 2012. "A Two-Edged Sword: The Differential Effect of Religious Belief and Religious Social Context on Attitudes towards Democracy." *Political Behavior* 34 (2): 249–276.

Bobo, Lawrence, and Frederick C. Licari. 1989. "Education and Political Tolerance: Testing the Effects of Cognitive Sophistication and Target Group." *Public Opinion Quarterly* 53 (3): 285–308.

Bradshaw, Matt, and Christopher G. Ellison. 2008. "Do Genetic Factors Influence Religious Life? Findings from a Behavior Genetic Analysis of Twin Siblings." *Journal for the Scientific Study of Religion* 47 (4): 529–544.

Canetti-Nisim, Daphna. 2004. "The Effect of Religiosity on Endorsement of Democratic Values: The Mediating Influence of Authoritarianism." *Political Behavior* 26 (4): 377–398.

Druckman, James N., and Cindy D. Kam. 2011. "Students as Experimental Participants." In *Cambridge Handbook of Experimental Political Science*, edited by James N. Druckman, Donald P. Green, James H. Kulkinski, and Arthur Lupia, 41–57. New York: Cambridge University Press.

Eisenstein, Marie A. 2006. "Rethinking the Relationship between Religion and Political Tolerance in the U.S." *Political Behavior* 28 (4): 327–348.

Eisenstein, Marie A., and April K. Clark. 2014. "Political Tolerance, Psychological Security, and Religion: Disaggregating the Mediating Influence of Psychological Security." *Politics and Religion* 7 (3): 1–31.

Francis, Leslie J. 2010. "Personality and Religious Orientation: Shifting Sands or Firm Foundations?" *Mental Health, Religion, and Culture* 13 (7–8): 793–803.

Gaddy, Beverly. 2003. "Faith, Tolerance, and Civil Society." In *Faith, Morality, and Civil Society*, edited by Dale McConkey and Peter Augustine Lawler, 159–195. Lanham, MD: Lexington Books.

Gibson, James L. 1992. "Alternative Measures of Political Tolerance: Must Tolerance Be 'Least Liked'?" *American Journal of Political Science* 36 (2): 560–577.

———. 2006. "Enigmas of Intolerance: Fifty Years after Stouffer's *Communism, Conformity, and Civil Liberties.*" *Perspectives on Politics* 4 (1): 21–34.

———. 2010. "The Political Consequences of Religiosity: Does Religion Always Cause Political Intolerance?" In *Religion and Democracy in the United States: Danger or Opportunity?* edited by Alan Wolfe and Ira Katznelson, 147–175. New York: Russell Sage.

Golebiowska, Ewa A. 1995. "Individual Value Priorities, Education, and Political Tolerance." *Political Behavior* 17 (1): 23–48.

Green, John C., James L. Guth, Lyman A. Kellstedt, and Corwin E. Smidt. 1994. "Uncivil Challenges: Support for Civil Liberties among Religious Activists." *Journal of Political Science* 22:25–49.

Guth, James, and John Green. 1993. "Salience: The Core Concept?" In *Rediscovering the Religious Factor in American Politics*, edited by David C. Leege and Lyman A. Kellstedt, 157–174. Armonk, NY: M. E. Sharpe.

Halperin, Eran, Daphna Canetti-Nisim, and Sivan Hirsch-Hoefler. 2009. "The Central Role of Group-Based Hatred as an Emotional Antecedent of Political Intolerance: Evidence from Israel." *Political Psychology* 30 (1): 93–123.

Hills, Peter, Leslie J. Francis, Michael Argyle, and Chris J. Jackson. 2004. "Primary Personality Trait Correlates of Religious Practice and Orientation." *Personality and Individual Differences* 36 (1): 61–73.

Jelen, Ted G., and Clyde Wilcox. 1991. "Religious Dogmatism among White Christians: Causes and Effects." *Review of Religious Research* 33 (1): 32–46.

Kellstedt, Lyman A. 1993. "Religion, the Neglected Variable: An Agenda for Future Research on Religion and Political Behavior." In *Rediscovering the Religious Factor in American Politics*, edited by David C. Leege and Lyman A. Kellstedt, 273–303. Armonk, NY: M. E. Sharpe.

Kellstedt, Lyman A., John C. Green, James L. Guth, and Corwin E. Smidt. 1996. "Grasping the Essentials: The Social Embodiment of Religion and Political Behavior." In *Religion and the Culture Wars*, edited by John C. Green, James L. Guth, Corwin E. Smidt, and Lyman A. Kellstedt, 174–192. Lanham, MD: Rowman and Littlefield. Kellstedt, Lyman A., and Corwin E. Smidt. 1993. "Doctrinal Beliefs and Political Behavior: Views of the Bible." In *Rediscovering the Religious Factor in American Politics*, edited by David C. Leege and Lyman A. Kellstedt, 177–198. Armonk, NY: M. E. Sharpe.

Koenig, Laura B., and Thomas J. Bouchard Jr. 2006. "Genetic and Environmental Influences on the Traditional Moral Values Triad—Authoritarianism, Conservatism, and Religiousness—as Assessed by Quantitative Behavior Genetic Methods." In *Where God and Science Meet: How Brain and Evolutionary Studies Alter Our Understanding of Religion*, edited by Patrick McNamara, 31–60. Westport, CT: Praeger.

Kuklinski, James H., Ellen Riggle, Victor Ottati, Norbert Schwarz, and Robert S. Wyer, Jr. 1991. "The Cognitive and Affective Bases of Political Tolerance Judgments." *American Journal of Political Science* 35 (1): 1–27.

Layman, Geoffrey C., and John C. Green. 1998. "The Changing Religious Voter: The Political Impact of Belonging, Believing, and Behaving." Paper presented at the annual meeting of the Midwest Political Science Association, Chicago.

Leak, Gary K., and Brandy A. Randall. 1995. "Clarification of the Link between Right-Wing Authoritarianism and Religiousness: The Role of Religious Maturity." *Journal for the Scientific Study of Religion* 34 (2): 245–252.

Marcus, George E., W. Russell Neuman, and Michael MacKuen. 2000. *Affective Intelligence and Political Judgment*. Chicago: University of Chicago Press.

Marcus, George E., John L. Sullivan, Elizabeth Theiss-Morse, and Daniel Stevens. 2005. "The Emotional Foundation of Political Cognition: The Impact of Extrinsic Anxiety on the Formation of Political Tolerance Judgments." *Political Psychology* 26 (6): 949–963.

Marcus, George E., John L. Sullivan, Elizabeth Theiss-Morse, and Sandra Wood. 1995. *With Malice toward Some: How People Make Civil Liberties Judgments.* New York: Cambridge University Press.

Mondak, Jeffery J. 2010. *Personality and the Foundations of Political Behavior.* New York: Cambridge University Press.

Mondak, Jeffery J., and Karen D. Halperin. 2008. "A Framework for the Study of Personality and Political Behaviour." *British Journal of Political Science* 38 (2): 335–362.

Nunn, Clyde Z., Harry J. Crockett, Jr., and J. Allen Williams, Jr. 1978. *Tolerance for Nonconformity.* San Francisco: Jossey-Bass.

Saroglou, Vassilis. 2002. "Religion and the Five Factors of Personality: A Meta-analytic Review." *Personality and Individual Differences* 32 (1): 15–25.

Sears, David O. 1986. "College Sophomores in the Laboratory: Influences of a Narrow Data Base on Social Psychology's View of Human Nature." *Journal of Personality and Social Psychology* 51 (3): 515–530.

Skitka, Linda J., Christopher W. Bauman, and Elizabeth Mullen. 2004. "Political Tolerance and Coming to Psychological Closure Following the September 11, 2001, Terrorist Attacks: An Integrative Approach." *Personality and Social Psychology Bulletin* 30 (6): 743–756.

Stark, Rodney. 2001. "Reconceptualizing Religion, Magic, and Science." *Review of Religious Research* 43 (2): 101–120.

———. 2002. "Physiology and Faith: Addressing the 'Universal' Gender Difference in Religious Commitment." *Journal for the Scientific Study of Religion* 41 (3): 495–507.

Stouffer, Samuel A. 1955. *Communism, Conformity and Civil Liberties: A Cross Section of the Nation Speaks Its Mind.* New York: Doubleday.

Sullivan, John L., George E. Marcus, Stanley Feldman, and James E. Piereson. 1981. "The Sources of Political Tolerance: A Multivariate Analysis." *American Political Science Review* 75 (1): 92–106.

Sullivan, John L., James Piereson, and George E. Marcus. 1982. *Political Tolerance and American Democracy.* Chicago: University of Chicago Press.

Vance, Todd, Hermine H. Maes, and Kenneth S. Kendler. 2010. "Genetic and Environmental Influences on Multiple Dimensions of Religiosity: A Twin Study." *Journal of Mental and Nervous Disorders* 198 (10): 755–761.

Wilcox, Clyde, and Ted G. Jelen. 1990. "Evangelicals and Political Tolerance." *American Politics Quarterly* 18:25–46.

III

How Religion Shapes Responses to Intolerance

11

Carriers of the Creed?

The Effects of Urging Tolerance on Persuasion

PAUL A. DJUPE
JACOB R. NEIHEISEL
LAURA R. OLSON

Scholars who concern themselves with the quality of public deliberation in democratic societies ask a variety of questions about the necessary and sufficient conditions for productive, meaningful discourse among citizens. Some of these questions concern the processes (rules of the game) that are and should be used in deliberation. Other questions have to do with persuasion: Who is persuasive in communicating values and policy preferences, and under what circumstances? There are good reasons to ask questions about democratic processes and persuasion separately. A democratic process with integrity should neither boost nor undermine any particular bias. If one perspective deserves the right to be freely expressed, that right must extend to all perspectives. Persuasion, however, usually is presumed to be particular not to any given process but rather to the press for fulfillment of particular agendas. Constitutional guarantees are necessary, but are also not sufficient; many among us see maintaining reliable democratic processes and pursuing ebullient persuasion as twin responsibilities of responsible citizenship.

Political scientists indeed have treated process and persuasion as distinct and separable concepts. Recognizing that they often accompany each other in public debate, however, this chapter puts the two matters on the same canvas. Many elites urge tolerance *while* attempting to advance ideas in public debate; this contention has driven studies dating to Samuel Stouffer's (1955) claim that elites are more tolerant than the masses (see also Gibson and Duch 1991; Sullivan et al. 1993). Therefore, for more than fifty years, political scientists have viewed elites as "the major repositories of the public conscience and as carriers of the Creed" (McCloskey 1964: 374; see also Stouffer 1955). If the mass public was (is) essentially intolerant (but see Sniderman et al. 1989), at least educated elites who negotiate significant differences in public life could be relied on to exercise restraint and keep the demons of faction at bay. There are exceptions, including one that finds conservatives (elite and mass) significantly less tolerant than liberal citizens, not to mention liberal elites (Sniderman et al. 1991; see also Duch and Gibson 1992).

To be sure, an elitist theory of democracy can function without public disclosure. Elites do not have to inform the public that they are choosing restraint, and they may opt instead to maintain order through private (in)actions. However, there are times when elites do decide to talk about tolerance—almost always in the midst of a policy debate. One example would be when George W. Bush spoke on tolerance for Muslims in the midst of discussion of how and toward whom to respond to the September 11, 2001, attacks. We suspect that public campaigns for tolerance often have their desired effects, but since they happen during policy debates, it is entirely possible that calling for tolerance is not a neutral choice but rather bears on the efficacy of persuasion attempts.

No study to our knowledge has turned the usual formulation around to assess whether persuasive attempts accompanying pleas for tolerance can also be effectual, although some have used tolerance as an independent variable (Gibson 1992; Gibson and Anderson 1985). Elites are not just more tolerant in their decision making; at times in their public address they explicitly plead for tolerance in the context of advancing policy arguments they find compelling. If tolerance is important to the fair conduct of democracy, then how do citizens react to pleas for tolerance when evaluating policy arguments?

More concretely, we decided to undertake the present study in light of a set of findings we obtained from a survey of South Carolina clergy regarding their political communication about immigration. We found that almost all respondent clergy urged tolerance of immigrants in addition to their (at times) ideologically charged arguments. The results of this previous survey, shown in Table 11.1, demonstrate that even clergy members who reported mentioning anti-immigrant arguments to their parishioners also exhorted their flock to be tolerant of illegal immigrants at a very high rate. Of the religious leaders who mentioned that "immigrants drain our community of scarce resources," nearly nine out of ten accompanied that particular argument with a plea for greater tolerance of illegal immigrants. The same percentage (87) of those who reported presenting their congregation with the argument that "immigration increases competition for already scarce jobs" also urged tolerance.

Given the sometimes shrill tone of debate about immigration in South Carolina (e.g., Preston 2014) and elsewhere, we were surprised by our finding that clergy seem to almost universally urge their publics to hate the sin and not the sinner—that is, to maintain basic respect for persons even while arguing with their decisions. We wondered whether the addition of a tolerance statement would affect how clergy's ideological arguments are received in the context of the immigration debate. In this chapter, we pursue this question experimentally in the specific context of clergy communication. We argue that how these

TABLE 11.1 SOUTH CAROLINA CLERGY COMMUNICATION OF AND AGREEMENT WITH IMMIGRATION ARGUMENTS AND THE ATTENDANT MENTION OF A TOLERANCE ARGUMENT (AMONG THOSE MENTIONING THE ARGUMENT)

Argument	*Proportion Mentioning the Argument*	*Proportion Agreeing with the Argument*	*Proportion Mentioning Tolerance Argument*
Regardless of how people immigrated, we need to treat all people with dignity and respect.	0.77	0.94	—
Regardless of how people immigrated, we need to make all people feel welcome in our community.	0.54	0.77	1.0
Given desperate social and economic conditions, it is understandable why someone would immigrate illegally.	0.54	0.89	0.97
Illegal immigration threatens the economic security of the community.	0.32	0.42	0.95
Immigrants are welcome in my community if they make an effort to learn about the community and integrate themselves.	0.53	0.76	0.94
Immigration should be encouraged because people deserve the chance at a better life in America.	0.44	0.69	0.93
Immigrants fill jobs other Americans don't wish to perform.	0.44	0.67	0.93
We need to crack down on individuals and businesses that hire illegal immigrants.	0.42	0.60	0.92
Illegal immigration leads U.S. businesses to exploit immigrants for their labor.	0.42	0.84	0.92
Immigrants deserve to have access to education, health care, and welfare just like any other Americans.	0.37	0.62	0.91
To uphold the law's integrity, we must work harder to stop illegal immigration.	0.34	0.69	0.90
Illegal immigration threatens the historic traditions and values of my community.	0.27	0.46	0.88
Immigration should be tolerated because diversity is healthy for a community.	0.41	0.67	0.88
Immigration increases competition for already scarce jobs.	0.24	0.40	0.87
Immigrants drain our community of scarce resources.	0.26	0.43	0.87
N	~62	~65	~62

arguments are received will depend on individual tolerance predispositions as well as threat context. We first review our approach to the problem before turning to the nature of our experiments and the results from two samples.

Tolerance and Social Legitimacy

There are a number of vantage points from which to consider the effect of tolerance pleas. Tolerance is widely acknowledged as a cornerstone of liberalism and liberal democracy. Without tolerance, individuals will not be free to express their views; neither will citizens be able to assert control over elites (Dahl 1971; Gutmann and Thompson 1996). But if one side argues that liberalism enables debate, the other side argues that liberalism precludes debate. The essence of the argument lies in the hierarchy of value systems.

Liberal theorists famously argue that people must set aside comprehensive perspectives before engaging in dialogue with others (e.g., Gutmann and Thompson 1996; Rawls 1993; Rorty 1994). Doing so acknowledges that disagreement is likely to be persistent—and that it is in fact the modal condition of living with others in a free society. It is easy to see how embracing reciprocity means abandoning truth claims that many hold dear: "A deliberative perspective . . . must reject the unqualified quest for agreement because it must renounce the claim to comprehensiveness" (Gutmann and Thompson 1996: 92). Exchanging "religious certainty" for "comprehensiveness" makes the nature of the conflict clear. Therefore, it is not surprising that religious people have been the most vociferous critics of liberalism (e.g., Carter 1991; Hauerwas and Willimon 1989; Sandel 1996; see also Fish 1999),[1] arguing that liberalism demands that the faithful not reason from religious bases yet allows nonbelievers to argue from their enlightenment perspectives. Putting it more starkly, Republican U.S. Representative Todd Akin of Missouri suggested in an interview that "at the heart of liberalism really is a hatred for God. And a belief that government should replace God" (McCrummen and Farenthold 2012). Thus, liberals argue that democracy continues only on the basis of shared norms that enable unbiased debate, while some conservatives see those norms as tipping the scales toward a particular, liberal perspective. Liberals are satisfied with "Jefferson's compromise" of stability in exchange for secularity, while many conservatives would significantly change the equation.

Our own approach to this fundamental question is guided by the order of importance of concerns about process. Social scientists have long recognized that whoever writes the rules writes the outcome (North 1990). That is, tolerance and other matters of political process are temporally prior to actual debates about the direction of government (Hibbing and Theiss-Morse 2002). While support for the government typically depends on perceptions of fairness, legitimation of various public ends often is coupled with the perceived fairness of a group's status (see Tyler 2006 for a review). Important to our work here, Matthew Hornsey and colleagues (2003) show that perceptions of the legitimacy of high or low status (some groups deserve to have high or low status) drove bias, not the status level itself. Threats to the social order that upend status hierarchies that people perceive to be legitimate generate negative assessments.

We conceive of tolerance judgments as constructions of the social order that best preserve an ingroup in question. In essence, this is a basic self-preservation assumption. Threatening groups are awarded unequal rights and lower status, which helps inoculate the ingroup from further social harm. Because of things that threatening groups have said or done, targets of intolerance are set up to be perceived as legitimately having low status. Communists attempt to undermine a democratic United States; racists attack individuals for their skin color; atheists reject God—the groups seen as legitimately of low status vary widely (Sullivan, Piereson, and Marcus 1982). Tolerance pleas are issued precisely to shift the status of a targeted low-status group and change the social order. Because they grant or restore equal political status and rights, pleas for tolerance are deliberate arguments *against* the ascribed legitimacy of low group status and are an attempt to elevate a group's status. It is easy to see how controversial such a claim might be and how it might taint associated claims. In fact, claims associated with an illegitimate claim to recast the social order may themselves be considered illegitimate.

We suspect that urging tolerance can be used as a heuristic to understand the rest of an argument, particularly when group boundaries are salient. One way to understand how this dynamic might work is by considering the role of threat. Threat has been a staple of tolerance explanations from the beginning (Stouffer 1955). Advances since then have examined the etiology of threat (Gibson 2006), the target level of threat (Chanley 1994; Green and Waxman 1987; Huddy et al. 2002), and the relation of threat to anxiety (Brader, Valentino, and Suhay 2008; Marcus et al. 2005). An additional line of work, particularly in cross-national studies, finds that territorial threat is a particularly potent force undermining tolerance levels (Hutchison and Gibler 2007; Inglehart, Moaddel, and Tessler 2006). Studies in the United States also have found powerful evidence about the role of threat, such as after the attacks of September 11, 2001 (Davis and Silver 2004; Huddy et al. 2005). When threat activates group identity, calls for tolerance have the potential to hijack a conversation depending on how people judge the legitimacy of social arrangements. Those who see a group's status as legitimately low would react negatively to arguments attached to an attempt to boost the group's status (toward equality). Those who want to shift the group's low status because of its illegitimacy (that is, they are tolerant) would be more likely to adopt arguments that contain a call for tolerance.

When little threat is present, almost every study has found higher tolerance (e.g., Marcus et al. 1995; Nunn, Crockett, and Williams 1978; Gibson 2006). Furthermore, in the absence of threat, a call for tolerance can be a powerful norming force. Tolerance, through its association with democracy, is a powerful idea that American citizens hold as a core value (McClosky 1964; McClosky and Brill 1983). Either way, without the sense that being tolerant of a particular group would upend the social order, individuals should be willing to go along with arguments attached to a founding ideal (see Marcus et al. 1995).

Research Design

We generated data to evaluate the effect of clergy urging tolerance of illegal immigrants through two studies: one of students and one of a national sample of adults. For the first, we administered an experiment embedded within a larger survey to 222 students at a large southern university in introductory political science courses. Several versions of the survey were prepared for delivery, each containing a different experimental condition. The design varied the content of the arguments as well as the presence of the tolerance frame, which constitutes a 4×2 design. The particular combinations of arguments regarding immigration were generated from the survey of clergy in South Carolina mentioned at the outset of the chapter. We took the full set of arguments listed in Table 11.1 and subjected them to factor analysis (and some logic) to splice together sets of arguments. Though there were other combinations, we employed four groups of them. We labeled these four groups *tradition*, *justice* (for social justice), *integrity* (for legal integrity), and *community* (as in community standards).

Each cell of the experimental design involved presenting three arguments set in the final paragraph of a newspaper article reporting a conflict between illegal immigrants and citizens, the full text of which is provided in the online appendix.[2] In half of the cells, one of the article's three arguments was a statement urging tolerance of illegal immigrants: "Regardless of how people immigrated, we need to treat all people with dignity and respect." In the other half of the cells, the third argument consistent with the other two was presented to substitute for the tolerance frame. The rationale for replacing the tolerance argument with more substance was to control for the possibility that more support is built simply because one condition provided more arguments.

The justification for such a complicated design is manifold. First, we hoped to stay as close to nature as possible, thus incorporating the multitude of ways that clergy might have been engaging the immigration debate, especially when the frame urging tolerance was included in most clergy's argument repertoires. Second, we wished to test whether the tolerance frame interacted with the direction of the clergy's arguments. And, as developed above, we thought about this in two conflicting ways that reflect the tension within liberalism about whether urging tolerance tips the scales or provides a neutral playing field. In one vision, the tolerance frame could add more liberalism, amplifying arguments that affirm the dignity of the immigrant (the social justice argument package) while undercutting arguments to limit immigration on the basis of tradition or the economy. It is also possible that the tolerance frame is used as a negative since no one likes to be told (in a patronizing way) to play nice. In this view, the presence of the tolerance frame should boost opposition to the policy views of the clergy.

We also reasoned that the participant's preexisting level of tolerance would affect how a tolerance message is received. To measure tolerance, we employed the content-controlled approach pioneered by John Sullivan, James Piereson, and George Marcus (1982), asking first for the participant's least-liked group and then assessing whether the participant would extend political liberties to members of that group. For ease of use in interacting with the treatments, we split the resulting tolerance index at its mean.

The dependent variables consist of an index of attitudes on policy toward immigrants and feelings toward "illegal immigrants" taken from a battery of feeling thermometer items that came late in the survey, both of which closely followed the news article hosting our treatments. The immigration attitudes index uses responses to six statements regarding immigration policy and immigration-related effects on the economy. For each statement, we asked participants to indicate on a scale ranging from 0 to 10 how many arguments there are to support and oppose the statement. We took the difference between them such that the highest score is most conservative and then averaged the scores across the six statements.

This is not the standard way of gathering attitudes in political science, though several literatures recommend this approach. This measurement scheme builds on the psychological research by John Cacioppo, Wendi Gardner, and Gary Berntson (1997) indicating that positive and negative assessments of an attitude object can move independently. This logic is at least implicit in the research on ambivalence that incorporates distinct measures of positive and negative evaluations (e.g., Craig and Martinez 2005; Gainous 2008; Thompson, Zanna, and Griffin 1995). Our measurement scheme is also complementary to Joseph Capella, Vincent Price, and Lilach Nir's (2002) measure of opinion quality that they term "argument repertoire": the ability to list the relevant reasons for one's own opinion and the reasons someone with the opposite opinion might hold.

Our second study was conducted on the panel maintained by Qualtrics, administered October 21–27, 2011, to 631 respondents in a nationally representative sample. The structure of the instrument closely mirrored the one we used with our student sample, though we simplified the number of conditions to a 2×2. Half of the sample was presented with a tolerance call, and half was not. The other two conditions varied the context of the tolerance call, with half receiving a conservative set of arguments and the other half receiving more liberal arguments.

Perhaps a key difference between the two studies is the location of the scenario described in the treatment. James Gibson (1987) argues for setting tolerance work in local contexts, especially those with actual incidents, to allow researchers to see how tolerance attitudes function on the ground when called on. Local incidents should ramp up threat. Given the importance of threat in priming the legitimacy of the social order, we kept the same location (in Greenville, South Carolina) for the incident reported in the article seen by the national sample. In our scheme, this means that the national sample should have reacted as if in a low-threat situation; the student sample should have reacted as if in a higher-threat situation because of the students' location in the South. Following this logic, the national sample should follow the direction of clergy's arguments, while the local student sample may be more likely to polarize in the context of the tolerance frame. This setup is not ideal, of course, since the sample varies along with the construction of the experiment.

Experiment 1

Our analysis of the two dependent variables from the student sample is generated from models including interaction terms between the tolerance treatment and preexisting tolerance levels given one of the four argument packages; that is, we examine the interaction term separately for each argument package. Although randomization was successful and there were no significant differences across cells in demographic variables, we include several controls to help clean up the estimates: gender, grade point average, and born-again/evangelical identification. The role of the controls here is to maintain balance in the comparison of treatments; the controls themselves have almost no substantive meaning, since our focus is on differences between randomly assigned groups.

As it turns out, the treatments and interactions with the preexisting tolerance levels were insignificant in three of the four argument packages. The tolerance frame in the integrity, justice, and community treatments produced almost no variation in attitudes about either immigration or illegal immigrants (results not shown).

One set of arguments did support treatment effects, however: the tradition treatment. In this treatment article, the clergyperson argues, "Immigrants are welcome in my community if they make an effort to learn about the community and integrate themselves" and "Illegal immigration threatens the historic traditions and values of this community." This language marks clear advocacy of ingroup status, which may make the threat to the social order posed by a tolerance statement particularly salient. The marginal effects of the tolerance statement treatment are shown in Figure 11.1. A significant effect is shown when the 90 percent confidence interval does not overlap with the line drawn at 0 (a null effect). Both dependent variables are coded so that their full range is 0–1: Higher values represent more liberal attitudes and warmer feelings toward illegal immigrants.

In the case of immigration attitudes (see the left side of the graph), exposure to a tolerance frame drives the less tolerant portion of the sample to express even more conservative attitudes. The addition of the tolerance frame led these respondents to become considerably less tolerant of immigrants (by about 13 percent). And although the result is not significant strictly speaking ($p = .12$), the addition of the tolerance frame nonetheless led the more tolerant portion of the

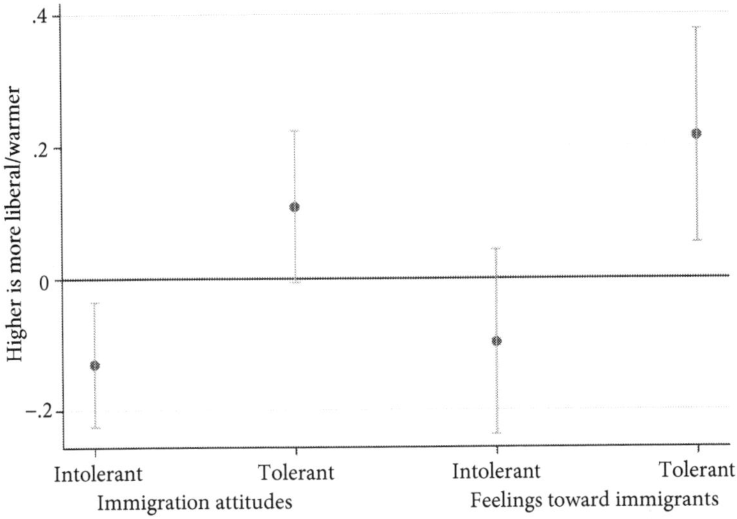

Figure 11.1 Marginal effects of the tolerance frame given predispositional tolerance on immigration attitudes and feelings toward illegal immigrants in the context of arguments supporting tradition

Note: $N = 50$ (attitudes), $N = 55$ (feelings); 90 percent confidence intervals.

sample to become 11 percent more liberal in their immigration attitudes. What is notable is that these two groups did *not* differ in their immigration attitudes in the absence of the tolerance frame; that is, when presented with three arguments favoring "maintenance of tradition" (not shown). They polarized only when exposed to a plea for tolerance of illegal immigrants.

The right side of Figure 11.1 shows the marginal effects of the tolerance frame on feelings toward illegal immigrants. Though the significance level changes slightly, it is clear that the results are essentially in accord with the previous set. The intolerant respondent feels cooler toward illegal immigrants when exposed to a tolerance frame (by about 10 percent), while the already tolerant respondent feels warmer toward them when so exposed (by about 21 percent). Thus, the two groups polarized when the clergyperson advanced a call for tolerance, but they did not polarize as a direct response to a conservative argument against illegal immigration.

Experiment 2

We administered our second experiment, which closely mirrored the first, to a national sample of adults by embedding the experimental manipulations within a Qualtrics survey. Given that the Qualtrics survey was designed for respondents across the United States, the newspaper article in which the treatments were delivered described events that took place at a considerable distance from most respondents compared to the one given to the student sample, which described hypothetical events taking place in close physical proximity to them. This aspect of the treatment in the second experiment represents more than just a practical consideration; it also offers a chance to investigate the effect of a nonthreatening (distant) context on respondents' reception of and reactions to tolerance frames.

We followed the same analytic procedure as in experiment 1. We estimated models for each argument package separately, looking specifically for the interaction between the tolerance frame and preexisting levels of tolerance to be significant. We also included several controls, again not because randomization failed but because of small variations across cells that the introduction of controls can help equalize. The controls have no substantive importance to the investigation, but they help produce crisper estimates of the treatment effects.

In the case of our national sample, the conservative, tradition-maintaining argument package produced no treatment effect—but the liberal arguments did. Figure 11.2 presents those results in the same manner as Figure 11.1. The results are directly opposed to those in Figure 11.1. Here, the views of less tolerant respondents move consistently in the direction of the clergy's arguments, but only when accompanied with a tolerance plea. These respondents shift their immigration attitudes in a more liberal direction and express warmer feelings toward illegal immigrants, both by about 6 percent. Tolerant respondents, on the other

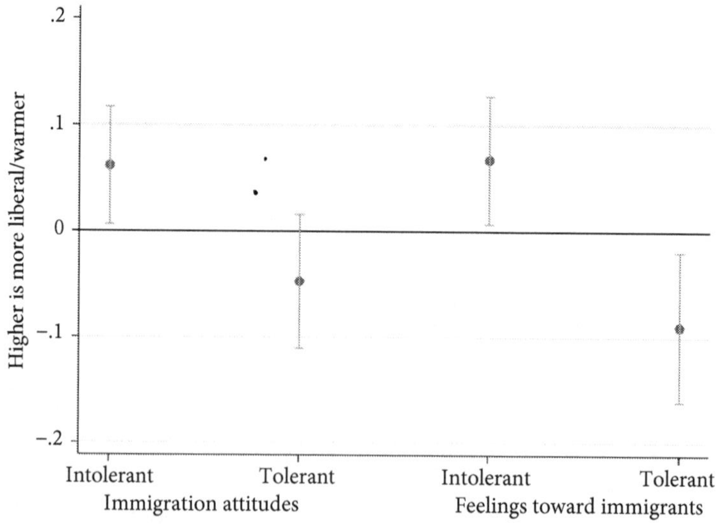

Figure 11.2 Interactive effects of urging tolerance and preexisting tolerance judgments on immigration attitudes and feelings toward illegal immigrants when given the liberal argument package (nationally representative sample)

Note: $N = 284$ (attitudes), 297 (feelings); 90 percent confidence intervals.

hand, shift their attitudes in a more conservative direction (an insignificant 5 percent in attitudes and a significant 9 percent in warmth). In contrast to the student sample, the gap between the tolerant and intolerant remains sizable no matter the treatment, indicating that tolerant respondents are moving from very liberal policy attitudes/feelings to a slightly less liberal point of view, while the intolerant are moderating their opposition to welcoming policies toward immigrants. We suspect that the tolerance frame has no effect on tolerant respondents and simply takes the place of any other pro-immigration argument. For intolerant respondents, however, a tolerance plea from a clergyperson marks a call to attention that urges them to reconsider pro-immigration arguments. The difference in results across the studies is probably a reflection on the context of the threat, a point to which we turn in the conclusion.

Conclusion

Discussing tolerance is not simply a matter of understanding the rules of the game but instead can *be* the game under some conditions. Calls for tolerance can be important buoys to the formation of citizens' attitudes about policy priorities and solutions, especially in instances when tolerance is perceived to have potential effects on the social hierarchy. Our findings here indicate that there are real costs involved in urging tolerance when arguing about public policy. Such calls, depending on the contexts within which they are made, may hijack how people view policy arguments. As we show using our student sample, such calls can help build support for the elite's policy preferences among the already tolerant—but simultaneously serve to weaken support among those with lower than average levels of tolerance.

Only in the national sample did the presence of a tolerance frame appear to aid in religious leaders' efforts at persuasion. Intolerant respondents exposed to a liberal package of arguments concerning the immigration debate in conjunction with a plea for greater tolerance of illegal immigrants expressed more liberal attitudes toward immigration and more positive feelings toward illegal immigrants than those who did not receive the tolerance frame. Of course, some respondents might be more susceptible to social desirability effects—or simply more persuadable—given the relatively nonthreatening, distant context of our experimental frame.

We believe that the results of our analyses of these two samples differ because of the divergent contexts within which the experiments were administered. In the national sample, the news story in which the experimental manipulation was embedded was (necessarily) generic. For the students, however, the hypothetical events described in the article were happening in close proximity to them. It is this proximity that points to the moderating influence of threat and anxiety (see Brader, Valentino, and Suhay 2008; Marcus et al. 2005). It may be that debates hitting particularly close to home result in a heightened sensitivity to cues. The presence of a tolerance frame appears to provoke respondents in the student sample into pure social identity theory responses, rejecting that which is inconsistent with the ingroup's interests (Tajfel 1970).

Our study also suggests some reconsideration of the usefulness of relying on the American case in studying the role context plays in shaping tolerance judgments. James Gibson and Amanda Gouws (2001), for instance, conclude their study of tolerance in South Africa with a plea for more cross-national work on the subject, arguing that politics in the American context adheres to particular democratic norms that center around tolerance of competing viewpoints (see also Sullivan et al. 1985). With respect to the question of illegal immigrants, however, perceptions of threat vary widely across the American states. In our national sample, the effect of threat appears to have been sufficiently diluted so as to allow pleas for tolerance to have an effect, whereas the same experiment conducted in a different regional context (and political climate) uncovered a polarizing relationship. This result reaffirms the utility of treating states as essential laboratories of democracy.

While we did not study the effect of elites advocating tolerance on tolerance itself, respondents' attitudinal responses suggest a defensive reaction to such calls among those whom the elite is trying to reach under circumstances when their attitudes matter the most. It would be too cynical to think that clergy, especially, use tolerance as a tool to mobilize a constituency. Most clergy truly care about establishing rules for debate that affirm the dignity of all people. This impetus, however, leaves clergy—and indeed any elites who care about promoting a tolerant society—in a difficult position. When elites advocate for their own preferred policies and for tolerance, they risk polarizing their audience along just the rift they hoped to heal. When they avoid calls for tolerance, they simply advocate for their policy preferences without raising awareness about the dignity of the individuals affected (see also Kuklinski et al. 1991).

Perhaps the supreme irony of our findings is that clergy appear to be successful in coupling pleas for greater tolerance with a persuasive line of argumentation only in the abstract. When addressing a population that has experienced conflict over the issue of immigration, religious leaders' efforts at urging tolerance of illegal immigrants effectively negated subsequent attempts at persuading the audience of their preferred policy stance. Although clergy can, and do, issue public statements on matters that extend beyond the confines of the communities they serve, they are most commonly called on to minister to their own flocks in place. It is in the latter context, however, where they are perhaps the least capable of simultaneously pushing for a particular policy and issuing a call for tolerance, because the issue is salient and immediate.

This bleak portrait affirms Alexis de Tocqueville's ([1840] 1994) formulation of the role of religion in a democracy. His famous observation was that religion provided Americans a common set of values and practices that maintained peace and order, prevented "experimentation" in social behavior, and permitted political freedom within a narrow band. The results of this study suggest that organized religion and its elites may have a difficult time healing the rifts among themselves over the treatment of minorities in society, which serves to maintain the status quo. Preexisting preferences of the application of political liberties may impede calls for change (but see Friedrichs 1971). In short, our study provides still more evidence that religious leaders are highly constrained by the distribution of preferences in their congregations and face considerable obstacles when they attempt to fulfill a prophetic role (see also Neiheisel and Djupe 2008).

However, there are several scenarios in which organized religion is capable of overcoming the problem of localism. First, clergy with a national audience may indeed act as opinion leaders on pressing issues of the day while at the same time preaching tolerance of all peoples. Few examples of this kind of public figure come readily to mind, however, aside from perhaps Dr. Martin Luther King, Jr., who wisely chose to target white moderates away from the front lines of the civil rights movement (Findlay 1993). Second, local congregations can carry prophetic sway through the organizational superstructures to which they are connected (though decreasingly so): denominations. Denominations, especially the more hierarchical ones, encourage member congregations to address certain issues at salient times. For example, denominations pushed to address gun control in the wake of the 2012 Sandy Hook school shootings, have encouraged environmental protection, have pressed for racial reconciliation, and have even banded together to lobby for comprehensive immigration reform. Put another way, denominations are national networks that can encourage the widespread address of problems with populations that may not otherwise have incentives to learn about them—and thus may be more susceptible to persuasion including the sorts of appeals for tolerance we have analyzed here. Therefore, denominations may play an especially important role in policy diffusion (Djupe and Olson 2010) and in the maintenance of democratic values, at least to the extent that denominations proffer these ideas.

In this way, our results also engage existing research on clergy political behavior. Some studies of clergy political behavior tend to treat clergy as if they are policy maximizers who use the bully pulpit to press an agenda, held in check only by constraints that could threaten their position (e.g., Calfano 2009, 2010; Calfano, Oldmixon, and Gray 2013; Glock and Stark 1965; Guth et al. 1997; Hadden 1969; Quinley 1974). Although clergy do express themselves on political matters in and out of the pulpit, bullies they tend not to be. Clergy care deeply about individual empowerment, safeguarding basic rights and liberties, and boosting participation in civic life (Djupe and Gilbert 2003). They often have an abiding concern for the sustenance of democracy (Djupe and Calfano 2012; Djupe and Neiheisel 2008), one of the foundations of which is tolerance of people of different backgrounds.

Notes

Acknowledgments: This work is supported by a Jack Shand Research Award from the Society for the Scientific Study of Religion granted to Djupe and Olson. We thank George Marcus for comments on an earlier draft. All errors are our own.

1. We can find opposition in the "sin of tolerance" speech from Billy Graham from 1959 in which he complains, "We have become tolerant about divorce; we have become tolerant about the use of alcohol; we have become tolerant about delinquency; we have become tolerant about wickedness in high places; we have become tolerant about immorality; we have become tolerant about crime; and we have become tolerant about godlessness. We have become tolerant of unbelief." (For an updated version of the speech, see http://billygraham.org/story/the-sin-of-tolerance/). One popular culture illustration is the book *The New Tolerance: How a Cultural Movement Threatens to Destroy You, Your Faith, and Your Children* (Hostetler and McDowell 1998); the book description on Amazon.com informs us that "this book will help readers discern truth from error and to withstand the pressure—even persecution—to conform to a relativistic culture."

2. The full text of each set of arguments as well as all variable coding notes are provided in the online appendix at http://pauldjupe.com/s/Appendix.docx.

References

Brader, Ted, Nicholas A. Valentino, and Elizabeth Suhay. 2008. "What Triggers Public Opposition to Immigration? Anxiety, Group Cues, and Immigration Threat." *American Journal of Political Science* 52 (4): 959–978.

Cacioppo, John T., Wendi L. Gardner, and Gary G. Berntson. 1997. "Beyond Bipolar Conceptualizations and Measures: The Case of Attitudes and Evaluative Space." *Personality and Social Psychology Review* 1:3–25.

Calfano, Brian R. 2009. "Choosing Constituent Cues: Reference Group Influence on Clergy Political Speech." *Social Science Quarterly* 90 (1): 88–102.

———. 2010. "Prophetic at Any Price? Clergy Political Behavior and Utility Maximization." *Social Science Quarterly* 91 (3): 649–668.

Calfano, Brian R., Elizabeth A. Oldmixon, and Mark Gray. 2013. "Strategically Prophetic Priests: An Analysis of Competing Principal Influence on Clergy Political Action." *Review of Religious Research* 56 (1): 1–21.

Capella, Joseph N., Vincent Price, and Lilach Nir. 2002. "Argument Repertoire as Reliable and Valid Measure of Opinion Quality: Electronic Dialogue during Campaign 2000." *Political Communication* 19:73–93.

Carter, Stephen L. 1991. *The Culture of Disbelief.* New York: Anchor Books.

Chanley, Virginia. 1994. "Commitment to Political Tolerance: Situational and Activity-Based Differences." *Political Behavior* 16 (3): 343–363.

Craig, Stephen C., and Michael D. Martinez. 2005. *Ambivalence and the Structure of Political Opinion*. New York: Palgrave MacMillan.

Dahl, Robert. 1971. *Polyarchy: Participation and Opposition*. New Haven, CT: Yale University Press.

Davis, Darren W., and Brian D. Silver. 2004. "Civil Liberties vs. Security: Public Opinion in the Context of the Terrorist Attacks on America." *American Journal of Political Science* 48 (1): 28–46.

Djupe, Paul A., and Brian R. Calfano. 2012. "The Deliberative Pulpit: The Democratic Norms and Practices of the PCUSA." *Journal for the Scientific Study of Religion* 51 (1): 90–109.

Djupe, Paul A., and Christopher P. Gilbert. 2003. *The Prophetic Pulpit: Clergy, Churches, and Communities in American Politics*. Lanham, MD: Rowman and Littlefield.

Djupe, Paul A., and Jacob R. Neiheisel. 2008. "Clergy Deliberation on Gay Rights and Homosexuality." *Polity* 40 (4): 411–435.

Djupe, Paul A., and Laura R. Olson. 2010. "Diffusion of Environmental Concerns in Congregations across U.S. States." *State Politics and Policy Quarterly* 10 (3): 270–301.

Duch, Raymond, and James L. Gibson, 1992. "'Putting Up With' Fascists in Western Europe: A Comparative, Cross-Level Analysis of Political Tolerance." *Western Political Quarterly* 45 (1): 237–273.

Findlay, James F., Jr. 1993. *Church People in the Struggle: The National Council of Churches and the Black Freedom Movement, 1950–1970.* New York: Oxford University Press.

Fish, Stanley. 1999. *The Trouble with Principle.* Cambridge, MA: Harvard University Press.

Friedrichs, Robert W. 1971. "Decline in Prejudice among Church-Goers Following Clergy-Led Open Housing Campaign." *Journal for the Scientific Study of Religion* 10 (2): 152–156.

Gainous, Jason. 2008. "Ambivalence about Social Welfare: An Evaluation of Measurement Approaches." *American Review of Politics* 29:109–134.

Gibson, James L. 1987. "Homosexuals and the Ku Klux Klan: A Contextual Analysis of Political Intolerance." *Western Political Quarterly* 40 (3): 427–448.

———. 1992. "Alternative Measures of Political Tolerance: Must Tolerance Be 'Least Liked'?" *American Journal of Political Science* 36 (2): 560–577.

———. 2006. "Enigmas of Intolerance: Fifty Years after Stouffer's *Communism, Conformity, and Civil Liberties.*" *Perspectives on Politics* 4 (1): 21–34.

Gibson, James L., and Arthur J. Anderson. 1985. "The Political Implications of Elite and Mass Tolerance." *Political Behavior* 7 (2): 118–146.

Gibson, James L., and Raymond M. Duch. 1991. "Elitist Theory and Political Tolerance in Western Europe." *Political Behavior* 13 (3): 191–212.

Gibson, James L., and Amanda Gouws. 2001. "Making Tolerance Judgments: The Effects of Context Local and National." *Journal of Politics* 63 (4): 1067–1090.

Glock, Charles Y., and Rodney Stark. 1965. *Religion and Society in Tension.* Chicago: Rand McNally.

Green, Donald P., and Lisa M. Waxman. 1987. "Direct Threat and Political Tolerance: An Experimental Analysis of the Tolerance of Blacks toward Racists." *Public Opinion Quarterly* 51 (2): 149–165.

Guth, James L., John C. Green, Corwin E. Smidt, Lyman A. Kellstedt, and Margaret Poloma. 1997. *The Bully Pulpit: The Politics of Protestant Clergy.* Lawrence: University of Kansas Press.

Gutmann, Amy, and Dennis Thompson. 1996. *Democracy and Disagreement: Why Moral Conflict Cannot Be Avoided in Politics, and What Should Be Done about It.* Cambridge, MA: Harvard University Press.

Hadden, Jeffrey K. 1969. *The Gathering Storm in the Churches.* Garden City, NY: Doubleday.

Hauerwas, Stanley, and William H. Willimon. 1989. *Resident Aliens.* Nashville, TN: Abingdon Press.

Hibbing, John R., and Elizabeth Theiss-Morse. 2002. *Stealth Democracy: Americans' Beliefs about How Government Should Work.* New York: Cambridge University Press.

Hornsey, Matthew J., Russell Spears, Iris Cremers, and Michael A. Hogg. 2003. "Relations between High and Low Power Groups: The Importance of Legitimacy." *Personality and Social Psychology Bulletin* 29 (2): 216–227.

Hostetler, Bob, and Josh D. McDowell. 1998. *The New Tolerance: How a Cultural Movement Threatens to Destroy You, Your Faith, and Your Children.* Wheaton, IL: Tyndale House.

Huddy, Leonie, Stanley Feldman, Theresa Capelos, and Colin Provost. 2002. "The Consequences of Terrorism: Disentangling the Effects of Personal and National Threat." *Political Psychology* 23 (3): 485–509.

Huddy, Leonie, Stanley Feldman, Charles Taber, and Gallya Lahav. 2005. "Threat, Anxiety, and Support of Antiterrorism Policies." *American Journal of Political Science* 49 (3): 610–625.

Hutchison, Marc L., and Douglas M. Gibler. 2007. "Political Tolerance and Territorial Threat: A Cross-National Study." *Journal of Politics* 69 (1): 128–142.

Inglehart, Ronald, Mansoor Moaddel, and Mark Tessler. 2006. "Xenophobia and In-Group Solidarity in Iraq: A Natural Experiment on the Impact of Insecurity." *Perspectives on Politics* 4 (3): 495–505.

Kuklinski, James H., Ellen Riggle, Victor Ottati, Norbert Schwarz, and Robert S. Wyer, Jr. 1991. "The Cognitive and Affective Bases of Political Tolerance Judgments." *American Journal of Political Science* 35 (1): 1–27.

Marcus, George E., John L. Sullivan, Elizabeth Theiss-Morse, and Daniel Stevens. 2005. "The Emotional Foundation of Political Cognition: The Impact of Extrinsic Anxiety on the Formation of Political Tolerance Judgments." *Political Psychology* 26 (6): 949–963.

Marcus, George E., John L. Sullivan, Elizabeth Theiss-Morse, and Sandra Wood. 1995. *With Malice toward Some: How People Make Civil Liberties Judgments*. New York: Cambridge University Press.

McClosky, Herbert. 1964. "Consensus and Ideology in American Politics." *American Political Science Review* 58 (2): 361–382.

McClosky, Herbert, and Alida Brill. 1983. *Dimensions of Tolerance*. New York: Russell Sage.

McCrummen, Stephanie, and David A. Farenthold. 2012. "Akin's Congressional Legacy Small, but His Support among Christian Groups Is Big." *Washington Post*, August 22. Available at http://www.washingtonpost.com/politics/akins-congressional-legacy-small-but-his-support-among-christian-groups-is-big/2012/08/22/b2c2d98e-ec75-11e1-aca7-272630dfd152_story.html.

Neiheisel, Jacob R., and Paul A. Djupe. 2008. "Intraorganizational Constraints on Churches' Public Witness." *Journal for the Scientific Study of Religion* 47 (3): 427–441.

North, Douglass C. 1990. *Institutions, Institutional Change and Economic Performance*. New York: Cambridge University Press.

Nunn, Clyde Z., Harry J. Crockett, Jr., and J. Allen Williams, Jr. 1978. *Tolerance for Nonconformity*. San Francisco: Jossey-Bass.

Preston, Julia. 2014. "G.O.P. Congressman in South Carolina Takes a Risk with Foray into Immigration." *New York Times*, February 21. Available at http://www.nytimes.com/2014/02/22/us/politics/gop-congressman-in-south-carolina-takes-a-risk-with-a-foray-into-immigration.html.

Quinley, Harold E. 1974. *The Prophetic Clergy: Social Activism among Protestant Ministers*. New York: Wiley.

Rawls, John. 1993. *Political Liberalism*. New York: Columbia University Press.

Rorty, Richard. 1994. "Religion as a Conversation-Stopper." *Common Knowledge* 3:1–3.

Sandel, Michael J. 1996. *Democracy's Discontent: America in Search of a Public Philosophy*. Cambridge, MA: Harvard University Press.

Sniderman, Paul M., Philip E. Tetlock, James M. Glaser, Donald Philip Green, and Michael Hout. 1989. "Principled Tolerance and the American Mass Public." *British Journal of Political Science* 19 (1): 25–45.

Stouffer, Samuel A. 1955. *Communism, Conformity and Civil Liberties: A Cross Section of the Nation Speaks Its Mind*. New York: Doubleday.

Sullivan, John L., James Piereson, and George E. Marcus. 1982. *Political Tolerance and American Democracy*. Chicago: University of Chicago Press.

Sullivan, John L., Michal Shamir, Nigel Roberts, and Patrick Walsh. 1985. *Political Tolerance in Context: Support for Unpopular Minorities in Israel, New Zealand, and the United States*. Boulder, CO: Westview Press.

Sullivan, John L., Pat Walsh, Michal Shamir, David G. Barnum, and James L. Gibson. 1993. "Why Politicians Are More Tolerant: Selective Recruitment and Socialization among Political Elites in Britain, Israel, New Zealand and the United States." *British Journal of Political Science* 23 (1): 51–76.

Tajfel, Henri. 1970. "Experiments in Intergroup Discrimination." *Scientific American* 232:96–102.

Thompson, Megan M., Mark P. Zanna, and Dale W. Griffin. 1995. "Let's Not Be Indifferent about (Attitudinal) Ambivalence." In *Attitude Strength: Antecedents and Consequences*, edited by Richard E. Petty and Jon A. Krosnick, 361–386. Mahwah, NJ: Lawrence Erlbaum.

Tocqueville, Alexis de. (1840) 1994. *Democracy in America*. 2 vols. New York: Alfred A. Knopf.

Tyler, Tom R. 2006. "Psychological Perspectives on Legitimacy and Legitimation." *Annual Review of Psychology* 57:375–400.

12

Going to Extremes

Stereotypes, Constitutional Violations, and Support for Religious Elites

BRIAN R. CALFANO
PAUL A. DJUPE

This chapter is a companion piece to Chapter 11, which investigates the effect of calling for tolerance on the ability of elites to persuade an audience. Here, we assess whether a call for intolerance can affect how elites and their arguments are evaluated by audience members. The premise behind elitist theories of democracy obviates the need for mass tolerance (e.g., Prothro and Grigg 1960; Stouffer 1955). But confirmation that elites generally have a greater commitment to basic democratic principles does not mean that intolerant elites are imaginary figments. Perhaps because of their relative rarity, intolerant elites may gain more media attention than conforming tolerant ones. Therefore, one of the fallback mechanisms of maintaining democracy is for the public to push back on elites who espouse intolerant policy positions. The key question we investigate in this chapter is whether citizens factor in democratic norms when evaluating policy arguments attached to norm-violating calls.

Theories of Elite-Mass Relations

The relationship between group members and elites has been assessed from a variety of perspectives in political science, social psychology, and related disciplines (e.g., Downs 1957; Hogg and van Knippenberg 2003; Page and Shapiro 1992; Zaller 1992). Much of the theoretical interest of the connection between elites and citizens centers on the role elites play in acting as guideposts for the articulation of citizen political preferences. Many studies examine the public's reliance on heuristics, and scholars have found these information shortcuts to be essential determinants of a range of political actions, including vote choice and opinion articulation (e.g., Brady and Sniderman 1985; Lau and Redlawsk 2001;

Darmofal 2005). The heuristic function may be one of the central acts of shaping public opinion, perhaps even politics itself (Gamson 1992).

But elites can serve in more than a heuristic-providing role. Elites attempt to provide people with new things to think about (agenda setting—MacKuen 1984), they give them new lenses to use in evaluating the world (e.g., priming—Iyengar and Kinder 1987), and they can provide context for events that encompass what is important about the event by highlighting relevant considerations (such as framing—e.g., Druckman 2001; Nelson, Clawson, and Oxley 1997).

Elite communication does not occur in a vacuum, however. Indeed, both the simple cues and complex stories they offer are often available to both a wider public and an intended audience. This reflects the stuff of politics, as parties and other groups vie for public opinion and decision-making control. But the evaluation of elite communication does not stop at cue or story adoption. Instead, there is a feedback loop in which elite communication builds considerations that may affect how elites are evaluated in their cue-giving role (Lodge, McGraw, and Stroh 1989; Peterson 2005) and even identity choices (e.g., Green, Palmquist, and Schickler 2002).

Social psychology has gone further than political science in investigating the bounds of elite ingroup credibility. Scholars have found that higher levels of prototypical behavior associated with group elites give these leaders the flexibility to articulate views that may not be in keeping with traditional group-held views but that are influential nonetheless (Tyler and Lind 1992; Hogg 2001). There is also a large literature on source effects, which primarily assesses whether there is an identity match across, for instance, racial, gender, age, and religious groups (e.g., Campbell, Green, and Layman 2011; McDermott 2007, 2009; though see, e.g., Djupe and Calfano 2013: chap. 6). We argue that a focus on elites outside the traditional political sphere may be instructional. Without the rigidity often imposed by party identity, elites operating outside partisan political environments may have greater latitude in offering political cues. With greater potential freedom to offer cues on political issues, clergy may be well positioned to offer cues on controversial topics without incurring an influence interruption among targeted audiences.

This suggests that identity is a prime mover in how elite communication is assessed. If elite communication over time bears on identity selection, then in the short run group members will be interested in identity maintenance and policing imagined group boundaries (see Anderson 1993). Groups realize what Geoffrey Cohen and Julio Garcia (2005) refer to as the "I am us" problem—that how individuals are evaluated depends on how the group they are associated with is viewed. The proposition that people use stereotypes to evaluate groups is not a new idea, but a noteworthy point is that group members may be wary of others in the group who support the (presumably negative) stereotype or who make it worse. This is what Cohen and Garcia (2005) refer to as "collective threat"—that poor individual behavior may be used to build and reinforce negative group stereotypes (see also Tyler and Lind 1992).

The idea of collective threat and identity maintenance potentially complicates the potential for elite influence through the standard routes discussed above. Arguably, the heuristic value of cues from elites whose behavior redounds poorly for the group (i.e., the "elite behaving badly") changes. The frames may be the same, the primes could remain unchanged, but the source providing those cues changes in a demonstrable way that may affect how those cues are perceived. That leaves us with two questions. First, is the elite behaving badly recognized as such—is the behavior seen as a collective threat? Second, does the collective threat affect whether the elite's persuasive communication is adopted?

Research Design

The collective threat we assess is the call for stripping away rights and liberties from a political opponent. Given that Americans almost universally appreciate and support rights and liberties (McCloskey and Brill 1983; Prothro and Grigg 1960), we presume that an elite calling publicly for restricting the rights and liberties of a group would be embarrassing to the ingroup. Of course this is an empirical question. To test this, we conducted an experiment in which participants were randomly assigned combinations of three conditions embedded in mocked-up news articles on the topic of gay rights. Gay rights represents an "easy" issue that has long been at the center of the "culture wars," thus providing a policy on which ingroup opinion change should be more difficult (Carmines and Stimson 1980). We focus on the conditions where people grant support to a religious elite cue-giver by shifting the elite's source cue attributes and the message conveyed.

We variably provided the elite's religious tradition to our randomly assigned subjects in a survey experiment—either identifying the clergyperson as evangelical or providing no information. We also altered the issue argument direction. Half the subjects read about our experimental elite—"Reverend Olson"—arguing for gay rights, while half read about him arguing against said rights. Importantly, and as evidence that elites do not have carte blanche to say whatever they like while maintaining their credibility, our subjects did not find the story of a pro-gay-rights reverend credible. Using a trust measure as the outcome assessment, the trust score for the frame of a pro-gay-rights clergyperson was 3.9 versus 5.4 for the frame of an anti-gay-rights clergyperson (0–10 scale; the difference is significant at $p < .01$). The difference is a bit smaller for the credibility item but still significant ($p < .01$). More important, the treatments were ineffective in the half of the sample that read the pro-gay-rights frame. Given these results, we focus our analysis below on the half of our subject pool that received the anti-gay-rights frame. Last, we varied the inclusion of a proposal to strip activists of the right to advocate for gay rights. With all conditions included, the statement looked like the following stimuli reproduction, with the two conditions noted by their typeface (**bold** for the evangelical cue and *italics* for the unconstitutional "violation" cue):

May 14, 2007

The Oregonian

Gay Rights Initiative Draws Fire
By Kate Morrisey, Staff Writer

The war to advance the rights of gays and lesbians in the United States is progressing like the Battle of the Bulge. Two sides are entrenched, evenly matched, and making little movement. That is why supporters of gay rights were encouraged Wednesday when a new bill was introduced into the Oregon House of Representatives that would grant same-sex partners the same status as spouses in making health care decisions. The bill faces an uncertain and rocky future, especially in the Senate, but Governor Kulongonski has expressed tentative support.

Not all are pleased, of course. Reverend Matthew Olson, who hosts a prominent **evangelical Christian** television ministry in Oregon, has taken a tough stance against the bill: "Providing special rights to homosexuals does nothing more than undermine our most important, sacred institution—marriage—and threatens the stability of this great nation founded upon Christian values. *In fact, instead of giving them new special rights, we should pass a law to stop homosexuals from lobbying for their immoral agenda.*"

We administered the survey experiment to introductory political science undergraduate students at a variety of universities around the United States. Though concerns have been raised about using student samples (e.g., Sears 1986), recent research suggests that student samples are a problem in only a few situations, none of which are at issue here (see Druckman and Kam 2011). Given that we have diversity on the key moderating measure—37 percent self-identified as born again or evangelical—we have sufficient information to estimate differences in how ingroup members evaluate available elite cues.

We asked subjects about their perception of the clergy's credibility, the number of positive and negative arguments they could personally think of regarding the clergy's anti-gay-rights argument, and whether the subject would adopt the clergy's argument as his or her own. The question wording and process for these measures was as follows:

- "Do you find Rev. Olson's comments credible? Use a 0–10 scale, where 0 means the comments are not at all credible, and 10 means they are extremely credible."
- "Thinking about Rev. Olson's position, are there *positive* arguments you can think of to back that position? Use a scale from 0–10, where 0 means you can think of no positive arguments to back his position and 10 means there are very many arguments in support." And second, "How about *negative* arguments against Rev. Olson's position?

Use a scale from 0–10, where 0 means you can think of no negative arguments to back his position and 10 means there are very many arguments in opposition." We then took the difference of the first minus the second, so the measure ranges from −10 (all negative arguments) to +10 (all positive and no negative).

- "If you were having a discussion about the issues discussed in the article, how likely would you be to adopt Rev. Olson's arguments as your own? Pick 0 if there is no way you would adopt his argument and 10 if it is very likely."

Results

The key hypotheses we explore involve conditional effects of our experimental conditions. In particular, the social identity literature suggests that evangelicals will react more positively to a clergyperson identified as an evangelical. We are ambivalent about the effects of a constitutional rights violation cue, however. On the one hand, an elite advocating for taking away an outgroup's rights highlights boundaries that might augment ingroup solidarity. Conversely, Americans demonstrate at least rhetorical support for civil rights and liberties, and clergy advocating outside of that framework may lose support as a consequence. This may be especially true when an elite represents the ingroup, as group members may be particularly sensitive to negative sentiments accruing toward their group because of their elite's incongruence with dominant norms (such as the right of political activism). Still another possibility is that ingroup members only react differently and negatively to *outgroup* elites acting against social norms. Thus, for instance, evangelicals would react negatively to a nonevangelical elite calling for a rights violation against political activism by gay rights lobbyists but not an evangelical clergyperson advocating the same.

These hypotheses call for the estimation of a triple interaction—among (1) the individual evangelical identity, (2) the clergy evangelical cue, and (3) the appearance of a constitutional violation. We explore these graphically in Figures 12.1–12.3.[1] We also control for gender and political ideology in our models to better balance the sample.[2] In each figure, the gray lines indicate confidence intervals around the estimated prediction for nonevangelicals; the black lines show the estimates with confidence intervals for evangelicals.[3] The columns are otherwise labeled for the combinations of treatment conditions that they represent.

In Figure 12.1, we explore the interactive effects of the significant triple interaction on assessed clergy credibility. As seen, the differences between evangelical and nonevangelical subjects are negligible for all elites except the nonevangelical Rev. Olson who does not advocate a rights violation (seen in the first column). Nonevangelicals rate this version of Rev. Olson the most credible, while evangelicals see him as the least credible. Otherwise, it is notable that credibility drops precipitously for the nonevangelical Rev. Olson calling for a

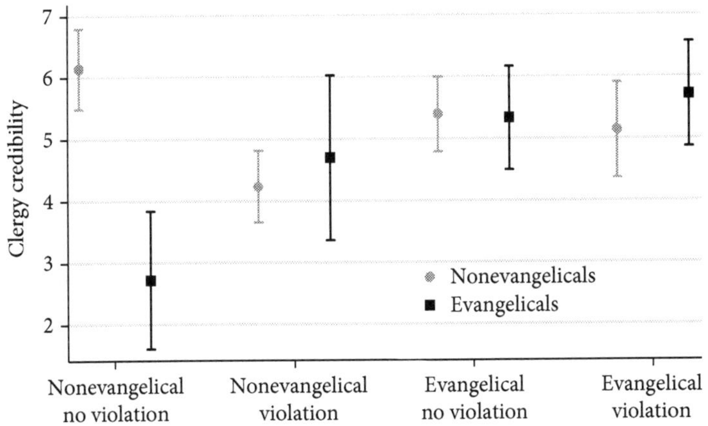

Figure 12.1 Interactive effects of evangelical ID, clergy evangelical cue, and a constitutional violation argument on assessed clergy credibility

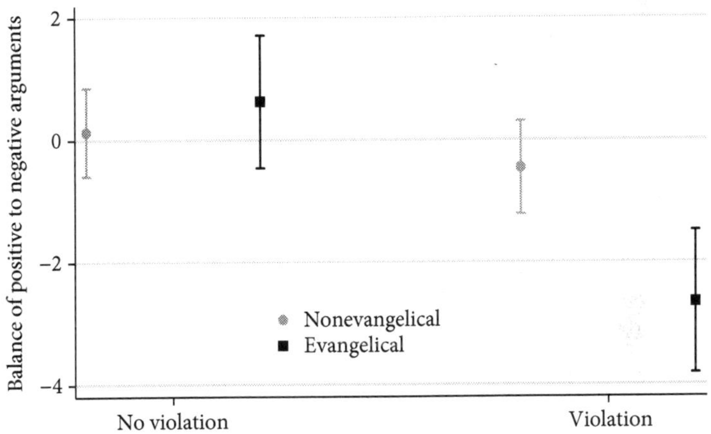

Figure 12.2 Interactive effects of advancing a constitutional violation on the balance of positive (versus negative) arguments held by evangelicals and nonevangelicals

rights violation, which is suggestive evidence that the ingroup rejects elites when they violate group norms. Rev. Olson's credibility jumps among evangelicals when he calls for a rights violation or when he is an evangelical—subjects apparently used both interchangeably to assess credibility. Clearly, an anti-gay-rights clergyperson cue fits the leadership stereotype held by both evangelical and nonevangelical subjects, and the cue of an outgroup rights violation is consistent with that (since they are evaluated similarly).

Our second dependent variable is the balance of arguments that subjects hold about the clergy's anti-gay-rights arguments. Here, the triple interaction is

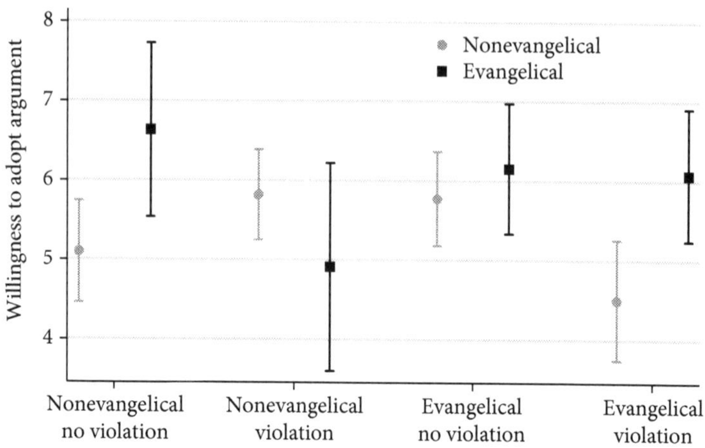

Figure 12.3 Interactive effects of evangelical ID, clergy evangelical cue, and a constitutional violation argument on the willingness to adopt the clergy's argument as one's own

not significant, but one of the two-way interactions is. This suggests that evangelical subjects react differently to a rights violation than nonevangelicals, and Figure 12.2 demonstrates how. Nonevangelicals actually do not change the balance of positive arguments regarding the anti-gay-rights clergyperson's claims when he advocates for a rights violation, whereas evangelicals' balance of *negative* arguments grows. That is, while the credibility given to this Rev. Olson grows for evangelicals, they actually gain more negative arguments (i.e., against his position) than without the civil rights violation. These results seem the best evidence yet that ingroup elites occasion the biggest subject reactions, especially when they advocate against social norms.

With its significant triple interaction ($p < .06$), Figure 12.3 shows how evangelicals and nonevangelicals react differently to the clergy conditions on elite argument adoption. In all cases but one, evangelicals are at least somewhat more likely to say they would adopt Rev. Olson's argument as their own in a conversation. But the particulars of subject movement toward this end of the adoption scale are revealing. Evangelicals' willingness to adopt the arguments of Rev. Olson drops when the nonevangelical Rev. Olson calls for a rights violation. Importantly, nonevangelical subjects do the opposite. They are generally on the fence about adopting Rev. Olson's arguments (a 5 would be on the fence), but their likelihood of adopting his argument is reduced when the outgroup (evangelical-identified) Rev. Olson calls for a rights violation. It is important to remember that the core argument against gay rights does not change when a rights violation or evangelical label is added. Thus, from both perspectives, the least amount of subject support is generated by the outgroup elite who violates social norms regarding the right of political activism (which is generally in line with intergroup relations theory).

Conclusion

Our experiment provides a balanced assessment of the ingroup reactions that clergy encounter when offering issue positions to selected audiences. We draw three basic insights from these findings that should drive future research on latitude for elite cues. First, clergy cannot assume that cue content offered to match conventional wisdom about their ingroup's ideological preferences will be welcomed by members prima facie. Indeed, clergy cannot offer just any position on a social policy issue and expect to be considered a credible source. Half of our sample bears this out in the low level of trust expressed in Rev. Olson offering the pro-gay-rights frame, which then translated into inattention to the remainder of the treatment. Clearly, elites have a credibility threshold to overcome before they can command attention (Lupia and McCubbins 1998).

The second insight from these results concerns ingroup member willingness to stick with clergy (and presumably other elites as well) despite friction generated over calls for restriction of an opponent's civil liberties. What is particularly interesting is that the ingroup elite who calls for the constitutional violation faces reduced credibility and increases the stock of negative arguments the ingroup has. If Samuel Stouffer was concerned with the "sober second thought" (1955: 27) that elites were able to provide in decision making on civil liberties, then it seems clear that these subjects are affording that here. They do not uncritically adopt anything offered by the ingroup elite. In fact, they appear to grant their own elite more scrutiny than the outgroup counterpart.

The puzzle, therefore, and the third conclusion, is that if clergy lose credibility and increase arguments against their position in the eyes of ingroup members, why should these same members stick with the clergyperson and express willingness to adopt his position in conversation? The explanation lies in the fact that the elite person's policy arguments are still likely in line with the group adopting them, at least in a broad sense. So, while the extremist elite gives ingroup members pause, they are still armed with policy arguments that help make their case. What we do not know from our questioning is whether they use the specific argument that their opponents' advocacy rights should be restricted. Presumably they would not, given the rise in negative arguments in our results, but that result is not ensured. After all, though ingroup subjects demurred elite arguments perceived to be outside certain plausibility bounds, the position elites have in shaping mass political preferences and perspectives remains substantial. These leaders are not easily replaced. Hence, whatever disagreement ingroup members might have with the cues their elites offer, it is not necessarily the case that elites and their overall issue influence are so easily discarded.

Chapter 11 demonstrates that attaching a call for tolerance to a policy argument helped its public adoption, especially among less tolerant portions of the public (in the national sample). Here we find that calls for intolerance do not appear to undermine persuasion attempts as measured by the indication that participants would raise the elite's arguments in discussion, though elites' calls for intolerance do raise the potential of ambivalence by boosting the number of arguments against their position. In this way, Figure 12.3 represents something close to the ideal democratic interaction between elites and the mass public. In broader discussions about liberalism as a political philosophy (e.g., Rawls 1997), the implications of tolerance and mutual respect are controversial. We can revisit these notions from Chapter 3 and Chapter 11. Recall that we discussed the possibility that tolerance is a procedural maneuver to achieve particular kinds of policy changes (Chapter 3) and democracy's dependence on leaving out comprehensive arguments (Chapter 11)—religion is a "conversation stopper" (Rorty 1994). In ideal form, procedural norms like tolerance do not impinge on people's pursuit of their political interests. Thus, debates about civil liberties are separable from debates over policy directions. While Chapter 11's results suggest that calls for tolerance affect what opinions people express, they largely do not in this chapter. Calls for constitutional violations weaken elite credibility and raise objections to what they say, but they do not prevent the use of ingroup policy argumentation. However, when the outgroup calls for rights restrictions, that elite's argumentation is considered less desirable. This makes sense in a world in which power shifts across time and group enmity may shift with it.

Of course, the other way to view the results is as a narrow form of identity politics. The identity match between the recipient and elite appears to be sufficient to overcome whatever negative sentiments arise over the call for a constitutional violation. Our subjects do not establish a bright line about what is appropriate democratic procedure, especially when the elite has ingroup status. Thus, we continue to have doubts that citizens can be relied on to maintain a clean democratic process, especially when elites do not model ideal behavior.

Notes

Acknowledgment: We thank a great group of people who assisted in gathering the data on which our paper is based: Tim Johnson, Anand Sokhey, Sarah Sokhey, Justin Vaughn, and Sarah Fulton. An earlier version of this chapter was prepared for delivery at the 2011 annual meeting of the American Political Science Association in Seattle.

1. The specific estimates are available in Table 12.A in the online appendix at http://pauldjupe.com/s/Appendix.docx.

2. There are small (though nonsignificant) differences in the composition of the various treatment groups, which indicate that controls may help generate more accurate effect estimates.

3. The confidence intervals are composed so that the comparison between evangelicals and nonevangelicals represents a 95 percent level test—see Schenker and Gentleman (2001).

References

Anderson, Benedict. 1993. *Imagined Communities: Reflections on the Origins and Spread of Nationalism*. Rev. ed. New York: Verso.

Brady, Henry E., and Paul M. Sniderman. 1985. "Attitude Attribution: A Group Basis for Political Reasoning." *American Political Science Review* 79 (4): 1061–1078.

Campbell, David E., John C. Green, and Geoffrey Layman. 2011. "The Party Faithful: Partisan Images, Candidate Religion, and the Electoral Impact of Party Identification." *American Journal of Political Science* 55 (1): 42–58.

Carmines, Edward G., and James A. Stimson. 1980. "The Two Faces of Issue Voting." *American Political Science Review* 74 (1): 78–91.

Cohen, Geoffrey L., and Julio Garcia. 2005. "'I Am Us': Negative Stereotypes as Collective Threats." *Journal of Personality and Social Psychology* 89 (4): 566–582.

Darmofal, David. 2005. "Elite Cues and Citizen Disagreement with Expert Opinion." *Political Research Quarterly* 58 (3): 381–395.

Djupe, Paul A., and Brian R. Calfano. 2013. *God Talk: Experimenting with the Religious Causes of Public Opinion*. Philadelphia: Temple University Press.

Downs, Anthony. 1957. *An Economic Theory of Democracy*. New York: Harper and Row.

Druckman, Jamie N. 2001. "The Implications of Framing Effects for Citizen Competence." *Political Behavior* 23 (2): 225–256.

Druckman, James N., and Cindy D. Kam. 2011. "Students as Experimental Participants." In *Cambridge Handbook of Experimental Political Science*, edited by James N. Druckman, Donald P. Green, James H. Kulkinski, and Arthur Lupia, 41–57. New York: Cambridge University Press.

Gamson, William A. 1992. *Talking Politics*. New York: Cambridge University Press.

Green, Donald, Bradley Palmquist, and Eric Schickler. 2002. *Partisan Hearts and Minds: Political Parties and the Social Identities of Voters*. New Haven, CT: Yale University Press.

Hogg, Michael A. 2001. "A Social Identity Theory of Leadership." *Personality and Social Psychology Review* 5:184–200.

Hogg, Michael A., and Daan L. van Knippenberg. 2003. "Social Identity and Leadership Processes in Groups." In *Advances in Experimental Social Psychology*, edited by Mark P. Zanna, 1–52. San Diego, CA: Academic Press.

Iyengar, Shanto, and Donald R. Kinder. 1987. *News That Matters*. Chicago: University of Chicago Press.

Lau, Richard R., and David P. Redlawsk. 2001. "Advantages and Disadvantages of Cognitive Heuristics in Political Decision Making." *American Journal of Political Science* 45 (4): 951–971.

Lodge, Milton, Kathleen M. McGraw, and Patrick Stroh. 1989. "An Impression-Driven Model of Candidate Evaluation." *American Political Science Review* 83 (2): 399–419.

Lupia, Arthur, and Matthew D. McCubbins. 1998. *The Democratic Dilemma: Can Citizens Learn What They Need to Know?* New York: Cambridge University Press.

MacKuen, Michael. 1984. "Exposure to Information, Belief Integration, and Individual Responsiveness to Agenda Change." *American Political Science Review* 78 (2): 372–391.

McClosky, Herbert, and Alida Brill. 1983. *Dimensions of Tolerance*. New York: Russell Sage.

McDermott, Monika L. 2007. "Voting for Catholic Candidates: The Evolution of a Stereotype." *Social Science Quarterly* 88 (4): 953–969.

———. 2009. "Religious Stereotyping and Voter Support for Evangelical Candidates." *Political Research Quarterly* 62 (2): 340–354.

Nelson, Thomas E., Rosalee A. Clawson, and Zoe M. Oxley 1997. "Media Framing of a Civil Liberties Conflict and Its Effect on Tolerance." *American Political Science Review* 91 (3): 567–583.

Page, Benjamin, and Robert Y. Shapiro. 1992. *The Rational Public.* Chicago: University of Chicago Press.

Peterson, David A. M. 2005. "Heterogeneity and Certainty in Candidate Evaluations." *Political Behavior* 27 (1): 1–24.

Prothro, James W., and Charles M. Grigg. 1960. "Fundamental Principles of Democracy: Bases of Agreement and Disagreement." *Journal of Politics* 22 (2): 276–294.

Rawls, John. 1997. "The Idea of Public Reason Revisited." *Chicago Law Review* 64 (3): 765–807.

Rorty, Richard. 1994. "Religion as a Conversation-Stopper." *Common Knowledge* 3:1–3.

Schenker, Nathaniel, and Jane F. Gentleman. 2001. "On Judging the Significance of Differences by Examining the Overlap of Confidence Intervals." *American Statistician* 55 (3): 182–186.

Sears, David O. 1986. "College Sophomores in the Laboratory: Influences of a Narrow Data Base on Social Psychology's View of Human Nature." *Journal of Personality and Social Psychology* 51 (3): 515–530.

Stouffer, Samuel A. 1955. *Communism, Conformity and Civil Liberties: A Cross Section of the Nation Speaks Its Mind.* New York: Doubleday.

Tyler, Tom R., and Edgar A Lind. 1992. "A Relational Model of Authority in Groups." *Advances in Experimental Social Psychology* 25:115–191.

Zaller, J. R. 1992. *The Nature and Origins of Mass Opinion.* New York: Cambridge University Press.

13

Stigma Management by Midwestern Secularists

CHRISTOPHER GARNEAU

An emerging body of research is demonstrating that secular Americans face stigmatization—being perceived as outside the mainstream, unpopular, or even dangerous. Secularists (and atheists in particular) encounter low levels of trust from the public (Edgell, Gerteis, and Hartmann 2006; Harper 2007) and self-report discrimination because of their lack of religious affiliation and belief (Hammer et al. 2012). While research documenting the stigmatization of secularists is growing, less is known about how secularists manage their stigmatized status. In this chapter, I use a mixed-methods approach to explore how secular individuals in the Midwest manage a highly stigmatized status in a particularly religious region of the United States.

Stigmatization can have serious consequences for secular individuals. Prior research shows that stigmatization has been linked to psychological distress and lower levels of well-being (Allport 1954; Lee and Craft 2002). Evaluating how secularists deal with stigma could help empower individuals who may struggle with their own stigmatization because it can provide insight into how stigmatization affects their mental well-being and hinders social acceptance. Also, this research extends the body of literature on stigma management strategies of other stigmatized groups including gays and lesbians, ex-offenders, and those with mental health issues, to name a few (e.g., Cain 1991; Couture and Penn 2003; Winnick and Bodkin 2008). Understanding how secularists deal with stigma may assist in helping other social outgroups deal with societal stigma. This study is also timely given the increase in the percentage of Americans professing a nonreligious identification (Hout and Fischer 2002; Putnam and Campbell 2010; Schwadel 2010).

This chapter focuses on secular individuals located in the Midwest region of the United States (as defined by the U.S. Census Bureau). I define a "secularist" as an individual who (1) claims to have no religious or supernatural belief or (2) makes no claims to knowledge of the existence of religious or supernatural entities and phenomena. This definition of secularists includes those who would identify themselves as atheists, agnostics, secular humanists, Brights, and free-thinkers, among other labels.

The Stigmatization of Secularists

A good deal of evidence suggests secularists are a stigmatized group in the United States. Americans commonly rely on religious affiliation or religious belief as a proxy for morality (Edgell, Gerteis, and Hartmann 2006). Therefore, having no religion is often associated with a lack of morals in terms of public perception (Hood et al. 1996). Additionally, Americans tend to feel that religious belief of any kind is important to social belonging (Bellah 1967; Herberg 1960). It is not surprising then that atheists are one of the least, if not the least, trusted of all stigmatized groups in the United States (Edgell, Gerteis, and Hartmann 2006). Public distrust of atheists is likely because of extreme negative feelings that come from the label "atheist," which many Americans have traditionally viewed as a pejorative term (Edgell, Gerteis, and Hartmann 2006; Jacoby 2004). The stigmatization of atheists has also been linked to their lack of belief, which is often interpreted as a flaw in their moral character (Harper 2007). While some research shows that Americans have become more willing to grant civil liberties to atheists (e.g., Bobo and Licari 1989; Schafer and Shaw 2009; Schwadel and Garneau, forthcoming; Whitt and Nelson 1975), other research shows that atheists have not experienced the dramatic increase in tolerance that has been noted among other stigmatized groups (Edgell, Gerteis, and Hartmann 2006).

Secular stigma has also been noted in research in which secular individuals self-report stigmatization. A growing body of work demonstrates various contexts in which atheists and other secularists experience prejudice and discrimination related to their secularism (e.g., Hunsberger and Altemeyer 2006; Cimino and Smith 2011; Heiner 1992; Smith 2011). Using nationally representative data from the American Religious Identification Survey, Ryan Cragun and colleagues (2012) find that 41 percent of theological atheists and 44 percent of theological agnostics report secular discrimination. Other research finds that secular discrimination is a common experience for atheists (Hammer et al. 2012). Overall, this burgeoning field of research demonstrates not only that secularists perceive stigma but that these perceptions are pervasive and have a substantial effect on secularists (e.g., Cragun et al. 2012; Hammer et al. 2012; Smith 2011).

Stigma Management

As with other stigmatized groups, secularists often employ strategies to mitigate the impact of stigmatization. Researchers generally classify stigma management as either inward or outward management strategies. Inward stigma management strategies include secrecy and passing while outward stigma management includes strategies like disclosure, educating others, and the use of contact outing (making a contact aware of one's secular status).

Secrecy is a stigma management strategy that results from fear related to perceived stigma (Blinde and Taub 1992). Individuals choose not to disclose their secular identities to others because it might cause unnecessary friction in their personal and professional lives (Cain 1991; Kalichman et al. 2003). I expect that midwestern secularists, the subjects of this chapter, employ secrecy in several dimensions of their social lives. Because religious identity is not outwardly visible, it is relatively easy for secularists to conceal their nonreligious status. As with other stigmatized groups, secularists probably keep their secular status a secret if they anticipate conflict with close social network ties like family members and coworkers.

Passing is a strategy by which stigmatized individuals identify themselves or allow themselves to be identified as having a status other than their actual status. For instance, James Lee and Elizabeth Craft (2002) report that individuals with genital herpes often pass themselves as unafflicted. Changing company or associations accommodates passing. For example, transsexuals commonly hold onto both sex statuses to pass themselves as their original sex around those who may not be privy to their sex transformation (Kando 1972). Passing is a stigma management technique that could be common for midwestern secularists, and they might try to pass as religious. Passing as religious is especially likely for secular individuals brought up with religion because they can use their prior religious identity as a passable identity if necessary. Secularists might also "soften" their label. For example, an atheist may try to pass as an agnostic or claim to be a humanist to avoid the negative connotations of the word "atheist."

Disclosing a stigmatized status is a common outward stigma management strategy. Disclosure often relieves the stress of keeping a stigmatized status a secret (Rosario et al. 2001). Disclosure is an attractive stigma management strategy because it is often easier than maintaining a hidden identity (Cain 1991). Several factors either facilitate or suppress the likelihood of disclosing a stigmatized status. Perceiving oneself as stigmatized decreases the likelihood of disclosure and increases the use of inward stigma management strategies (Herman 1993). Social support is also important; research shows that stigmatized individuals who perceive the support of family and friends are more likely to disclose their status (e.g., Kalichman et al. 2003).

Educating others is another outward stigma management technique. The goal of educating others is to reduce stigma in society by changing attitudes toward a stigmatized group (Blinde and Taub 1992). One way of educating others is through contact, which entails purposely being open about a stigmatized status to reduce stigma. Stigma is reduced when the experience with the stigmatized person is inconsistent with stereotypes about the stigmatized group (Corrigan and Matthews 2003; Couture and Penn 2003; Link and Cullen 1986). Secularists likely educate others to change attitudes and perceptions by addressing inaccuracies and stereotypes about secular individuals. For instance, an atheist may educate a friend about how atheists are good people and are able to live moral lives. Secularists are also likely to use contact outing in an attempt to change the prejudiced attitudes of people they know.

General Expectations

Because of the exploratory nature of this work, I do not propose any specific hypotheses for my analyses. I do, however, have some general expectations for the analyses with regard to the stigma management strategies of midwestern secularists. I expect to find that midwestern secularists commonly employ the aforementioned inward (secrecy and passing) and outward (disclosure, educating, and contact) stigma management strategies.

In addition to assessing the prevalence and nature of stigma management strategies, I also explore the effect of subjective secular self-identity on the likelihood to manage stigma. Atheists should be more likely than other secularists to use stigma management strategies because they are more prone to experience stigmatization, considering the high level of societal distrust of atheists. It is possible, however, that the strong secular identity of more hard-line atheists would make them less likely to use inward stigma management strategies and more likely to employ outward strategies. I anticipate that perceived support from networks (family and coworkers) increases the use of disclosure and decreases the use of secrecy. I also expect that secularists with a previous religious identity are more likely to "pass" as religious. Finally, I anticipate that secularists who perceive greater stigmatization are more uncomfortable disclosing their secular status.

Data and Methods

I use a mixed-methods approach. In addition to quantitative analyses from survey data, I use qualitative methods to add context and breadth. Including qualitative methods is generally preferred for conducting comprehensive research in a largely understudied subject area (Creswell 2007), which would include research on secularists. I employ a parallel convergent mixed methods research design in which quantitative and qualitative data are collected and analyzed concurrently. Both strands of data are given equal weight in analyses, and neither strand is dependent on the other (Cresswell and Plano Clark 2011).

Quantitative Data

Quantitative data are obtained from a web survey. The sample for this survey is nonrepresentative. Previous work has documented the usefulness of web surveys to collect data on nonrepresentative groups that are difficult to find through national, representative sampling (Gosling et al. 2004). This approach comports with other recent research on atheists (e.g., Hammer et al. 2012). The population for this study is composed of secularists in the Midwest region of the United States.[1]

The sample is based on members of secular social groups in the Midwest. I conducted Internet searches for groups in Midwest cities and universities with search terms like "atheists," "secular humanists," "skeptics," "freethinkers," and "Brights." I then contacted group leaders from these groups and asked them to forward an e-mail to members of their respective groups. Of the 307 group leaders I e-mailed, 134 (44 percent) replied with confirmation that they would distribute the e-mail to their group members. The e-mail contained a link to my web survey. The e-mail also requested that group members forward the message to any secularists they may know in the Midwest. Thus, I employed purposive as well as "snowball" sampling methods (Creswell and Plano Clark 2011).

I deleted cases for individuals who do not live in the Midwest region of the United States, are not secular, or have missing data on any of the dependent variables in the quantitative analyses. The final sample size is 2,242. I imputed data for all missing data on variables that are not used as dependent variables in regression analyses. Multiple imputation is a useful strategy for dealing with missing data when missing cases cannot be avoided (Acock 2005).

Stigma Management Variables

The *secrecy* dummy variable assesses whether respondents have purposely kept their secular status a secret to avoid negative judgment.[2] *Passing* is a dummy variable that assesses whether a respondent has tried to pass as religious to avoid negative judgment. I measure disclosure with the Secular Disclosure Index (SDI), an additive index that measures how comfortable a respondent is with disclosing secular status. The index is constructed using a series of survey items in which respondents indicate how comfortable they are disclosing their secular status to friends, family, neighbors, casual acquaintances, and strangers. Responses for these items are "very comfortable," "somewhat comfortable," and "not very comfortable." The α value, an estimate of the lower bound of reliability, for this index is .78.

Two measures assess the stigma management strategy of educating others. *Educated other* is a dummy variable based on the question "Have you ever informed a religious friend or relative about seculars to give them better insight about the true nature of seculars (for example tried to tell someone religious that seculars can also have morals)?" For the *contact* dummy variable, respondents are asked, "Have you ever 'come out' as secular to someone with the intent of showing them that seculars are good people?"

Religious Identification and Identity

Religious identification is measured with a typology that splits secularists into four groups based on primary secular self-identification and level of nonbelief. Self-identifying atheists are accordingly referred to as "atheists." Respondents who identify with any secular identification other than atheist (agnostic, humanist, or freethinker, for example) are referred to as "non-atheists." In terms of nonbelief, secularists who say they do not believe in god or a higher power are referred to as "nonbelieving." Respondents who say they do not know if there is a god or higher power, only sometimes believe in god, or believe with some doubts are referred to as "uncertain." Using this typology, I create a secular identity scheme with four categories: (1) *nonbelieving atheists* (those who self-identify as atheist and do not believe in god or a higher power), (2) *uncertain atheists* (those who identify as atheist but are unsure about the existence of god or a higher power), (3) *nonbelieving non-atheists* (those who self-identify with a secular identity other than atheist and do not believe in god or a higher power), and (4) *uncertain non-atheists* (those who self-identify with a secular identity other than atheist and are unsure about the existence of god or a higher power). In all regression analyses, *nonbelieving atheists* are the reference category.

Qualitative Data

The data for qualitative analyses come from in-depth interviews with twenty-four group leaders of secular organizations in the Midwest. I found interview participants by asking group leaders to participate in a phone interview (all those asked agreed to participate). While I used a basic structure for the interview schedule, I also allowed enough flexibility in an interview to ask supplementary questions. I coded interviews to correspond to specific expectations, but I also allowed for open coding to capture emergent themes (Creswell 2007).

Quantitative Results for Inward Stigma Management

I begin by looking at the prevalence of inward stigma management. The majority (72 percent) of respondents report having intentionally kept their secular status a secret, which demonstrates that secrecy is a common stigma management strategy for midwestern secularists. However, fewer secularists (21 percent) report passing as religious. While only one-fifth of the sample reports passing as religious, these results indicate that a sizable proportion of midwestern secularists have directly dealt with stigma by pretending to be religious.

Next, I examine logistic regression results for inward stigma management strategies. I begin regression analyses with the measure of keeping a secular status a secret. The results in Table 13.1 show that neither category of non-

TABLE 13.1 ESTIMATES FOR PURPOSELY KEEPING A SECULAR STATUS A SECRET TO AVOID JUDGMENT AND PASSING AS RELIGIOUS TO AVOID NEGATIVE JUDGMENT (LOGISTIC REGRESSION)

	Secrecy		*Passing*	
	Odds Ratio	*p*	*Odds Ratio*	*p*
Religious at 16	—		1.56	***
Perceived Support				
Supportive family	0.43	***	—	
Coworkers might judge	3.18	***	—	
Secular Status				
Nonbelieving atheist (ref)	—		—	
Uncertain atheist	2.32	***	1.54	
Nonbelieving non-atheist	1.17		1.13	
Uncertain non-atheist	0.95		1.89	***
Control Variables				
Age	0.99		0.98	***
Female	1.68	***	0.96	
Nonwhite	0.57	***	0.96	
Bachelor's degree	1.17		1.14	
Income	1.04		1.02	
College student	1.27		1.14	
Rural residence	1.01		1.27	
Urban residence	0.89		1.07	
Great Plains region	1.16		1.25	**
–2 log likelihood	1,602.57		2,012.21	
Bayesian information criterion	1,705.96		2,112.51	

Note: Regressions using "perceived support" variables use a smaller sample of those who are employed at least part time (N = 1,612).

** $p \leq .05$, *** $p \leq .01$ (two-tailed test)

atheists differs meaningfully from nonbelieving atheists in their use of secrecy. An interesting finding is that uncertain atheists are twice as likely as nonbelieving atheists to keep their secular status a secret. Moreover, social support is strongly associated with secrecy. Compared to those who do not perceive family support, the odds of keeping a secular status a secret are 57 percent less for those who say their family would likely support them if their family found out they are secular. Similarly, compared to secularists who do not anticipate negative judgment from coworkers, the odds of secrecy are three times greater for those who say they fear negative judgment from coworkers. These results show that secularists who perceive support from family are particularly unlikely to use secrecy. The positive effect of fearing judgment from coworkers on keeping a secular status a secret is even more robust. These findings emphasize that in deciding whether to use secrecy, the support of family and peers for one's secularism is important.

Next, I explore logistic regression results for passing as religious (column 2 of Table 13.1). Uncertain atheists and nonbelieving non-atheists are no different from nonbelieving atheists with regard to passing as religious. The odds of passing as religious are nearly twice as great for uncertain non-atheists compared to nonbelieving atheists. As I proposed, secularists with a previous religious affiliation are also relatively likely to pass as religious. Specifically, the odds of passing as religious are 56 percent greater for those who had a religious affiliation at age 16 compared with those who were raised with no religious affiliation. This finding may suggest that formerly religious secularists can use their prior religion as an identity resource to facilitate passing as religious. It is also plausible that these individuals pass as religious more often because they are likely to have family members who are religious.

Qualitative Results for Inward Stigma Management Strategies

In assessing the use of secrecy, I asked secular group leaders if they had ever used secrecy to avoid negative judgment. Ten of the twenty-four interview respondents reported keeping their secular status a secret from others (about half the rate found among survey respondents). Avoiding the stigma associated with their secularism was a motivating factor for those who used secrecy. In most cases, secrecy was employed to avoid negative interactions with religious family members and coworkers. While avoiding negative interactions was the most cited motivation for secrecy, professionalism was also a prevalent theme. Several respondents said they kept their secularism a secret from coworkers because discussing their nonbelief at work would be unprofessional.

Group leaders were also asked questions about passing as religious as a way to manage their stigma. As with results from the survey data, a minority of qualitative respondents (one-fourth) reported passing as religious to avoid negative interactions. In most instances, interviewees said that passing as religious involved passing with family members during religious activities such as praying before dinner or attending religious services during the holidays. A few respondents discussed that passing as religious was a way to "keep the peace." Natalie, a thirty-six-year-old atheist from Illinois, discussed passing with her in-laws to alleviate stress:

> My husband's parents don't know [we are atheists]. When we visit them, they go to church every day. We would do the rosary together. In the last year, we said we're not going to pretend that we go to church when we don't. Since then, they stopped asking us to pray the rosary. But we never had a conversation. My daughter is five . . . coming up on the age of first communion. That weighs heavily on my mind because they [the in-laws] will have to know at that point.

This quotation from Natalie also highlights passing by compartmentalization, which was another common way that group leaders reported passing as religious. Natalie is open about her secularism with most of her friends and family but not with her in-laws. Similarly, ten out of the twenty-four group leaders reported passing with certain individuals while remaining out with others. This selective passing is a common stigma management strategy for other stigmatized groups (Kando 1972). The most common reason for passing through compartmentalization was to avoid conflict with family or because the respondents felt that someone would be hurt to hear about their secularism. This sentiment was articulated by Alex, a thirty-one-year-old atheist from Kansas:

> I tend to be fairly open. It's easier to be around people who do know [that I am an atheist]. I'm never going to break it to my grandma, though. I'd like her to go to her grave thinking I'm Catholic. It's more upsetting to her than the benefit of me being an open and out atheist. I hold my tongue in situations where it's going to be an issue.

A common strategy for "passing" among group leaders was the use of a "softer" secular status to mitigate negative judgment. Two-thirds of the qualitative interview respondents reported softening their label in one way or another. Nearly all respondents who had softened a secular label did so with a vague statement like "I'm not religious" or "I don't go to church." Roughly half of the group leaders said they had passed as something other than an atheist because they were afraid of the response that the term "atheist" would elicit. This was exemplified by Charlie from Minnesota, who said:

> I've used the word "nontheist." . . . "Atheist" has negative connotations of being immoral. The words are so close together in definition, but the term "nontheist" . . . that takes the edge off. A lot of times I say I'm a member of the UU fellowships.[3] "Atheist" is a loaded term. For a lot of people, it means more than "without a belief in theism." The word has some semantic baggage.

Quantitative Results for Outward Stigma Management Strategies

A majority of midwestern secularists report using educating techniques. Specifically, 81 percent of respondents report having educated someone else about secularists and 59 percent report having "outed" themselves as secular as a way to reduce stigma.

Secular Disclosure Index

Table 13.2 displays results from ordinary least squares (OLS) regressions for the Secular Disclosure Index (SDI). The SDI is an additive index that measures a respondent's comfort in disclosing their secular status. The index has a range of 5 to 25 with a mean of 18.1 and a standard deviation of 4.6, indicating a fairly high degree of comfort with self-disclosure. The results demonstrate that uncertain

TABLE 13.2 ESTIMATES OF THE SECULAR DISCLOSURE INDEX WITH STIGMA AND SUPPORT VARIABLES SEPARATELY (OLS REGRESSION)

	With Stigma Variables		*With Support Variables*	
	β	p	β	p
Support Factors				
Supportive family	—		1.83	***
Coworkers might judge	—		−2.69	***
Perceived Stigma				
Prejudice	.07		—	
Discrimination	−.76	***	—	
Secular Status				
Nonbelieving atheist	—		—	
Uncertain atheist	−1.45	**	−1.51	**
Nonbelieving non-atheist	−.39		−.48	*
Uncertain non-atheist	−.77	**	−.81	**
Control Variables				
Age	.00		.01	*
Age-squared	.00	***	—	
Female	−1.40	***	−1.28	***
Nonwhite	.32		.15	
Bachelor's degree	−.65	**	−.75	***
Income	−.07		−.12	
College student	−.47		−.49	
Rural residence	−.50	*	−.37	
Urban residence	.87	***	.81	***
Great Plains region	−.49	*	−.32	
R^2	.07		.15	

Note: Regressions using "support factor" variables use a smaller sample of those who are employed at least part time (N = 1,612).

*$p \leq .05$, **$p \leq .01$, ***$p \leq .001$ (two-tailed test)

atheists and uncertain non-atheists score significantly lower than nonbelieving atheists on the SDI. Midwestern secularists with an uncertain belief about god are less comfortable in disclosing their secular status compared to more ardent nonbelievers. I also assess the relationship between perceived stigma and levels of disclosure. I anticipate that secularists with high levels of perceived stigma have relatively low levels of disclosure. While perceived prejudice is not associated with levels of disclosure, perceived discrimination is associated with a 0.76 reduction in the SDI. I also assess the importance of family and peer support for levels of disclosure. I expect that secularists who perceive greater support from family and coworkers have higher levels of disclosure than secularists who perceive less support. Indeed, the results from the model in the second column of Table 13.2 show that those who perceive family support score 1.83 higher on the SDI.[4] Similarly, those who fear potential negative judgment from coworkers because of their secular status score, on average, 2.69 points lower on the SDI. Perceived social support from family and peers is an important factor in how comfortable secular individuals are in disclosing their secular status.

Another notable finding is that the addition of support variables increases the coefficient size and significance for the secular identification variables (column 2 of Table 13.2). Nonbelieving atheists are even more comfortable disclosing their secular statuses than all other categories of secularists when including controls for social support. This suggests that compared to other secularists, ardent atheists are more likely to "out" themselves when they feel that family and friends will support their nonreligious identity.

Educating Others and Contact Outing

Compared to nonbelieving atheists, uncertain non-atheists are 31 percent less likely to educate others about secularists.[5] Nonbelieving non-atheists and uncertain atheists, however, are no different from nonbelieving atheists when it comes to educating others. It is worth noting that a fully controlled model explains little of the total variance. Shifting to a different form of educating others—namely, through contact—results show that compared to nonbelieving atheists, the odds of using contact are 47 percent less for uncertain non-atheists. Uncertain atheists and nonbelieving non-atheists, however, do not differ from nonbelieving atheists with regard to the use of contact. Overall, these results show that nonbelieving atheists are significantly more likely than uncertain non-atheists to use outward stigma management techniques, which suggests that the more hard-line stance of nonbelieving atheists is conducive to the use of more proactive forms of stigma management.

Qualitative Results for Outward Stigma Management

One-third of the interview participants reported disclosing their status because of complications associated with keeping it a secret. Six of the eight respondents who said they used disclosure in this way cited online social networking or Internet involvement with secular groups as a problem for keeping their secular status a secret from relatives and coworkers. In many cases, respondents were confronted by acquaintances who discovered their secular status on a social networking website like Facebook. One respondent said someone searched for his name on the Internet and found out about his atheist activism. In these cases, the secularists felt they had no choice but to disclose their secular status. Some of them knew that they might be found out because of their online secular activist activity and decided that maintaining secrecy about these activities from family and peers was too difficult. These sentiments are exemplified by Nathan from Nebraska who said, "I don't want to live in secret; it's frustrating to live with discrimination, but I don't want to lead a double life."

Turning to the idea of educating others about a stigmatized status, I asked interviewees if they could recall educating someone else about secular individuals.

The majority (nineteen of the twenty-four) of group leaders reported educating someone about secularists to manage stigma. Representative comments included "I look forward to opportunities to talk to religious individuals," "I have to do it all the time," and "I constantly try to explain how my moral compass operates to others."

I also asked the secular group leaders if they had ever used contact outing, or purposely outed themselves to others to reduce stigma toward secularists. Fifteen of the twenty-four respondents reported outing themselves as secular with the intent of reducing societal stigma toward secularists. Responses from interviewees suggested that outing was a common occurrence. Representative comments included "I do it all the time," "I've outed myself in the community," and "I declared [my atheism] on Facebook." Jason, a twenty-three-year-old atheist from Illinois, said, "I had a friend who was talking about being a Christian, and she assumed I had Christian values, and I said, 'No, I just have human values.'" While many instances of outing occurred in an organic fashion between the secular individuals and their acquaintances, such as the example from Jason, a few respondents discussed outing themselves to as many people as they felt comfortable to reduce stigma. Common tactics for public outings included using social media as well as newspapers to announce a secular status in order to reduce societal stigma.

While the secular group leaders used diverse methods in outing themselves, the reason for outing was consistent among the responses: The interview participants wanted to reduce stigma and make secularism more socially acceptable. This was often accomplished by outing themselves to acquaintances with the goal of demonstrating that there are "a lot of seculars out there" (as a group leader in Missouri put it).

Conclusion

In this chapter, I show that midwestern secularists use both inward and outward forms of stigma management. The quantitative results for inward stigma management show that the secrecy strategy is far more common than passing as religious. Results from qualitative interviews show that among group leaders, passing as religious is not as common as passing with a "softer" status (e.g., identifying as agnostic instead of atheist). I also find that outward forms of stigma management are far more prevalent among secularists in general. Qualitative results show that midwestern secular group leaders are particularly out and open with their secular statuses, which is not all that surprising given the fact that group leaders tend to be more visible in their communities in an attempt to find other secularists who might want to join their organizations.

I find that nonbelieving atheists are less likely than uncertain non-atheists to use secrecy and to pass as religious. This finding suggests that the more hard-line secular status of atheists makes them more likely to be out about their secularism. These findings are also reflected in results for outward stigma management, as nonbelieving atheists are more likely to use education and contact strategies compared to uncertain non-atheists. These results imply that a stronger secular identity is associated with a more outward orientation when dealing with stigma.

The results in this study show that midwestern secularists generally report high levels of outward stigma management—the mean score on the SDI (with a range of 5 to 25) is 18.1. Additionally, a majority of midwestern secularists use contact outing to manage stigma, and more than four out of five survey respondents report having educated someone else about secularists. The prevalence of outward stigma management aligns with findings from the qualitative data. Interviews with group leaders reveal that most of these individuals had participated in outward forms of stigma management. A majority of interviewees cited regular involvement in civic activities for secular causes and educating another person about secularists. Taken together, the quantitative and qualitative data paint a picture of midwestern secularists as active and outgoing with regard to their secularism. Despite some evidence of inward stigma management, outward forms of stigma management appear to be more commonplace among secular individuals.

While outward forms of stigma management are common, there are differences in disclosure levels across secular self-identifications. Uncertain atheists and uncertain non-atheists scored significantly lower than nonbelieving atheists on the SDI. This finding suggests that uncertainty about theistic belief decreases comfort in disclosing a secular status. This is an interesting finding because prior research—for example, by Penny Edgell, Joseph Gerteis, and Douglas Hartmann (2006)—suggests that the "atheist" label is important in determining the decision to be out about a stigmatized status. However, Edgell, Gerteis, and Hartmann (2006) do not distinguish between secular identity and theological belief in their study. The findings in this study add to this conversation by providing a more robust view of secular identities with regard to stigmatization.

Another prevalent theme from this chapter is that perceived social support is an important factor for the use of both secrecy and disclosure. Results show that perceived support from family correlates with less secrecy and more comfort in disclosure. Additionally, perceived negative judgment from coworkers is associated with more secrecy and less comfort in disclosure. Secularists gain a great deal of comfort from having the support of family and friends. Moreover, knowledge of a supportive social network facilitates the ability to be out, which is important because past research on stigmatized groups shows that being out provides psychological benefits for stigmatized individuals (Cain 1991; Rosario et al. 2001).

An additional finding with regard to being "out" as secular is that midwestern secularists who perceive discrimination are less comfortable disclosing their secular status. This comports with research that asserts that individuals who perceive themselves as stigmatized are more hesitant to disclose their stigmatized status (e.g., Herman 1993). Recent research on atheist discrimination adds some complexity to this particular finding. Joseph Hammer and colleagues (2012) find a positive correlation between perceived discrimination and outness of an atheist status, but they propose that it is atheist outness that leads to greater perceived discrimination. They theorize that the brazen attitudes of out atheists elicit hostility from others, resulting in stigmatization. While the findings of Hammer and colleagues (2012) seem to contradict the findings from this chapter, it is likely a difference in measurement of outness that accounts for this particular discrepancy. The findings from this chapter focus on secular individuals' comfort in disclosure, while Hammer and colleagues (2012) assess atheist outness. It is possible that atheists who are open and out about their secular status experience stigmatization, which may lead to greater discomfort in disclosing their atheism. More research is needed to assess the relationship between stigmatization and the willingness to be out as secular.

An interesting result from this chapter is the seemingly contradictory finding that a majority of secularists report using secrecy (72 percent) and a majority also report outing themselves to others to reduce stigma (59 percent). Clearly, many secularists report using both of these stigma management strategies. A plausible explanation for the finding that some secularists report both secrecy and self-outing is that the survey items for these measures are retrospective questions asking respondents if they had *ever* done these things. So it makes sense that over long periods of time, secular individuals have had the opportunity to use both inward and outward strategies. Furthermore, qualitative results from interviews with secular group leaders show that stigma management strategies tend to change over time from a general inward orientation to an outward orientation. These results suggest that the process of achieving a secular status accompanies a more outward orientation, a finding that is supported by prior qualitative work on secular identity construction (e.g., Smith 2011; Zuckerman 2012). Thus, seculars may be more prone to use secrecy during the early stages of secular identity development but more likely to use outing during the later stages. It is also possible that these individuals are using both of these strategies simultaneously and compartmentalizing who they are out to and who they are not, a strategy noted in research on other stigmatized groups (e.g., Kando 1972). Additional research is needed to examine how stigma management strategies change throughout the process of constructing a secular identity.

There are several limitations to this study. As previously mentioned, many of the focal variables are derived from retrospective questions about lifetime experiences. Hammer and colleagues' (2012) work on atheists asks respondents about discrimination experienced in the previous five years. Employing a similar strategy might be more meaningful to studies in this line of research, especially when dealing with individuals who have been secular for several decades.

There are also important limitations to the qualitative component of this research. Because I use secular group leaders as my target population, I likely have a sample of interviewees that are not representative of midwestern secularists.

They are members of secular groups, which means they are probably quite different from secularists who have not sought out membership in a secular group. Moreover, the fact that they are group leaders suggests that they are more engaged in group activities and have more salient secular identities. Future research could incorporate qualitative work on secular individuals who are not active participants in secular groups to assess the impact of having a secular status with fewer social support systems.

A final limitation worth mentioning is that I examine secularists in only one region of the United States. Prior work (Hammer et al. 2012) shows that perceived discrimination varies by region and that secularists living in coastal regions experience less discrimination than those living in the Midwest and the South. It is likely that the prevalence and nature of stigma management strategies also vary by geographic region. Furthermore, because many of the participants in this study come from secular groups, there is probably an underrepresentation of secularists from rural areas, where secular groups are less common. With the exception of university groups, few of the secular groups that I contacted were located in cities with a population under fifty thousand. It is likely that secularists who live in rural areas and small towns as well as those who are not part of secular groups have different experiences with secular stigma. Many of these individuals would likely have been missed by the sampling strategy. For this reason, representative data including more secular respondents would be helpful in identifying possible differences in lived experiences of secularists.

Despite these limitations, the current research is a timely study given the rapid increase of religious nonaffiliates and nonbelievers in the last twenty years (Hout and Fischer 2002; Sherkat 2008). As the numbers in the secular ranks continue to grow, social science researchers should broaden studies of religion to include these Americans. Additionally, the recent momentum of secular movements such as New Atheism increases the salience of secularism in the United States. These recent trends should provide ample opportunities for new scholarship in the field of secular research.

Notes

1. As defined by the United States Census Bureau, the Midwest includes Ohio, Indiana, Michigan, Illinois, Wisconsin, Missouri, Iowa, Minnesota, Kansas, Nebraska, South Dakota, and North Dakota.

2. Descriptive statistics for quantitative measures, along with full variable coding for all independent variables, are shown in Table 13.A in the online appendix at http://pauldjupe.com/s/Appendix.docx.

3. UU stands for Unitarian Universalist. This is a denomination that is friendly to secular individuals. Consequently, several participants in this study reported some kind of affiliation with a Unitarian Universalist congregation.

4. Because one of the items for the SDI asks about comfort in disclosing a secular status to family members, I ran separate regressions to distinguish the statistical

importance of family effects in the event that comfort in family disclosure might drive the relationship between perceived family support and overall levels of disclosure. Separate OLS regression results (not shown) reveal that while the "comfort in telling family" item has a stronger correlation to perceived family support than the overall SDI, the omission of this item from the index does not meaningfully change the results shown in model E in the online appendix.

5. These results are available as Table 13.B in the online appendix.

References

Acock, Alan C. 2005. "Working with Missing Values." *Journal of Marriage and Family* 67:1012–1028.

Allport, Gordon W. 1954. *The Nature of Prejudice*. Cambridge, MA: Addison-Wesley.

Bellah, Robert. 1967. "Civil Religion in America." *Daedalus* 96 (1): 1–21.

Blinde, Elaine M., and Diane E. Taub. 1992. "Women Athletes as Falsely Accused Deviants: Managing the Lesbian Stigma." *Sociological Quarterly* 33 (4): 521–533.

Bobo, Lawrence, and Frederick C. Licari. 1989. "Education and Political Tolerance: Testing the Effects of Cognitive Sophistication and Target Group." *Public Opinion Quarterly* 53 (3): 285–308.

Cain, Roy. 1991. "Stigma Management and Gay Identity Development." *Social Work* 36:67–73.

Cimino, Richard, and Christopher Smith. 2011. "The New Atheism and the Formation of the Imagined Secularist Community." *Journal of Media and Religion* 10 (1): 24–38.

Corrigan, Patrick W., and Alicia K. Matthews. 2003. "Stigma and Disclosure: Implications for Coming Out of the Closet." *Journal of Mental Health* 12 (3): 235–248.

Couture, Shannon M., and David L. Penn. 2003. "Interpersonal Contact and the Stigma of Mental Illness: A Review of the Literature." *Journal of Mental Health* 12 (3): 293–305.

Cragun, Ryan T., Barry A. Kosmin, Ariela Keysar, Joseph H. Hammer, and Michael E. Nielsen. 2012. "On the Receiving End: Discrimination toward the Non-Religious." *Journal of Contemporary Religion* 27 (1): 105–127.

Creswell, John. W. 2007. *Qualitative Inquiry and Research Design: Choosing among Five Approaches*. Thousand Oaks, CA: Sage.

Creswell, John W., and V. L. Plano Clark. 2011. *Designs and Conducting Mixed Methods Research*. 2nd ed. Thousand Oaks, CA: Sage.

Edgell, Penny, Joseph Gerteis, and Douglas Hartmann. 2006. "Atheists as 'Other': Moral Boundaries and Cultural Membership in American Society." *American Sociological Review* 71 (2): 211–234.

Gosling, Samuel D., Simine Vazire, Sanjay Srivastava, and Oliver P. John. 2004. "Should We Trust Web-Based Studies? A Comparative Analysis of Six Preconceptions about Internet Questionnaires." *American Psychologist* 59 (2): 93–104.

Hammer, Joseph H., Ryan T. Cragun, Karen Hwang, and Jesse M. Smith. 2012. "Forms, Frequency, and Correlates of Perceived Anti-Atheist Discrimination." *Secularism and Nonreligion* 1:43–67.

Harper, Marcel. 2007. "The Stereotyping of Nonreligious People by Religious Students: Content and Subtypes." *Journal for the Scientific Study of Religion* 46 (4): 539–552.

Heiner, Robert. 1992. "Nones on the Run: Evangelical Heathens in the Deep South." *Deviant Behavior* 13 (1): 1–20.

Herberg, Will. 1960. *Protestant-Catholic-Jew.* Garden City, NJ: Anchor Books.

Herman, Nancy J. 1993. "Return to Sender: Reintegrative Stigma-Management Strategies of Ex-Psychiatric Patients." *Journal of Contemporary Ethnography* 22:295–330.

Hood, Ralph W., Bernard Spilka, Robert Hunsberger, and Richard Gorsuch. 1996. *The Psychology of Religion: An Empirical Approach.* 2nd ed. New York: Guilford Press.

Hout, Michael, and Claude S. Fischer. 2002. "Why More Americans Have No Religious Preference: Politics and Generations." *American Sociological Review* 67 (2): 165–190.

Hunsberger, Bruce, and Robert Altemeyer. 2006. *Atheists: A Groundbreaking Study of America's Nonbelievers.* Amherst, NY: Prometheus Books.

Jacoby, Susan. 2004. *Freethinkers: A History of American Secularism.* New York: Metropolitan.

Kalichman, Seth, Michael DiMarco, James Austin, Webster Luke, and Kari Difonzo. 2003. "Stress, Social Support, and HIV-status, Disclosure to Family and Friends among HIV-Positive Men and Women." *Journal of Behavioral Medicine* 26:315–332.

Kando, Thomas. 1972. "Passing and Stigma Management: The Case of the Transsexual." *Sociological Quarterly* 13 (4): 475–483.

Lee, James David, and Elizabeth A. Craft. 2002. "Protecting One's Self from a Stigmatized Disease . . . Once One Has It." *Deviant Behavior* 23 (3): 267–299.

Link, Bruce G., and Francis T. Cullen. 1986. "Contact with the Mentally Ill and Perceptions of How Dangerous They Are." *Journal of Health and Social Behavior* 27 (4): 289–302.

Putnam, Robert D., and David E. Campbell. 2010. *American Grace: How Religion Divides and Unites Us.* New York: Simon and Schuster.

Rosario, Margaret, Joyce Hunter, Marya Gwadz, and Raymond Smith. 2001. "The Coming-Out Process and Its Adaptational and Health-Related Associations among Gay, Lesbian, and Bisexual Youths: Stipulations and Exploration of a Model." *American Journal of Community Psychology* 29:113–160.

Schafer, Chelsea E., and Greg M. Shaw. 2009. "The Polls—Trends: Tolerance in the United States." *Public Opinion Quarterly* 73 (2): 404–431.

Schwadel, Philip. 2010. "Period and Cohort Effects on Religious Non-Affiliation and Religious Disaffiliation: A Research Note." *Journal for the Scientific Study of Religion* 49 (2): 311–319.

Schwadel, Philip, and Christopher R. H. Garneau. 2014. "An Age-Period-Cohort Analysis of Political Tolerance." *Sociological Quarterly* 55 (2): 421–452.

Sherkat, Darren. 2008. "Beyond Belief: Atheism, Agnosticism, and Theistic Certainty in the United States." *Sociological Spectrum* 28:438–459.

Smith, Jesse. 2011. "Becoming an Atheist in America: Constructing Identity and Meaning from the Rejection of Theism." *Sociology of Religion* 72 (2): 215–237.

Whitt, Hugh P., and Hart M. Nelson. 1975. "Moral Traditionalism, and Tolerance of Atheists." *Social Forces* 54 (2): 328–340.

Winnick, Terri A., and Mark Bodkin. 2008. "Anticipated Stigma and Stigma Management among Those to Be Labeled 'Ex-con.'" *Deviant Behavior* 29 (4): 295–333.

Zuckerman, Phil. 2012. *Faith No More: Why People Reject Religion.* New York: Oxford University Press.

14

American Muslim Political Responses to Threat

PATRICK SCHOETTMER

On December 27, 2012, Sunando Sen was waiting on the 7 train platform in New York City when Erika Menendez pushed him in front of a northbound train. Sen was struck by the train and killed instantly. The attack was widely publicized, and by the next day, Menendez had been both identified and arrested. When she was brought in for questioning, Menendez admitted to the attack, stating, "I pushed a Muslim off the train tracks because I hate Hindus and Muslims ever since 2001 when they put down the twin towers I've been beating them up" (Reuters 2012). While Menendez is clearly an outlier in a number of ways (including a history of mental illness and violence—see Santora and Hartocollis 2012), the sentiments she expressed were not unique. Indeed, anti-Muslim sentiment is fairly widely held in the United States, with Muslims ranking as one of the least-liked religious groups in the country (Putnam and Campbell 2012). While a number of researchers have begun examining how this perceived threat from Muslims has affected political behavior for the American majority (Benson, Merolla, and Geer 2011; Davis 2007; Kalkan, Layman, and Uslaner 2009; Sides and Gross 2013), it is equally important to examine the Muslim response to the perceived threat emanating from the general public.

In this chapter, I examine the Muslim response to the perception of threat by examining the response to different sources of threat, how the threat perception affects the level of civic and political participation from the Muslim community, and Muslims' level of tolerance for outgroups. Though the nascent literature on the topic has found Muslim Americans distinctly more likely to engage in politics in response to perceived threat, the evidence we provide suggests qualifiers and limitations to this observation.

Threat Perception and Muslim Americans

Muslims in Europe (Fetzer and Soper 2005; Klaussen 2005; Mythen, Walklate, and Khan 2009) and in Australia (Amath 2013; Dunn, Klocker, and Salabay 2007; Mason and Poynting 2006) have generally perceived the government and publics in which they live to be hostile toward them. This perceived hostility has, particularly in the case of European Muslims, been associated with political disengagement and social isolation. Indeed, Robert Leikin's (2005) description of "Europe's angry Muslims" has typified how people have thought about Muslim enclaves in Europe. Muslims make up a significantly larger percentage of European populations than they do in the United States.[1] Thus, their political behavior has been scrutinized longer in Europe than in the United States, and much of what was initially assumed by American political scientists was at least in part informed by the understanding scholars have developed of Western Muslims based in Europe. However, Muslims (and ethnic groups generally associated with Muslims, such as Arab Americans) in the United States have not responded to the perceived hostility in the wake of the terrorist attacks of September 11, 2001, with disengagement. Instead, American Muslims have generally increased their political engagement (Djupe and Green 2007; Jalalzai 2009; Tam Cho, Gimple, and Wu 2006) and ingroup solidarity (Dana, Barreto and Oskooii 2011; Jamal 2005).

Part of the explanation for this difference lies in the nature of the immigrants coming into Europe (lower-educated, rural labor migrants) and North America (the children of elites looking for education or entrepreneurial opportunities) (Voas and Fleischmann 2012), and part of it is certainly the scale of the immigration as compared to the overall population. However, that would not help explain the rising level of political participation we have seen among American Muslims since 2001. Clearly, something more must be in play. Threat perceptions play a role in shaping the community response, but the nature, intensity, and scope of the threat response from the general public varies across national lines.

The Role of Threat

Threats can serve as either a deterrent or an opportunity to individuals and communities that perceive themselves as being in the crosshairs of public and governmental scrutiny (see Goldstone and Tilly 2001). The fundamental role threat plays in encouraging political participation is in stimulating a defensive action to protect the community (Huddy et al. 2002). This can help the community to consolidate a shared political identity that can facilitate cooperation across ethnic and national lines (Dana, Barreto and Oskooii 2011; Jalalzai 2009). However, the perception of threat also undermines the sense of trust necessary to support a robust civil society (Sullivan and Transue 1999). Trust is a cornerstone of the creation of social capital (Putnam 2000), which in turn facilitates the capacity to respond to social and political troubles. However, when trust is lacking, social capital formation breaks down. Groups that do not trust others to treat them fairly respond with defensive mechanisms—creating insular, more homogenous networks and responding with their own intolerance (Gibson 1992). This sense of distrust and the defensiveness that accompanies it may be quite sensitive. Paul Djupe and Brian Calfano (2012), for example, find that Muslims who disagree with a non-Muslim in their discussion network are more intolerant than those who agree across group lines. Along these lines, Amaney Jamal (2007) finds that participation in pro-democracy civil groups in authoritarian states actually drives down the level of generalized trust. When threatened groups perceive an inability to pursue a legitimate and fair resolution through official means, they look to extralegal, perhaps violent remedies. So the nature of the threat, coupled with trust in the institutional forces regulating or otherwise keeping such threats in check, matter. Personal threats are much more likely to elicit a stronger, more negative, and more sustained response than are sociotropic threats (e.g., Davis 1995; Gibson 2006), though the political response to this threat is importantly shaped by the level of trust in the government (Davis and Silver 2004).

Muslim Americans, for their part, tend to report high levels of trust in the government. Tom Tyler, Stephen Schilhofer, and Aziz Huq (2010) report that trust in the legitimacy of city police shapes the level and degree of Muslim cooperation with government investigations. Other measures of acceptance of American norms (such as the belief in American exceptionalism) suggest that these sentiments might not be evenly distributed across the Muslim American population, though.

Muqtedar Khan (2012) argues that the central driver for norm acceptance among many Muslims is their immigrant status. Native-born and, particularly, African American Muslims are both more willing to criticize the government and more skeptical of the state's intentions. Immigrant Muslims' attitudes, on the other hand, tend to depend much more on whether they are focused on the immigrant experience or whether they are focused on U.S. foreign policy. Immigrants thinking in terms of personal experiences tend to be much more supportive of American norms (ideas of American exceptionalism, in this case) than are Muslims primed to think about American foreign policy (Khan 2012; see also Djupe and Calfano 2013). An important dividing line, then, for understanding Muslim responses to the perceived threat originating from outgroup sources is both their ethnic and national origin. This is not dissimilar to the situation Latinos find themselves in. Those bearing the label "Latino" are a highly diverse collection of nationalities brought together largely by the social forces—particularly perceived threat—that encourage alliances and political identities that they might not otherwise have adopted (Pantoja, Ramirez, and Segura 2001; Pantoja and Segura 2003; Ramirez 2013). Contextual sensitivity is needed, then, to understand the mobilizing effect we expect to see from perceived external threat, as well as to understand potential civic consequences for threat-based mobilization.

Islamic Theology, American Exceptionalism, and the *Dar al-Kufr*

Of course, Muslims in the United States are organizing around a religious identity rather than an ethnic identity constructed by the government. Thus, one cannot fully equate ethnic mobilization against a threat with a religious community's response to the same. Western Muslims have a rich religious tradition to draw from in order to navigate the modern environment, from religious texts (the *Qur'an*) and parables of the life of the prophet Muhammad (*hadith*) to the juridical traditions and rulings of scholars accumulated over centuries. Wasif Shadid and Pieter Koningsveld (1996) raised this very issue when they discussed the various concerns regarding theology and *shari'a* (laws based on the Qur'an) that Western Muslims needed to consider when weighing the extent of loyalty they owed to a non-Islamic government. The division of the world into an Islamic world (*dar al-Islam*) and the world of the unbelievers (*dar al-kufr*, also called *dar al-harb*—the world of conflict) raised potential concerns that certain strains of theology would argue that even integration into a non-Islamic society is a threat to the religious values of the community. Indeed, in my interviews with religious leaders in the city of Indianapolis, Indiana, I heard frequent mention among immigrant leaders that participation in U.S. politics was considered *haram* (discouraged by religious law) by many members of their community before 2001.

It was these concerns that shaped, in part, Tariq Ramadan's (2004) discussion of the distinct leadership role Western Muslims had to play in the global *ummah* (Islamic religious community). Ramadan was concerned about the traditional interpretations of Islam that might limit the participation and weaken the social position of Western Muslims. Far from urging withdrawal, Ramadan instead argued that Western Muslims needed to develop a Western Islam that could then be returned to predominantly Islamic countries to better equip them both to engage with the twenty-first century and to build authentically Islamic democratic institutions in their own lands. While this seems to have had only limited impact on the behavior of European Muslims, Khan's (2012) research suggests that an embrace of American exceptionalism among U.S. Muslims has fostered a sense of American *Islamic* exceptionalism as well. This sentiment suggests that American Muslims have a special role to play in shaping and remolding the global *ummah* for the twenty-first century and beyond. I heard this sentiment discussed as well, with some native-born religious leaders going so far as to argue that veil-wearing, arguably the most distinctive symbol of Islamic identity to non-Muslim Westerners, should not be considered acceptable in the United States under the standards of Islamic modesty as it serves to draw far more attention to the wearer than would leaving one's hair uncovered.

It appears that religious belief is a highly flexible resource that can either encourage and enhance religious participation in society or serve as an isolating force that encourages inward-looking orientations among its believers. What seems to matter for how the belief system will shape the participation of

Muslims in the West is the acceptance of a spiritual framework that at least permits, if not encourages, political and civic engagement. This needs to be coupled with a belief in the legitimacy of the institutions through which Muslims will be acting and trust in the strength of civil society to tolerate and even welcome their participation. The perception of threat gives this ethnically and nationally diverse religious community in the United States the impetus to come together to try to develop a common political identity through which they can mobilize. However, the perception of threat can also serve to reinforce notions of being in "the world of conflict." The cultural and religious memory of Muslims operating as a minority in Western settings has generally encouraged isolation and disengagement. So, while the perception of threat can help an identity to coalesce, it also can have the effect of encouraging Muslims to circle the wagons.

A Question of Motivations

We generally think of religion playing a formative role in shaping political behavior because of the distinctive institutional and conceptual structure surrounding religious institutions (see Putnam and Campbell 2012). The social ties (Djupe and Gilbert 2009; Lim and Putnam 2010), resource mobilization (Verba, Schlozman, and Brady 1995), and even the psychological sense of divine sanction and protection (Harris 1999) religion can inspire are all ways in which religious commitment can influence the degree and scope of individual civic participation. However, the case of American Muslims leads us to ask how much of their civic behavior is explained by religious orientation itself and how much of what we observe among Muslims is a result of situational concerns. It is likely that the role Muslim theology and religious belief plays in shaping political participation is dependent on contextual information such as information flow, trust, and even the perceived salience of Muslim identity itself (as opposed to the ethnic identities that have generally shaped and defined Muslim political participation in the United States—see Saeed 2003 for a discussion of pre-9/11 Muslim political behavior in the United States). I surmise that Islam contains within it the seeds for spurring both participation and isolation. The question, then, is why we see American Muslims participating as we do in the United States. Is it faith qua faith that plays the decisive role in mobilizing Muslims, or is it threat perception and other dynamic contextual factors that shape the interpretation of the faith?

Data: The IMPAS Study

To answer the question, I turn to a survey of Muslims living in the state of Indiana. The survey relies on a convenience sample, drawing from the mailing list of the Muslim Alliance of Indiana (MAI). The MAI is a civic engagement group that seeks to contact and encourage civil and political participation among Muslims living in the state of Indiana. The initial mailing list contains 10,824 names of individuals in the state of Indiana identified by the organization as having a high probability of being Muslim. The list draws its names from a number of sources, though the largest sources of names are voter registration rolls and mosque registration rolls.

Paper surveys were sent out to all names on the organization's mailing list, providing paper ballots and return envelopes as well as information for replying online. Subsequent analysis of the return mail suggests that roughly one-third of all letters received were from non-Muslims.[2] The survey is a mixed-mode survey that solicited participation through both e-mail and post invitations to participate. The online list provided by the organization is redundant to, though significantly smaller than, the mailing list provided. It was also considerably more accurate in identifying practicing Muslims. I relied on e-mail follow-ups and targeted postal mail responses to try to boost the number of responses from individuals believed to be of the ethno-religious background of interest as well as to accommodate cost constraints. The survey was conducted from July to September in 2012. The data below are drawn solely from the 261 self-identified Muslims who responded to the survey request (I refer to this survey as the Indiana Muslim Political Attitude Survey, or IMPAS for short).

The survey was based on a number of previous surveys of the Muslim community. In particular, the survey drew from elements of the Pew Research Center surveys of Muslims in 2007 and 2011, the Muslim American Public Opinion Survey (MAPOS) conducted by Matt Barreto and Karam Dana (e.g., Dana, Barreto, and Oskooii 2011), and the social network surveys of Djupe and Calfano (2012). The survey looks at three distinct aspects of respondents' lives: political engagement and preferences, religious and communal engagement, and social network communication. Social network items contain both an egocentric inventory focused on political discussion and a description of the general composition of their close social network in both ethnic and religious terms (i.e., "How many of your close friends would you say are the same X as you?"). The following analysis relies on this self-reported network diversity.

The survey data distinguish between a number of different sources of threat. To account for the different types of threat an individual might encounter, I examined the perception of anti-Muslim hostility from respondents' neighbors, perceived anti-Muslim bias on the part of the government, and the perception of threat from what the survey described as "Christian extremists." This final item was part of a battery inquiring about a number of sources of potential group threat, and it was paired with "Islamic extremists," a group that Muslims are frequently asked about. Muslims are, however, rarely asked about their concerns over Christian extremist activity in the United States, so this survey allows us to examine this distinctive source of religious as opposed to personal threat to the Muslim community.

The survey is supplemented with a series of interviews and participant observations conducted at five mosques in the Indianapolis area in June and July of 2013. At each mosque, I conducted structured formal interviews with a member of the leadership of each center, as well as casual conversations with congregants, and I cite observations at three of the five centers. These interviews and conversations were oriented toward developing an understanding of the social context of the mosque communities, how their sociopolitical position shaped internal relations, and their level of interest in engagement with those outside the community. The interviews also help give more nuance to the distinctive characteristics of the Indianapolis Muslim community, which is reflective of the diversity of the Hoosier *ummah*.

The Muslims of Indiana are diverse, and the demographics of their community generally reflect those of the national community as a whole. Northern Indiana is home to one of the oldest Muslim communities in the United States: The Shi'a community of Michigan City, Indiana, incorporated in 1914 and built one of the first specifically Shi'a mosques in 1924 (Takim 2009). Likewise, northern Indiana serves as a crossroads between the two centers of black Islam in the United States: Chicago and Detroit. Owing to this distinctive location, old and well-established communities dedicated to the Nation of Islam and its successors, as well as the Moorish Sciences Temple of the Noble Drew Ali (the predecessor of the Nation of Islam) can still be found in the Gary, Indiana, area. One of the first Muslim Student Associations in the country was established at Indiana University in Bloomington, and in part because of this, the Islamic Society of North America was located in suburban Indianapolis at the time of its creation (a location it maintains to this day). The majority of Muslim communities are concentrated either in Indianapolis or northern Indiana or are otherwise clustered around colleges (such as in West Lafayette, Bloomington, or Muncie), though a rising number of smaller communities are located away from academic centers and large cities (such as in the small community of Columbus, Indiana). The demographic distribution generally reflects national norms, though there is an atypically large population of Bosnian Muslims in the area of Fort Wayne, Indiana, and the well-established Lebanese communities in and around Michigan City, Indiana, have much in common with the more well-known Lebanese community of Dearborn, Michigan.

Indianapolis is home to numerous Muslim communities, most of which are interconnected in one way or the other. The oldest Islamic community in Indianapolis is the Nur Allah Islamic Center, which was founded in the 1950s as a chapter of the Nation of Islam. This religious community followed the same vicissitudes that other chapters of the Nation of Islam have and is today an orthodox Sunni community, though one that is still centered in and focused on the needs and concerns of the African American community. Masjid al-Fajr is the oldest continuously existing Muslim community in Indianapolis. It was founded in the 1970s and today is a central touchstone for the Muslims of the area. Even those unaffiliated with al-Fajr are familiar with it, and many were members of this community before leaving to join or found other Islamic communities throughout Indianapolis.

To take advantage of some of the more distinctive characteristics of the Indiana Muslim community, the IMPAS survey targeted members of four ethnic communities: African Americans, Arabs, south Asians, and Bosnians. Together, these four ethnic groups make up 83 percent of the IMPAS sample. While south Asians, Arabs, and blacks each make up about a third of the overall national Muslim community (Pew Research Center 2011) and are fairly representatively balanced in the overall sample, the Bosnians in the sample are significantly overrepresented. However, their inclusion is fortuitous, for this community is notable for being one of the only Muslim ethnic groups of European origin. Bosnians are also distinctively more secular in their outlook than other Muslims. This is likely in part because of the effects of having lived several generations under Communist rule in their homeland. While the mean level of religious attendance for Arabs and south Asians is statistically indistinguishable from the overall mean, the Bosnian and black levels of religious participation are significantly different. On a six-point scale measuring religious attendance, Bosnians are a full point lower on the scale than the mean level of participation, while blacks are a half-point higher (and generally report the most frequent mosque attendance rates). Both differences are statistically significant deviations from the group mean.

Civic Participation

To begin with, I examine the correlates of engagement among the respondents to the 2012 IMPAS survey, focusing on how threat perception, faith, and identity shape the level of engagement across three modes of engagement: political acts associated with political campaigns (volunteering time, donating money, displaying yard signs); expressive actions that express individual views and preferences (contacting media or elected officials, engaging in online political discussions, signing a petition, and participating in a protest or boycott); and community engagement (whether respondents volunteer within their religious community, work within their community to solve problems, and have attended a play or a PTA meeting). These measures capture a broad range of types of engagement and allow us to better understand when the perception of threat and intolerance is likely to elicit a mobilizing response and when it is going to promote threatened individuals to circle the wagons.

I discuss the independent variables of interest across the three modes of engagement, and the data analysis is shown in Table 14.1. Religion is generally seen as a tremendous source of mobilization for civic engagement. Communal religious participation in particular is seen as a tremendous source of civic skills acquisition and political recruitment (Verba, Schlozman, and Brady 1995), though this observation is qualified by the fact that skills and recruitment opportunities are not equally available to all members of the religious community (Djupe and Gilbert 2009) and that it is the social ties (and particularly the church-based

TABLE 14.1 PERCEIVED PERSONAL THREAT HAS A PERSISTENT NEGATIVE EFFECT ON CIVIC ENGAGEMENT

	Campaign		*Voice*		*Community*	
	β	p	β	p	β	p
Religious						
Guidance	.07		.05		.09	*
Attendance	.10		.11		.39	*
Prayer	.04		.12		.34	*
Network religious homogeneity	–.04		.03		.01	
Discussion religious homogeneity	–.03		–.02		–.02	
Threat						
Government hostility	–.22	*	–.06		–.09	
Neighbor hostility	–.27	*	–.16	*	–.17	*
Christian "extremists"	.17	*	.06		.11	
Identity						
Muslim identity	.07		.02		.14	*
American identity	.41	*	.20	*	.25	*
Muslim linked fate	.09		.08	*	.08	
Ethnicity						
Arab	.09	*	.06	*	.06	*
Black	.00		.01		.04	*
Bosnian	–.10	*	–.08	*	–.12	*
Control						
Generalized trust	.17	*	.09	*	.13	*
Trust in government	.13	*	.01		.07	
Education	.40	*	.31	*	.43	*
Income	.43	*	.24	*	.32	
Political interest	.32	*	.25	*	.28	*
Born in the U.S.	.03		.04	*	.09	*

Source: 2012 IMPAS Study.
Note: Models developed using maximum likelihood estimation. $N = 261$.
$*p < .05$

friendships) individuals have that explains most of the civic mobilizing capacity of religious institutions (Lim and Putnam 2010). Even so, we do see some measures of religious commitment positively correlating with community involvement. The community engagement measure is a mix of ingroup and outgroup activities. Even when disaggregated, however, one sees religious commitment correlating with greater community involvement across a number of different types of apolitical civic engagement. However, religious commitment variables show no significant correlation with more overtly political modes of engagement, and neither does the relative religious homogeneity of either respondents' reported friendship networks or their reported discussion networks.

While religious commitment measures have a powerful positive correlation with one particular mode of civic engagement, measures of identity have more sustained significance across a broader array of engagement modes. Looking first at self-reported ethnicity (south Asians are the excluded category in this analysis), we see that Arabs are consistently the most engaged Muslims in the sample while Bosnians are the least engaged. Blacks are somewhat more engaged within their community than are south Asians, but in general these two groups seem to have similar levels of civic participation. These observations confirm others' observations of Arab mobilization (Tam Cho, Gimple, and Wu 2006) and Bosnian disengagement (Jalalzai 2009). More interestingly, those who more tightly embrace their American identity have higher levels of engagement across all three measures of civic engagement. One's reported strength of religious identity is, like other variables tapping into religiosity, correlated with higher levels of apolitical and more often ingroup engagement. The strength of linked fate sentiments, on the other hand, is correlated with a greater propensity to engage in activities that give voice to the respondent, though not necessarily with particular campaign activity on behalf of individual candidates.

However, what is striking is the observed relationship between threat perception and civic engagement. The level of perceived threat from Christian religious extremists has a significant and positive relationship with electoral modes of engagement measured in the survey. This resonates with the literature finding Muslims responding to perceived political threats (or, as it is more often operationalized, those who feel greater anxiety about outgroup behavior) with increased levels of political participation (Ayers and Hofstetter 2008; Gimple, Tam Cho, and Wu 2007; Jalalzai 2011; Tam Cho, Gimple, and Wu 2006; Sinno 2012).

This also resonated with the interviews held in Indianapolis. The concern about religious entrepreneurs using religious divisions to strengthen their appeal was raised by several discussants. A few of the respondents singled out Franklin Graham as exacerbating tensions between the two communities.[3] Individuals who raised these concerns about evangelical Christians in particular tended to be born in the United States and active in politics. It would seem that a certain level of political awareness and sophistication is needed to make the connection between evangelical Christianity and anti-Muslim sentiment. However, given the seemingly widespread awareness of Tea Party hostility toward Muslims among interviewees, many Muslims seem to meet or exceed this minimum level of awareness.

In contrast, those who express the belief that the government itself is hostile toward Muslims are less likely to participate in specifically electoral activities (see also Gibson 1992). Threat perception has direct as well as indirect effects. Structural equation modeling suggests that governmental threat also has an indirect role in shaping political voice activities, as governmental threat perception is an important factor in shaping a sense of linked fate among American Muslims.

Those who express a belief that their neighbors—the non-Muslim people they see on a daily basis—are hostile to Muslims are significantly less likely to engage in all three spheres of civic participation. This, too, resonated with what was heard during interviews. One interviewee in particular expressed his belief that in the eyes of his neighbors, "Muslims are guilty until proven innocent," and that he was tired of always feeling under a cloud of suspicion. While a clear majority of respondents reported either positive or neutral experiences with their neighbors, coworkers, and the other people they see frequently in the community, those who felt hostility from their neighbors were the ones who were most withdrawn from the general public.

The importance of intolerance in activating a defensive mobilization to protect the community, then, depends on the source and the type of participation in question. If one is concerned about intolerance stemming from a rival religious community that might be perceived as more distant, then intolerance can be an important catalyst for political and civic engagement. This sort of threat, after all, is a political challenge that can legitimately be responded to in the political arena. On the other hand, if one believes that their neighbors view them with hostility, they are not going to get involved and risk exposing themselves to these potentially hostile others.

Threat, Social Networks, and Outgroup Tolerance

American Muslims are themselves a group with a relatively recent sense of common purpose. Because of this, they are still in the process of negotiating common identities and shared beliefs (Ali 2011; Leonard 2003). One area of particular importance for understanding how the perceived threat environment affects Muslim political behavior is their attitudes toward other ethnic and racial groups. Djupe and Calfano (2012) find that exposure to disagreement within social networks lowers tolerance for acts against religious groups, except when that disagreement is coming from ingroup sources. Understanding how threat perception and social closure among Muslims affects their tolerance is critical for understanding how contextual information shapes the religious group's perception of others. One of the advantages of the IMPAS study is that it included a battery of feeling thermometer scores, which enables an examination of how the perceived threat from various sources affects Muslim tolerance and warmth for individuals in the outgroup and ingroup.

Figure 14.1 presents the mean feeling thermometer score for the religious and ethnic groups asked about in the survey. The feeling thermometer scores have been standardized against each respondent's mean score among these groups, which means the scores presented are the average distance from each respondent's mean feeling thermometer score and not the distance from the mean of the whole survey.[4] Perhaps unsurprisingly, the group Muslims feel warmest toward is themselves. However, Muslims are almost equally as warm to the various ethnic groups asked about in the survey (except for Jews). Of

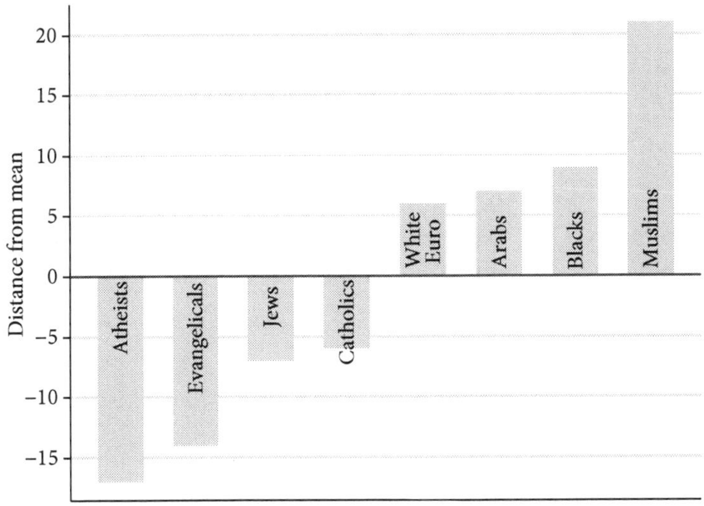

Figure 14.1 Distance from mean for ethnic and religious feeling thermometer scores
Source: 2013 IMPAS Study.

course, given the mean feeling thermometer for Jews, it would be reasonable to suggest that they are being evaluated by Muslims more as a religious group than an ethnic group. Religious groups are, on a whole, less warmly evaluated than ethnic groups, with Jews and Catholics viewed equivalently. The least-liked groups in this set are atheists and evangelical Christians. Evangelical Christians and atheists are commonly among the least-liked groups in the United States (Putnam and Campbell 2012), so the real question is not so much whether they are disliked but why.

To address that question, I turn to regression models to evaluate feeling thermometer scores (see Table 14.2). The models are structured similarly to Djupe and Calfano's (2012) study of social network disagreement and tolerance among Muslims. Thus, the primary interest is examining the impact of social network composition and the perception of hostility in shaping the tolerance of Muslim respondents. As with the analysis of civic engagement, I note differences across ethnicities within the sample.

Turning first to the role of social networks, the effect of the respondents' political discussion partners varies considerably across groups. Most notably, discussion networks seem to have their most significant impact only on the evaluation of ingroup sentiments and in the evaluation of evangelical Christians. Evangelicals are associated with the Republican Party as well as the Tea Party movement[5] (Campbell, Green, and Layman 2011) and, therefore, can reasonably be seen as the primary religious and political rival of American Muslims. Furthermore, evangelical Christians seem to be more likely to make efforts to reach out to American Muslims specifically for the purpose of conversion.

TABLE 14.2 NETWORK HOMOGENEITY, THREAT PERCEPTION ARE TIED MOSTLY TO FEELINGS TOWARD MAJORITY, NOT MINORITY, GROUPS

	Evangelicals		*Catholics*		*Jews*		*Atheists*		*Muslims*	
	β	*p*	*β*	*p*	*β*	*p*	*β*	*p*	*β*	*p*
Social Networks										
Muslim discussant	.000		–.003		–.002		–.001		.003	*
Disagreement	–.006	*	.002		.001		–.001		.003	
Muslim × disagreement	–.002		–.004		–.003		–.003		.006	*
Discussant expertise	.005	*	–.001		.001		–.002		–.001	
Political talk	–.006		.005	*	.002		.002		–.003	
Network size	–.009		–.005		–.004		–.001		.001	
Threat Perception										
Government hostility	–.007	*	–.012	*	–.010	*	–.001		.012	*
Local hostility	.007		–.011	*	–.007		–.002		.008	*
Christian "extremism"	–.016	*	.005		.004		.005		.006	
Ethnicity										
Arab	–.002		.005	*	.006	*	.003	*	–.006	*
Black	.001		–.004	*	–.001		–.002		.004	*
Bosnian	.002		–.006	*	–.005	*	–.003	*	.005	*
American identity	–.008		.022	*	.008		.000		–.009	*
Demographics										
Female	.002		.003		.008	*	.003		–.006	*
Education	–.019	*	.028	*	.017	*	.009	*	–.012	*
Religious attendance	–.009		–.002		–.014	*	–.009		.027	*
Prayer frequency	–.005		.006		.005		–.005		.005	
Income	–.018	*	.016	*	.001		.007		–.006	
Political Interest	–.014	*	.016	*	.013	*	.008	*	–.010	*
Born in the U.S.	.000		.000		.005	*	.000		–.003	
Age	.167	*	–.268	*	–.201	*	–.067		.130	*

Source: 2012 IMPAS Study.

Note: Models developed using maximum likelihood estimation. $N = 261$.

$*p < .05$

One example of this can be seen at the annual Dearborn Arab International Festival. The celebration of Arab culture has traditionally been held on Warren Avenue in Dearborn, a center of the Arab Muslim community in the American city with the densest concentration of Muslims. However, the mayor and the Arab American Chamber of Commerce moved the festival from a public to a private venue starting in 2013 after rising tensions between locals and evangelical missionaries who frequented the event to proselytize to attendees and proclaim "that they were going to hell because they were Muslim" (Warikoo 2013). For both these political and religious reasons, we would expect conversation to shape evangelical evaluations more. I find that the more frequently respondents name a same-faith political discussant, the warmer they feel toward members of their ingroup. Exposure to disagreement, on the other hand, seems to vary depending on the source. Exposure to political disagreement within the social network is correlated with lower levels of warmth for evangelical Christians and higher levels of warmth toward Muslims. However, in the latter case, it is only ingroup disagreement that seems to elicit this warmth (the interaction is significant). Additionally, those who report more informed political discussion partners tend to feel somewhat warmer toward evangelical Christians, while those who talk more frequently about politics within their discussion partners feel warmer toward Catholics.

Threat perception, however, has a more consistent effect across models. Interestingly, it is not threat perceptions pertaining to local hostility that are the most consistently correlated with more negative outgroup evaluations but rather perceptions of government hostility. The more intensely one believes the state is hostile to Islam, the more likely respondents are to have more negative evaluations of other religious groups and more positive evaluations of their co-religionists. Beyond that, evaluations of the two Christian traditions asked about are shaped by different factors. Warmth toward Catholics is correlated with evaluations of local anti-Muslim sentiment, while intolerance toward evangelicals seems to be governed by the broader concern about Christian "extremism." Meanwhile, positive ingroup evaluations seem to be significantly correlated with local perceptions of hostility as well.

It is worth noting that anti-atheist sentiment is not significantly correlated with either social network factors or the perception of threat. This is expected. While Muslims in America do not see secular or atheist people as threats, the creeping threat of *secularism* might be a concern for Muslim parents. In my interviews, I repeatedly heard about the importance of youth ministers in particular and youth outreach in general. The ability to relate to younger members of the congregation was considered to be among the most important qualifications for a prospective imam by people I spoke with. One mosque leader even went so far as to say, "In my opinion, the position of youth leader is more important than the imam." Yet even if Muslim parents are concerned about the possibility of their children losing their faith, they quite reasonably do not blame secularists and atheists for this potential problem.

While there does seem to be a growing sense of Islamic community among the Muslims of the United States (Jamal 2005; Dana, Barreto, and Oskooii 2011), ethnic differences persist within the group. While ethnicity is not significantly correlated with anti-evangelical sentiments, it plays a strong role in shaping intolerance toward Catholics. In particular, Arabs and those who feel more strongly attached to their identity as Americans are friendlier toward Catholics while blacks and Bosnians are less tolerant of Catholics. Interestingly, while Arabs show greater warmth across a broad range of groups and Bosnians feel cooler toward outgroup members, Arabs are somewhat less likely to evaluate Muslims as warmly as other ethnic groups in the sample. Furthermore, for all respondents evaluations of their fellow Muslims decline somewhat as respondents rate their identity as Americans as more important.

American Muslims: Standing Center Stage or Circling the Wagons?

Social discrimination and persistent inequality have the capacity for provoking considerable violence from the minority discriminated against, depending on the social and political circumstances of the nation (Cederman, Wimmer, and Min 2010; Crighton and Mac Iver 1991; Gurr 2000; Piazza 2011). While resource competition (Piazza 2011) and group image maintenance (Fein and Spencer 1997) play important roles in creating the incentive for discrimination and derogation of outgroup members, Ted Gurr (2000) argues that regime type and regime strength likewise play important roles in understanding the ultimate consequence of minority discrimination—autocratic and weak regimes are more likely to inspire a violent response from disaffected minorities, while strong democratic states are more likely to inspire peaceful protest. However, while democratic polities might offer an institutional route for conflict resolution, the willingness of minority groups to pursue this option may well be conditional on their beliefs in the legitimacy and neutrality of the state in question.

As noted at the beginning of this chapter, Muslims in the United States are generally more civically and politically engaged with the general population than are European Muslims. Formal church-state relations help explain the varying degrees of Muslim political integration (Fetzer and Soper 2005). The willingness of states to negotiate and compromise with their religious minority populations is dependent on formal state relationships with previously existing religious institutions, which in turn shapes the state's capacity for compromise and negotiation with religious minorities. For example, Germany has experienced generally more peaceful relations with its Muslim minority than France because the institutional framework in Germany allows for more compromise with religious groups (Fetzer and Soper 2005). Following this pattern, religious minorities in the United States have received at least some protection from the state; also, the state does not give a strong preference to any religious group.

The American tradition of friendly public secularism has long been held up as an ideal type (Tocqueville [1840] 1994). The deep enmeshing of civil society and civil religion has afforded religious traditions broad latitude to engage with the public and mobilize in defense of their interests. Yet in the United States, deep hostility and intolerance have also historically played a role in demobilizing certain religious groups and promoting a preference for separatism. Most notably, some strains of fundamentalist Christianity essentially withdrew from the public sphere following the Scopes trial of 1925 in the face of considerable denigration and intolerance (Hunter 1983; Wald and Calhoun-Brown 2007). While American Muslims have shown a considerable level of engagement following the September 11 attacks, becoming considerably more engaged with civil and political society, the examples of both the Muslims in Europe and fundamentalist Christians in the United States suggest that is not necessarily the only outcome we might expect. The findings in this study suggest that sustained suspicion and perceived hostility from the federal government can have a deleterious effect on the currently robust response we have seen from the American Muslim community.

American Muslims may very well, as Ramadan (2004) proposed, have a special and distinctive role in leadership in the global *ummah* in the coming years. Yet if the American Muslim community loses confidence in the essential fairness and neutrality of the U.S. government, we may be looking at the disengagement of European Muslim minorities not as a counterexample of the American case but rather as an example of things to come.

Notes

1. Demographic information on religion is sometimes difficult to measure, particularly since some countries (notably France and the United States) do not ask about religious affiliation in official censuses. Our best estimates of the size of the American Muslim minority is somewhere between 0.5 and 1 percent of the population (Pew Research Center 2011; Gallup 2011). The Central Intelligence Agency (2014) estimates that about 5–10 percent of the French population is Muslim.

2. Indeed, the considerable hostility some recipients demonstrated at receiving the mailing was telling. Some respondents replied with telephone calls or letters denouncing the study, pleading for a conversion to Christianity, or denouncing terrorism, while others expressed anger or fear at being associated with Islam. Several non-Muslim respondents specifically mentioned fear of encountering travel difficulties if they were to be associated with Muslims. Others took more artistic approaches in expressing their opinions, including one respondent who opted to reply by stuffing the return envelope with pictures of pork products.

3. Graham notably described Islam as a "very evil and wicked religion" and has frequently inveighed against the faith on various media platforms ("Graham Disinvited" 2010).

4. The justification for this is that some may "like it hot" (Wilcox, Sigelman, and Cook 1989) and have high (or low) thermometer ratings across the board. Thus, the more appropriate comparison is to gauge feelings relative to each individual's baseline (average) feeling.

5. Feeling thermometer evaluations of evangelical Christians in the IMPAS sample are correlated with feeling thermometer scores toward the GOP at a modest $r = .32$ and with evaluations of the Tea Party at $r = .43$.

References

Ali, Muna. 2011. "Muslim American/American Muslim Identity: Authoring Self in Post-9/11 America." *Journal of Muslim Minority Affairs* 31 (3): 355–381.

Amath, Nora. 2013. "The Impact of 9/11 on Australian Muslim Civil Society Organizations." *Communication, Politics, and Culture* 46:116–135.

Ayers, John W., and C. Richard Hofstetter. 2008. "American Muslim Political Participation Following 9/11: Religious Belief, Political Resources, Social Structures, and Political Awareness." *Religion and Politics* 1 (1): 3–26.

Benson, Brett V., Jennifer L. Merolla, and John G. Geer. 2011. "Two Steps Forward, One Step Back? Bias in the 2008 Presidential Election." *Electoral Studies* 30 (4): 607–620.

Campbell, David E., John C. Green, and Geoffrey Layman. 2011. "The Party Faithful: Partisan Images, Candidate Religion, and the Electoral Impact of Party Identification." *American Journal of Political Science* 55 (1): 42–58.

Cederman, Lars-Erik, Andreas Wimmer, and Brian Min. 2010. "Why Do Ethnic Groups Rebel? New Data and Analysis." *World Politics* 62 (1): 87–119.

Central Intelligence Agency. 2014. "The World Factbook: France." Available at https://www.cia.gov/library/publications/the-world-factbook/geos/fr.html.

Crighton, Elizabeth, and Martha Abele Mac Iver. 1991. "The Evolution of Protracted Ethnic Conflict: Group Dominance and Political Underdevelopment in Northern Ireland and Lebanon." *Comparative Politics* 23 (2): 127–142.

Dana, Karam, Matt A. Barreto, and Kassra A. R. Oskooii. 2011. "Mosques as American Institutions: Mosque Attendance, Religiosity and Integration into the Political System among American Muslims." *Religions* 2 (4): 504–524.

Davis, Darren W. 1995. "Exploring Black Political Intolerance." *Political Behavior* 17 (1): 1–22.

———. 2007. *Negative Liberty: Public Opinion and the Terrorist Attacks on America*. New York: Russell Sage Foundation.

Davis, Darren W., and Brian D. Silver. 2004. "Civil Liberties vs. Security: Public Opinion in the Context of the Terrorist Attacks on America." *American Journal of Political Science* 48 (1): 28–46.

Djupe, Paul A., and Brian R. Calfano. 2012. "American Muslim Investment in Civil Society Political Discussion, Disagreement, and Tolerance." *Political Research Quarterly* 65 (3): 516–528.

———. 2013. *God Talk: Experimenting with the Religious Causes of Public Opinion*. Philadelphia: Temple University Press.

Djupe, Paul A., and Christopher P. Gilbert. 2009. *The Political Influence of Churches*. New York: Cambridge University Press.

Djupe, Paul A., and John C. Green. 2007. "The Politics of American Muslims." In *From Pews to Polling Places: Faith and Politics in the American Religious Mosaic*, edited by J. Matthew Wilson, 213–250. Washington, DC: Georgetown University Press.

Dunn, Kevin M., Natascha Klocker, and Tanya Salabay. 2007. "Contemporary Racism and Islamophobia in Australia: Racializing Religion." *Ethnicities* 7 (4): 564–589.

Fein, Steven, and Steven J. Spencer. 1997. "Prejudice as Self-Image Maintenance: Affirming the Self through Derogating Others." *Journal of Personality and Social Psychology* 73 (1): 31–44.

Fetzer, Joel S., and J. Christopher Soper. 2005. *Muslims and the State in Britain, France, and Germany*. New York: Cambridge University Press.

Gallup. 2011. *Muslim Americans: Faith, Freedom, and the Future*. Available at http://www.gallup.com/poll/148931/presentation-muslim-americans-faith-freedom-future.aspx.

Gibson, James L. 1992. "The Political Consequences of Intolerance: Cultural Conformity and Political Freedom," *American Political Science Review* 86 (2): 338–356.

———. 2006. "Enigmas of Intolerance: Fifty Years after Stouffer's *Communism, Conformity, and Civil Liberties*." *Perspectives on Politics* 4 (1): 21–34.

Gimple, James G., Wendy K. Tam Cho, and Tony Wu. 2007. "Spatial Dimensions of Arab American Voter Mobilization after September 11." *Political Geography* 26:330–351.

Goldstone, Jack A., and Charles Tilly. 2001. "Threat (and Opportunity): Popular Action and State Response in the Dynamics of Contentious Action." In *Silence and Voice in the Study of Contentious Politics*, edited by Ronald R. Aminzade, Jack A. Goldstone,

Doug McAdams, Elizabeth J. Perry, William H. Sewell, Jr., Sidney Tarrow, and Charles Tilly, 179–194. New York: Cambridge University Press.

"Graham Disinvited from Prayer Event over Islam Comments." 2010. *CNN*, April 23. Available at http://www.cnn.com/2010/US/04/23/graham.islam.controversy/.

Gurr, Ted Robert. 2000. *Peoples versus States: Minorities at Risk in the New Century*. Washington, DC: United States Institute of Peace.

Harris, Fredrick C. 1999. *Something Within: Religion in African-American Political Activism*. New York: Oxford University Press.

Huddy, Leonie, Stanley Feldman, Theresa Capelos, and Colin Provost. 2002. "Disentangling the Effects of Personal and National Threat." *Political Psychology* 23 (3): 485–509.

Hunter, James D. 1983. *American Evangelicalism: Religion and the Quandary of Modernity*. New Brunswick, NJ: Rutgers University Press.

Jalalzai, Farida. 2009. "The Politics of Muslims in America." *Politics and Religion* 2 (2): 163–199.

———. 2011. "Anxious and Active-Muslim Perceptions of Discrimination and Treatment and Its Political Consequences in the Post 9-11 United States." *Politics and Religion* 4 (1): 71–107.

Jamal, Amaney. 2005. "The Political Participation and Engagement of Muslim Americans: Mosque Involvement and Group Consciousness." *American Politics Research* 33 (4): 521–544.

———. 2007. *Barriers to Democracy: The Other Side of Social Capital in Palestine and the Arab World*. Princeton, NJ: Princeton University Press.

Kalkan, Kerem Ozan, Geoffrey C. Layman, and Eric M. Uslaner. 2009. "'Bands of Others'? Attitudes toward Muslim in Contemporary American Society." *Journal of Politics* 71 (3): 847–862.

Khan, M. A. Muqtedar. 2012. "American Exceptionalism and American Muslims." *Review of Faith and International Affairs* 10 (2): 59–65.

Klaussen, Jytte. 2005. *The Islamic Challenge: Politics and Religion in Western Europe*. New York: Cambridge University Press.

Leiken, Robert S. 2005. "Europe's Angry Muslims: An American Concern." *Foreign Affairs*, July/August. Available at http://www.foreignaffairs.com/articles/60829/robert-s-leiken/europes-angry-muslims.

Leonard, Karen Isaksen. 2003. *Muslims in the United States: The State of Research*. New York: Russell Sage Foundation.

Lim, Chaeyoon, and Robert D. Putnam. 2010. "Religion, Social Networks, and Life Satisfaction." *American Sociological Review* 75 (6): 914–933.

Mason, Victoria, and Scott Poynting. 2006. "'Tolerance, Freedom, Justice, and Peace'? Britain, Australia, and Anti-Muslim Racism since 11 September 2001." *Journal of Intercultural Studies* 27 (4): 365–391.

Mythen, Gabe, Sandra Walklate, and Fatima Khan. 2009. "'I'm a Muslim, but I'm Not a Terrorist': Victimization, Risky Identities, and the Performance of Safety." *British Journal of Criminology* 49 (6): 736–754.

Pantoja, Adrian D., Ricardo Ramirez, and Gary M. Segura. 2001. "Citizens by Choice, Voters by Necessity: Patterns in Political Mobilization by Naturalized Latinos." *Political Research Quarterly* 54 (4): 729–750.

Pantoja, Adrian D., and Gary M. Segura. 2003. "Fear and Loathing in California: Contextual Threat and Political Sophistication among Latino Voters." *Political Behavior* 25 (3): 265–286.

Pew Research Center. 2007. "Muslim Americans: Middle Class and Mostly Mainstream." Available at http://www.pewresearch.org/2007/05/22/muslim-americans-middle-class-and-mostly-mainstream/.

———. 2011. "Muslim Americans: No Sign of Growth in Alienation or Support for Extremism." Available at http://www.people-press.org/2011/08/30/muslim-americans-no-signs-of-growth-in-alienation-or-support-for-extremism/.

Piazza, James A. 2011. "Poverty, Minority Economic Discrimination, and Domestic Terrorism." *Journal of Peace Research* 48 (3): 339–353.

Putnam, Robert D. 2000. *Bowling Alone: The Collapse and Revival of American Community*. New York: Simon and Schuster.

Putnam, Robert D., and David E. Campbell. 2012. *American Grace: How Religion Divides and Unites Us*. New York: Simon and Schuster.

Ramadan, Tariq. 2004. *Western Muslims and the Future of Islam*. New York: Oxford University Press.

Ramirez, Ricardo. 2013. *Mobilizing Opportunities: State Contexts, Mobilization, and the Evolving Latino Electorate*. Charlottesville: University of Virginia Press.

Reuters. 2012. "Subway Pusher Charged with 'Murder as Hate Crime.'" *Otago Daily Times*, December 30. Available at http://www.odt.co.nz/news/world/240887/subway-pusher-charged-murder-hate-crime.

Saeed, Agha. 2003. "Muslim-American Politics: Developments, Debates, and Direction." In *Muslims in the United States: Demography, Beliefs, Institutions*, edited by Phillipa Strumm and Danielle Tarantolo, 39–44. Washington, DC: Woodrow Wilson International Center for Scholars.

Santora, Marc, and Anemona Hartocollis. 2012. "Troubled Past for Suspect in Fatal Subway Push." *New York Times*, December 30. Available at http://www.nytimes.com/2012/12/31/nyregion/erika-menendez-suspect-in-fatal-subway-push-had-troubled-past.html.

Shadid, Wasif A. R., and Pieter S. van Koningsveld. 1996. "Loyalty to a Non-Muslim Government: An Analysis of Islamic Normative Discussions and the Views of Some Contemporary Islamicists." In *Political Participation and Identities of Muslims in Non-Muslim States*, edited by Wasif A.R. Shadid and Pieter S. van Koningsveld, 84–115. Louvain, Belgium: Peeters.

Sides, John, and Kimberly Gross. 2013. "Stereotypes of Muslims and Support for the War on Terror." *Journal of Politics* 75 (3): 583–598.

Sinno, Abdulkader H. 2012. "The Politics of Western Muslims." *Review of Middle East Studies* 46 (2): 215–230.

Sullivan, John L., and John E. Transue. 1999. "The Psychological Underpinnings of Democracy: A Selective Review of Research on Political Tolerance, Interpersonal Trust, and Social Capital." *Annual Review of Psychology* 50:625–650.

Takim, Liyakat Nathani. 2009. *Shi'ism in America*. New York: New York University Press.

Tam Cho, Wendy K., James G. Gimple, and Tony Wu. 2006. "Clarifying the Role of SES in Political Participation: Policy Threat and Arab Mobilization." *Journal of Politics* 68 (4): 977–991.

Tocqueville, Alexis de. (1840) 1994. *Democracy in America*. 2 vols. New York: Alfred A. Knopf.

Tyler, Tom R., Stephen Schilhofer, and Aziz Z. Huq. 2010. "Legitimacy and Deterrence Effects in Counterterrorism Policing: A Study of Muslim Americans." *Law and Society Review* 44 (2): 365–402.

Verba, Sidney, Kay Lehman Schlozman, and Henry E. Brady. 1995. *Voice and Equality: Civic Voluntarism in American Politics*. Cambridge, MA: Harvard University Press.

Voas, David, and Fenella Fleischmann. 2012. "Islam Moves West: Religious Change in the First and Second Generations." *Annual Review of Sociology* 38:525–545.

Wald, Kenneth D., and Allison Calhoun-Brown. 2007. *Religion and Politics in the United States*. Lanham, MD: Rowman and Littlefield.

Warikoo, Niraj. 2013. "Dearborn Arab Festival Being Moved after Attendees Antagonized." *Detroit Free Press*, April 29. http://www.freep.com/article/20130429/NEWS02/304290024/dearborn-arab-american-festival-moving.

Wilcox, Clyde, Lee Sigelman, and Elizabeth Cook. 1989. "Some Like It Hot: Individual Responses to Group Feeling Thermometers." *Public Opinion Quarterly* 53 (2): 246–257.

Conclusion

Reflections on the Study of Religion and Political Tolerance

TED G. JELEN

The essays that make up this volume are based on an old hypothesis—that religion and political tolerance are somehow incompatible. The classic formulation of this hypothesis is based on epistemological considerations. Religious insights are considered to be both authoritative and unverifiable (hence, the importance of "faith" in most Western religious traditions). Tolerance for opposing and perhaps unpopular ideas is desirable for both intrinsic and instrumental reasons. Intrinsically, since the ultimate truth of any idea is ultimately unknowable, a respect for the autonomy of each person requires that no idea, or its public expression, be eliminated from public discourse a priori. Instrumentally, because human reason is fallible and human experience necessarily limited, exposure to alternative ideas and perspectives is likely to have an educative effect and bring society closer to whatever truths may be accessible to humans (see especially Mill [1869] 1975).

Such considerations are thought to be incompatible with religious belief, in which truth is largely revealed through interactions between humans and the divine, and in which theological beliefs and values are infallible and nonnegotiable. As Pope Pius IX argued in his 1864 "Syllabus of Errors" (1999), error has no rights with respect to (revealed) truths. That is, individuals simply do not have the right to be wrong on matters in which religious beliefs and values are regarded as authoritative. Thus, the incompatibility of religion with democratic discourse is arguably basic and methodological.

The studies contained in this book provide more nuanced and less parsimonious accounts of the relationship between religion and political tolerance. Both general variables in this set of relationships are shown to be much more complicated than might be imagined. Indeed, the study of political tolerance, and the presence or absence of religious antecedents to tolerance, might well be characterized as "post-paradigmatic." As the studies in this volume show, descriptions and explanations of political tolerance involve different combinations of several sets of variables, whose conceptualization and measurement are not the subject of general scholarly agreement. For this reason, as Paul Djupe suggests in the Introduction to this collection, it is an exciting time to be studying political tolerance. However, the cost of such excitement may be a lack of a theoretically parsimonious, empirically verifiable understanding of the relationship between political tolerance and religion.

The Nature of the Dependent Variable

What, precisely, is meant by the concept of political tolerance? The chapters in this volume take a variety of approaches to answering this question. In the classic formulation sketched above, religiously based intolerance is a general predisposition, and perhaps an element of a broader concept of personality—a concept admirably analyzed by Marie Eisenstein (Chapter 10). Intolerance is based on epistemological or methodological traits, in which attitudes based on faith supersede those based on reason or experience. In addition to aspects of religiosity and religious affiliation, intolerance has traditionally been linked to other psychological predispositions (perhaps even pathologies) such as authoritarianism or dogmatism.[1] Indeed, since some studies (see, for example, Jelen and Wilcox 1991) have shown that such traits are related to religious variables, the difficulty in isolating the effects of religion becomes even more acute.

Perhaps beginning with the classic work of John Sullivan, James Piereson, and George Marcus (1982), the literature on political tolerance has suggested that tolerance is a more nuanced, limited, and contextual variable. That is, the same person may be tolerant or intolerant of ideological or behavioral outgroups depending on several considerations, including (but not limited to) the identity and nature of the group being tolerated, the seriousness of any threat posed by members of the outgroup, the manner in which the issue is framed, and the political environment. That is, tolerant or intolerant responses may not reflect deep personality characteristics but may depend on time, place, or circumstance.

Although the jury is still out, the weight of the evidence presented in this volume generally supports the contextual approach. First, the chapters by Paul Djupe, Jacob Neiheisel, and Laura Olson (Chapter 11) and by Brian Calfano and Paul Djupe (Chapter 12) suggest that tolerant responses can be affected by experimental manipulations, such as differences in the manner in which an issue is framed. Were tolerance a more basic psychological trait, it seems unlikely that responses would be sensitive to experimental treatments. Second, as is addressed in the following section, several chapters suggest that the variables that predict political intolerance vary across the types of tolerance being considered. The effects of such standard variables as education and religiosity differ across a range of possible specifications of the dependent variable, as shown in the chapters by Paul Djupe and Stephen Mockabee (Chapter 7); Marie Eisenstein (Chapter 10); Paul Djupe and Brian Calfano (Chapter 2); Joby Schaffer, Anand Sokhey, and Paul Djupe (Chapter 9); and Marie Eisenstein and April Clark (Chapter 5).

Finally, specific political contexts seem to matter. In the comparison of the United States and Israel by Pazit Ben-Nun Bloom and Marie Courtemanche (Chapter 6), the most important predictor of religious intolerance is a dummy variable measuring country of residence. Even in the face of fairly elaborate multivariate controls, Israelis are less tolerant of religious outsiders than are residents of the United States. This is not surprising, since the contexts in which citizens may be called on to make tolerance judgments are markedly dissimilar in the two nations. Nevertheless, the sole cross-national comparison in this collection makes it clear that political contexts make a difference.

Conversely, Eisenstein's chapter, as well as her earlier work (Eisenstein 2008), suggests that more general personality traits are plausible intervening variables between manifestly religious variables and tolerance judgments, although the usual suspects (such as dogmatism) do not seem as important as other, less directly political, psychological variables. Although the targets of political intolerance are variable, Eisenstein's analysis suggests the possibility that such intolerant attitudes may have more basic psychological roots.

Several of the authors whose work is included in this book use the least-liked-group, or content-controlled, method pioneered by Sullivan, Piereson, and Marcus (1982). The fact that this method often results in diverse outgroups about which respondents are asked to make tolerance judgments offers further, if indirect, support for the contextual approach to political tolerance. However, this approach, while arguably superior to the preselection of outgroups by the researcher, is itself beset with certain problems. Most importantly, the procedure in which respondents are asked to select their first and second least-liked groups entails the assumption that the groups to be singled out for intolerance differ across individual respondents. In other words, few studies using the content-controlled method analyze tolerance for an individual respondent's third, fourth, or fifth least-liked group (for a prominent exception, see Gibson 1992a). It does not seem implausible to imagine that the scope of intolerance at the individual level is a variable, with some respondents being general intolerants, others specializing in intolerance for specific groups, and others targeting general groups based on ethnicity, race, religion, or some other characteristic. Put more simply, there is a paucity of empirical work on the *organization* of tolerance/intolerance judgments, although James Gibson (1989, 1992b, 2006) has suggested that the differences between the content-controlled measures and the older measures used by Samuel Stouffer (1955) are not particularly large or substantively important.

Moreover, the least-liked-group approach to the measurement of political tolerance assumes that tolerance judgments are made primarily on the basis of identity of the group under consideration. While such an assumption is plausible, it is certainly not uncontroversial. In earlier work using the standard

General Social Survey (GSS) battery of preselected outgroups, members of some religious traditions exhibited an attitude structure based on the activities in which outgroups were engaged, rather than on the identity of the outgroups themselves (Jelen and Wilcox 1990). Specifically, some religiously defined populations were less likely to permit a Communist, racist, or homosexual to teach in a public school than to publish a book or to make a public speech. While results of this study can scarcely be regarded as definitive, it seems clear that tolerance judgments can be made on the basis of elements beyond an outgroup's identity. In particular, tolerance may be more difficult in the context of the education of pre-adults. People who are quite willing to permit the public presentation of controversial, even harmful ideas in public discourse may balk at the idea that such ideas would be presented to children, whose beliefs are by definition still undergoing a process of formation.

This raises the final consideration concerning the content-controlled method. If the issues surrounding political tolerance are regarded as *political* (as opposed to psychological) phenomena, the actual targets of political intolerance are generally dictated by the political environment, and, perhaps more specifically, by the actions of members of the outgroups themselves. For example, perhaps few readers are old enough to remember the controversy over the rights of members of the American Nazi Party to hold public demonstrations in the (primarily Jewish) Chicago suburb of Skokie and the Marquette Park neighborhood of Chicago (which stood at the boundary of two distinctive, racially homogeneous communities) in the mid-1970s. Not surprisingly, the propriety of a Nazi march in a municipality inhabited by a large number of Holocaust survivors was quite controversial, and it was contested in public opinion, the courts, and within interest groups. For example, the American Civil Liberties Union lost a large number of members because of its support of the assembly rights of the Nazis (see Gibson and Bingham 1985).

During the Skokie controversy, it would likely have seemed quaint or irrelevant to wonder whether Muslims should be allowed to build mosques, or whether adherents of Islam should be subject to monitoring by law enforcement officials. Four decades later, of course, the Nazi march on Skokie seems primarily of historical interest, while the civil liberties of Muslim Americans (or, for that matter, undocumented immigrants) is an ongoing controversy in mid-2014. The willingness to tolerate the activities of one's least-liked group may have a different meaning depending on the political environment. In 2014, tolerating Nazis may seem an abstract or hypothetical proposition, while perceived "threats" posed by Muslims in the post-9/11 era may seem much more salient. In part, this problem may be ameliorated by including a "perceived threat" variable (as do several of the entries in this collection), but even the most carefully constructed research design cannot simulate variations in the political environment.

In summary, the notion of political tolerance seems to lack a clear conception among scholars addressing the topic. Is tolerance one variable or several? Does the answer to this question differ among respondents? To what extent are intolerance judgments dependent on time, place, and circumstances, and how do contextual variables interact with more stable demographic, psychological, or attitudinal individual characteristics? The chapters in this book raise such questions with unusual clarity, and they contribute to advances in the conceptualization and measurement of the dependent variable.

The Nature of the Independent Variable

If the characterization of political tolerance can be described as "post-paradigmatic," the specification of the independent variable(s) of interest in this collection might well be described as "pre-paradigmatic." It is by now commonplace to assert that religion is a multidimensional concept that defies straightforward definition or measurement. The essays in this collection both clarify and complicate our understanding of the relationship between religion and political tolerance, and they illustrate three general points.

First, standard measures of religion and religiosity (including the "three Bs" of belonging, believing, and behaving) that are often used by political scientists (see especially Green 2007) are of limited value in accounting for variations in political tolerance. Indeed, in the several studies in which the content-controlled method of measuring tolerance is used, conventional measures of religious belief and practice are virtually useless (see especially Chapter 5). The studies by Pazit Ben-Nun Bloom and Marie Courtemanche (Chapter 6) and by Daniel Cox, Robert Jones, and Juhem Navarro-Rivera (Chapter 8) show that more conventional religious variables have the greatest explanatory power in analyses in which the target of tolerance judgments is specifically religious in nature. This is not surprising, and it should draw scholarly attention to more systematic inquiries of religion as a source of target group selection, although Djupe and Calfano (Chapter 2) have shown that there is no relationship between the least-liked groups of clergy and laity at the congregational level.

Second, religious socialization on tolerance judgments is both possible and problematic. The experimental work by Calfano and Djupe (Chapter 12) suggests that people respond to religious cues in making tolerance judgments.[2] Religious leaders may have credibility among certain respondents, which permits the transmission of tolerant (or possibly intolerant) value judgments (but see Chapter 2). Again, a promising line of inquiry may be to examine denominational or theological differences in the credibility of religious leaders (see especially Djupe and Calfano 2009).

The issue of the credibility of religious leaders also raises questions of context and pastoral priorities. While the experimental work described above suggests that religious elites may have substantial potential to influence tolerance judgments, many may make rational decisions not to mobilize this potential. Ministers, rabbis, and even Catholic priests (who may not be directly accountable to the congregation) have multiple tasks and values, of which the inculcation of political tolerance is only one. Paul Djupe and Jeffrey Kurtz (Chapter 3) raise issues of organizational maintenance, in which clergy may need to satisfy the preferences of lay members in order to prevent attrition or (in extreme cases) termination of the congregation's religious leader. This insight dovetails nicely with earlier work (Campbell and Pettigrew 1959; Hadden 1969; Jelen 1993; Quinley 1974) finding that ministers were occasionally reluctant to confront their congregations about the racism of some church members or that they encountered resistance among the laity when advocating social or political engagement. Further, as shown by Djupe and Kurtz (Chapter 3), and by Paul Djupe, Brian Calfano, and Ryan Burge (Chapter 1), some clergy may place a high value on the application of democratic values in the internal operations of their congregations and may see direct socialization (even in defense of an ostensibly democratic value such as tolerance) as a violation of that norm.[3] This, of course, reiterates the old paradox of whether tolerant citizens must tolerate the expression of intolerant beliefs. This is a problem that some religious leaders may resolve by being as open and nondirective as possible, especially when more assertive responses may have psychological or organizational costs. However, Djupe and Calfano (Chapter 2) and Djupe and Kurtz (Chapter 3) show that clergy who hold democratic norms tend to have more tolerant congregations, which suggests that the socializing effect of clerical communications may be subtle and nuanced. Perhaps the modeling of tolerance in clerical behavior is a more effective teaching technique than direct socialization, or perhaps indirect methods, such as value framing or agenda setting, may be more useful in inculcating democratic values. It may be necessary to conduct intensive research at the level of individual congregations to analyze this set of phenomena more fully.

Finally, several of the chapters suggest the possibility that standard religious variables (such as the three Bs) may influence political tolerance through the intervening mechanism of religious worldviews. Of course, religious worldviews may have different, and manifestly secular, sources as well. In addition to familiar concepts such as authoritarianism or dogmatism, the use in this volume of variables such as "inclusive" versus "exclusive" religious values, or attitudes toward the social role of religion, or openness to dialogue (Clyde Wilcox and Christine Kim [Chapter 4]; Djupe and Mockabee [Chapter 7]) is extremely promising. The success of these conceptual and methodological innovations (or more accurately, contemporary adaptations of older concepts from sociology and social psychology) suggests two avenues for future research. First, the variety of such variables would benefit from systematic comparison along the lines suggested by Eisenstein. To what extent are "inclusiveness" and "openness to dialogue" (for example) empirically related? Second, what are the cognitive, affective, and behavioral antecedents of religious worldviews? Although Schaffer, Sokhey, and Djupe (Chapter 9) suggest that few denominational differences can account for variations in inclusive and exclusive worldviews, the religious sources of such perspectives clearly merit more systematic investigation. Similarly, are adherents of particular religious traditions more or less likely to endorse a visible public role for religion? Again, Eisenstein's study (Chapter 10) provides an excellent start in that direction and suggests paths that future research might profitably follow. The success of these variables in accounting for differences in political tolerance has rendered the study of tolerance considerably more complicated but much more interesting.

Some Consequences of Political Intolerance

Does it matter whether democratic citizens are tolerant or intolerant of ideological or behavioral minorities? Perhaps surprisingly, some literature suggests it may not. The theory of "democratic elitism," which is mentioned several times in this volume, suggests that the attitudes of mass publics are not as important to the maintenance of democracy as the attitudes of elites, or the quiescence of mass publics (see especially Bachrach 1967). Some analysts (see especially Herson and Hofstetter 1975) have suggested that the same traits that predict political intolerance are also associated with political inactivity. That is, the least tolerant citizens are also the least likely to participate in politics, and to act on those intolerant beliefs. Further, decisions as to whether the activities of ideological or behavioral outgroups are to be permitted are often made by courts and not by elected officials. Indeed, the entire notion of a Bill of Rights, including freedom of religion, expression, and assembly, is predicated on the idea that certain prerogatives are so important as to require being placed out of the reach of elected officials, and, by extension, of popular majorities. To this extent, an intolerant mass public may not pose much of a problem for the practice of democratic politics.

While this volume does not offer a definitive set of answers to this concern, two of the studies—Chapter 13 by Christopher Garneau and Chapter 14 by Patrick Schoettmer—add a dimension to this normative issue. These chapters show that the *targets* of intolerance are often inhibited in their participation in the public dialogue. Garneau shows that atheists often engage in coping strategies, including quiescence and deception, while Schoettmer demonstrates that American Muslims who perceive discrimination based on their religious beliefs are less likely to engage in political participation than those who do not perceive discrimination. These chapters provide contemporary reminders of Alexis de Tocqueville's ([1840] 1994) insight that the "tyranny of the majority" has a sociological, as well as a legal, component, and that restrictions on liberty and full citizenship are not limited to the consequences of government policies. A hostile climate of public opinion does not require legal enforcement to effectively limit the freedom of citizens whose beliefs and values lie outside the political or cultural mainstream.

Changes in the Nature of Opinion Research

A final set of considerations is methodological in nature. At the most basic level, the studies presented in this book represent the culmination of a basic change in the manner in which research in public opinion is conducted. Scholars of an earlier generation (myself included) were often limited to secondary analyses of large-scale national surveys, such as the General Social Surveys (GSS) or American National Election Studies (ANES). Although a good deal of excellent work has been and continues to be done using these sources, the measurement of certain key variables was often not ideal, and too often, analysts of public opinion data routinely included apologetic footnotes to the effect that secondary analysts cannot be choosers.

The studies in this volume take advantage of newer communications technology to devise more customized surveys, in which the individual researcher has much more control over question wording and format. Indeed, technology such as the Internet and newer social media has made large-scale experimental designs feasible, and several of the contributors to this collection have taken advantage of such opportunities (as illustrated in Chapters 6, 7, 11, 12, and 13). For this reason, the ability to conceptualize, measure, and test alternative approaches to political tolerance (and, for that matter, religion) has increased almost exponentially.

However, the increased control over measuring instruments has not come without costs. In particular, the sampling designs of many Internet surveys can occasionally lead one to question the external validity (or generalizability) of the results. Even under the best of circumstances, electronic surveys overrepresent the technologically sophisticated, who may differ from nonrespondents in politically meaningful ways. Further, the sampling issue becomes particularly problematic when samples are drawn from lists of organization members (see especially Chapters 4, 13, and 14), who, by definition, are more active (and perhaps, as a result, are more tolerant) than potential respondents who belong to the target population but lie outside the sampling frame.

The chapters in this volume demonstrate that the external validity problem is not insurmountable, and that the methodological innovations that have occasioned this concern may provide means to ameliorate the issue of generalizability. The authors whose work is included in this book are well aware of the problem of generalizability, and they have addressed this issue in appropriate, intellectually honest, and occasionally imaginative, ways. Chapter 11 illustrates the problem and an appropriate approach to the issue nicely. Moreover, the problem of external validity may be mitigated to some extent by the use of experimental designs (see Chapters 11 and 12), in which the representativeness of the sample to a larger population is not as important as the comparability of various treatment and control groups.

Although the ability to control the measurement of key variables in the study of political tolerance may have been purchased at the cost of exacerbating the problems associated with statistical inference, the potential of low-cost electronic data gathering may provide unprecedented opportunities for replication, which is an area in which the social sciences historically have been deficient. Further, the possibilities created by electronic publishing certainly enable scholars to publish replications without sacrificing precious journal space.

Thus, aside from the content of the individual chapters, the studies in this volume provide something of a map of the future for opinion research generally. Political science is poised at the beginning of a major transition in the conduct of empirical research on mass publics. Although the decentralization of the research enterprise is likely purchased at the cost of theoretical parsimony (at least in the short run), the conversation is expanding in ways that will add more voices to the scholarly dialogue.

Concluding Thoughts

As is often the case in the social sciences, the insights offered by each contributor to this volume have raised more questions than they have answered. As Paul Djupe suggests in the Introduction, these are indeed exciting times to be studying the relationship between religion and political tolerance. The contemporary period is one of intellectual and political challenge.

As noted earlier in the chapter, the studies in this volume make it clear that the relationship between various conceptions of religion and of political tolerance are not grounded in a single set of theoretical or methodological traditions. Different approaches to the study of political tolerance have quite diverse theoretical roots. That is, there is little consensus on the proper understanding (and, therefore, the proper measurement) of either dependent or independent variables. Is tolerance a psychological predisposition, a response to social and political environments, or some combination of the two? Under what circumstances do the standard measures of religious affiliation, belief, and behavior exert direct influence on tolerance judgments? Under which circumstances are religious variables mediated by attitudinal variables, and under which circumstances is religion simply irrelevant? While the essays that make up this collection do not offer final answers to any of these questions, they provide a solid basis for more focused ongoing research in the area of political tolerance. What the study of political tolerance has come to lack in parsimony, it has gained in verisimilitude.

The study of religion and tolerance is both exciting and challenging for political reasons as well. In the second decade of the twenty-first century, American politics seems to be characterized by increased levels of both ideological polarization and religious and ethnic diversity. If some consensus on at least procedural fundamentals is necessary for democratic discourse (Rawls 1993), political tolerance becomes an increasingly important citizen characteristic. Absent general agreement on the substance of public policy or the moral and ethical bases on which such judgments might be made, common understandings of the manner in which political disagreements are negotiated and (at least provisionally) settled is vital to the maintenance (or restoration) of democratic civility. That is, given the apparently increased inability of Americans to agree on matters of social and political substance, agreement on the rules of engagement, such as tolerance for opposing viewpoints, seems more important than ever.

Is religion a positive or negative influence on political tolerance and, by extension, democratic discourse? One might as well ask if fire is a positive or a negative force in human technology. Some of the studies in this volume offer some support for the conventional wisdom that religion and tolerance are not compatible, but the work of most of the contributors suggests that the effects of religious values on tolerance judgments are often subtle and indirect and, indeed, that religion can enhance the tolerance of ordinary citizens. From the standpoint of democratic theory and practice, this is good news. The fact that the United States is a religious country, relative to other industrialized nations, does not mean that intolerance is an intrinsic characteristic of Americans (even among highly religious members of doctrinally conservative denominations or other stereotypically intolerant populations). The religious pluralism for which the United States is often noted seems to provide its citizens with exposure to diversity, competition, and social capital. As these chapters show, religion is a source of alternative worldviews, social and congregational interactions, and engagement with transcendent values.

With this reminder of the normative stakes of research in political tolerance, we have come full circle. Whether religion, in any of its manifestations, contributes to or detracts from a democratic political culture is a central question for democratic theory and practical politics. We hope that the studies in this volume make a contribution to a continuing scholarly and public dialogue.

Notes

Acknowledgment: I thank Paul Djupe for helpful comments on an earlier draft of this chapter.

1. For an analysis and critique of these concepts as applied to religion, see Wald, Owen, and Hill (1989).

2. This finding lends further support to the conceptualization of tolerance as a context-dependent variable.

3. This dilemma will seem quite familiar to readers who teach and who seek to combine open classroom discussions with the desire to encourage the mastery of course material.

References

Bachrach, Peter. 1967. *The Theory of Democratic Elitism: A Critique.* Boston: Little, Brown.

Campbell, Ernest Q., and Thomas F. Pettigrew. 1959. *Christians in Racial Crisis: A Study of Little Rock's Ministry.* Washington, DC: Public Affairs Press.

Djupe, Paul A., and Brian R. Calfano. 2009. "Justification Not by Faith Alone: Clergy Generating Trust and Certainty by Revealing Thought." *Politics and Religion* 2 (1): 1–30.

Eisenstein, Marie A. 2008. *Religion and the Politics of Tolerance.* Waco, TX: Baylor University Press.

Gibson, James L. 1989. "The Structure of Attitudinal Tolerance in the United States." *British Journal of Political Science* 19 (4): 562–570.

———. 1992a. "Alternative Measures of Political Tolerance: Must Tolerance Be 'Least Liked'?" *American Journal of Political Science* 36 (2): 560–577.

———. 1992b. "The Political Consequences of Intolerance: Cultural Conformity and Political Freedom." *American Political Science Review* 86 (2): 338–356.

———. 2006. "Enigmas of Intolerance: Fifty Years after Stouffer's *Communism, Conformity, and Civil Liberties*." *Perspectives on Politics* 4 (1): 21–34.

Gibson, James L., and Richard D. Bingham. 1985. *Civil Liberties and Nazis: The Skokie Free Speech Controversy*. New York: Praeger.

Green, John C. 2007. *The Faith Factor: How Religion Influences American Elections*. Westport, CT: Praeger.

Hadden, Jeffrey K. 1969. *The Gathering Storm in the Churches*. Garden City, NY: Doubleday.

Herson, Lawrence J. R., and C. Richard Hofstetter. 1975. "Tolerance, Consensus, and the Democratic Creed: A Contextual Explanation." *Journal of Politics* 37 (4): 1007–1032.

Jelen, Ted G. 1993. *The Political World of the Clergy*. Westport, CT: Praeger.

Jelen, Ted G., and Clyde Wilcox. 1990. "Denominational Preference and the Dimensions of Political Tolerance." *Sociological Analysis* 51 (1): 69–81.

———. 1991. "Religious Dogmatism among White Christians: Causes and Effects." *Review of Religious Research* 33 (1): 32–46.

Mill, John S. (1869) 1975. *On Liberty*. New York: Norton.

Pope Pius IX. 1999. "Syllabus of Errors." In *Popes against Modern Errors: 16 Papal Documents*, edited by Anthony J. Mioni, 27–39. Charlotte, NC: TAN Books.

Quinley, Harold E. 1974. *The Prophetic Clergy: Social Activism among Protestant Ministers*. New York: Wiley.

Rawls, John. 1993. *Political Liberalism*. New York: Columbia University Press.

Stouffer, Samuel A. 1955. *Communism, Conformity and Civil Liberties: A Cross Section of the Nation Speaks Its Mind*. New York: Doubleday.

Sullivan, John L., James Piereson, and George E. Marcus. 1982. *Political Tolerance and American Democracy*. Chicago: University of Chicago Press.

Tocqueville, Alexis de. (1840) 1994. *Democracy in America*. 2 vols. New York: Alfred A. Knopf.

Wald, Kenneth D., Dennis E. Owen, and Samuel S. Hill, Jr. 1989. "Habits of the Mind? The Problem of Authority in the New Christian Right." In *Religion and Political Behavior in the United States*, edited by Ted G. Jelen, 93–108. New York: Praeger.

Contributors

Pazit Ben-Nun Bloom is Assistant Professor of Political Science at Hebrew University of Jerusalem. She holds a 2010 Ph.D. from Stony Brook University and explores religion from a political psychology perspective. She has published in a growing number of widely respected outlets including *British Journal of Political Science*, *Political Psychology*, and *Political Behavior*, among others.

Ryan P. Burge is an instructor of political science at Eastern Illinois University. His research investigates the effect of religious influence on public opinion and the politics of the emergent church movement. He has published in *Politics and Religion*, *Journal for the Scientific Study of Religion*, and *Review of Religious Research*.

Brian R. Calfano is Associate Professor of Political Science at Missouri State University. He is coauthor of *God Talk* (Temple, 2013) and has published numerous pieces on various facets of religion and politics using diverse research methodologies. His articles have appeared in many political science and sociology outlets, including *Political Research Quarterly*, *Political Behavior*, and *Political Communication*.

April K. Clark is Assistant Professor in the Department of Political Science at Northern Illinois University. Dr. Clark is also a senior research associate at the Center for Governmental Studies and specializes in the development of political attitudes and behavior with a particular focus on group differences. She has published on a number of topics including social capital, interpersonal trust, and democratic norm support.

Marie Courtemanche is Assistant Professor at Thiel College. Marie is a 2010 Ph.D. from Stony Brook University and investigates the determinants of immigration attitudes. She has published in *Political Behavior*.

Daniel Cox is a doctoral candidate at Georgetown University and is Research Director of the Public Religion Research Institute. He is widely published and cited in the mass media and in academic journals regarding religion and contemporary American politics.

Paul A. Djupe is Associate Professor of Political Science at Denison University and the coeditor of *Politics and Religion*, a Cambridge journal for the Religion and Politics section of the American Political Science Association. He has published six books—four as author and two as editor—including *The Political Influence of Churches* (Cambridge, 2009) and *God Talk* (Temple, 2013).

Marie A. Eisenstein is Associate Professor of Political Science at Indiana University Northwest. She has published a book, *Religion and the Politics of Tolerance* (Baylor, 2008), and several articles and book chapters on religion and political tolerance appearing in such outlets as *Politics and Religion*, *Political Behavior*, and *Interdisciplinary Journal of Research on Religion*.

Christopher Garneau is Assistant Professor of Sociology at the University of Science and Arts of Oklahoma. His primary research areas are in the sociology of religion and political sociology. His most recent publications include articles on religious measurement as well as political tolerance.

Ted G. Jelen is Professor of Political Science at the University of Nevada, Las Vegas. He is the founding coeditor of *Politics and Religion* and former editor of the *Journal for the Scientific Study of Religion*. He is the author of several books and numerous articles on the relationship between religion and public opinion, especially regarding abortion and church and state.

Robert P. Jones holds a Ph.D. from Emory University and is chief executive officer of the Public Religion Research Institute. He is widely published and cited in the mass media and in academic journals regarding religion and contemporary American politics.

Christine Kim is a Ph.D. candidate in government at Georgetown University. Her research interests include religion and politics, public opinion, and age-period-cohort effects.

Jeffrey B. Kurtz is Associate Professor of Communication at Denison University. His work is at the intersection of religious and civic discourse in American public life. His articles and review essays have appeared in the *Quarterly Journal of Speech*, the *Review of Communication*, *Rhetoric and Public Affairs*, and the *Journal of Communication and Religion*.

Stephen T. Mockabee is Associate Professor of Political Science and Graduate Program Director at the University of Cincinnati. His research interests include elections, public opinion, survey research methodology, and religion and politics. His work has appeared in a variety of journals such as *Political Research Quarterly*, *Political Analysis*, *Political Behavior*, *Journal for the Scientific Study of Religion*, and *Politics and Religion*, as well as in numerous edited volumes.

Juhem Navarro-Rivera is a Ph.D. candidate in political science at the University of Connecticut and research associate at Trinity College's Institute for the Study of Secularism in Society and Culture. Formerly, he was a research associate at Public Religion Research Institute. He has published widely on secularism in American politics. His current research focuses on the impact of increasing racial diversity on nonreligious Americans' political views.

Jacob R. Neiheisel is Assistant Professor of Political Science at the University of Buffalo, SUNY. Jake received his Ph.D. from the University of Wisconsin, Madison, in 2013. He is the author of a number of journal articles on various facets of religion and politics, political advertising, and political parties, appearing in *American Politics Research*, *Journal for the Scientific Study of Religion*, *Political Research Quarterly*, and *Social Science Quarterly*.

Laura R. Olson is Professor of Political Science at Clemson University. Laura is the editor of *Journal for the Scientific Study of Religion*. She has published a number of journal articles along with seven books, including two edited volumes and four editions of a widely used textbook on religion and politics.

Joby Schaffer is a Ph.D. student in political science at the University of Colorado, Boulder. He specializes in comparative politics, with a particular focus on developing countries. In addition to his research on political tolerance, his work examines the social and psychological aspects of clientelism and informal sector incorporation.

Patrick Schoettmer is Assistant Professor of Political Science at Southeastern Oklahoma State University. His research areas are religion and politics, civic engagement, and the politics of American Muslims. He has published in *Politics and Religion* and *Politics, Groups, and Identities*.

Anand E. Sokhey is Assistant Professor of Political Science at the University of Colorado, Boulder. He holds a 2009 Ph.D. from Ohio State University and has published widely on the nature of social influence. He also has several publications on religion and politics, and his work has appeared in *American Political Science Review*, *American Journal of Political Science*, *Journal of Politics*, and others.

Clyde Wilcox is Professor of Government at Georgetown University. He is an internationally known scholar with scores of articles and books on religion and politics, campaign finance, political parties, gender politics, and public opinion more broadly.

Index

Religion and Political Tolerance in America

In the series *The Social Logic of Politics*, edited by Scott D. McClurg

Also in this series:

Paul A. Djupe and Brian R. Calfano, *God Talk: Experimenting with Religious Causes of Public Opinion*
Krista Jenkins, *Mothers, Daughters, and Political Socialization: Two Generations at an American Women's College*
J. Celeste Lay, *A Midwestern Mosaic: Immigration and Political Socialization in Rural America*
Casey A. Klofstad, *Civic Talk: Peers, Politics, and the Future of Democracy*
Simon Bornschier, *Cleavage Politics and the Populist Right: The New Cultural Conflict in Western Europe*
Alan S. Zuckerman, ed., *The Social Logic of Politics: Personal Networks as Contexts for Political Behavior*
James H. Fowler and Oleg Smirnov, *Mandates, Parties, and Voters: How Elections Shape the Future*